THE BRIDESMAIDS

The Bridesmaids

Grace Kelly,
Princess of Monaco,
and Six Intimate Friends

Judith Balaban Quine

WEIDENFELD
& NICOLSON
New York

Published by Weidenfeld & Nicolson, New York
A Division of Wheatland Corporation
841 Broadway
New York, New York 10003-4793

Published in Canada by General Publishing Company, Ltd.

Due to limitations of space, permissions and
acknowledgments appear on page 498.

Library of Congress Cataloging-in-Publication Data
Quine, Judy.
The bridesmaids / Judith Balaban Quine. — 1st ed.
p.   cm.
Includes index.
ISBN 1-55584-067-1 (alk. paper)
1. Grace, Princess of Monaco, 1929–   —Friends and associates.
2. Quine, Judy—Friends and associates.   3. Weddings—Monaco.
4. Rainier III, Prince of Monaco, 1923–   . 5. Upper classes—
United States—Biography. 6. Monaco—Princes and princesses—
Biography.
DC943.G7Q56   1989
944'.949'00994—dc19
[B]   89-30855
CIP

Manufactured in the United States of America

This book is printed on acid-free paper

Designed by Christine Swirnoff/Libra Graphics

First Edition

1 3 5 7 9 10 8 6 4 2

To Grace

Acknowledgments

Without the loving support of a great many friends, I would never have written this book, could never have written it. Princess Grace herself gave me her initial blessing when I first discussed the idea for *The Bridesmaids* with her in 1978. From then until her death in 1982, she encouraged me to start writing. Prince Rainier, too, evidenced his continuing friendship along the way with countless acts of kindness and generosity of spirit, as did Prince Albert, Princess Caroline and Princess Stephanie. I will be ever grateful for their trust and their affection.

My husband, Don Quine, and our children, Amy Kanter Thiele, Victoria Kanter Colombetti, Nina Franciosa, Robert, James and Sean Quine, and Bob Thiele, Jr., gave me far more than most authors' families are asked to give. For in addition to unfailing patience and inspiration, they gave me pieces of their lives they might just as soon have forgotten. They gave me love. They will always have mine.

The same is true of five other people and their families—the bridesmaids. I am deeply moved when I think of Rita Gam and her children, Kate and Mike Guinzburg; of Bettina Gray and her Lizzie and Sam; of Maree Rambo and Linda Pamp Farnum and Louise Rambo Adams; of

if I thought about what she had said to me long enough and hard enough.

Nowadays, life often seduces us with quick fixes. It invites us to be the worst of ourselves by making celebrities out of scam artists, heroes out of manipulators and deities out of dollar signs. Perhaps the mythology of our earlier era laid too big an ethical burden on many of my contemporaries. But the era, like Grace who was so much a part of it, always inspired us to try to be the best of ourselves. That was a gift, and we have tried to give it to our children. They will try to give it to theirs.

Contents

THE BRIDESMAIDS

life. But it happened that late in 1955 MGM had finally offered Grace a part in an acceptable film project, the movie version of Ferenc Molnár's *The Swan.* During the previous two years the studio had repeatedly sent her a series of dreary, second-rate scripts, all of them for B movies. *The Swan,* however, had a certain elegant charm, and Grace had gone off to spend the late-autumn months of 1955 portraying a beautiful, shy and sensitive heiress cautiously waiting for her love life to begin. In *The Swan* two men compete for Grace's hand: one a wealthy, witty, slightly stuffy and overly eager prince, portrayed by Alec Guinness; the other a handsome, intelligent and soulfully romantic "Mr. Right," played by Louis Jourdan. It took MGM two and a half months to film the story, during which time Grace traveled from New York to North Carolina to Hollywood.

She completed *The Swan* on December 23, caught a plane out of L.A. for a pre-Christmas party at my apartment in New York, sped off to Philadelphia the next morning to spend Christmas with her family at the Kelly home, and returned to New York before New Year's Eve—engaged to a wealthy, witty, slightly stuffy and eager prince who *also* happened to be a handsome, intelligent and soulfully romantic "Mr. Right." What MGM had taken ten weeks to do Grace accomplished in five days. And her prince had a capital P and an existing fairy-tale nation to which her life would become inextricably bound. Movies end; marriages—or some of them—go on.

Once their engagement was formally proclaimed, had a Martian landed on earth, that alien would surely have believed that the sun rose and set and the tides rolled in and out on the basis of the lives of two earthlings named Grace and Rainier, or of anything or anybody with even the remotest connection to either of them. Stories about the engaged couple, about their past, present and projected future lives, appeared every day, everywhere, in all media. The infant industry of television journalism reported on them nightly and again at the crack of dawn. "Here's Grace driving into the studio lot in Hollywood." "There's Prince Rainier signing a document at his desk in the palace Grace will soon call home." Radio reporters announced with breathless excitement that Grace had been seen in I. Magnin's on Wilshire Boulevard while her prince was charming dignitaries at a society ball in Monte Carlo. The morning newspapers, along with the less significant afternoon journals, reported on them in the columns devoted to celebrities and socialites, amid advice to the lovelorn, local shopping tips, regional criminal activities and national scandals.

But the 1950s were also the era of the *serious newspaper.* Every major and minor city still had at least one such journal that printed only *serious news.*

From the moment the betrothal of the Oscar-winning film star and the world's most eligible royal bachelor was announced, even serious newspapers became frivolous. *The New York Times* had consistently consigned announcements of engagements, weddings and births to a discreetly placed page at the rear of its first or second section. To "make" the *Times* society page, one of the principals or certain family members had to be people of wealth, accomplishment, social standing, or commercial or intellectual success. Actresses were usually excluded from the society page, as it was called. Yet even *The New York Times* wrote about Grace and Rainier's betrothal on its serious front page. This public obsession with Grace and Rainier continued well into the New Year of 1956, infiltrating the psyches, hearts and dreams, as well as the dining rooms, bedrooms and offices, of nearly every American over the age of five.

Then, on the morning of April 4, the real hoopla began. The entire American press corps converged with tens of thousands of New Yorkers onto Pier 84 on the Hudson River to watch the U.S.S. *Constitution* embark, carrying friends and family, bridesmaids and their husbands, selected members of the press, and guests and gawkers bound for Monaco and what was being called "The Wedding of the Century." At the pre-sailing press conference on shipboard, frenzied reporters and photographers started to trample on Grace. The police had to evacuate the massive salon, carrying Grace out over the heads of the stampeding throng like a ballerina concluding a *pas de treize* with a dozen male dancing partners. When it was time to depart, an extra forty-five minutes were needed to clear the visitors from the dozens of stateroom cocktail parties.

I had made many transatlantic crossings and had often seen the throngs at pierside, but this embarkation was different. Beneath my mental snapshot of the event appear the words "What's wrong with this picture?" Every one of the thousands of faces on Pier 84 is turned in one direction. With necks craned, bodies hung over the railings, eyes squinted against the glare of the haze and the hearty April wind, everyone watches the ship's most precious cargo, a slender and shy young blond actress in a pillbox hat, holding a wiry-haired French poodle named Oliver. They are destined to become, respectively, the reigning princess and favorite household pet of an enchanted land called Monaco.

It is better if you do not notice the tears that well in the young woman's gray-blue eyes or the lump she visibly keeps swallowing every five seconds. Smile and wave. Cheer, sing and throw your red, white and blue confetti into the Manhattan sky. Grace Kelly is going to Monaco to become a princess. American romance hits the big time.

Grace's journey begins here. In many ways, so do mine and those of the five other young women who smiled and waved at the disappearing coastline from the top deck of the steamer. For we were the chosen, Grace Kelly's six closest, dearest and most intimate friends, her bridesmaids.

Actually, only three of us sailed with our world-famous friend on that April day thirty-three years ago. Maree Frisby Pamp of Philadelphia was on board, accompanied by a current beau, Karl Dodge. Maree and Grace's friendship dated back the furthest of any of our relationships, to Grace's freshman year in high school at Stevens School in Germantown, Pennsylvania. From Dedham, Massachusetts, came Bettina Thompson Gray with her husband Francis, called Frank. Bettina had been a classmate of Grace's at the American Academy of Dramatic Arts and her onetime roommate at the Barbizon Hotel for Women. I, Judy Balaban Kanter, was the newest of Grace's friends to be chosen as an attendant, the only one who had come to her in a package deal along with movie stardom. My husband, Jay Kanter, also making the voyage, was Grace's agent and friend; and my father, Barney Balaban, was president of Paramount Pictures, the studio at which Grace had played many of her choicest film roles, including Georgie in *The Country Girl* for which she won her Oscar.

Grace's three other bridesmaids, who flew to Europe, were Sally Parrish Richardson, a young but already retired actress who had also been both at the Academy and the Barbizon with Grace in her pre-Hollywood days. Sally and her husband John traveled with bridesmaid Carolyn Scott Reybold, a successful model who had also made the Barbizon her first New York home, and with Carolyn's husband Malcolm. The sixth and most famous of the bridesmaids, Rita Gam, Grace's fellow film actress and former roommate, had married Viking Press publisher Tom Guinzburg in New York the previous week. They were honeymooning in Italy and were to join us in Monaco upon our arrival.

The three young women who were to land with Grace in Monaco, the two who would come by plane, and the one who would motor in from her own Italian honeymoon were, in 1956, very much the product of their time. Other than Rita Gam, only Carolyn Scott Reybold was known to the public. Her face had appeared on the front covers of *Seventeen* magazine and other widely read periodicals dozens of times. It was a face that sold you Lux or Ivory soap. The body that went with this face was not that of the *haute couture* models of the day—elongated, emaciated, unreal—but rather that of an average, well-assembled American girl who was good at team sports, won class elections, and had a lot of dates. My recollections of Carolyn, however, remain misty, vague and focus mainly on her appearance. For more than anything else, what she seemed to be was the wife of Malcolm Reybold, a man a good deal her senior.

Malcolm was tall, slender, ruddy-faced and blondish (perhaps it was actually light brown hair, but I remember a faint tinge of apricot and gray). He was well tailored, poised and socially available. He was easy to be with, a regular guy, a man among men. When Carolyn married him I thought of him as a "playman," somewhat too old to be called a playboy. Malcolm and Carolyn lived in Manhattan but were building an impressive house in Lloyd Harbor on Long Island, adjacent to the even more impressive house owned by Sherman Fairchild, the definitive "playman" of that era.

At the time I was never too sure exactly what Malcolm did, nor where he had gained the fortune that allowed him his planned house next to Sherman's, and the conviviality of their shared frolics. I only recall him speaking about playing tennis, though not professionally. For Carolyn, however, it seemed that whatever Malcolm was and whatever he did were just fine. At parties she would stand next to him, looking beautiful, gaze up at him respectfully, smile enigmatically and say little. Of all the bridesmaids, Carolyn was the one I was to see the least of over the coming years. It still seems odd that I can remember so little about the sound of either her voice or her laugh, except that both were especially modulated. At the time I read this as self-containment.

Sally Parrish Richardson also came from New York. She had been a fellow actress of Grace's in the early days of their careers, studying to- gether at the American Academy of Dramatic Arts and pounding the pavement, looking for parts in Broadway shows and on live television. Sally had married long and lanky John Richardson sometime earlier, seemed extremely content with him, and always had a good time at a party. Sally was a no-nonsense young woman, attractive, somewhat preppy and Connecticut-looking (though she was a brunette), likable, outgoing and direct, a person you felt you could trust to be herself. John was less gregarious. I do not remember him laughing a lot, as Sally did infectiously, but think of John with the corners of his mouth always turned downward and with somewhat sad eyes. He, like Malcolm Reybold, was a tall man, but that was the only similarity I could detect between them.

Bettina Gray, another alumna of the American Academy and the Barbizon, was New England's contribution to the bridesmaids. After drama school she had abandoned all notions of acting and moved to the outskirts of Boston as the wife of Francis Gray, whose Brahmin back- ground echoed the American aristocracy of her own. I had met Bettina only once or twice before the *Constitution* sailed. I liked her, though some found her too outspoken—the very quality that endeared her to me. Bettina had a slightly eastern-prep-school accent. She was attractive—not beautiful or pretty, but attractive. Her husband Frank, from a banking family, was tall with a ruddy complexion, prematurely portly with slightly receding light brown hair, and very much the affable Bostonian. When Bettina laughed, the pleasant, hearty sound that issued from her resem- bled a horse's neigh. Whereas Sally's humor was consistently good- natured, Bettina's sometimes contained an edge that could approach bitterness. She was not, however, a malcontent. It was years before I was to understand exactly *what* she was.

The bridesmaid closest to the bride, Maree Frisby Pamp, came from the bride's hometown of Philadelphia. Grace's friend since high school, Maree was stunning, with blond hair that always behaved correctly, a nice tall body, and a pair of eyes that seemed to see right through the world at large. Maree was consistently well turned out, conservatively but styl- ishly, and her view of things was always cast in an original and humorous perspective. Maree told it the way she saw it, which was pretty much the way it was. She just didn't tell it so too many people could hear.

In those days I considered her enormously sophisticated, very self-assured, a touch cynical. It was clear that Maree's roots with Grace went deeper than those of the rest of us. The younger and less defined people are when they meet, the closer the ties between them often become. Maree and Grace had not grown apart when Grace left Philadelphia for New York and Hollywood. Maree's daughter Linda had been born a few years before Grace's wedding. Divorced from Linda's father, Arvid Pamp, Maree had invited Karl Dodge to journey to Monaco as an appropriate escort for the festivities.

Rita Gam was the honeymooning bridesmaid. I had met Rita a few years earlier, during the last stage of her previous marriage to director Sidney Lumet. Rita, stepdaughter of New York dress designer Ben Gam, was an original, exotic beauty. Dark-haired, implacable and mysterious, Rita was, like Grace, an emerging actress on the New York and Hollywood scenes. Both were represented by my husband, Jay Kanter, by John Foreman and by various other agents at MCA (Music Corporation of America), then the largest and most powerful talent agency in show business. When we met, Sidney Lumet was enjoying growing respect as a young director of live television drama, then the staple of prime-time TV. Rita and Sidney were the odd couple: she, tall, erect, sphinxlike and regal; he, the consummate New York Jewish artist, small, wiry, always in motion, gesturing, grimacing, passionate almost to the point of frenzy, his energy like a torrent of small electrical charges. At parties Sidney would dart about, touching every base, while Rita sat, usually as though waiting for her portrait to be painted, her posture perfect, her eyes roaming the room slowly, uncommunicative unless forced out of herself.

By the time of Grace's wedding, Rita and Sidney had divorced. Rita worked in New York, where she had met Grace, and also overseas and in Hollywood, where she and Grace had shared a house. There had been, it was rumored, a love affair in Paris—not a good one. And then Rita met Tom Guinzburg. Tom's father had founded Viking Press, to which Tom was the heir apparent. Tom's was an elegant, New York German-Jewish family, conservative, proper almost to the point of Victorian, with a lovely townhouse nestled in foliage adjacent to the East River on Sutton Place. Tom himself was not unexotic in appearance. Tall, foreign-looking, quiet, reserved, stilted, nervous, shy, he spoke as though he was never sure he had the right to express himself, as though self-expression might, in fact, violate some proprietary rule of the society in which he had been raised.

party had originally been promised to other passengers. Back in the States, sixty-six grumpy people who had previously booked space on this crossing of the *Constitution* were busy grumbling about the misfortune of having been "bumped" from the voyage. Many of them had been rebooked in larger rooms on grander ships, but other ships were not bound for Monaco for the most glamorous wedding of the century, and other ships did not list Grace Kelly and her guests on the passenger log.

I am told that the *Constitution* did carry a large number of previously booked "civilians." There were many more of them than us, it turns out, but I cannot remember seeing or hearing any of them during the eight hectic days and nights that followed. I was convinced that everyone on board was bound for the big event, that each face I saw was a familiar one, that each voice was a voice I had heard dozens of times before. In my then limited perception of the universe, I was so dazed by the wedding-related activity (as were most of the other wedding guests and participants) that I was thoroughly convinced I knew every single person in the entire world, that each of them figured somehow into Grace's existence in ways I could not quite recall at the moment, and that all of them were en route to attend the wedding in Monaco.

Once the *Constitution* hit the open seas, we returned to our staterooms. Unpacking turned out to be the major logistics challenge of the day. All the Kelly group, but especially the family and we bridesmaids, who were to be included in the largest number of activities on the *Constitution* as well as in Monaco, had shopped our hearts out.

Just imagine our situation. Newspapers in seventy countries had recently announced that you had been selected to be a bridesmaid at the world's most publicized wedding. They had sent reporters and photographers to be sure that everyone who could hold a newspaper knew exactly how you looked, where you came from, why you had been chosen, and what you knew about the bride and groom. For several weeks members of the press had followed you to restaurants, to the movies and to your neighborhood butcher, where they recorded you on film, together with your single-ribbed French-cut lamb chops. Journalists had lounged for hours in the lobby of your apartment building, waiting to pop another question or another flashbulb at you as you wheeled your baby to the park, your hair rolled in pin curls and poorly concealed under your school scarf.

Imagine, too, that a few weeks earlier, before you packed for this trip, you had received reams of letters and directives from the royal protocol office of a distant nation, written in a foreign language, notifying you of the series of events you were to attend during your seven-day visit to that country and listing the "house rules" for wardrobe at the Princely Palace. Add to that the stack of invitations you had received to planned affairs on shipboard en route to the wedding. Remember, too, that you could expect to be photographed nearly anytime and everywhere. And do not forget that every picture taken and every story written would disclose and analyze every item of clothing you would wear, from the tops of your hats to the tips of your shoes, and that every bit of this evidence would appear in every newspaper and magazine of every developed nation in the world. Armed with a great excuse, we went on full-blown shopping orgies.

Staterooms aboard the *Constitution* became almost unlivable. Massive steamer trunks filled every inch of space, opened suitcases spilled their contents onto bureaus and beds. Ball gowns and cashmere sweater sets were draped and flung over every chairback and door handle. Each of us had to identify every piece of clothing that might be needed during the eight-day journey ahead of us, remove it from its case, pack everything else neatly back in place, summon porters and stewards to remove most of the luggage to the ship's hold, and then try to find somewhere to set all the required apparel so that it would not be destroyed and so that two people who had to live in the space for more than a week might also be able to sleep, bathe and remain free from acute attacks of claustrophobia. The latter turned out to be more than any of us had the right to ask.

All this had to be accomplished inside an hour. On the normal first night out of the average sailing, nobody dressed for dinner. This did not mean that people sallied forth into the high-ceilinged dining room in disarray. It meant, merely, that the men did not have to don dinner jackets and that the women were permitted to wear street-length cocktail dresses rather than dinner dresses or "formals" that touched the floor. It was presumed that the average passenger, exhausted from preparing for the trip and the excitement of departure, deserved a brief respite from the social whirl that would govern the ensuing days at sea. That was the theory behind the relaxed dress code on the first night of a normal Atlantic crossing in those times. But you can forget the word "normal" from here on out because it bears not the remotest connection to the events at hand.

With our unpacking rituals completed, we bridesmaids now faced the luxury of an additional fifteen minutes during which we could fluff up our coiffures, spruce up our faces, whip into our cocktail clothes, and report (on time) to the first of four post-sailing, pre-dinner cocktail parties we were expected to attend. Our husbands managed to sandwich in their shaves using teaspoons as reflectors ("Sorry, honey, I need the mirror for mascara"), to locate their comparatively few and meager belongings amid the rubble ("Your white dress shirts are right under my shoes on the floor of the closet, sweetie pie"), and to remain gracious and chivalrous as they raced us down the ship's corridors and helped us shoulder our way into the crush of the first romp of the evening.

The press, having been assigned cabin-class quarters, was not free to roam the first-class area of the ship; thus we were spared cameras and questions in the hallways. It seemed, however, that once inside the cocktail reception, there were about four hundred people from Philadelphia whose noses had small, black, box-shaped objects attached to them with strobe-sharp lights that blinded everyone in the room once every ten seconds. Conversation was almost impossible. You couldn't see who it was you were talking with, and it turned out that the Philadelphia shutterbugs were all would-be directors heavily bent on "blocking." "Judy, stand next to Grace with Jay on the other side of her and Bettina on the other side of you." . . . "No, Jay, stand next to Maree with Judy and Frank—come on in there, Frank—on the other side of Grace." . . . "I think it would be better if Grace sat down with the Kanters and the Grays stood behind her."

Through all this the guest of honor smiled, affectionately kissed the cheeks of the older guests, and hugged the shoulders of the few Kelly family children who had come along on the trip. She winked conspiratorially at her friends, patiently answered any question asked of her, and generally created the impression that she wanted to be nowhere else on earth at this very moment but here, in this exact room, with every single one of these people, doing whatever it was any of them would have her do. Had she been acting, it would have been considered a bravura performance. She was not acting.

Grace's mother busied herself, flapping about the room, drumming up excitement, pausing to relate anecdotes of the past few days, and suggesting new groupings for the snapshots. I had known Margaret Kelly for nearly three years before she and Grace's father had announced their middle daughter's engagement to the Prince of Monaco. She had always seemed to be a stalwart, no-nonsense, pragmatic matriarch, with her sensible Teutonic background and polite if somewhat distant smile. Though she was nowhere near old enough for the role, I always thought of her as my friend's grandmother, not as her mother. Over the last few months, Margaret Kelly's instant fame as the world's most publicized mother-in-law-to-be had transformed her into a giddy and babbling girl, never sure when to hold her tongue, fluttering like a butterfly. Only occasionally, late at night, did I glimpse the spine that supported her and the toll she had paid during all those years when she had maintained herself, her home and her children in the image that her German family and John B.'s Irish one had etched into their respective psyches in the early decades of the twentieth century.

While Grace's mother skitted about, John B. Kelly, Grace's dad, continued to control everything from on high. It was business as usual for John B. He was a tall man who appeared even taller because of the ease with which he held himself. John B., owner of a successful Philadelphia construction business, was a self-made man. By the time the *Constitution* left Pier 84 for this crossing, there was not a soul in the universe who had not read of his rise from poverty and oblivion to a position of exalted wealth and respect in his community. He had, we knew by then, even managed to gain retribution over the people who had snubbed him in his early life. Ostracized from competition in the 1920 Henley Diamond Sculls, the prestigious rowing event on London's Thames River, he had seen to it that his son, John B., Jr. (known as "Kell"), would become a champion oarsman like himself. With the senior Kelly's acquired prestige and position, and under his grueling tutelage, Kell had not only entered the race his father had been denied entry to more than twenty years earlier, he had won it. Twice. John B. Kelly was, indeed, a self-made man. He was also quite accustomed to "making" anyone else he cared to. This included his wife (and a number of other women, we have been told), his children and others he deemed worthy of his attention. As he circulated among the crowds at the shipboard parties, he was puffed with joviality and pride. He had, in some way, made all this happen, he thought. What he didn't know was that the power he had become accustomed to wielding was about to slip away from him. A force even greater than John B. Kelly was to challenge his omnipotence.

Lizanne, Grace's younger sister, was at home in Philadelphia, decorating a nursery, shopping for layettes, and trying to get ready for the baby she and her husband, Donald LeVine, expected within a matter of weeks. Though I did not think about it at the time, it must have been a difficult period for Lizanne. She was, after all, Grace's sister and should have been a part of the glamour and excitement that attended her famous sister's nuptials. Or, under other circumstances, it would have been Lizanne's time to shine. It was she who was about to bring another Kelly grandchild into the world. Dynastic parents such as hers would normally have created a great to-do about this expected offspring. Kelly friends in Philadelphia would have focused on Lizanne and her imminent motherhood.

Everyone was too busy, though, thinking about, dreaming of and planning for Grace's wedding. Neither the Kellys themselves nor their Philadelphia circle gave Lizanne her due. It was Grace's hour, shared by everyone the world over, not Lizzie's. While there was a great deal of love between the two girls, I cannot help wondering if the attention Lizanne did not get toward the end of her pregnancy left her feeling like a fat girl sitting out the biggest party of the decade.

While Lizanne propped pillows under the small of her back in Philadelphia, Grace's two other siblings, Peggy and Kell, were ensconced in our summer camp on the high seas. Kell, as I recall, was pleasant and amorphous, rather like a genial, overgrown puppy made of Play-Doh. Since birth his father had shaped and reshaped Kell to his liking. In the early part of one's life that kind of thing can be seductive. It can take you off the hook about decisions other kids have to make for themselves, give you a sense of freedom from responsibility, keep you eternally young, rob you of your soul. And so Kell smiled and mixed and was pleasant. Always pleasant. That is what I remember about him throughout the entire journey and the days that followed in Monaco.

Peggy, however, was another kettle of fish. She, along with her then husband, George ("Gabby") Davis, was the life of every party. Full of beans, lean, long-legged, blond-bobbed Peggy was Daddy's delight. She had excelled at the sports Mummy and Daddy had encouraged. She had grown into the kind of girl who, at school, was always the group leader.

Peggy had that brittle edge of sophistication girls of the Forties aspired to. She was tanned, capable and thin. She could make you laugh. She laughed at your jokes. She laughed at life.

Peggy and Gabby danced, sipped champagne and cocktails, smoked and joked, and organized us and their children, Meg and Mary Lee, on the historic crossing. Gabby was a good-time guy. Peggy was the child who knew her father best, the child he liked best because she was so damned adept, the way he wanted her to be. Peggy was secure, sure about herself. Perhaps Peggy thought that her own good looks and adeptness would stand her in good stead now that her movie-star sister was going off to live the life of royalty in a small foreign country. Perhaps Peggy had dreams even she would not admit: dreams of approval that went beyond her childhood, when only Daddy's approval had mattered; dreams of the kind of approval her sister Grace had achieved. World-wide acclaim. Perhaps not. Peggy wasn't the kind of girl who would let you think, for a moment, that she wanted anything else out of life other than exactly what she had. Besides, what she had that Grace didn't was their father's approval. At the time that was enough.

And so the Kelly kids and grandkids, Kelly aunts and uncles and cousins, Kelly family friends and "Gracie's group" (as Mrs. Kelly used to call us) partied across the Atlantic. All the cocktail parties were just like the one before and just like the one after. The shutterbugs shot endlessly like swarms of click beetles. The directors posed photo groupings of key players as though this granted them the power to create a moment in history.

Throughout every gathering of the clan, Gracie beamed and blessed and patted affectionately. She grew alternately amused or wistful at every reminiscence anyone wanted to share with her. A good part of it came from Grace's ability to focus in a way others could not, no matter how many distractions there were. Perhaps another part of it was her will to cling greedily to each memory as though it were a comfort she would need desperately to hug in the coming months.

Our party spirit was not noticeably dampened by the presence of the press. Denied free access to all the first-class decks, the journalists amused themselves amidships and waited for the few scheduled interviews or photo sessions with the bride, and one or two "cattle calls" attended by as many of the wedding guests and participants as wished to be memorialized. Other than that, most of us kept forgetting they were there with us. Perhaps forgetting is the wrong word. The near-subliminal knowledge of their presence provided the vaguely itchy edge that reminded us this was not your average transatlantic crossing with an American wedding party. For the most part, we tried not to think about that and what it would really mean once we disembarked in Monaco.

Following the nightly cocktail receptions, evenings were given to dining and parties. Dinner on shipboard is always akin to the last supper before an execution, one staggeringly rich course after another. The chefs felt compelled to outdo themselves for the illustrious passengers. I, for one, consumed enough cream and oil during the voyage to have been milked with a herd of Guernseys and to have kept my joints lubricated well into the next decade.

Each dinner was the occasion for toasts. Some were long, boring and pointless, others were hilarious, but all ultimately produced tears in the wedding party. It was not only that the tributes reminded us that we were en route to the wedding of two young people very much in love but also that we could begin to feel the nostalgia we would learn to live with for the rest of our lives once Gracie left home. She felt it more than any of us.

After dinner each night "Gracie's group" would head off to an enclosed public room that had been set aside for our use. Here we would visit, drink coffee and more champagne ("More champagney, Judybird?" Grace would ask, with a bottle of bubbly poised over the widemouthed glass, a picture that would repeat itself often over the coming years), listen to music, dance and play games. On one such evening Grace decided on a sing-along. Every one of us was a devotee of both standard and lesser known songs from the movies and Broadway. In our sing-alongs, one-upmanship was measured not by who had the best voice but by how many lyrics one could remember. Jay and I were close to several of the era's best singers, and we counted Jule Styne, Betty Comden and Adolph Green, Harold Rome, Harold Arlen, Frank Loesser, Stephen Sondheim and Leonard Bernstein among our friends. At almost weekly New York parties I had taken to singing familiar show tunes as well as those written by our friends for as-yet-unproduced Broadway musicals. All this gave me an edge. Besides, in those days I had a head filled mostly with phone numbers and song lyrics.

While I may have paced the crowd on lyric retention, at our oceango-
ing sing-along all the cats joined in. The flat and raspy voices mingled with
the sweet, clear ones. Harmonies were attempted, sometimes successfully,
often not. Sounds did not matter, though. Camaraderie did. Our hearts
were young and gay, and we were bound by the shared experience of
traipsing off together for this great adventure with our darling friend. I
remember Grace's voice clearly that night. The song she sang alone was
"True Love" from the movie *High Society,* the remake of *The Philadelphia Story,* the last Hollywood motion picture Grace Kelly ever made. In
some people's lives even the titles are propitious.

Charades were also very popular then; there was even a weekly television show featuring celebrities who played for audiences across the nation.
Grace was an avid charades buff. We split into teams, wrote our charades
and began to play. The teams were running neck and neck, midway
through the first round, when it was Jay's turn at bat. For a good part of
the charade his team managed to get what he was doing, but then he
began to act out something that none of them could understand. Frustra-
tion turned to frenzy. Grace cajoled, pleaded and screamed for Jay to give
her and his other teammates something they could understand. Try as he
might, nothing was getting through—and the clock was ticking. Grace
was tearing her hair, jumping up and down, waving her arms, shrieking
for a better clue. Finally she threw herself to her knees directly at Jay's
feet, her eyeglasses skewed across the bridge of her nose, her arms raised
in prayer, mouth agape in a cry of anguish, looking for all the world like
a cockeyed supplicant at Lourdes. For those who devoured by the hundreds photos of a woman believed to be the world's coolest cucumber, this
picture (which I hold even now in my mind's eye) belied the publicized
self-containment. The truth was that just like the rest of us, Grace wanted
desperately to win the game. Perhaps more than the rest of us.

If evenings were spent in large groups, the daylight hours were composed, in the main, of private moments. Grace was a big "group person,"
but she was also exceedingly private. This duality permitted her to maintain her balance during hectic times such as these days at sea. In the
mornings Grace walked Oliver, the French poodle that was to become a
fixture in Grace's and Rainier's lives, and perhaps, other than Franklin
Delano Roosevelt's Fala, the world's most photographed dog. He already
knew he was special to Grace, and he behaved accordingly. But something

about the way Oliver strutted along the *Constitution*'s upper decks said he also knew he was palace-bound. Dogs know about these things.

Before and after walks with Oliver, Grace busied herself writing personal thank-you notes to each host of each cocktail reception and to every giver of any type of gift she had received. Hundreds of presents, letters and telegrams had been pouring in since her engagement was announced, and as her wedding day grew nearer the volume increased. All of Grace's notes identified the specific gift in question, were written promptly and by hand. Her longtime secretary/companion/friend Prudy Wise, a young, larger-than-life brunette eccentric with a powerful Southern accent, a huge supply of energy and the longest legs in the Western world, had recently been succeeded by another young woman who accompanied Grace on this journey to help organize her life. Nobody but Grace, though, was ever to run it.

Between walks and letter writing came the review of schedules, instructions and protocol details of what was to occur once the bride-to-be had landed in Monaco. There was also a hasty brushup course in French. Grace went over everything carefully, hoping to avoid confusion by intense planning. Many things were, of course, out of her hands. The bulk of the arrangements rested with the Prince's Palace staff and Monaco's government officials. It was presumed that this group had everything under control, except for those personal touches that Grace herself would add. At the time I believed this took a great deal of the pressure off Grace. Only now do I realize, as she likely did then, that it also made her rather like a guest at her own wedding. She may have been the co-star of the event, but—whether we realized it or not—like the rest of us, she was just an American commoner en route to her first royal wedding.

Though Grace still behaved like Gracie on our crossing, cloaking her in my own awe, I had already cast her in her new role. Unconsciously, I began to withhold myself from her in small ways, expecting her to do the same with me as though her impending title demanded this distance between us. While it was meant respectfully, it was a dreadful thing to do to a friend, especially one as vulnerable as Grace at that moment. Unfortunately, I was young enough and sufficiently impressed by the glamour of the events at hand that only my own vulnerability seemed real to me. In my mind, Grace (a mere twenty-six years old at the time) had already begun her ascent into the serenity of highnessness.

Grace had this other problem—her hair. It was extremely fine, and it was not abundant. That was an era when we didn't put much store in the casual look, except for days in the country. People were expected to behave themselves, and their hair was expected to do the same. If your hair didn't do this easily, you had to allow sufficient time each day to bring it under control.

Fortunately for Grace, one of the passengers aboard the *Constitution* was Virginia Darcy, her hairdresser from MGM. Virginia, possessed of her own flaming ruby mane, had done Grace's hair for her last two films and was on loan-out from the studio to fluff up the famous golden tresses—what there was of them. What there wasn't, Virginia compensated for with the attachment of "pieces." Braids entwined into configurations that looked like deli Danish were among the day's popular options, as were chignons rolled inward like cannolis or bunches of curls poised at the rear of the head like a small waterfall of grapes. On certain of the less gala shipboard evenings, Grace's freshly shampooed hair was held back with a plain headband or merely pinned behind her ears. These variations—along with a proclivity for what our mutual friend John Foreman used to call her "sensible shoes" and horn-rimmed glasses—often gave Grace the semblance of a prissy New England schoolmarm. During the daytime at sea her hair was, as it would be for a great deal of her life, concealed under a scarf.

Movie stars are often extremely close to their hairdressers. They see them at ungodly hours and between frustrating retakes when things aren't going right. In those days we who were around show business knew that often a celebrity truly confided only in her hairdresser. (Joan Crawford, for one, who had bizarre relationships with her friends—and even stranger ones with her children—had what amounted to a chattel-mortgage ownership on her hairdresser's life.) Virginia Darcy had a raucous laugh, a big heart and a warm spirit. She was joined at the hip to Grace during this crossing and would remain so for the entire wedding week in Monaco.

It was like Grace to include during each day at sea an intimate hour or more with one or a cluster of her friends or immediate family. She would send a little note, asking if we were free for tea and would join her in her cabin. Once there we would chat, compare impressions of the trip, giggle, or discuss some detail of the wedding plans that concerned her. In addition to the bridesmaids, and sometimes our husbands, these gabfests included Grace's other friends, Gant Gaither, then a theatrical producer with a heavy Southern accent and an incisive wit (both of which he retains to this day), and Donald Buka, a broodingly handsome, black-haired actor who had become a close chum of Grace's over the years.

One afternoon when I appeared for my teatime summons, there were just the two of us. As Grace poured, she began, "Judybird . . ." (I was "Judybird" because I was married to Jay, who was, of course, "Jaybird," which then made her "Graciebird," Gant Gaither "Gantbird" and John Foreman "Johnbird." Our small group of bird-persons took to greeting one another not in the accustomed English language, but merely with a few simulated chirps.) ". . . there is something I want to give you, now that I am getting married." She drew a small leather jewel box from her lap, opened its lid, and turned the box toward me. Nested within a slit in the puffy Van Cleef & Arpels satin lining was an exquisite brooch. "This is particularly appropriate for you, Judybird, which is why I want you to have it now that I am getting married and leaving the nest." There was a slight crack in Grace's voice.

The pin was made of gold, a delicate birdcage with a tiny, barred door that opened and closed on a minuscule hinge. Inside the cage, on a swing, sat a diamond bird with pavéed wings and eyes of bright blue sapphires. "Brrip, brrip," Grace added, our bird noise sounding not silly now but sad. While I oohed and aahed over the jewel, I told Grace I couldn't possibly take it from her. She must keep it for herself. "I can't," was her only reply. No further explanation. Many years later, in 1984, some two years after Grace's death, I read in a biography of her that the pin had been a somewhat controversial pre-Rainier gift to her from the Shah of Iran. Of course, she would not wear it as the Princess of Monaco. I felt a bit queasy as I read about the brooch, handed to me so lovingly in a cabin aboard the *Constitution* nearly thirty years earlier, to think that Grace had chosen not to explain its origins to me. But that was not unlike her. She probably wanted to save us both from the vague sense of disapproval one or both of us might have felt about the original giver of the gift and the surrounding circumstances, whatever they were.

I wore the pin well into the Sixties, until it fell off a suit lapel some-where on the grounds of Versailles. The brilliant little diamond bird trapped in its golden cage by nearly invisible bars tumbled into the autumn leaves near the historic French palace and was gone. It wasn't until many years later that I realized even the life of the pin was prophetic.

So the time at sea passed with parties, games, songs, walks, letter writing, review of arrangements, and late-afternoon confidences and exchanges. By the middle of the trip everyone seemed comfortably settled in a cloud of suspended reality. We all had come from somewhere to be on this ship together and were warmly enjoying our time on board. I think that most of us forgot, for a while, what was about to happen once we got to where we were going. The one who could not have forgotten was Grace.

As we passed through the Straits of Gibraltar, leaning over the ship's railings to glimpse the misty mountains rising high above Algeciras, a mood, both exotic and threatening, invaded our cozy nest. The familiar Atlantic had been traversed. America was far behind us. What lay ahead was foreign. Our history was in America, our legend in things American. We bridesmaids, along with the bride, were a part of the melting pot. The conscience of our generation had been formed by a broad variety of influences, and we were adept at shifting our perspectives in order to survive as we grew. But we were sailing toward a land with a history different from any we had ever been a part of, a land with legends and perspectives of which we knew little except what we had read in books. Would we be as adaptive in these new surroundings where Grace was going to live? Would any of us fit in? The questions hung in the fog, dampening our customary self-assurance as the air grew heavier.

Moving farther into the waters of the Mediterranean, each of us began preparing for what was to come. We reviewed our stacks of invitations and lists of coordinated wardrobes we had fussed over for months. We knew that additional notices of events would be waiting for us in Monaco, and we wished we had been given even clearer and more precise information, particularly about protocol.

Europeans of certain social strata are presumed to have been raised with some knowledge of proper etiquette in the presence of royalty. Part of such behavior is to be found, of course, in common good manners. But other aspects of protocol are absent from the life of the average American. True, this was an era when manners were in. Thus most of us either had been raised with good ones or, in order to move on with our lives, had

that made her think of me as "the Queen of the May." It was the era of big weddings (Senator Jack Kennedy married Jacqueline Bouvier that same year). But as weddings marked the vital milestones in our lives as time progressed, and as mine made such a strong impression on Grace on the day we met, it deserves some description here.

On Wednesday afternoon, April 15, 1953, I moved into a huge suite at the Plaza Hotel, bringing with me my wedding gown, my veil, my mother, Jay's mother, my flower girl niece, my four bridesmaids, my maid and matron of honor, my mother's personal maid, my hairdressers, my florist and my own personal beader.

There had, in fact, been several beaders who had labored for months on my gown. The dress was of lace-trimmed white silk organza, its bodice framed by a low-cut, sweetheart neckline with pleated sleevelets just covering my shoulders. Fortunately, at that time my unbound waist measured eighteen inches. The voluminous skirt culminated in a train you could have laid between the Plaza and Columbus Circle, three blocks west. The bodice, front panels of the skirt, entire hem and train were embroidered with white chalk beads and seed pearls in the shape of lilies of the valley. My tiara duplicated the pearl and chalk beaded lily motif and trailed enough silk tulle to drape Yankee Stadium. This was underpinned by eleven layers of petticoats, silk tulle on the bottom layers, silk chiffon on top, with the topmost layer embossed with lace woven in France to replicate the lily of the valley theme.

My mother, hell-bent on extravagant perfection for the marriage of her only daughter, was not satisfied with the selection of tablecloths offered through the Plaza's banquet department and ordered ecru lace topcloths over peach underskirts. Among my bridal party of seven was former child star Peggy Ann Garner *(A Tree Grows in Brooklyn);* the era's most popular female songstress, Rosemary Clooney; and Patsy Reuben, whose father owned the restaurant after which the Reuben sandwich was named. They, along with my two sisters-in-law, my oldest friend and my niece, had all been fitted for custom-made peach organza gowns.

Jay's attendants had only to own or rent a set of white tie and tails, topping these with black yarmulkes, the traditional Jewish skullcaps that we provided for them. For my brothers and the other ushers, this wardrobe did not seem unusual. But as his best man, Jay had chosen his client and closest friend Marlon Brando. By 1953, Marlon had already taken the

wore a cinnamon-colored, lace-trimmed dress that twirled yards of chiffon round her feet. The breathtaking beauty I had seen under her bonnet in *High Noon* was not a trick of magic performed by Hollywood cameras. It was all there in the perfection of her features as she wafted across the ballroom floor. Ted Stauffeur's orchestra played its hit, "The Most Beautiful Girl in the World," and though I was the bride and quite happy with my own appearance, it was clear who qualified for that designation.

Just before the wedding cake was served, Grace and Marlon danced by, directly in front of our table. As the music stopped, the song ended, and something Marlon said to Grace made her laugh. In one split second, gone was the liquid Grace, the one who appeared to be carried by clouds as she danced a moment before, her face wreathed in the enigmatic and cinematic half-smile. In her place was another Grace, a child dissolved and swept away by her own glee, her body collapsing in laughter, arms and legs all gangly. It was only an instant before she regained control, composing herself, but in that instant I began, from close range, to do what millions of people around the world would do for the next few decades—I began trying to figure out Grace Kelly.

We were not to see each other again for a month or so. Pelted by the traditional rice and flower petals, Jay and I left for our honeymoon. The only nontraditional aspect of our departure was that Marlon was lying on the floor of our limousine, unseen by our friends and families but uttering obscene punch lines to us as we waved our farewells.

We flew first to Mexico City, then on to Acapulco, where we were met by a message from Yul Brynner saying that he and Gary Cooper (with whom he'd been hunting Gila monsters in the Mexican jungles) were expecting us for dinner the following night. While we sipped margaritas with Yul and Coop on the terrace of their bungalow at the El Mirador Hotel the next evening, something happened that was to be repeated each time we dined with them on this trip. Coop brought a telephone extension outside, placed it near his feet, and waited for "a call from Europe." When the call came, Coop went inside to talk privately. I knew that Coop had been separated from his wife of many years, Rocky, near the time he and Grace had made *High Noon* together. It was not Grace, though, but another friend of ours from New York, the actress Patricia Neal, with whom Coop had been in love. Their relationship had begun when they co-starred in *The Fountainhead*, and its intensity had caused havoc in

country by storm playing the T-shirted Stanley Kowalski in both the stage and screen versions of Tennessee Williams's *A Streetcar Named Desire*. Appearing in white tie and tails made him the brunt of endless jokes.

Rounding out the principals in the cast were a noted rabbi flown in from Washington, D.C., and the hottest male singer in America, Eddie Fisher, who sang the *broche*, or traditional Jewish ritual blessings. Eddie had been a cantor's assistant in his Philadelphia neighborhood synagogue. He was starring that week in the live stage show at the nearby Paramount Theater and had agreed to dart to the Plaza between shows to bless us, hurry back to the Paramount to knock 'em dead with a chorus of his big hit "Oh, My Papa," and then join us again for our wedding dinner-dance.

The set and wardrobe were great, and the extras—those four hundred distinguished guests seated on gold-leaf Victorian chairs—behaved in exemplary fashion. Only the leading characters blew the scene, making it nearly impossible for the rabbi to behave rabbinically. For a variety of reasons, Jay and I and all of our attendants erupted in fits of giggles throughout the ceremony. We all bit our lips and tried not to laugh so our shoulders wouldn't shake up and down. Just as we finally had it under control it was Eddie Fisher time, and midway through the *broche* he hit one of the flattest notes ever to issue from the mouth of man. Our convulsions were contagious. Soon all but the rabbi appeared to be shaken with emotion or stricken with Saint Vitus's dance.

Grace was there for all of this. Following the ceremony, she and the other guests waited to congratulate our families in the long receiving line outside the Plaza's Grand Ballroom. From the comments of most of the guests, we realized our laughing fits had been misinterpreted as crying jags by those sitting behind us. As I turned to acknowledge another person's greeting, I saw Grace was next in line. The person gushed, "I never saw anything so beautiful and emotional in all my life, Judy. Why, every one of you young people up there was moved to tears!" As I was being hugged, I peeked at Grace. She stood perfectly erect and still like an alabaster statue. Her face was a model of composure. Then she gave me a long, slow wink.

Jay leaned across me to grab her hand. "Judy," he said, "this is Gracie." It had begun.

I watched Grace when possible throughout the wedding dinner. When she danced by our table, she floated. Her golden hair was pulled straight back from her face, wound in coils at the nape of her neck. She

both their lives. Rocky Cooper was ready to kill Patsy, it was said. When the relationship ended some months before our wedding, Patsy herself had not much cared whether she lived or died. However, Pat was in New York and these calls were from Europe, so I couldn't guess who might be at the other end.

One night at the local bullfights, Coop seemed particularly depressed and withdrawn. He had not snapped out of this mood after the evening's overseas phone call. I asked Yul if Coop was all right. Yul answered, "Sort of. He's friendly with a French actress who has another crisis going on abroad, a very tragic and complicated situation. Her name is Gisèle Pascal and she's been in love for a long time with Prince Rainier of Monaco. It's all very sad and dramatic." At the time it meant little to me. Years later I would recall that I had heard these unfamiliar names just days after first meeting Grace. At the time I wondered exactly where Monaco was and why I had never, before this night, heard of someone called Prince Rainier.

Jay spoke with Marlon from Acapulco to learn he had walked off a picture at Twentieth Century Fox and was heading back to New York to hide out from the press and the studio until Jay got back to the States to settle things. Believing Marlon should go somewhere where no one would look for him, Jay called my mother and asked her to give Marlon the keys to our new apartment. Then we flew on from Acapulco to Beverly Hills for the last leg of our honeymoon.

Arriving back in New York at our fifteenth-floor Sutton Place apartment, we found Marlon grinning, waiting for us at the front door. A mock argument ensued over whether he or Jay would carry me over the threshold, with Marlon insisting the term "best man" was not without significance. The matter was quickly settled when Marlon and I hoisted Jay across the doorsill. The following morning, after waking up for the first time in our new bed, Jay kissed me goodbye to head for the office, and I fell back to sleep. A bit later I stirred, vaguely aware that I was not the sole occupant of my nuptial bed. I opened one corner of one eye to see Marlon curled up on the other side. "The couch isn't great," was all he said before we both slipped back into dreamland. I had grown up with two older brothers and a house full of their boyhood chums. Platonic sleepovers were nothing unusual.

During the first few months of our marriage, we saw Grace only when she and Jay arranged to have dinner out, or take in a play or a movie. There was also one evening when we were invited to a small, informal gathering at her Manhattan House apartment, which she shared with her companion/secretary Prudy Wise.

On our evenings out, Grace would usually be accompanied by one of her close male friends. Donald Buka was a dark and handsome actor with the smile of an angel. Grace had met him two years earlier, in the summer of 1951, when she had been cast as the ingenue Isabelle in Jean Anouilh's play *Ring Around the Moon.* Donald had played the leading male role in the Ann Arbor Drama Festival's production, and while he and Grace worked together in Michigan they formed a friendship that would last for life. Another actor from that same production, Bill Allyn, cemented the same kind of liaison with Grace. Both of them knew Grace's true goal, to establish herself as an actress in the New York theatre world, even though she was already one of the six leading women appearing in important live television drama of that period along with Rita Gam, Mary Sinclair, Neva Patterson, Maria Riva (Marlene Dietrich's daughter) and Felicia Montealegre (Leonard Bernstein's wife).

If Donald did not escort Grace on a particular night, she might bring Gant Gaither. A small Southerner with a wicked sense of humor and exquisite manners, Gant was the producer of the Broadway musical version of *Seventh Heaven.* Like Grace, he knew many people in and around the New York theatre and was obviously a close friend and confidant.

A fourth man who frequently accompanied Grace was John Foreman. Jay and John were ex–apartment mates. John and I, as I have said, were also close friends. So the evenings with just the four of us were cozy and intimate. John had come to us from Pocatello, Idaho, via Stevens College in Missouri, where he had briefly taught dramatic literature to classes of young women from fine families. John was handsome, reasonably tall with a graceful yet athletic body. Like Jay, he was in love with show business. I was not convinced, in those days, that his and Grace's relationship was purely platonic, because John was both romantic and sensual, making it hard to know where the lines were drawn on any of his relationships when we were young.

Through John's eyes, I began to notice another contradiction within Grace. He teased her mercilessly about her transformation from a glamorous movie queen one night to a dowdy school marm on another. One evening Grace would appear in a décolleté or strapless dress, her hair coiffed immaculately, her makeup subtle yet enticing. The next time we would meet, granted in a less formal setting, Grace would be wearing her "sensible" shoes. Grace's "sensible" shoes were so sensible that the only other persons I had ever seen wearing them were old maids who taught compulsory Latin in eastern prep schools. At my wedding I had noticed the serene and elegant Grace who became awkward as a newborn colt when laughter overtook her. Now I could see, too, a Grace who was lusciously provocative on one night and decidedly frumpy on the next.

From her conversations and her companions I learned that Grace was loyal to a fault. Nobody who ever made it past the boundaries of her built-in reserve would be expelled from her heart. She had impeccable manners, born not of affectation but of her fundamental desire to be kind to people and to make every moment in a social situation as pleasant as possible. It also became clear that Grace was deeply serious about her work, constantly looking for challenges so that she could grow as an actress. What had not shown in her face in *High Noon* showed clearly in real life. A vital concern for people (she was a dedicated listener), compassion for the downtrodden (her eyes teared instantly at tales of true misfortune), and a love of laughter leavening her otherwise serious and purposeful approach to life were all qualities that endeared her to me, even in these early days of our friendship.

Grace adored jokes. She liked clean jokes, dirty jokes, practical jokes, puns and even sick jokes, anything so long as it was really funny. She loved telling jokes with accents and jokes that required her to play several parts as the characters of the joke appeared. She delighted in others' ability to tell jokes well and do dialects accurately or amusingly. She loved to giggle at Gant Gaither's slightly Victorian, somewhat snappy, Southern, butter-wouldn't-melt-in-your-mouth asides about any subject or person being discussed. John Foreman's literate, elitist manner of describing a situation or person filled her with delight, as did Jay's one-liners that came from out of the blue and amused as much for their extraordinary accuracy as for the fact that they were delivered with such subtlety.

One night Grace, John Foreman, Jay and I went to the theatre to see our friends John Forsythe and David Wayne in *Teahouse of the August Moon*. Grace was looking particularly dazzling. During intermission we moved to the side of the lobby and stood next to the box-office window to get her out of the way of the curious stares of others in the audience.

Once there, we encircled Grace to protect her from public scrutiny. "Sometimes it doesn't bother me to have so many people stare at me," Grace commented. "Other times, like tonight, I feel just awful when it happens, as though I'm expected to be doing everything right and somehow I'm doing everything wrong."

Not a minute after she spoke, a loud bell went off to signal the end of intermission, startling everyone.

"Grace," Jay yelled at her with mock urgency, "get off the bell." Grace looked about in panic, trying to discern how she could be causing this hideous din. "Grace," Jay pressed, "you're standing on the bell!" She jumped, lifting both feet off the ground as though to escape burning coals. Miraculously, the bell stopped ringing as her feet left the ground. For an instant she looked relieved. Then, noticing our expressions, she realized Jay had "gotten" her. She tried to pummel his chest but was too weak with laughter to succeed. Grace could not stop giggling once we were back inside the theatre. The four of us spent the second act like kids in church trying not to laugh hysterically.

At Grace's apartment, I began to meet her other friends. Carolyn Scott Reybold and her husband Malcolm also lived in the Manhattan House complex. The Reybolds had one baby daughter, Jyl, now nearing two, as her mother swayed about pregnant with her second child. It was Carolyn who had encouraged Grace to start modeling to support herself during Grace's early days in New York at acting school when the two women lived across the hall from each other at the Barbizon Hotel for Women. Sally Parrish came with a new beau, John Richardson. Sally and Grace had met in the autumn of 1948 as both entered their second year at the American Academy of Dramatic Arts, and Sally had been Grace's first roommate at Manhattan House when both moved out of the Barbizon. Rita Gam had worked with Grace in television, and was the only one of Grace's friends I had met before.

If I had expected to understand Grace better through her apartment, this was not the case. Only the bedroom and bath revealed that its tenants were female. The living room was without charm, character or gender. It wasn't ugly; it was utterly bland. Furniture, fabrics and colors alike were all resolutely practical. Everything seemed brown. The room could have belonged to a Boston graduate of Katharine Gibbs who had gone on to do secretarial work in Cleveland, but surely not to a budding New York movie star such as Grace.

My own apartment, nine blocks south on Sutton Place, was all gray and tweedy. This had been my reaction against my mother's penchant for rose and gold brocades. I had also rejected her passion for formal and feminine French antiques, turning instead to the clubby masculine look of seventeenth- and eighteenth-century English wood pieces. I could not tell how Grace came to be surrounded with the setting I saw. Had her mother selected this decor as fitting for a room where careless young people might congregate (a salon version of a rumpus room), and had Grace allowed her mother a free hand because she herself was unsure of her own taste? Had she been raised amid pastel froufrou and was this her way of asserting herself? Or was the "sensible" flat merely an extension of the person who wore such "sensible" flats?

In July 1953, a few months after we had met, Grace headed to California to co-star with Ray Milland and Robert Cummings in Alfred Hitchcock's movie version of the successful Frederick Knott play *Dial M for Murder.* During the months after that, she worked again with Hitchcock, this time co-starring with James Stewart in *Rear Window.* On her brief returns to New York, we would dine together again, but still shared no afternoon "girl" time. All I learned about her forays west was that she never soloed in The Big Orange Grove. Grace was always accompanied either by her secretary or one of her sisters. Or she would ask Rita Gam to share an apartment with her if she found Rita filming in Hollywood at the same time.

Grace's Los Angeles apartments were inevitably inexpensive flats in middle-class buildings on Sweetzer Street and other neighboring boulevards of broken dreams. She consistently turned down invitations to "A"-rated dinner parties where she was meant to be fodder for the sophisticated and jaded bachelors who prowled Hollywood looking for new game. Her evenings were often spent at home studying, cooking or munching on something she and her roommate would throw together to avoid starvation. This economic lifestyle was mandated both by her rigorous shooting schedule and by the fact that she wasn't rolling in money.

Though certain concessions (including her right to work periodically in the theatre) were granted to her, Grace had signed a term contract with

Metro-Goldwyn-Mayer as a condition of doing *Mogambo.* MGM paid her a regular salary and then, having no projects of their own in which to cast her, had loaned her out to Warner Brothers and Paramount for the two Hitchcock films. As her price per picture began to escalate, MGM continued to pay her her flat stipend, while they themselves pocketed the extra money other studios were willing to pay for her services.

Grace was enthusiastic about the experience of working with Hitch-cock. She was also thrilled to be co-starring with such huge Hollywood stars as Gary Cooper, Clark Gable, Ray Milland and James Stewart. Though she still wanted desperately to be a major theatrical actress, the material, directors and co-stars of her first few films were in a class most neophytes would need years to rise to. Within less than two years, from the start of her twenty-second year to the end of her twenty-third, Grace had risen from an unheralded bit player in *Fourteen Hours* to one of the nation's most prestigious female movie stars. The only people in town who seemed not to notice this were at the one studio that had exclusive rights to her services, MGM.

Grace never discussed her personal relationships with her co-stars with me. I had read rumors about Grace and Clark Gable before and after I met her, and had subsequently heard that Mal Milland, Ray's irate wife, was bemoaning her husband's infatuation with his young blond *Dial M* co-star to several Hollywood columnists. But Grace offered nothing and I did not ask. I knew by this time that as warm and cozy as Grace was, there was an enormous sense of reserve about her. The media speculation on her personal life was just beginning to get out of control, and she remained closemouthed with me. Besides, we were not really friends, merely friendly acquaintances whose relationship was forged by my husband, Grace's friend and agent.

Then, too, we must remember that this was the 1950s. None of the girls I knew, even those who had a sex life, sat around talking about it. It was just nobody else's business. It was also possible in those times to have an intense and serious relationship without going to bed. Sometimes even non-virgins selected this option. Abstinence often had the effect of making the relationship more compelling. Longing, after all, is a principal component of romance, and we were a most romantic generation.

On the other hand, the myth that we were all virgins is just that.

Though our mothers told us men didn't want spoiled goods, except for my friends who married *very* young, I believe I would have been hard-pressed to raise a quorum for a Board of Virgins meeting in my neck of the woods.

What I did not know was any girl who indulged in what has come to be called "casual sex." Sex without love was only for bohemians (arty types believed to be found in Greenwich Village) or nymphs (females stricken with some tragic disease that allowed them to enjoy sex for its own sake). For the former, all my friends lived uptown. For the latter, in this era of miracle drugs it was hoped some cure could be found.

Accordingly, those of us who did "it," did "it" only because we were in love. In this state, we were sure the person we did "it" with was the person we would marry. One did not have to be in this state for any prescribed period of time. Twenty minutes would have been frowned upon, two weeks was okay. But this being-in-love state of affairs took doing "it" as far away as possible from being perceived as the dreaded casual sex, legitimizing the act with prenuptial and thus purified intent. It was one thing to see oneself as an incurable romantic, giving one's all to one's beloved, quite another thing to be "the town pump" or "the community chest." Even if our closest friends (or in rare cases our mothers) knew we had done "it," everyone behaved as though "it" had never happened. I had been "engaged" six or seven times before I married Jay Kanter. But Grace would not have known that unless I told her. I didn't. I would not have known what Grace had been up to unless she told me. She didn't.

Late one afternoon in the midwinter of 1953–54, after we had known each other for nine months, Grace, Jay and I boarded a train from Penn Station heading for Philadelphia, where *Dial M* was to be previewed. Our first stop was the Henry Avenue home of Grace's parents in Germantown. Here I saw the genesis of her Manhattan House decor. And here I met the family in which she had been raised. We ate a rather hurried, early dinner, then gathered in the Kellys' living room. Jay was leaning against the mantel talking with Grace's brother Kell. Grace sat on a sofa with her sisters, Peggy and Lizanne, as her father, Jack, lowered himself onto the arm of my chair. At that instant Peggy said something that made Grace whoop with laughter. "Baba's a sketch," said Jack Kelly to me, his eyes smiling proudly as he beamed at his oldest daughter, Peggy, whose nickname he had used.

"Isn't it exciting what's happening with Gracie's career?" I offered. I knew that Jay had told him at dinner about even more impressive picture offers that were coming in for his middle daughter, who had left this house five years earlier to study acting.

"She was a weak little thing," Grace's father sighed dismissively, his smile fading. "I don't understand why she'd want to be an actress, never did, but I told her she could go to New York when she asked because I couldn't think of anything else she could do. Not even getting into college. Oh, well, I'm glad she's making a living." It was clear that in Jack Kelly's eyes, his daughter Grace was an unprofitable and unexceptional investment. To her dad, Grace was a write-off.

Throughout the screening of *Dial M*, as I watched this apparently secure young actress on screen, I would see the sensitive little girl whose father didn't think much of her and didn't mind saying so even now when she was starting to distinguish herself as a professional. It was familiar territory. We daughters who didn't want to develop exactly as our fathers saw fit were mysteries to them. It wasn't that we weren't loved. It was just that we had chosen the wrong way, a way they couldn't understand. We loved our fathers and tried to understand them. They loved us but could not begin to think of understanding us. It was not the generation gap we would hear so much about in later years as we raised our own children. It was the gender gap, and its message had been written indelibly into our souls.

This insight into Grace's childhood remained with me as we all shared a nightcap before boarding the milk train for our return to New York. It had begun to rain, and when we got to the station someone handed us a bottle of champagne and paper cups "for the road." Within twenty minutes Jay fell asleep. Grace motioned me to move with her and the champagne bottle to seats a few rows away so we could talk without disturbing him. We were both reflective as the wet, black night streaked past our windows, an occasional streetlamp spotlighting an isolated mailbox here, a fire hydrant there in the tucked-in villages of New Jersey. As we sipped our champagne out of wilting Dixie cups, I thought again about Grace's father. Sitting across from each other in double seats, I became aware of Grace leaning forward, then felt her hand tapping lightly on my knee.

"Judybird," she said emotionally, "I'm so glad you married Jay. Sometimes you have a friend and they get married, but you don't *really* like the person your friend marries. Of course you don't make it uncomfortable to be together because that person is, after all, married to your friend." Her sentences were beginning to run together now but she tobogganed on rapidly. "And it would be awful to make it difficult for all of you to spend time together, so you won't ever say you didn't *like* the person your friend married, because it isn't your business after all to judge the person your friend wants to be married to." I nodded somewhat dimly, as I wasn't sure what had prompted this outburst or where it was leading. "But with you and Jay it's *completely* different because you know how much I love Jaybird and now I want you to know how much I *really* love you and how close I *really* feel to you as my friend—not because of Jay, but because of us."

Truly surprised and confused, I told Grace I was very pleased to hear her say what she had, but that while I *really* liked her, too, I didn't think she felt at all close to me or that we knew each other very well.

"Oh, I'm so glad you like me," she replied. "I was worried that because I'm so shy you'd think I was dull when you're so gregarious and full of personality. People are always criticizing me for sitting like a board, alone in a corner of a room at a party, not joining in the way you do, and I'm aware of that, too, and wish I could stop doing it." My expression told her that I dismissed such nonsense.

"What's odd about what you said, Grace," I told her, "is that I always thought you felt I was too outgoing, not reserved enough. I thought you watched me at parties wondering what I was doing gadding about like a moth." After thinking for a moment I added, "Probably we're both shy. Your defense is to withdraw quietly. Mine is to 'put the lampshade on my head and dance on the tables.' Both things work to get each of us past our shyness. They're just different defenses." It was two o'clock in the morning on a jiggling milk train smelling of wet newsprint and beery breath. It was the moment that Grace and I became friends.

After that, whenever Grace was in New York we would see each other in the daytime, as well as on evenings with Jay and others. We ran errands together, shopped, ate chicken sandwiches at her apartment or mine, had tea and cookies at Schrafft's, and gabbed our heads off. We realized that though Grace had been raised in Germantown, Pennsylvania, saying catechism and going to Mass, while I had spent Saturday mornings in synagogue and taken Hebrew lessons in Manhattan and Rye, New York, our childhoods and our families shared much in common.

Press coverage on Grace led me to believe that her family moved in circles known as Main Line Philadelphia. Until I visited her home that recent night, I hadn't realized that Grace was raised in the upper-middle-class suburb of Germantown. The Main Line is a series of suburban enclaves that protectively house Philadelphia's oldest families, those who make up the local elite and whose money has been accumulated over several generations. In New York, where I avidly read the society columns, the Main Line represented an even more conservative version of Manhattan's own "Four Hundred." Surrounded by proud fathers and escorts from the leading military schools and colleges of the nation, Main Line daughters made debuts at Assembly Balls in enormous formal gowns that swept the floor as they curtsied their introductions to polite society.

Grace told me she used to fantasize about her own coming-out party when she was in her early teens, but had never even been invited to an Assembly and thought them quite dumb by the time she was old enough. I told her that my mother, in a flight of fancy in 1950 when I was seventeen, had asked me if I wanted a coming-out party. As I'd been dating since I was thirteen and had already been engaged twice, I asked her what we could say I was coming out of. The subject was dropped. Perhaps, I thought, the press knowingly misled us into thinking Grace's family had been Main Line aristocracy. Perhaps Grace's own patrician demeanor, her elegant voice with its quasi-British accent (only recently acquired at the American Academy of Dramatic Arts), and the propriety with which she conducted her public life had helped the media to their presumption. Anyway, it made a better story and they had stuck with it.

The Kellys, however, were Irish and Catholic, which, by definition, meant they could not be on the Main Line. And the money that permitted Grace's family to live as pleasantly as I had seen had been made, not by Jack Kelly's forefathers, but by Jack himself. Grace's father was one of ten children born to a family of humble farmers who had migrated to America in the latter half of the nineteenth century from County Mayo in western Ireland. The Kellys had settled in the Falls of Schuylkill, on the shores of Philadelphia's Schuylkill River, where a great many of the able-bodied adults and children had labored for Dobson's textile mills. With fierce determination and no small amount of skill, Jack Kelly had become a two-time Olympic champion oarsman. He had risen from teen-age jobs as a construction worker to become the owner of a successful family building enterprise known as "Kelly for Brickwork." He was active in city politics and had been a serious but unsuccessful mayoral candidate some years earlier.

Grace's mother, Margaret Majer, was also the child of first-generation immigrant parents. But her family had come from Germany, where, before financial reverses, they had been sizable landowners. While Jack Kelly had been raised Catholic, his wife had been raised in the Lutheran Church, converting to Catholicism only when she and Jack were married.

My own father, Barney Balaban, the oldest of a family of ten, had also been born to immigrant parents, but from Odessa, Russia. My father's childhood was spent in a Jewish ghetto in Chicago called Maxwell Street, where he, his parents and his siblings shared two rooms above a fish and produce market his mother ran on the floor below. The two jobs he had held since the age of nine made it difficult for my father to keep up at school. At fourteen he had quit to devote his full energies to helping his family survive. His longest hours were spent at the Western Cold Storage Company. Fortunately, he and his brothers and one living sister had pioneered the motion picture theatre business in Chicago, urged on by their mother, who saw this as a window of opportunity. They had built a large theatre chain called Balaban & Katz, and in 1936 my family had moved to New York, where my father became president of Paramount Pictures, a position he would hold for nearly thirty years.

Both Grace's father and my own had been born in the era when the commercial development of the United States had been up for grabs. Those who reached for the gold ring had not all emanated from one culture, one religion or one ethnic background. Though of diverse origins, they were young men of exceptional drive and energy who had recognized the needs of the burgeoning society, created businesses to serve those needs, and then labored with purpose, intelligence and guts to make their businesses work. As children, Jack Kelly and Barney Balaban had been imbued with near-reverential respect for their parents. Grace and I each had paternal grandmothers of uncommon strengths whose spirits, ambi-

weather, they had made camp by firelight in desolate reaches. Large animals prowled nearby, while their tents were filled with smaller creatures that flapped, whirred or slithered overhead and underfoot.

I thought of what it must have been like for Grace, just turning twenty-three, a few years out of her family home in Philadelphia, with one starring movie role under her belt, halfway across the world in Africa with Clark Gable. It must have been nice to know she was not as frail as her father had suspected. What Jack Kelly had missed is that Grace was never chicken. It was merely that she insisted upon deciding which games were worth playing in, and what stakes were worth winning.

Grace told me, "I was unable to stop crying when I left Clark at the London airport the morning I flew home for your wedding." Many years later, when it was too late to tell Grace, a mutual friend of ours who had also been a friend of Gable's told me that "The King" had been seriously in love with Grace. He had, I was told, determined they should part only as friends because he sadly believed their age difference would bring them unhappiness and distance in too few years.

In that era I was told by a Hollywood hostess that Mal Milland, Ray's wife, did not wish to be seated at the same dinner party table with me because she heard that Grace and I were friends. The gossip was that Milland had fallen in love with Grace and had left his wife for her. The stories ended by saying that the moment Milland presented himself at Grace's doorstep, she withdrew.

One day while lunching together at Hamburger Heaven on Madison Avenue, I told Grace about the first two Academy Awards shows I had attended with my parents. In both years Paramount had nominees who won. Because of my father's position at the studio, I found myself at age twelve in 1944 alongside Bing Crosby when he rose to claim his Oscar for *Going My Way,* and in 1945 two seats down from Ray Milland when he heard his name called for *The Lost Weekend.* I must have been embarrassed when I mentioned Milland's name, for Grace caught me first looking up at her and then quickly down at my food. "It was," she said ever so quietly, "a bad mistake."

From mid-1953 through mid-1954, though Grace was still not twenty-five years old, she made an amazing number of prestigious and successful films. With *Fourteen Hours* and *High Noon* already released, she had just finished filming *Mogambo* when we met. Then she headed for Hollywood in the summer of 1953 to make *Dial M* for Hitchcock at Warners. It was Hollywood again to make *Rear Window* at Paramount, again for Hitch, then Hollywood made to look like Tokyo for her co-starring role with William Holden in *Bridges at Toko-Ri* (her second consecutive loan-out to Paramount), under the producer/director team of William Perlberg and George Seaton. The Perlberg/Seaton exposure came at the perfect time for Grace. In early 1954 Jennifer Jones, who was to have played Georgie Elgin in *The Country Girl* opposite Bill Holden and Bing Crosby, informed them and the studio that she was pregnant. Though every major and minor actress in show business wanted to play the part, Perlberg and Seaton wanted Grace to replace Jennifer.

The only people who did not want Grace to make *The Country Girl* were Bing Crosby and her home studio, MGM. Crosby, though an established star for years, felt he was over his head when it came to playing Frank Elgin in *The Country Girl*. The part of Frank Elgin was the toughest kind of role for an actor of Crosby's previously limited depths. It required him to play himself, an alcoholic with little self-esteem, the self he had carefully hidden from the public throughout his career. Bing wanted to be sure that the actress who played his courageous and loyal wife Georgie was experienced, mature and strong. In Grace he saw a glamorous youngster with a glossy surface, a cool flirtatiousness and not much else. If she were to be his co-star, the entire film, he felt, would rest on his shoulders. Perlberg and Seaton convinced Crosby to give Grace a chance, assuring him that they would replace her if early shooting proved them wrong.

MGM had begun to look foolish for not coming up with its own property for Grace, and was slowly waking up to the fact that it could make more money by starring her in a film of its own than by loaning her out to others. So her home studio submitted two scripts as alternatives to *The Country Girl*. Both were inferior to the films she had already completed. Both were laughable by comparison to the prestige and brilliance of Clifford Odets's movie adaptation of his *Country Girl*. Grace turned them down, insisting she be allowed to make the film of her choice. So MGM played its strong suit. The studio notified Grace through her agents that if she would not appear in one of its films, she would be placed on suspension, meaning she could not work for any other film company. And Grace played her trump. She told Jay and Lew Wasserman to give MGM the following message: If she would not be loaned out for *Country Girl*, a suspension was academic. She intended to tear up her MGM contract, walk away from the movie business forever, and make her career in the theatre, where MGM could not stop her from working.

MGM was rocked to its core. So was the rest of Hollywood as the story spread. The notion that a young actress with only a few films to her name, some unreleased, was thumbing her nose at Hollywood was unthinkable. The only explanation the industry could offer was that Grace was a spoiled rich kid with money from her father. In fact, her family had pledged only minimal support when Grace left Philadelphia to become an actress. Yet, Hollywood reduced her act of bravery by an artist to an act of folly by an heiress. It was a better script. It made the Tinsel Townsfolk feel better to tell it that way. Grace herself made no public statements to correct the impression. She simply smiled and went off to do the most challenging work of her career, playing Georgie Elgin in *The Country Girl*. The myth that was building around her was erroneous, but even an erroneous myth is better for an actress than no myth at all. And Grace knew that.

In the spring of 1954, a year after we met, Grace agreed to make *Green Fire* for her home studio. It was scheduled to be shot amidst the emerald mines and coffee plantations of Colombia and co-starred Stewart Granger. Grace made the movie as much to cheer herself and her oldest friend as to mollify Metro.

Maree Frisby Pamp, Grace's close friend from high school at Stevens in Germantown, had a small daughter, Linda, by Arvid Pamp, the husband she had married while very young. Arvid had been sent to Barranquilla, Colombia, to open a Sears store there, taking Maree and Linda with him. Grace knew from Maree's letters that she was miserable, so being a loyal friend, Grace decided she would accept *Green Fire* and surprise Maree by arriving unannounced in the hinterlands of Colombia to keep her company. However, when Grace arrived in South America, she discovered Maree had already returned to Philadelphia.

Having committed herself to make a movie she disliked, Grace stuck out the location in the country from which Maree had fled. In the late spring of 1954, though, packing to leave for Paris and the French Riviera to co-star with Cary Grant, again under Hitchcock's aegis, in *To Catch a Thief*, Grace was excited, enthralled and exhausted. She was also ready for romance.

Either Grace herself or the rumor mill spoke of intense relationships between Grace and her co-stars on four of the six movies she had completed in the first year of our friendship. In Africa, it was Grace and Gable on *Mogambo*. In Hollywood, Grace and Milland on *Dial M*. In Hollywood again, Bill Holden was said to have gone gaga for Grace on *Toko-Ri*. Though he reportedly assured Crosby the romantic coast was clear at the start of *Country Girl*, while Bing and Grace dated platonically and publicly, always chaperoned by one of Grace's sisters or other protectors, Bill's car was said to be seen almost nightly in front of Grace's apartment. In the year since we met, Grace had done six of the hottest movies and reputedly four of the hottest male stars in the business. Quite a heady and potent legend was emerging.

Years later, however, it would be said that the greatest personal obsession over Grace existed in every corpulent cell of the director she was about to work with for the third time, Alfred Hitchcock. It was, Grace told me, while working for Hitch that she had discovered what moviemaking was all about. She recognized that the theatre was the playwright's medium because actors and director were primarily beholden to serving the writer's words, but that the screen was the director's medium. No matter what elements were contained in the plot, dialogue or performances, the audience would see the film through the eye of its director. Working with Hitch and Edith Head (Paramount's great designer), Grace had even come to accept film costuming as an art. "Every small detail of a single piece of wardrobe becomes another thread in the developmental texture of my character," she would say.

In Grace, Hitchcock found the perfect filmmaking partner. Where he led—with only a word, gesture or raised eyebrow—she followed. It was a director's and actor's dream. Whether they knew it or not, at the same time that they were creating movies and characters, they were producing a legend. Before Hitch, Grace was a girl. By the time she returned from Europe after making *To Catch a Thief*, Grace had become the movie star version of the ideal Fifties woman—and she knew it.

We had come through the era of the war babies, the dancing darlings like Betty Grable. Pony-tailed girl scout Debbie Reynolds was too girlish to entice us. Elizabeth Taylor had given a remarkable performance in *A Place in the Sun*, but we were not sure yet whether she was just a remarkably beautiful, lucky, headstrong child or a real actress. Katharine

Hepburn, in a universe all her own, Jane Wyman and Susan Hayward were all doing revitalizing work on screen, but were too well known for too long to epitomize our era. Deborah Kerr was too British; Audrey Hepburn so fastidious and rarefied she might break if you touched her. We liked Doris Day for the same reason we liked fortified breakfast cereal. And though Marilyn Monroe tickled our boyfriends' fancies and broke our hearts, not one of us wanted to be her.

Grace did not start the fashion for wearing polite, white kid gloves. She merely confirmed that we could continue doing so without cramping our style. It was exactly what we wanted to hear. For the Fifties woman— at least her idealized vision of herself in the first half of that decade—was based entirely upon our male contemporaries and what they wanted us to be. The young men we dated and hoped to marry had been raised with two classifications for all womanhood. On the one hand, there were girls you sleep with; on the other, girls you take home to mother. However, what they really wanted was a girl you could both sleep with *and* take home to mother. So that's exactly what most of us wanted to be. Grace, both in *The Country Girl* and under Hitchcock's guidance in his movies, became the film and then real-life representation of our desires.

What you saw on screen and read in the press revealed a woman who was as beautiful and refined as she was sexy. She spoke with cultured reserve, yet she told you tantalizing things. Though she worked at her career, she was available whenever her man wanted or needed her. Like Nancy Drew, she aided her partner in solving crimes yet abetted him in his mischief. While she dressed immaculately, she undressed with the graceful seductiveness of an upper-crust stripper. She mocked life but cried easily. She called a spade a spade even when she dealt it to herself, but stood by her failing man unfailingly. She was your playmate, your sister, your girlfriend, your hot potato and your puppy dog. She was the best of all 1950s worlds. If she could be all that, maybe we could, too.

As this movieland Grace was being concocted for our viewing plea- sure, the real-life Grace was also growing into womanhood. The difference between the legend and the reality was not always that great, but contra- dictions abounded.

The diffident, standoffish public Grace was privately warm and demonstrative. The guileless, capable Grace we saw was guilty of the subtlest manipulation, consistently seeing to it that others performed her unwanted tasks. Accommodating and pliable, Grace was also as willfully self-directed as could be. She had extremely high standards and was visibly judgmental on occasion, yet when it came to her friends she was indulgent almost to a fault. She was an optimist with a reserve of protective pessimism, but she was not a cynic.

Grace's meticulous caution commanded our respect while our hearts secretly yearned for her reckless bravery. We admired her faithful practice of Catholicism as much as her mischievous irreverence. We wanted to be as tranquil, well-ordered and unhurried as she appeared to be, but recognized that she thrived on excitement, chaos and overcrowded scheduling. Grace was mature, and prematurely grown-up, yet we loved in her the dizzy, dopey, melting and swooning schoolgirl who was never out of sight for long.

We were amazed at the apparent lack of self-consciousness in an extraordinary beauty who considered herself merely "nice looking." But we could not help wondering just how perfect Grace would have to be before she admitted to herself that she was exceptional. For a fortunate girl with blessings too countless to enumerate, it would have been unseemly to appear to need anything. So Grace appeared not to. Yet how could such a girl be so ambitious, aspiring and relentless?

As we watched Grace living her life and doing her work, we did not realize the enormity of the task she had undertaken. For what she was creating, frame by frame, was the most consistently compelling home movie of the mid-twentieth century. It was "The Grace Kelly Story," and she was its writer, producer, director, star and editor. As the latter, she alone would cut out the parts that didn't play, the pieces that offended or confused, to assure a strong central character both she and we could identify with as we played it over in our fantasies. She would also leave in just enough mystery to hook us forever into wanting to see more.

What she left on screen was the lucky little flower—the one who could watch the pain of living without so much as the bat of an eye, the one on whom the sun shone with unfailing regularity. What she excised from view, in those outtakes that lay tangled around her feet at the end of the day, in the cold bleak darkness of every night, were the battle scenes. For Grace was going to fight her wars in private, all by herself.

Perhaps she knew even then, perhaps she would not realize until she ran and reran the footage of "The Grace Kelly Story" in her own mind over the years to come, that it was only she who had been playing all the parts—the little flower and the warrior, the favorite and the underdog, the victorious and the vanquished, the heroine and the villain. What I believe she did know at the time was that this epic saga was in process and that its creation was a job that would last all the rest of her life. In that alone, Grace was light-years ahead of many of us. In my case, I was far too enthralled to find myself a featured player in her invention to begin the work of inventing myself. Like many of us then—perhaps now as well—I was not even aware that I possessed either the talent to do that, or the right.

Scott traveled the farthest of us, coming all the way from Steubenville, Ohio, to the Barbizon, where she met Grace and began her modeling career. Rita Gam had the shortest distance to go. She merely had to leave home and head downtown with her talent for acting—which led her to Grace. I had been flirting with the city since adolescence, using my parents' Hampshire House *pied-à-terre* as often as possible, only thirty-seven minutes by rail from my home in Rye.

Every one of us bridesmaids was privileged with good looks or money, with talent or charm, with humor or intelligence, or with some combination of these. Our teenage years had been a time of great optimism and high, strong energy when our nation was being revitalized, rebuilding itself for the peacetime economy we thought would be ours forever. The possibilities seemed limitless, not merely for us—the fortunate few—but for truck drivers and construction workers charged with moving goods and erecting the accommodations for the boom in housing and business, for factory workers, secretaries and civil servants—almost everyone who had his health. There was money to be made, money to be spent. The Dow Jones industrial average had risen from around 64, where it had been the year I was born, to 400. The average price of an automobile had tripled in twenty years so that what you could buy for $600 in 1932 might cost almost $1,500. But with rationing ended, there were enough tires and gasoline for all the shiny, automatic, fin-tailed cars Detroit was promising for our travel fantasies. This new message—you can go wherever you wish—permeated every aspect of our belief in our own potential.

We danced, flirted, studied, worked and dreamed—with glorious good faith—about the beautiful and joyous lives every one of us expected to live. As we finished our schooling, located our interim jobs, our husbands and one another, we never attached particular significance to the fact that we were the six best friends of Grace Kelly.

There is one other important thing, though, about Grace and the other six of us: We were the last generation of children raised on this planet without ever having to imagine that someday, some unknown maniac might press his finger on a button and blow the whole damn earth out from under us.

World War II was no small part of our childhood. It lasted from our pre-teen years well into our adolescence. Most of us saw someone we loved

CHAPTER 3

Out of the Everywhere

$\mathcal{N}$ot unlike our friend Gracie, we were the girls who busied ourselves appearing to be the person who we wanted to think we were. We were just trashing our training bras when our older sisters welcomed home the heroes from the last of this century's noble wars. As the 1940s gave way to the Fifties, we packed away our pleated plaid skirts, our penny loafers with the squashed counters and our angora bobby sox. Cinching our tiny waistlines into crinolined, *peau-de-soie* cocktail dresses, we fastened every last pearl button on our white kid gloves and, properly uniformed, hit our own beachhead—New York City.

Bettina Thompson had lived in a different place nearly every two years of her life as a Marine Corps brat when she settled into the Barbizon and the American Academy of Dramatic Arts and found Grace. Sally Parrish backed into Manhattan from Richmond, Virginia, while attending her first two years of college in suburban Bronxville at Sarah Lawrence. When she enrolled with Grace at the American Academy, it became the thirtieth school she had attended during her short lifetime. Maree Frisby, who had been close to Grace since high school in Philadelphia, settled in New York for a brief spell after she had married her first husband. Carolyn

go off to war. Grace and Maree in Philadelphia, Carolyn in Steubenville, Sally and Bettina in cities throughout the country, and Rita and I in New York and Rye all sold war bonds in school drives. We pasted decals on Woolworth's glasses, knitted or crocheted pot holders, arranged flowers from our gardens, and sold our wares at fairs for neighboring families to raise money for the war effort. There was a job to be done by everyone, even small children, and we were enriched by the experience of making our contribution.

But the war also gave many of us our first lessons in sex education. It was during this period that I learned about lovemaking and rape from war movies, war stories and Errol Flynn. In the movies, wartime love and sexuality were vested with patriotism. The actual sex scenes were, of course, only vaguely implied, but a romantic union became—on the silver screen—an act of majesty, a blessing of sanity in an insane world, the ultimate aid to the war effort. In reality, we girls made vomiting sounds when one of us described a soul-kiss with tongues touching as we knitted argyle socks for our first boyfriends. But in our fantasies, we contemplated giving our all as a bon voyage present to a handsome young soldier departing for foreign shores.

Lovemaking was never discussed in our presence. From the dirty jokes we overheard on occasion, we could imagine that women's sexual roles were relegated to smut, stupidity or—at best—a capacity for titillation. Men were entitled to a basic sexual drive, one in which tension, charge, release and, therefore, pleasure were acceptable. Women were their receptacles. Men did sex; women had it done to them. And in a time of war, behind the cupped hands of adults, the talk was of atrocities being committed in distant lands among masses of human beings. One of those atrocities was rape. In this act, the enemy took your all whether or not you had any intention of giving it. Then, when daily newspapers featured headlined stories of Errol Flynn, of all people—the movies' heroic swashbuckler—being accused of statutory rape (had he done it on the Lincoln Memorial or on horseback in Pershing Square, my tender mind reeled), a new sexual dilemma arose. Looking up statutory rape, I discovered it meant that rape was illegal—against a statute—only with minors. Did that mean that once we grew up we could be legally raped? (Reviewing some recent court decisions tells me the question is still a valid one.)

Certainly there were no adults we could ask. Four-letter words were verboten, twelve-letter words unknown, our mothers were posing as married virgins and our fathers hoping we would never have sex anyway.

The bridesmaids shared with the bride these common childhood imprints—war, peace and sex education. But though the times wrote upon us as a group, our immediate surroundings and families placed their own indelible impressions separately on each of us as we came to the years when we met Grace and formed our friendships with her.

❧ MAREE ❧

Maree Frisby was raised by her mother in Chestnut Hill, an exclusive suburb of Philadelphia. Though Maree herself would grow enviably tall and willowy, her mother was barely more than five feet in height. Maree's parents divorced when she was only one year old, and her father moved to Florida shortly afterwards. Maree may have seen the man who sired her a few times when she was very small, but those occasions were so rare that by the time she was grown she had no recollection of him.

Living alone together, Maree and her mother were extremely close. Maree attended local elementary schools and enrolled at Stevens School in Germantown at the start of junior high school. When she was twelve, and just entering Stevens, her mother met and married Dr. Strawbridge. After a brief episode of resentment Maree decided he was a welcome addition to their small family. The three spent a happy year together. Unfortunately, the doctor died shortly thereafter. Widowed so soon, Maree's mother could have beaten her breast, railed against fate, and weakened her link to her only child. Instead, she bravely carried on, leaving with her daughter a message that was loud and clear: Women may be dealt a bad hand, but they are expected to suffer in silence and to keep things running as smoothly as usual, both for the benefit of their children and for the outside world.

Three years after Maree's enrollment at Stevens, when she entered tenth grade, Grace Kelly joined the ninth-grade class. The two girls had no classes together, nor did they sit with each other during lunch recess. Their friendship began at the dances and parties that were held at the drop of a hat in those postwar years. Maree was already popular. Soon, so too was the new blond high schooler from Germantown who had learned to hide the intense shyness that had been so evident in her earlier childhood years. Gracie was in great demand, both as a date and a dancing partner. She was not yet a raving beauty, but she could not have looked in the mirror without realizing that she was, to say the least, extremely pretty. In spite of her chronic bouts with sinus trouble, she had something strong inside her which shone, glowingly, on the outside. Both her fellow bobby-soxers and their roster of escorts recognized that the new girl was special. It helped that she had beautiful, white, straight teeth and that the blemishes which erupted with regularity on the faces of other girls never once dared to mar her perfect complexion.

Maree had a lively and accurate sense of humor, even as a girl. She was kind and observant. She had her mother's strength and was able to roll with the punches as she made her way through the all-girls' school and the social life that filled both weekends and vacation periods. Her new friend had grown up somewhat outside the Kellys' boisterous activity, developing her own sensitive, rare and very private personality. As a child Grace recognized her basic sound health and fundamental good fortune. Once in high school she discovered that she was also talented, pretty and popular. No decent girl could have asked for more. In fact, a decent girl—counting her blessings as we had been taught to do and as Grace did regularly—knew that if you were healthy, affluent, adept, pretty and popular, you owed the world.

Maree watched her new friend as she tried out for and was cast in plays within the class, the school at large and the local community playhouse. It was clear to her that Grace learned her lines more quickly and delivered them with far greater meaning than her fellow student actors. The same conscientiousness and talent showed itself in Stevens's compulsory Saturday-morning modern dance classes.

Once Maree got out of school she had no intention of going back. She hated schools of all kinds, but the only acceptable alternative to college was work or engagement. Maree busied herself with nightly dates, random inconsequential jobs and multiple fiancés. Though she and Grace were living entirely different lives—the one out every night, the other still doing high school homework—they maintained and strengthened their friendship. Maree, however, had little to distract her from her journey to all the best places to dine and dance, to moor one's boat and to houseguest for country weekends. It was at the Lloyd Harbor estate of his close friend, inventor/industrialist/Pygmalion Sherman Fairchild, that Malcolm first met Grace.

The tycoon of Fairchild Industries had built Eastfair, his astonishing country house, by transporting a thirteenth-century castle, stone by stone, from Europe to Long Island. Sherman had tennis courts, swimming pools, a moat, a large orchard, a harborside view and an entire herd of young women whom he personally was grooming for life in upscale New York society. Sherman saw to it that these budding socialites learned all the amenities that were required for the good life. We used to refer to Sherman's trainees as the "Sherman Fairchild Finishing School for Young Beauties." Its motto, we believed, was, "If Sherman doesn't finish you, the school will."

Grace and Malcolm met over a tennis game one weekend afternoon at Eastfair. Malcolm was having a good time playing the field and had no intention of being tied down by anyone. Grace, for her part, had little interest in Malcolm, though the two later found themselves members of a larger group on a couple of nights on the town back in Manhattan.

One evening another current date of Malcolm's asked him to join her party as the escort of yet another girl. At the Lexington Hotel, where the group assembled, Malcolm met his blind date. He must have looked pretty good to the junior model from Steubenville. For a time Carolyn was just another phone number to be listed in Malcolm's little black book. Gradually, as Carolyn and Malcolm began seeing more of each other, they double-dated with Grace or joined together with her and other chums. Carolyn and Malcolm were both impressed one evening when they went to see Grace perform in an evening of one-act plays in the Academy basement. But Malcolm was more impressed with Carolyn.

By 1949, Grace and Carolyn were prepared to leave their teens. Having completed her two years at the Academy, Grace appeared in several stock productions at the Bucks County Playhouse and had been cast in her first Broadway play, *The Father,* by its director and star, Raymond Massey. Carolyn was successful on two counts. She had risen to the top of her field and had eliminated the rest of the field for Malcolm. He stopped playing the dating game when they were married in Florida.

No member of the bride's family was present, nor had Malcolm ever met any one of them prior to that day.

Carolyn, though, did know Malcolm's daughter Pat. In *Seventeen* magazine, Carolyn appeared as a teenage girl. Now she had become a stepmother to a full-blown adolescent daughter. By introducing the two, Malcolm was making no attempt to conceal from Carolyn that he was older than she. With Carolyn's unhappy childhood associations about fathers, the twelve-year age difference Malcolm admitted to might well have been one of his attractions. He told Carolyn he was "about thirty-two." Not really an older man. Not a boy. Just a nice mature person you could trust.

Not long after their marriage, Carolyn and Malcolm, accompanied by Grace and a mutual friend, Jack Duff, took off for a weekend at the Scenery Club in Canada. As Grace and Jack were not "involved," and as these were still years when house detectives evicted single occupants for entertaining even a daytime visitor of the opposite sex for more than five minutes, they booked two rooms—one for the men, the other for the girls.

Malcolm had presented Carolyn with a brand-new Buick as a wedding gift and decided they should break it in on the trip. Once in Canada, the two young women took off for an afternoon of exploration. During their drive they needed to look at the automobile registration. Malcolm had left it in the glove compartment with his driver's license, which he had forgotten to remove, on the back of the slip. When Grace and Carolyn saw the license, they discovered the new groom's actual birthdate. It turned out that the nice mature person you could trust was more mature than expected. In reality, Carolyn's "thirty-two"-year-old husband turned out to be nearly forty, not twelve but nearly twenty years her senior. Infuriated and hurt, the two drove back to the lodge, where Malcolm and Jack Duff were scheduled to meet them at the bar for drinks. Aided by Grace, Carolyn confronted her husband. Malcolm only gave a big, hearty laugh, which would repeat itself each time he told the story for the rest of his life, and hers. It was a great story, he thought. A big joke. One of the best he had ever heard.

Carolyn moved into Malcolm's bachelor apartment while they hunted for a larger place to live. When Grace told them about Manhattan House, the huge complex on East Sixty-sixth Street which "Kelly for Brickwork" was helping to erect, Carolyn and Malcolm took a flat on the eighteenth floor while Grace signed up for one on the ninth floor of the same wing. In the beginning, life was very gay for the newlyweds. There were lots of parties to go to, Carolyn kept on with her modeling, Malcolm worked in advertising, and by 1951, their first daughter, Deborah Jyl, another god-child for Grace, was born. When Grace came back to her New York home from acting jobs in stock in Michigan, at Elitch Gardens in Denver and from her first Hollywood movie, *Fourteen Hours,* the Reybolds and their daughter Jyl were the family she came home to.

The year 1953, when I met Grace and the Reybolds, was a good one for Grace and for me, but not for Carolyn and Malcolm. They were happily awaiting the birth of their second child when Malcolm, flying home from a business trip, began spitting blood. He had been plagued with ulcers for more than ten years. An ambulance took him directly to Roosevelt Hospital, where the doctors removed three-quarters of his stomach, some of his upper intestine and part of his pancreas. With Malcolm out of work, Carolyn returned to modeling as quickly as possible after the birth of their second daughter, Robin. It was a while before Malcolm was well enough to work again. He began by starting his own business selling air conditioners to Manhattan House tenants. Business boomed for a short period, and Malcolm saw himself as a "big thing in air conditioners." Grace had watched Carolyn brave this storm. She admired her and turned to her friend, not only for companionship, but for strength and solidarity.

❧ SALLY ❧

Sally Parrish is a Southern girl. Born in Richmond, Virginia, she—like Maree, Rita and Carolyn—had parents who divorced. Sally's mother did not linger long enough for the children to notice much. She loved to travel, so travel they did. By the time Sally was nine, she was fluent not only in her native tongue but in two foreign languages as well. She would hit twenty-nine schools during her developmental years, starting with kindergarten in California. There would be classrooms in Mexico, in

Buenos Aires and other South American cities, and she would touch base at lycées in Switzerland.

In spite of the transient nature of her childhood, Sally always felt she had roots in Virginia. Though her father's parents had died before her birth, her maternal grandparents lived in Virginia, where Sally and her younger brother were taken each summer for a lengthy visit. Sally's mother apparently had no problem providing herself with money. Wherever it came from, there was enough of it for her to keep moving on and to go through several fortunes in the process.

Twice during Sally's childhood, the Virginia traveler landed in New York and enrolled Sally in the elite Spence School for girls. But this was in two separate years. The only two consecutive years she ever spent at one school were at Holton Arms in Washington, D.C. (I played left inner for Mount Vernon when we beat them in field hockey.) When it came time for college, Sally's family thought a nice conservative school like Sweet Briar would be just the ticket, but Sally had thoughts of her own. The only two eastern girls' colleges that were noted then for their theatre arts programs were Bennington and Sarah Lawrence. In Grace's case, she had wanted to go to Bennington. Either she did not apply in time, would not take her entrance exams, or took them and flunked. All three stories have been told over the years, but nobody knows for sure which is accurate. Sally, though, preferred Sarah Lawrence because it was near New York and the Broadway theatre.

Sally enjoyed two years at Sarah Lawrence, learning stage managing and other aspects of theatre. Dissatisfied, though, with the limited amount of acting available to the students in her program, she transferred to the American Academy of Dramatic Arts. Most of her Academy classmates had come directly from high school, giving Sally a two-year advantage in age, maturity and experience.

Though Sally and Grace enrolled at the Academy in the same year, it was at different times and in different sections. After one year the Academy sifted through its current students, separating the wheat from the chaff. Both Sally and Grace passed muster and enrolled together for their second, and senior, year in the autumn of 1948. Though they got to know and like each other during this period, their friendship did not blossom for another year. Sally had gone off to England immediately after graduation. In 1950 she returned to New York and checked into the Barbizon while looking for a place to live. There, she and Grace found each other again. By this time, Grace had her parents' permission to leave the Barbizon, had some money to support herself, and had selected her new location at Manhattan House. But her parents did not want her to live alone. They had contemplated an older companion, but when Grace learned that Sally was apartment hunting, she called home and got the Kellys' permission to enlist Sally as her roommate.

Sally's and Grace's careers were not on a parallel. Grace was performing on live television drama, doing *Studio One, Playhouse 90* and other top shows. Sally did not yet have an agent and was shopping for one as she sought out acting jobs on her own. As a child she had never needed to have a lot of drive. As a young woman she did not have it, and she knew it. Though she saw Grace's outward quietness and reserve, Sally recognized in Grace the fierce desire to succeed and the aggressiveness to accomplish that goal which she herself did not possess.

Sally's first professional opportunity came when one of the heads of the Academy called to tell her about a chance to participate in a backer's audition for an upcoming musical. Sally had studied voice with Lydia Chaliapin and had done some singing at the Academy. But she was far more secure as an actress than as a vocalist. On the morning of her tryout, Sally woke up with what part of her had prayed for—total, complete laryngitis. She had no voice at all and a body that was nearly paralyzed with fear. She rasped her cancellation into the phone.

Later the same afternoon, though, Sally got a fortuitous call from some friends who were doing winter stock in Albany, New York. Their company was planning to do *Strange Bedfellows* and other productions with roles Sally could play. Sally's friends insisted that she leave for Albany immediately. In her grating whisper Sally explained that she had no voice. Her callers told her to take the only train at four the next afternoon or her chance was over. Sally found her voice, hopped the train, got the job that led to her Equity card, acted in *Strange Bedfellows, Jenny Kissed Me* and *The Silver Whistle,* froze in Albany for the three winter months, and loved every minute of it. She had become an actress.

It was not uncommon for Sally or Grace or both of them to be out of town for protracted periods while they lived at Manhattan House. Sally suspected, though, that Grace had a career in mind, while Sally herself was only seeking jobs. When another Academy teacher, Bob Champlain, left to become head of casting for William Esty Advertising, he hired Sally for several episodes of the Ralph Bellamy television series *Man Against Crime*. Sally was grateful for this added opportunity, but near the end of 1953, when a friend called asking her to be a fourth for dinner and theatre as the date of her husband's law school classmate, Sally accepted with pleasure.

Five months later, on Valentine's Day of 1954, Sally's blind date, John Richardson, proposed marriage. Upon her acceptance, they planned an October wedding for three hundred and fifty guests, but in July of that year, when Sally's father died, they amended their plans for a smaller August wedding. There was a formal ceremony at Christ Church Methodist in Manhattan, but only one hundred friends and family members were in attendance. Grace was away, shooting one of the five films she made that year. Sally was eager for her own new role. Suspecting that she could not be all things to all people, and knowing how hard one needed to focus in order to achieve success as an actress, Sally had opted to put her energies into something she wanted even more than acting. She wanted to be married. She wanted to have children, and she wanted to make a home for herself and her family. She had no sense of sacrificing anything. It was a matter of choice and Sally made her choice happily.

✤ BETTINA ✤

Like Sally, Bettina Thompson was raised nearly everywhere, but did not feel rootless. She was the fifth of the six of us to have seen her parents divorce when she was a tiny child. Both of Bettina's parents remarried: her father, Lewis Steenrod Thompson, Jr., to a Philadelphia Main Liner, Loulie Gordon Thomson; her mother, Elizabeth Craighead Watson, to a career Marine Corps officer, Julian P. Brown, who would later become a general. As Bettina lived with her mother and stepfather during the nine months of every school year, she moved every two years when the General changed bases and attended dozens of schools in several states. Her mother and General Brown (Daddy to Bettina) produced one of her half brothers, six years her junior. Her other two half brothers were the children of her real father, whom she called Pop, and his wife, Loulie.

Bettina's maternal grandmother was French and Catholic, and had raised Bettina's mother in New Orleans, where her family first settled in the States. Her father's mother was a member of the noted Morgan family of New York and Hyde Park. Her summers were spent at Brookdale, the magnificent New Jersey estate owned by her father's family. Brookdale was so large that everybody had a different house on the estate, and it had its own racetrack—a mile and a quarter with training barns. Bettina felt it was the ideal place to grow up.

When the Japanese bombed Pearl Harbor in 1941, Bettina was attending Bishop's School in La Jolla, California. Her family had been scheduled to move to Hawaii that spring, but her stepfather was quickly reassigned to the aircraft carrier *Enterprise*, where he served as Marine Intelligence officer under Admiral "Bull" Halsey. After the Battle of Midway in the Pacific, General Brown, suffering from the great strain of combat, was sent back to California on sick leave. The family moved to Newport, where Bettina boarded for two years at the Mary C. Wheeler School. During her junior year in high school she received a letter from her mother saying, "Hold on to your hats—here we go again." It was thus that she came to complete her senior year of high school under the tutelage of Puerto Rican nuns.

Bettina loved the excitement of changing schools and addresses often, but as she got a bit older she became aware of feeling that she was always on the fringe of things. It became harder to make friends, and the effort expended in trying to belong was energy that did not go into her schoolwork. Bettina's school in La Jolla had a first-rate drama department. Upon graduation she decided that Bennington was the place for her. But when, like Grace, she made it only as far as their waiting list, the American Academy became her alternate selection.

Until that time Bettina had not felt any substantive change in her circumstances. She was aware that life near a marine base and life at Brookdale looked different from each other, but she did not find them dissimilar. The values, the way of life were the same. One appeared simple, the other grand. Both were where her family was, and neither was without her accustomed level of gentility. At three, when her parents divorced, in lieu of alimony for her mother, Bettina was presented with a trust fund. As a high school graduate, she knew she could maintain herself in New York while she studied acting. The Barbizon was automatic. Bettina's paternal grandmother was only an hour away in New Jersey. Her maternal grandfather and his second wife had an apartment nearby on Park Avenue. What the Barbizon would not watch over, her grandparents would.

Bettina and Grace grew friendly during class time at the Academy and at the hotel. During their second semester as acting students, they and a third girl, Jean Drouillard, combined one smaller room and a larger double at the Barbizon to form a suite. Bettina got the single because her housekeeping style left much to be desired. The neater Miss Drouillard came from Cleveland, ran a tight ship and went home again. Though Bettina and Grace were close friends, Bettina found herself a bit put off by Grace's seriousness. She adored Grace's sense of humor and knew she loved to play, but it sometimes annoyed her that Grace had her mind set on so straight a path. This was foreign to Bettina's way of looking at life, with her need to laugh at its twists and turns. Grace represented another way, which Bettina found unsettling. Her own need to filter life through a veil of irony was great and strong. She knew that others often perceived this as abrasiveness, but it did not seem to bother Grace.

The summer before Bettina came to the Barbizon, fresh from the Puerto Rican nuns, she met a rather portly fellow named Francis (Frank) Gray. Bettina had been vacationing on Martha's Vineyard when her second cousin and a few others, including Frank, had stopped by to visit with her godfather Charlie Hardy. Bettina and Frank played tennis together, but did not see each other again until a year or more later when Bettina attended the New York wedding reception of a friend, with her father and stepmother. Once at the reception, Bettina's father informed her that he and her stepmother would not be taking her on to dinner with them. They had already made "grown-up" plans to have dinner with friends. Bettina felt hurt, and when Bettina feels hurt she gets furious. Her father pawned her off with the suggestion that she find someone else to dine with. Thinking to her defiant self, "By God, I will!" she marched off in the direction of Frank Gray. He was the only other person at the party she knew.

Two years later, needing to decide between the place offered to her at the Royal Academy of Dramatic Arts in London (the result of a successful audition) and the marriage proposal of Frank Gray, Bettina (whom Grace called "Tiner" or "Tiners") chose the latter. She was tired of moving. She wanted to settle down in one place. She wanted to have the same dentist. Grace was present at St. Bartholomew's Church in New York City for the wedding. It was medium-sized, with two hundred guests, and traditional.

Bettina and Frank settled into a happy and typical young married life, in Hancock for a year, then in Belmont, Massachusetts. A year after Bettina and Frank were married, in the summer of 1951, Grace called to say she had been hired for a modeling job that was bringing her to Boston. The U.S.S. *Constitution,* a new ship, had been built in the Quincy boatyards. It was scheduled to make its maiden overnight voyage on a run to New York during which Grace would be photographed as a honeymooning bride as part of the liner's advertising campaign. Bettina hopped into her little Austin to join Grace at the boatyards so the two could enjoy a visit. After being apart for so long, they had a lot of catching up to do, and were so deeply enmeshed in their exchange that neither of them heard the "all ashore" calls. As Grace put the finishing touches on her newlywed outfit in preparation for a session before the cameras, Bettina looked out the porthole to discover that the ship was moving! They ran on deck to learn that, indeed, the ship had sailed with Mrs. Francis Calley Gray II as a stowaway. The seas were too rough for her to be taken off in the pilot boat and, while the two friends screamed with laughter, the eight or nine members of the press who were making the voyage got a story to fill their news wires. When they landed in New York, Bettina was terrified of what her Boston Brahmin husband would think when he saw her escapade featured in the papers. She waved goodbye to her reporter friends, who stood at the railing waving back as she disembarked, then ran to a phone booth to call her father. "Daddy, I'm in town," she announced when she heard his voice.

"I know," he replied, "I read it in the shipping news." Though Bettina and Grace giggled about the episode by phone in the months to come, neither of them had any notion that it was just the first of two momentous voyages they would make together on the *Constitution* in their young lives.

Bettina returned from her seagoing adventure and settled down to more normal activities. Adhering to the pattern of a two-year interval between plighting and parenthood, Bettina and Frank had their first child on July 23, 1952. Named Elizabeth Thompson Gray, Jr., after her mother, she was called Lizzie. The hospital staff that attended us when we delivered our early children seemed hell-bent on keeping our families apart. The first thing that happened when you arrived at the hospital was the instant removal of your husband. During labor only strange faces loomed ominously above you. Doped to the gills, you delivered someone they told you about and were sent to the recovery room, where you had to read the numerals on the clock before being allowed to return to your room. (This was hard on Bettina because—alas—she had forgotten to bring her glasses with her for the test.) You had already been advised not to nurse your baby as it would sense the resentment you'd surely feel for having your social life interrupted. (This was actually a ploy by the hospital nurses, who found it easier to feed the bottle in the nursery than to carry your infant down the hall to your room six times a day during the day and night.) It was the 1950s and everyone was busy being modern. Despite this, Grace had another goddaughter, and as the Grays went househunting, Bettina's days of wanderlust were nearing an end. She was getting what she wanted—Frank, children, a home and a regular dentist.

❧ JUDY ❧

At Chicago's Lying In Hospital, I was delivered by the noted Dr. Joseph DeLee, who had modernized the Caesarian section, though I was not the product of such a birth. We lived in an enormous apartment on Lake Shore Drive into which my father had moved when he, his brothers, their sister and brother-in-law had become successful pioneers of the motion picture theatre business. In 1936, before I turned four, my father accepted an offer to become president of Paramount Pictures, so we moved to New York. My brother Leonard, three years my senior, immediately enrolled in elementary school. Our older brother, Burt, eleven years ahead of me, went off to Cornwall-on-the-Hudson, some miles north of the city near West Point, as a cadet at the New York Military Academy. I spent my days in Central Park, weather permitting, with my nanny Decky, feeding the pigeons, cringing from the polar bears, chattering with the monkeys, roller skating, and climbing jungle gyms and random rock formations. When I wasn't at home or in the park I was being driven around the city with my mother by George Stengel, our family chauffeur, who had moved with us and his family from the Midwest.

Like Kay Thompson's Eloïse, I was a hotel brat. While Eloïse's escapades took place at the Plaza, mine evolved at the Savoy Plaza, directly across Fifth Avenue from Eloïse's haunt. Our family apartment there consisted of twelve rooms occupying the eleventh and twelfth floors which had been custom-designed for its original tenant when the hotel was built. That tenant, Adolph Zukor, was the founder and, for many years, the chief executive of Paramount. He and Marcus Loew, one of the founders of MGM/Loews, used to play "Can you top this?" with houses. If the first erected a new residential marvel in town, the second had to go him one better. When the second created his dream mansion as a country retreat, the first felt obliged to top that estate. When my father went to Paramount, we became the beneficiaries of Zukor's extravagance. The Savoy Plaza apartment, where we spent our winters, had a paneled library, a marble-floored living room, a huge marble staircase winding to its second floor, a dining room with a ceiling hand-painted by Tiepolo, and a downstairs powder room in which the toilet was encased by a celadon green gilded wooden throne.

Our summer house was also the product of the Zukor/Loew playoffs. It was on eighty acres in New City, ninety minutes north on the Hudson River. We had an eighteen-hole golf course, championship tennis courts, a wooded dell with a teahouse suspended over a fish-filled stream and two swimming pools, one Olympic in dimension. We lived in the guesthouse, with nearly thirty rooms, because the main house "was just not homey," according to my mother. Our gardener, along with his wife and several children (our best friends, of course, the Fritz kids), lived in the gardener's house. It was one of several buildings on "the farm," as this mini-empire was euphemistically known. Every weekend we screened new movies in the separate theatre, and larger entertainments were held in "the party house," some three floors of gathering spaces which included a bowling alley on one level and a miniature replica of the Hall of Mirrors at Versailles on another. Most of the places I lived in as a child have since become public facilities. "The farm" has long been Dellwood Country

Club. I once went to a wedding reception in "the Tiepolo Suite" of the Savoy Plaza before they razed it, looked up at the ceiling and realized, "My God, these folks are plighting their troth in my old dining room!"

At six years of age I joined my brother Leonard at the Ethical Culture School across Central Park in the West Sixties. Jointly we determined that George Stengel should discharge us from the town car around the corner from school so nobody would see us chauffeured to class. In the afternoons, when school was out, we rode horseback at Ayleworth Riding Academy near Ethical. We took Central Park's paths by storm or practiced in our identical habits indoors at Ayleworth for upcoming horse shows, where we won a variety of cups and ribbons.

I have always believed "Ethical Culture" is the best name for a school where children are to be educated. Ethical was affiliated with the Fieldston School, which Rita Gam attended, but we did not know each other then. I remember taking typing while sitting atop the New York phone directory because I had finished all my second-grade workbooks and Ethical did not believe in skipping. I am certain that I learned how to think thanks to this remarkable institution.

There are three particular people from Ethical who often come to my mind. The first, a boy named Trafford Alpass, was my age and notable because I have always felt fortunate to know someone with such an unusual name. The second was a budding scientist in my brother's class whose name was Saul. Whenever he visited us, he would pinch me while ordering, "Prove that you're alive!," a challenge that, in spite of my tender years, I found enormously provocative. The third was also a classmate of my brother's. An earnest, intelligent and kind boy, he used to speak to me in the hallways and on the stairs whenever we met. I was six and he was nine, so this was big stuff. His name was Allard K. Lowenstein, and we would have to wait nearly thirty years before we became true friends.

The summer before the war broke out, my family moved to a twenty-two-room house on seven acres on Long Island Sound in Westchester County. After one year at Greenwich Academy, I matriculated at Rye Country Day School, a coeducational private school, while my brother Leonard went off to the military academy where our older brother had preceded him. Burt, having already logged two years at Roanoke College, joined the Marines the week after Pearl Harbor.

We had a harrowing attack of Japanese beetles which laid waste to

the White House, appeared in my third production of *H.M.S. Pinafore*, and was inadvertently caught in action by my first newsreel cameras. My original visit to the White House occurred when I was barely more than three. My brothers, parents and I stood behind the Franklin Delano Roosevelt family in their private quarters as they welcomed, from their balcony, the throngs gathered on the White House lawn for the annual Easter festivities. While at Mount Vernon I accompanied my father there again, where we enjoyed tea by invitation of the Harry Trumans. During this same period my father had presented one of the fourteen original copies of the Bill of Rights to the Library of Congress. He had found it in the possession of a private Philadelphia collector and though he, too, had a formidable collection of Americana, believed it properly belonged to the American people. Then he and other citizens, aided by the government, organized something called The Freedom Train.

Because air travel was not then what it was to become, most Americans did not visit Washington, where they could see, firsthand, the great documents on which our country's independent heritage was based. So a special train was created, which would travel all around the country carrying those historic papers. Masses of people formed unending queues in cities and towns across the nation. The train arrived in Washington on an icy day, and we Mount Vernon students, along with those from every other school in the district, waited for our turn to board. The Marine Corps band played rousing marches to entertain us as we froze to death outside the station. To keep our circulation going, we formed a chorus line and did Rockette-like kicks to the tunes of John Philip Sousa. We did not know that a newsreel crew was shooting our performance. That Saturday night, when my family ran movies at home and reviewed Paramount's weekly edition known as "The Eyes and Ears of the World," there were my bloomers, along with those of my schoolmates, prominently featured for America's movie-going public in The Freedom Train segment. I had a close-up, but did not become a star.

The biggest shock about being in our nation's capital was the discovery of signs saying "Black Only" or "White Only" on restrooms and drinking fountains, even in church. I was appalled to learn right here at the seat of democracy that all the chairs were reserved for those of a certain color. At the close of my second year at Mount Vernon, I raced through a Saturday morning final so I could catch the pre-lunch bus to a "hop" I was attending at the nearby Naval Academy in Annapolis. I darted up the stairs of the bus just before its doors were to close, lugging my suitcase and my formal in a hanging bag. Knowing the bus was about to leave, I quickly scanned the length of it for a place to sit. As Annapolis was not a local route, there was no standing permitted.

Relieved, I spotted a seat on the aisle and hastily dragged myself and my luggage to it. Stuffing my suitcase under the seat and my garment bag on the overhead rack, I was unaware that a heavy silence had descended throughout the vehicle. Sitting down with a big "whew," I looked up to see a huge, enraged bus driver glowering at me. "What do you think you're doing?" he snarled. Politely I informed him that I was going to Annapolis and produced the ticket to prove it. "Not on this bus, you're not! There ain't no seats," he menaced. I pointed out to him that, indeed, there was a seat and that, as I was sitting in it, we could move along now.

The petrified stillness of the small body next to mine gave warning. I turned to see my neighbor, an ancient, wizened black man, staring straight ahead. I was in "the back of the bus" with the wrong skin! Hastily I decided that even if the rights of my seatmate were not as unalienable as I had thought, surely my rights must be secure. I informed the driver that I did not wish to wait ninety minutes for the next bus and that I was perfectly happy to ride to Annapolis in the seat I presently occupied. It did not dawn on me that I was tampering with the entire fabric of the driver's identity. But that is how I found myself, at fifteen-and-a-half, in June 1948, being lifted from the bus by two fat men who reeked of stale underarms and cheap cigars. They hurled my bags after me to the sidewalk. My former seatmate and I looked at each other long and hard as the bus pulled away. Aha, I reflected, this is how it works. For ninety minutes I remained on the sidewalk reviewing the most important lesson I learned during my two years at Mount Vernon: If that man had lost his rights, I, too, had lost mine.

By the time I left Mount Vernon, not yet sixteen, I had been seriously in love three times. It was an era of great circumspection and, one would presume, limited independence for teenage girls. But the eastern seaboard's planes, trains and buses bulged regularly with sweet young things like myself who were allowed to go away, unchaperoned, for the weekend. We made our own reservations, bought our own tickets, found the right gates, and got ourselves transported to our destinations. We also learned

almost all my waking hours talking and laughing with a man named Frank
Merlo and his traveling companion, Tennessee Williams. When I returned home, not yet seventeen, I headed straight to Haverhill, Massachusetts, for Bradford Junior College, where I spent one year of classes and
filled my weekends with visits from my boyfriend and secret fiancé.

After a summer trip to Beverly Hills and New Orleans with my college
roommates, I settled down at home in New York City. My parents moved
to a larger Hampshire House apartment. My father refused to fund acting
lessons, so I got a job with a fashion trade publication called *The Tobé
Report* owned by a friend of the family. I briefly dated an interior decorator. I also went out with a surly, overweight member of the New York
Stock Exchange, danced nightly at Gogi's LaRue, and ate a lot of family
charge account lunches with friends at "21."

When my vacation time came in January, I wanted to go to Nassau
as my stockbroker escort was going to be there with some other friends.
My parents insisted on chaperoning me before they continued on to Palm
Beach, where my mother would spend the rest of the winter. At dinner
the night before our trip, my father announced he had invited a young
actor he liked to join us in Nassau for the week. My parents did not
socialize with many actors, but my father had met this young man at a
Bonds for Israel luncheon, where the two of them were speaking. Learning that the young man had secretly gone off to Israel to fight with the
underground Haganah, my father was deeply impressed.

I met my father's friend, Montgomery Clift, at four in the afternoon
outside the British Colonial Hotel in Nassau. By eight that night I was
in love again. By eleven the same evening, Monty had defended my honor
against the insulting stockbroker from New York in a fistfight on the
terrace of the local casino. By the time we returned to New York together,
the path was clear. I quit my job soon afterwards, and when I wasn't
pounding the pavements looking for acting jobs, spent every waking hour
with Monty in a dreamlike trance. We ate nightly steaks at Gregory's Bar
& Grill on Lexington Avenue. We shopped the neighborhood butcher for
the best chickens, which Monty would broil at his brownstone apartment
on the night we gave beef a holiday. We looked for Danish modern
furniture and took endless hansom cab rides through Central Park. We
spent Memorial Day weekend at the Westhampton home of photogra-

pher Richard Avedon and his wife Evelyn. My father hardly spoke to Monty once it became clear that I had taken his advice and improved the quality of my male companions. This was not what he had in mind.

Seven months later it had become clear that Monty's and my incessant talk of our future marriage was nothing but a fantastic daydream on both our parts. We were still friends when I accompanied Mickey Israel, my brother's fiancée, to Gainesville, Florida, where Leonard was taking postgraduate university courses. I was the eighteen-year-old chaperone, carrying the ring that Lenny would present to bind them together. On the plane from La Guardia, I met Merv Griffin, who was singing with Freddy Martin's orchestra at the prom we were attending in Gainesville. You know the rest.

Apparently, I thought it was called "the seven-month itch" because that long after I met Merv, he and I broke up. It was during that period, though, that I acquired a new group of friends. During these months my friendships with Rosemary Clooney and Peggy Ann Garner began, as did my early acquaintance with publicist Ruth Cosgrove, who would later marry Milton Berle, whom I'd known since I was five. Other female singers I knew included Jane Harvey and Monica Lewis, as well as Polly Bergen, and two of my closest male pals were astonishing young talents, Harry Belafonte and Sammy Davis, Jr. When my parents were in the country, I'd give late-night parties at our apartment, where Harry gobbled plates of my scrambled egg specials while Sammy and I sang through the scores of the current Broadway hit musicals. First, he'd play all the men's parts while I played the females', then we reversed roles so I got the baritone songs while he did the soprano.

My father had not approved of Merv Griffin any more than he had of Montgomery Clift. A Catholic band singer and a WASP actor ranked equally low on his scale of desirable sons-in-law. He was not overjoyed when I got acting jobs on Robert Montgomery's weekly television anthology, nor when I appeared briefly in NBC's *A Christmas Carol* with three of Great Britain's finest thespians. He was even less than thrilled when I captured an occasional one-nighter as a singer or filled in for a few days for an ailing star at one of a couple of small midtown nightclubs. By the time Jay Kanter came along (though divorced from a brief early marriage), a Jewish show business executive rather than a gentile performer and one

ignored this fact and referred to his devoted lifelong companion as "his valet.")

Throughout her last years of high school and her stint at the American Academy, Grace was running her own Fiancé-of-the-Year club. Like me, when Grace loved she thought marriage. When she thought marriage she took the prospect home to her parents for approval. When she got none, she gradually fell out of love or outgrew the candidate. But before Grace became a movie star and embarked on her run-of-the-schedule leading man romances, the grown-up Grace had been seriously in love with only one man. A ruddy, reddish-blond actor of Irish descent, Gene Lyons met Grace when they were both cast in various plays during her summer at Elitch Gardens in 1951. Grace was twenty-one, Gene had just concluded a two-year affair of considerable depth with another actress, Lee Grant. Like Grace's Uncle George, Gene was serious about the theatre, and possessed an incisive and probing wit and the mature brand of elegance that consistently seemed to attract Grace. He was, she told me, "a good person with strong ethics." Grace had learned a great deal from Gene, as I had from Monty. In both cases, we felt ourselves far younger than they. In both cases, each of us had realized we were in over our heads. For with all the strength Grace absorbed from Gene and I from Monty, both men suffered from some internal pain, an unseen vacuum that neither Grace in her case nor I in mine had been able to cure or fill. Both of our families had objected to both of our relationships, but it was each of us who recognized what we could not handle.

Looking back, it is easy, of course, to say directly that both Gene Lyons and Monty Clift were full-fledged alcoholics. At the time, though, it would never have dawned on Grace or on me to use that word. In the 1950s we would not have recognized an alcoholic unless we tripped over him for ten nights running in a Bowery doorway. Alcoholics came from places we didn't even know existed. Alcoholics were human refuse. Our hearts bled that such a destiny could befall one of our fellow creatures, but they bled from a safe distance. The boys we dated or fell in love with had, at worst (and this was mandatorily accompanied by a dismissive wave of the hand), "a little drinking problem." They "drank like a fish" or "couldn't hold their liquor" (the latter sounded as though they had failed some tribal test). In fact, drinking, for both sexes, had been enormously popularized in the post-prohibition years when we grew up. It was chic and sophisticated to drink, boorish not to. In the original *Thin Man* movie, the adorable William Powell and irresistible Myrna Loy spent every single scene either talking about drinking, laughing about drinking, pouring drinks or drinking. We ourselves had graduated from eyedroppers full of gin in the Tom Collins our parents made for us on the patio in summertime, to the Baccardi and Pink Lady phase of our early dates, and moved on to whiskeys and mixes or scotch on the rocks. Vodka was just becoming the rage. Grace herself had taken to ordering vodka and soda, a variation on Commander Schweppes's theme, which became known to a number of bartenders as "a Kelly."

Drugs simply did not exist in our world. I was the only girl I knew who had actually smelled and seen grass. Since high school my brother had surrounded himself with both aging and contemporary Dixieland jazz musicians. When our parents left town for a weekend, he would give the household staff of six a few days off and toss a two-day, two-night jam session that found us cleaning like crazy to beat the clock for our parents' Sunday night return. On one such occasion, I smelled something that resembled the inside of the men's room at Grand Central Station, and found a skinny, wrinkled cigarette butt in an ashtray. "Marijuana," my brother whispered furtively, although there was nobody home on all seven acres besides the two of us. I did think my mother's doctors took the easy way out by providing her with masses of sleeping pills, wake-up tablets, painkillers and tension capsules, but what she ingested throughout the day were not drugs but "doctor's orders." Psychiatry was held in low regard. "They're for crazy people," my father noted in 1952 when I told him I wanted to go to an analyst.

In any case, neither Grace nor I had any idea that Gene Lyons and Monty Clift had an illness. As the joke goes, we knew they didn't have "a wellness," but it was quite beyond either one of us to confront that in any way. It wasn't polite to confront.

CHAPTER 4

Birds of a Feather

$\mathcal{T}$he early 1950s, when we got to know one another, when Grace rose to meteoric stardom and we all began our adult lives, were the Eisenhower years. As good children from nice families, we had all learned the lesson of our day: Confrontation of any sort was the key to immediate personal disaster.

It was unthinkable to argue with one's parents or teachers about the merits of any given rule, regulation, ideology or tenet. All authority was right and good. All challenge to authority was bad and wrong. Unfortunately, nearly everyone but you was an authority. Our politicians were still vested with the wartime glow of statesmanship. They were our leaders. Honest men. Our doctors were all sacrificial gentlemen who devoted their lives to healing and curing those less fortunate than they. They did not make mistakes. Our lawyers and judges were the vigilant sentries of our equity. They never slept lest they drop those firm, outstretched arms supporting the weighty scales of justice. Their valiant army was composed of those good and brave peacetime soldiers, the police. The clergy, of course, was beyond reproach. You just did not hassle a fellow who was in direct touch with the Almighty. History would label us as a generation of conformists. We appeared to conform. But what we became, out of necessity, is a generation of sneaks. Our willfullness, however, was tempered by a well-formed conscience that dictated kindness, self-preservation and a fundamental decency we tried hard to live by.

When General Eisenhower became President of the United States, like the good little soldiers we were raised to be, we swallowed answers to the questions we had only just developed a taste for, mistook complacency for serenity, and accepted nonconfrontation as the American way of life. The proof could be found in our marital dollhouses. The little boy figures were dressed in their gray flannel suits. When you wound them up they knotted their sincere ties, splashed themselves with Old Spice, and committed their lives to their companies. We girl dolls made the perfect company wives. When you turned our keys we sped directly to matronhood.

As families by the hundreds of thousands headed for the suburbs to build their bomb shelters, it was hard to know exactly from whom they were hiding. Was it from the maniacs in Moscow who threatened our bodies or the unchecked senatorial menace in Washington, Joseph McCarthy, who threatened our souls? We had just finished fighting a hot war against fascism. Then, no sooner than "the Korean conflict" ended, we were fighting the cold war against communism. We forgot that democracy, by definition, is a state of agitation. We were too embalmed in our soporific satisfaction to be stirred. No wonder Grace and the rest of us were so captivated by séances and "Bridey Murphy" parties. We had to contact somebody. Just as long as it wasn't ourselves.

There were glimpses of courage amidst all this fear. Most we rejected. Bohemians were the precursors to beatniks. We rejected them as too outside the mainstream to be taken seriously. Political activists were too risky. I talked serious politics and the need for substantive change only with selected people. John Forsythe and his wife Julie, on a cozy evening at their Peter Cooper Village apartment, did awaken in me a strong curiosity to know a lot more about Adlai Stevenson. But I was only twenty and too young to vote.

The only offbeat reference that gained wide acceptance was J. D. Salinger's *Catcher in the Rye*. Its hero, Holden Caulfield, became our idol, the honest kid we had not ever had the courage to be. Our secret soul. Grace became so enamored of Holden that her references to him appeared with almost annoying frequency. Jay and I were such devotees that we chose his given name as the middle name for our firstborn child.

In small groups (after checking the room around us) we did discuss Senator Joseph McCarthy, especially those of us in or around show business who saw that our friends' personal and professional lives might crumble under the weight of his mad vendetta. In the fall of 1952, just before my first date with Jay, during the same week that Rita Gam's face filled the cover of *Life* magazine, I met one of McCarthy's henchmen, Roy Cohn. It was eighteen months before the nationally televised Army-McCarthy hearings and my father had been pressured by some business associates to arrange a date with me for the young attorney who had just become the Senator's aide. I was temporarily between fiancés and agreed to have dinner at home on the night he was invited.

By the end of the soup course, I was convinced that if I lived to be a thousand I would never again see anyone as thoroughly ugly as Roy Cohn. It was neither the design of his features nor the placement of them. On those, he could, and did finally, have a touch of surgical assistance. What I saw was untreatable. I was nauseated by the perverse hatred I read in the distortion of his mouth and the unfathomable meanness in his eyes.

In a time of hidden truths, politics was not the only arena where we could not be individuals. Since childhood we had all been told that in everything we did, we were a reflection of someone else. Growing up, we had become used to thinking of ourselves solely as mirror images of something or someone outside ourselves. How we behaved in school, the grades we got, the sports we played, our popularity among our peers—all these were nothing but a confirmation that our parents were okay. If one of us failed, that failure was proof of our family's imperfection. Later we were told we were not only reflections of our parents but of our schools as well. When we young ladies from Mount Vernon Seminary left the campus, we were told to remember that we were Mount Vernon girls and to behave accordingly.

If we looked "the right way," spoke "the right way," and acted "the right way," life would run smoothly. A lifetime commitment to "the right thing" was a lifetime guarantee of happiness. We would safely move from being somebody's daughter to somebody's wife and somebody's mother. For a girl, life's segments ended with the expression, "And then you get married and have children."

We were expected to arrive at marriage and motherhood with all we ever needed to know. All we needed was love—the love of "the right man." Who was he? Nobody ever quite said. Our parents knew who he wasn't. But nobody ever quite said who he was. There were few clues.

He was to provide for you and the children. He was to be a good citizen. Preferably, he would come from the same background as you. Hopefully, he would be faithful (though Alfred C. Kinsey's 1948 book *Sexual Behavior in the Human Male,* known as "The Kinsey Report," made that less likely than we or our parents would have wished). If you fell in love with "the right man," the rest of your life would be a snap. Presumably, the right man would provide for your happiness, along with your survival and your overhead.

But who would *you* be during all those years while you loved your right man and raised your children? You would remain the still photograph of the person you had been on the very day that you married. The face in the photo would mature and wrinkle, the body would sag, but the mind, the heart and the spirit would be frozen into perpetuity. You would live and die as that same person, no matter what happened in your life, your husband's or your children's, no matter what occurred in the world around you. It was such a comforting promise that all of us wanted to get married as quickly as possible. Most of us did.

Maree Pamp, née Frisby, who had originally married the wrong man, was vamping until the right one came along. Sally Richardson, née Parrish, wife of John, had become mother to John Blair Richardson, Jr., known as Blair, yet another of Grace's godchildren. Sally and big John conceived him six months after their marriage, and he was born in November 1955. While Sally baked and mommied, John became an associate of a Wall Street law firm. Together they hunted for a larger apartment so their new family could continue to expand.

Carolyn Reybold, née Scott, had her Mr. Right, and also kept on with her successful modeling career while raising her two daughters. Malcolm, regaining his strength after a long post-surgical recuperation, was happily involved with the organization of The Town Tennis Club in Manhattan. Carolyn would rush home from her modeling jobs, feed their two daughters, and dress to play hostess for his tennis group's socials. She basked in her husband's approval. He had married a wife who was perfect. "Absolutely delightful. Party girl. Wonderful."

Bettina Gray, née Thompson, also found her family expanding. In March 1955, little Francis Calley Gray III ("Sam") was born as brother to Lizzie. When the Grays' boat was damaged by Hurricane Carol, they traded up by buying land in South Dartmouth and building a summer house for family vacations. Finally, in 1956, they settled into a hundred-year-old home in Dedham.

Rita Gam was, in the mid-Fifties, a woman without a man. This was only one of two factors that left her without an identity. The second was her career, which continued splendidly on the rise. Rita had grown accustomed to the life of a working actress. It felt very real. But by the middle of the 1950s, she had become a movie star. Life was not as real as before. From all quarters she heard talk of her image. Now jobs were to be evaluated on the basis of whether they might help or hurt this image. Rita had entered the world of career moves. She had no map. Instead of Kraft dinners, she was required to cook up a persona. She had no recipe. Rita the person and Rita the personage began to have a tough time sharing the insides of one skin.

There was only one woman friend in Rita's life whom she trusted. She felt that other women looked upon her with disapproval or suspicion because she was beautiful. So when Rita and Sidney were divorced, it was Grace who became her lifesaver. Grace would make the effort to find Rita wherever she was. She would call just to see how Rita felt, what was going on, if there was anything a pal could do to help. In this difficult time, Rita and Grace began to form a strong bond of loyalty.

At a party in 1955, Rita met Tom Guinzburg and was attracted to the patches on his Yale tweed jacket. It was barely more than six months since Rita's divorce when superficial electricity ignited their mutual desires. Rita may have appeared to Tom to be a steamy little number, defying tradition by leaving home so young, living in sin with her first husband before they married, but this sultry movie star whom *Life* described on its cover as "silent and sexy" was, in fact, an extremely straitlaced, almost prudish young woman.

During the 1953–54 year I did what any self-respecting young wife would: I submerged myself in my husband's business. *On the Waterfront* was going into production that year, and it played a significant part in our life. Budd Schulberg's script was to be directed by Elia ("Gadge") Kazan when its producer, Sam Spiegel, approached Jay about Marlon playing

Terry Malloy. Though Marlon thought the project was interesting, he harbored bad feelings toward its director because of Kazan's appearance before McCarthy's hearings of the House Un-American Activities Committee. Marlon felt a question of ethics was at stake. As good as *Waterfront* was, he turned it down.

At the time Marlon was living simply in a pleasant and roomy apartment on West Fifty-seventh Street with his pet raccoon Russell, and sometimes with Movita (his on-and-off longtime love who had starred in the 1935 version of *Mutiny on the Bounty*). So Jay was surprised when Marlon called him, not long after the *Waterfront* offer had been rejected, to say he needed money quickly. Marlon's father (Marlon, Sr.) was running the family's midwestern cattle farm and had some problems that could be solved only with an immediate cash infusion.

One year earlier Marlon had done a summer stock production of *Arms and the Man* at a theatre in Connecticut. He suggested that Jay book him to do a reading from this Shavian work on *The Ed Sullivan Show* to earn the money he required. Instead, Jay urged Marlon to shelve that idea and reconsider Spiegel's offer for *Waterfront*. The script was wonderful, its message important and a reflection of Marlon's ideals. The picture would shoot almost immediately. As Marlon and Kazan had produced such extraordinary work together in the earlier *Streetcar Named Desire*, Jay felt the two should meet and try to make peace. The meetings were arranged, and Jay called Sam Spiegel to tell him that Marlon was rethinking his earlier decision on the picture. Sam was ecstatic. Though he had already signed Frank Sinatra for the role of Terry Malloy, he entered the "get Marlon" fray with vigor and tenacity. (Frank wanted the part, as any actor would have. He had just made an astonishing comeback in the prior year's *From Here to Eternity*, winning the Best Supporting Actor Oscar for his portrayal of Maggio. When he learned that Sam had hired Marlon and was trying to break his contract for *Waterfront*, Frank sued Sam. I would have done the same had I been he. Frank might well have done a marvelous job as Terry, but it is hard to imagine the part as being anyone's but Marlon's.)

During the summer of 1954, Grace enhanced her career on the French Riviera, where she, along with the Cary Grants and the Alfred Hitchcocks, went to film *To Catch a Thief.* Oleg Cassini followed her to France, giving rise to rumors that an engagement announcement might be forthcoming imminently. Jay and I spent another summer at my parents' country home, cruised Long Island's inland waterways on our fifty-seven-foot mahogany boat called the *Judith R.*, and affirmed the potency of our generation in the best way possible. We made a baby.

When fall came, we moved back into town and proceeded to see everything that opened on Broadway. I was several months pregnant when we attended the opening of a new play, *Wedding Breakfast,* directed by Herman Shumlin and starring a cast of four—Lee Grant, Harvey Lembeck, Virginia Vincent and a fledgling from the Actors Studio, Anthony Franciosa. Backstage, after the premiere performance, we congratulated everyone involved. It was the first time I met Lee Grant. I told her I was so intimidated by the brilliance of her performance in the earlier *Detective Story* that I had turned down the opportunity to play her part in a summer stock production before I was married. When we congratulated Anthony Franciosa, whom we first met that night, I added, "You were wonderful. I'm sure we'll be seeing more of you." Little did I know how much more!

Jay and I found a larger apartment in our same Sutton Place building. I busied myself in the daytime with getting it ready for us and our baby-to-be. By this time, I had all but abandoned trying to prepare dinners at home. Whenever I'd have a roast half done, Jay would call to say we had a business date and had to go out for dinner. One evening, though, when he phoned, it was to say he needed to have dinner alone with the well-known fashion and celebrity photographer Milton Greene. He could not tell me more by phone. I did have a clue to this mystery. The papers were filled with news that Marilyn Monroe had disappeared from Hollywood, and her studio, Twentieth Century Fox, was looking for her everywhere. Rumor had it that Milton Greene was her new mentor, and that he had her hidden somewhere in the New York area. It was a Thursday night, meaning Nat Brandywynne's orchestra was playing mostly waltzes at the Waldorf-Astoria. I called my favorite waltzing partner and we went off to Strauss up a storm. Heads turned as Marlon and I danced the night away. He, along with Monty Clift and James Dean, were viewed as the "crude, crotch-scratching" new breed of American actors. No one who watched him, in his dark blue suit, whirling around the floor with the elegance of a Viennese nobleman, could put this together with his image. Though we stayed until closing, Jay did not return home until nearly four in the morning. When he did, he had a new client, Marilyn Monroe, and a date for us to go to Connecticut two days later.

That weekend at the Greenes' home in Westport, I met Milton and Amy and their houseguest Marilyn for the first time. The Greenes' baby son Josh, their standard poodle Bobo and the rest of the ménage were ruled over by a housekeeper who ran the place with the hand of an imperial Russian czarina. Milton was an odd man, either unbelievably brilliant or incredibly dense, I was never sure which. He was soft-spoken to the point of being inaudible. His tiny and beautiful wife Amy was as outgoing and effervescent as they came. Some years earlier Milton had been married to Evelyn, now the wife of the other photographic great, Richard Avedon. Avedon had discovered Amy in Central Park. By the time we met, Milton and Evelyn were divorced and Evelyn had long been married to Richard Avedon. Avedon's discovery, Amy, had married Milton Greene. You could hardly tell the players without a program.

On the drive back to the city, Jay and I talked about Marilyn. I said she seemed sweet but very scared. All I could think of was a comment Monty Clift had made to me some years earlier about the way Shelley Winters had played her character in *A Place in the Sun.* Monty had said, "She foredoomed her tragedy." On that first day I met Marilyn Monroe in Westport, throughout all the days to come in which she was a part of our lives, and on all the days afterwards until her own life ended, I was never able to wipe that phrase from my mind.

With Marilyn as Jay's newest client, our lives changed. We were joined at the hip with her, Milton Greene and his wife. The Greenes had always used Milton's studio as a *pied-à-terre* when they needed to stay in Manhattan. Now the city sleepovers became the rule rather than the exception, and their nights did not end until it was nearly morning. Milton still had his successful photography business, and when early morning came he had to dislodge Amy from her slumber so he could start working. That is why, when I opened my eyes one morning, I found not my old roommate, Marlon, but Amy Greene sharing my bed with me. Jay had given her a key so she could sleep and dress at our house, away from the vortex of Milton's activities.

As Marilyn began to study with Lee Strasberg at the Actors Studio, we started seeing a lot of Lee, his wife Paula and their daughter Susan.

Susan Strasberg was still in her mid-teens. She reminded me of my own precocious self at the same age, except that she was wildly talented. Our good friend John Foreman was also deeply enmeshed with the Greenes and Marilyn. Together, he and I spent hours looking for songs Marilyn could record for the new album she wanted to make.

During the first few months we knew her, Marilyn continued hiding out in Westport or in town, at a small East Side hotel apartment. She was still traveling incognito. Every move she made was planned with the secrecy appropriate for the landing on Omaha Beach. Periodically, muffled whispers informed us that "Joe is in town." Though she and Di-Maggio were officially separated, he was still making frequent trips east from California to be with her. When he arrived we got a bit of our lives back for ourselves.

On one of our nights off, Jay and I went with Grace to a sneak preview of her movie *Bridges at Toko-Ri*. Our baby kicked so hard during Grace's big scene that my purse fell off my lap, clattering to the ground. When I turned to Grace to mouth an apology, she leaned over, put her head near my belly and whispered, "Hush, now, baby-bird. Your Aunt Gracie's trying to get her licks in."

Aunt Gracie was getting her licks in everywhere during the early months of 1955. She was nominated for an Oscar as Best Actress for her role in *The Country Girl*, and was busy moving into a glorious new apartment on Fifth Avenue. Her mother had suggested a particular decorator, but Grace, growing more sure of her own taste, selected George Stacey, whose work she had admired in a *Vogue* magazine layout. Her new apartment, unlike the old one at Manhattan House, looked like Grace. A lovely foyer acted as a center hall to the large living room, formal dining room, and sizable pantry and kitchen. A long hallway led to the two bedrooms that faced Eightieth Street, while the entertainment areas all fronted on Central Park. The soft, fluid and feminine lines of newly acquired French antiques looked a great deal more like the tenant than the neutered brown flat she had left, as did the colors—primarily a rich but pale blue—that dotted her ivory living room. The first piece of living room furniture you saw as you came through the front door was a gilded S-shaped settee where two people could face each other for conversation. It was covered in fabric that had the word "love" woven into it, and we all called it the kissing chair. Grace always adored the sight and smell of fresh flowers. Now there were small and large clusters of them in vases on every tabletop. It was the home of a successful young woman grown more self-assured, the dwelling of a beauty, a movie star, a grown-up. It was so much a home that I think it worried Grace a bit to be living in it with only a female companion, not with a husband like all her friends.

Another friend, Sammy Davis, Jr., had worse things to worry about in the beginning of 1955. He had been driving along a highway from the desert late at night, in California, when an older woman backed her car out of her driveway without looking. Her carelessness landed Sammy in a hospital with broken bones, multiple lacerations and the loss of one eye.

Simultaneously the Actors Studio was planning its big New York fund-raising event. In early March the Studio would host the benefit premiere of *East of Eden,* the movie adaptation of John Steinbeck's novel. After the movie the guests would cross the street to dine, dance and be entertained at a gala post-premiere party at the Astor Roof, high atop the world-renowned hotel in the heart of Times Square. Elaborate plans were made for the roster of celebrities who would perform during the party. The longest, starring turn of the evening was to be provided by Sammy Davis, who would repeat a good portion of his nightclub act, the best in the country.

Two weeks before the planned event, one of the benefit chairmen called me to say that Sammy had just reneged on his appearance commitment even though he admitted he would be well enough, physically, to perform. It was mid-February when I phoned Sammy on the Coast to see what was happening. His spirits were terribly low. He told me he could not sing at the premiere party because, either way, the evening would be a mistake for him. If he was bad, he said, he would never have the courage to work again. "But," he added, "I'll never really know if I'm good, either. I wouldn't know it there, especially now, especially that night." I didn't understand so he explained: "Suppose I do the show and everybody applauds like crazy and yells 'rah-rah' and all that jazz. How do I know it's for my performance and not just to be kind to some dumb schmuck who's brave enough to stand up and sing in public with one eye?" We debated this question for twenty minutes, but Sammy could not see, for that moment, anything but his missing eye. No talent, no popularity, no respect. Nothing but what he no longer had. My heart ached for him, but I realized that further pleading would only be in vain.

together. Her eyes grew wide, terror-stricken. She shook her head vigorously to say she would not take the baby in her arms. I put Amy back in her crib and knelt at Marilyn's feet, stroking her as she shivered with fear. I knew from Marilyn that her own mother had been institutionalized; that Marilyn, as a small child, had seen her mother constrained in a straitjacket and taken away. After a few moments I asked her if I could help. She kept shaking her head and trembling, until finally she spoke. "I can't hold her. Because if I do," she whispered, "she'll be just like my mother, just like me." Secretly, Marilyn believed she had caught her mother's disease, believed, even then, that she could be the carrier of insanity. Even to my child. Watching Marilyn show Amy's picture on the Murrow show, I ached for her. Once again, I thought, "She foredoomed her own tragedy."

Our Easter vacation in Las Vegas was wonderful. Cary Grant had booked the three suites that constituted the private penthouse floor of the Sands Hotel's main building. Our own elevator emptied into a small central foyer, which meant we could dart between one another's suites in robes without seeing strangers. Grace had become very close to the Grants during the previous summer on the Riviera, where they filmed *To Catch a Thief*. She had visited them often during her subsequent Hollywood stays. Jay knew both Cary and Betsy from his pre–New York life in California. When I met them Cary was fifty-one years old. He was, as expected, warm, charming, amusing, outgoing, handsome and graceful. He was Cary Grant. I was twenty-two years old, Grace twenty-five, Jay twenty-eight and Betsy not much beyond that. But Cary was one of us. There was nothing paternalistic or patronizing about Cary, though he did take masterful charge of seeing to it that all our arrangements in Vegas went smoothly. Being with him felt more like a reunion of old pals than a first-time meeting of new acquaintances.

    We played endless word games. We sat poolside for the fresh air. We ordered enough room service to feed an army. When night fell we dined, gambled, and took in shows at the Sands and the other early Vegas casinos. Cary never gambled. He sat in the bar chatting with the constant stream of Vegas honchos and fans who came by to bid welcome and pay their respects.

    Grace ran around from table to table. She made exuberant, noisy stops just long enough to learn the rudiments of shooting craps. She abandoned craps for the roulette wheels. She settled in for long, serious sessions in front of the blackjack dealers. Later, when Grace moved to Monaco and, like all of its citizens, was forbidden to gamble in its local casinos, I would think back to her brief, enthusiastic stint at the U.S. gaming capital.

Secretly, Cary arranged an Easter morning surprise for us. He had ordered three immense Easter baskets with gigantic stuffed bunnies to top each one. He told the florist to deliver them late on Easter morning and wrote a card for each of our baskets. He signed all three cards "The Easter Bunny Away from Home."

That night was a late one. We went to two or three shows, hit the tables at every stop, and spent a good part of the evening dodging a young man in hot pursuit of Grace. As the first light of dawn appeared across the desert, Grace remembered, "I've got to hit the rail." She needed to take communion at an Easter service. We waited for her return, had a snack together, and went to bed, closing all our drapes against the full-morning sun. We agreed to leave wake-up calls for noon. As we caught our three-hour naps, the florist delivered Cary's Easter baskets.

Cary rose first, before his and Betsy's wake-up call. He went to shower. While he was sudsing, the rest of us woke up and opened our front doors to get the newspapers—all at the same time. We found our terrific Easter baskets and Cary's "Easter Bunny Away from Home" cards. It was irresistible. We hastily took our baskets inside, darted in and out of one another's suites, found hiding places for the baskets, and listened for sounds that Cary was coming out of the shower. Before he was done, we had all raced back into our beds. Ten minutes later, our wake-up calls came. We went directly to the Grants' suite and ordered brunch.

Not a word about the baskets. Cary had sent Betsy to their door, presuming she would find her basket. Nothing. Each of us entered with a holiday kiss, but not a word about the baskets. Nothing. We watched Cary's puzzled expression, saw him go to his own front door. He even opened a service door in the hallway to see if someone had put the baskets there. Nothing. When he returned to us, he asked if anyone had seen anything unusual outside their door this morning. We shook our heads and looked at one another as though trying to figure him out.

Finally, Cary rose, threw his napkin to the floor, and started cussing out the florist. He told us the whole thing, berating the hotel for their incompetence, going on at great length about how you just could not rely on people to do their jobs. Then, like a comic strip character with a light bulb over his head, he got an idea. "I know what happened. I put a card on each one of your baskets. I bet the florist did deliver them, but some tourists who weren't supposed to be on our floor came up here. They found the baskets with my cards on them and probably swiped them so they could show my autograph to the folks back home!" He did one of those nifty little Cary Grant walkabouts while muttering to himself, confirming his own logic.

Betsy broke our silence. "Cary," she said, "why would anyone steal your 'autographed' gifts? You signed the cards 'The Easter Bunny Away from Home.' How could a tourist ever convince his friends that really meant 'Cary Grant'?" There was a second's pause before he got it. When he did, he howled. Thirty years later he was still laughing with me, not only about the joke we played on him but even about his own "silly, puffy" presumption that someone wanted his autograph enough to steal his pseudonymous surprise.

There was more coming in the year that commenced in April 1955 than any of us even suspected. Grace was ensconced in her beautiful new apartment, giving occasional cocktail parties and small dinners. Sometimes these would be well-planned events with everything prepared and presented elegantly. On other evenings, perhaps a last-minute cocktail gathering before the theatre, Grace became the mistress of the heated-peanut butter-and-bacon-on-saltines brigade. There were lots of hamburgers for dinner because Gracie loved them. She was playing house, but had no playmate. It was beginning to get to her.

During a visit one afternoon Grace admitted, "I have been falling in love since I was fourteen." I acknowledged it was a pattern I knew well, having followed it religiously before my marriage to Jay. Noting another similarity, Grace added, "And my parents have never approved of anyone I was in love with." In my case, it was my mother who carried the bad news, but always, apologetically, on behalf of my father, who would not carry the message himself. In Grace's case, while her father and brother were invariably trying to show up the men she brought home, it was Margaret Kelly who lowered the boom. In her own name. Ma Kelly was the family disciplinarian. She got better and better at the role as her children grew up.

Gracie began a head count on the marital and family status of her sisters and closest friends. "Peggy and Gabby have been married for years and have Meg and Mary Lee both in school." Peggy was some years older, but she added, "Lizzie [her younger sister] and Donald have been going together for three years. My parents made them wait until she graduated from college, but now they're getting married." (Lizanne and Donald Caldwell LeVine were to be married at a big ceremony in Philadelphia.)

"Carolyn and Malcolm already have Jyl and Robin. Sally and John are expecting and you and Jay have Amy." She did not mention Bettina, as I had never met her, but Bettina and Frank already had Lizzie and Sam. "Rita's divorced, like Maree, but Maree has Linda who's almost ready to begin school," she concluded. "I seem to be the late bloomer." She paused, looking around the room. "I love this apartment. But am I going to be living in it alone for the next twenty years going back and forth from Los Angeles and movie locations like a yo-yo on a string?"

"Maybe it's time to fall in love again?" I suggested. I was looking for a statement from her about her on-and-off relationship with Oleg Cassini.

What I got for an answer was, "We'll see." I also got a look that was so provocative and mischievous that I couldn't help laughing. Nor could she.

By spring 1955, Grace had been playing cat-and-mouse games with Oleg Cassini for so long that though I thought the relationship had peaked and ended some time earlier, I could never be sure. It had begun a few years before and had woven in and out of Grace's life while she grew to stardom. An American citizen, Oleg had been born in Paris of Russian descent, and raised in Italy. When he and Grace met through a mutual friend, French actor Jean-Pierre Aumont, Oleg was twice divorced: first from heiress Merry Fahrney, next from the beautiful film star of *Laura*, Gene Tierney. This was one strike against him in the Kelly family. In addition, Oleg was a major café habitué. Hardly a day passed in the first half of the decade when we did not know exactly where Oleg Cassini had dined the night before, and with whom he had danced the night away on one coast or the other. Then there was Oleg himself. He was elegantly dressed, debonair, charming, suave, with slick manners and hair to match. This was strike three for the Kellys. There was no hope that Oleg could qualify as the fellow the Kelly men expected Grace to bring into the family.

In 1954 Oleg followed Grace to France, where she was making *To Catch a Thief*. Alone, or together with the Grants and Hitchcocks, Grace and Oleg had dined at all the most romantic restaurants along the Côte d'Azur. They danced under the Mediterranean moon. That September Grace took Oleg to the Kellys' Ocean City home for a week-long visit. Her brother and father were less than gracious. Her sisters tried to compensate. Her mother, as usual, lowered the boom. If Grace married Oleg there would be no more Christmases on Henry Avenue. It was not so much Oleg himself as the idea of Oleg which was unacceptable. It may sound strange to say but we still accepted that our families were entitled to such a position, still felt that their approval mattered. Good girls from nice families just didn't ever quite *leave* home.

Though Grace and Oleg shelved their plan to marry, they persisted in seeing each other throughout the winter of 1954–55. Grace was continuing to make her own movie in her head, "The Grace Kelly Story." In it, she was astonished to find that she, no less than all her more earthbound friends, wanted to do "the right thing." Wanted to marry "the right man." She was a quarter of a century old, and less and less sure of who might qualify for that position. It was also essential that she love him. Deeply. Completely.

In this mood Grace left for the Cannes Film Festival in May 1955. Rupert Allan had written three cover stories on Grace for *Look* magazine since his first meeting with her in London at the end of the *Mogambo* shoot. He cared about Grace as a person, not merely as a commercial entity. Rupert was bright, witty, well-educated, kind and savvy. When he spoke, Grace listened. She trusted that he had her best interests at heart. It was Rupert who pressed her to attend the film festival. Grace was by then a huge star, the rage of Europe as well as the States. Rupert thought it would be right for her, for the American film industry and for the festival for her to be in Cannes.

It was arranged that Gladys de Segonzac would join Grace for her stay in Cannes. Gladys had been Grace's wardrobe supervisor on *To Catch a Thief*, so at least Grace would have a friend and an aide while she raced in and out of the dozens of parties, receptions and screenings she would be obliged to attend. On the train from Paris to Cannes, Gladys ran into Pierre Galante, an important *Paris Match* journalist who was married to film star Olivia de Havilland. His boss, Pierre Bonheur, the *Match* editor, had urged Galante to set up a photo shoot that he believed would make hot copy. On the train, with Gladys making the introductions, Pierre Galante got Grace to agree to the layout Bonheur had in mind.

Bonheur's idea was a photo session of Grace Kelly, American movie queen, being shown around the Palace Gardens by His Serene Highness Prince Rainier of Monaco. Grace had resigned herself to being available for a variety of public relations activities. She had seen Monaco during filming of *To Catch a Thief.* She loved flowers. Princes were not bad either. The appointment was confirmed with the Palace for the first full day Grace was in Cannes.

When it came time to get ready for the *Paris Match* shoot, Grace rang for the maid and asked her to press a rosy-beige tea dress. There was a slight problem, the maid informed her. Surely Mademoiselle Kelly had heard about the many strikes plaguing France. Well, on this day, Mademoiselle Kelly learned, such a strike was taking place, leaving the Carlton Hotel, along with the rest of the nation, without electricity. Alas, there would be no pressing in France today.

Grace washed her hair while Gladys de Segonzac searched through the closets to see what frock might be substituted. "I was rubbing my head with a towel," Grace told me, "when Gladys handed me 'the dreaded taffeta dress.' " Grace said she could think of nothing but my warning that the dress made her look like a pear. Exasperated, she plugged in her hair dryer. When pushing the switch resulted in utter silence, Grace remembered the electrical strike. There she was with her most unbecoming dress and a wet head of hair.

Gladys helped to get her hair pulled back and fashioned a facsimile of a hat out of a circlet of fake flowers. "Well, at least it was only for *Paris Match,*" Grace told me. "They made a big deal out of the article, but it's not like anyone will ever see those pictures again—or 'the dreaded taffeta dress'!" Little did Grace know then that "the dreaded taffeta dress" would be memorialized in print in every medium known to man in every country in the world for the remainder of the century.

When Grace reached the Palace, the Prince had not yet returned from a luncheon he was hosting at his villa in Cap Ferrat. Recounting how she had rushed and how soon she was due back at the cocktail reception in Cannes, Grace told me, "I got very restless. It was making everyone else nervous. So they suggested I tour the Palace with their photographers,

or Minneapolis, with blue booties or pink ones. Just by your beeping in the month of your birth, the gypsy knows all. She needs no added information. Judging by the rather consistent diagnoses of Grace's love life, I cannot help thinking we live in an era of Freud as gypsy. For what is pronounced by the pseudopsychologists is that Grace had a father complex. Well, so did every girl then whose daddy paid her little attention. And so do most girls now who grow up with a father who cannot be intimate with his daughter.

The only men in Grace's life who were uncommonly older than she were her co-stars. They were among the most glamorous, amusing, intelligent men in the world. Women of all ages, everywhere, swooned at the thought of having their autographs, no less their hearts. Had Clark Gable been a paunchy, middle-aged haberdasher from Peoria who talked only about bowling scores, I doubt whether Grace would have been fascinated by him.

Once Grace started making movies, she quickly became the world's most important female movie star. She could earn enough money to support herself and any man in the style to which they wished to become accustomed. Whom was she supposed to fall for? We were the girls who dated twenty- to twenty-five-year-olds when we were sixteen and seventeen. By the time we were in our early twenties, with rare exceptions, we would have to wait years for our male contemporaries to catch up with us. Should Grace have selected some Main Line Philadelphia, Penn jock who reported every morning to his dad's business or the trainee program at General Electric? Grace did not want a boy just like the boy that was married to or had issued from dear old Mom.

When I think of Grace after her return from Cannes, during the summer of 1955, I can feel both her contentment and her restlessness. It was clear that her Cannes caper with Jean-Pierre had not blossomed into a serious prospect of marriage. Grace spent a good part of her six months away from the movie cameras visiting with her family and friends.

In the city Carolyn Reybold and Grace had lunch often. Then Grace would return to her friend's apartment to spend hours playing with her four-year-old goddaughter Jyl and Jyl's sister Robin, not yet one. She and Sally Parrish Richardson talked over the various layette items needed for Blair, whom Sally was expecting that autumn. When Rita came to town between her own movie assignments, she and Grace lunched and talked at length about Rita's post-divorce decline and recovery. Grace had dinner with Gant Gaither or John Foreman, with the Reybolds or the Richardsons at neighborhood restaurants. After dinner she and her friends took in a movie or strolled leisurely down Third Avenue, where the El rattled overhead and Grace could peer into the darkened windows of the dozens of antique stores in which she loved to browse.

Toward the end of June, Grace went to Philadelphia to be maid of honor when her younger sister, Lizanne, married Don LeVine. Their older sister, Peggy, was matron of honor. Peggy's two daughters, Meg and Mary Lee, were the flower girls. There is a photo of the women in the wedding party taken at the base of the Kellys' staircase. All the girls are attractive, the three Kelly girls beautiful. The five attendants are dressed exactly alike. You would be hard-pressed to know that one of them was the leading movie celebrity in the world. Grace looked merely like a very pretty girl from a nice family in Philadelphia who was one of the gang.

Grace had more of the same at Ocean City, where she relaxed throughout the summer at the sprawling family home just off the Atlantic. She played with her smaller relatives—her nieces, and first and second cousins. Together with her brother Kell and sister-in-law Mary, and with her two sisters and their husbands, they took the family's younger set for walks on the beach and the boardwalk, collecting souvenirs and seashells as they ambled. There were the inevitable barbecues, potato sack races, horseshoe games and other competitions, which reminded Grace of every childhood summer she had spent with her family at the shore.

Maree Frisby Pamp brought her daughter Linda down to the beach. That section of the New Jersey coast is where many affluent Philadelphians took their hot weather holidays. Together, she and Grace had long hours to reminisce about high school days and catch up on the more recent events of their lives. It was a summer of families, and Grace was deeply moved by the warmth of everyday life among those she loved and cared for.

One morning in September 1955, Grace called. She was going to spend the day selecting clothes to pack for her trip to Hollywood and Asheville, North Carolina, where *The Swan* would shoot. She asked me to come for lunch and spend the afternoon while she organized her suitcases. She apologized for asking me to sit through the packing, but she said she needed to talk. It was the first time Grace had ever admitted to needing anything, so I told her I would be there by noon. I added that I needed to talk, too, so the day sounded perfect to me.

During the early summer, shortly after Jay and I had moved to the country, I was told that "Marilyn was having trouble with Joe," and needed to be sequestered in a hideout—our place. We were not going to be there, so I was glad we could offer her the apartment. We had just moved back to town, and that's what I needed to discuss with Grace.

When I arrived at her apartment for lunch, though each of us wore blue jeans, men's shirts and tennis shoes, we sat in her large formal dining room for our chicken sandwiches. Grace opened by asking how it felt to be back in my own apartment. "I'm not even sure it is mine," I answered, describing the recent incident which produced that sentiment.

A few days earlier Jay and I had decided to spend one night in town before moving our baby back from the country. It was opening night of Arthur Miller's new play *A View from the Bridge*. Miller and Tennessee Williams were recognized as the two most important living American playwrights. What was whispered about, but not acknowledged, was that Arthur Miller and Marilyn had been seeing each other frequently and were more than casual friends. The relationship was important to Marilyn. Less than one year earlier she had been trapped in her image as a sex symbol. To escape, she had left her studio and moved to New York to study acting with Lee Strasberg. Now, the most talented actors, directors and producers on Broadway treated her with respect. And Arthur Miller was becoming seriously involved with her.

In the late afternoon, when Amy Greene and I got to my apartment to change, we were greeted by chaos. Marilyn was to have completed her toilette, makeup and coiffure by the time we arrived. Instead, she was running around in a ragged white terrycloth bathrobe, her hair dirty and straggly.

When I reached my door, a foppish man threw his arm across the entrance to block my way. Hissing through his waxed mustache he proclaimed arrogantly, "No pairsonnes air pairmeeted eento Mees Monroe's boudoir!" He rolled his French "r's" and his frosty eyes simultaneously. I informed him that this was, in fact, my boudoir, and that Miss Monroe was my guest. He lowered his arm as though reporting for duty, grasped my hand, clicked his heels, and bowed snappily, "Eyeam Antoinnnnnnne . . . auv Paris!"

"I'm Judy of New York," I responded, "and I'm going to my closet." But Antoine did a backstep lunge and flung himself in front of me, his arms outstretched again. He informed me that I could not go to my closet or open it because such a move would dislodge all the equipment he had set up and plugged in for the "breelyant coiffe" he had prepared for "Mees Monroe." We engaged in a minor physical skirmish. The round went Antoine of Paris, 10–8. Instead of going the distance with Antoine, I decided to run across town to my mother's apartment, where I had a black dress and shoes stored and could borrow a bag, stockings and a wrap.

When I returned to my apartment, some dozen people of assorted heights, ages and genders were laying out miles of black fabric and equal quantities of black and white fox fur across the length and breadth of my foyer and living room. I recognized only one face, that of John Moore, the protégé of America's leading fashion designer, Norman Norell, whom I knew socially. John proudly showed me the slinky but elegant straight black floor-length gown he had designed for Marilyn. He explained that all the black fabric and all the fur of both colors were for her wrap. I pointed out that the Russian army could be kept warm through the dead of winter with that amount of goods, and that this was only September in a still summer-muggy Manhattan. But it seemed that John and Marilyn had not been able to decide between a mile-long black stole trimmed in white fox and a mile-long black stole trimmed in black fox. So John had brought enough fur to do it either way, together with his workroom staff, and the fox would be stitched to the stole when Marilyn made her last-minute decision. I asked John, who looked anxious, if he'd like a drink.

At this point in my story, Grace stopped me. "I don't believe you, Judy. You can't get into your own bathroom to get your makeup out. Antoine's got you locked out of your bedroom. You've been crosstown to get clothes. There's a design workroom set up in your living room. And you're offering *drinks*?"

It got worse. I offered drinks to John Moore's entire staff. "Well," I told Grace, "they were in my living room—and that sort of made them guests." Within thirty seconds I realized I couldn't keep the drink orders straight in my head. I dashed to the kitchen for a pad and pencil, and returned to continue taking orders like a cocktail waitress. A scotch on the rocks, three gin and tonics with lime, two bourbons with soda, and a rum and Coke. I had gone this far, I told Grace, so I decided to see what

Antoine of My Bedroom, formerly of Paris, might want to whet his whistle. Mistake. "Vaudka and *jus d'orange.*"

I served the dozen or so people in my living room and headed for Antoine, pleased as punch that I had been able to accommodate his request. Marilyn had her own drink and was seated in front of my dresser mirror as Antoine fingered her wet hair. I set his drink down and started to leave. *"Mon Dieu!"* shrieked Antoine. I turned, shaken. *"Le jus d'orange."* He pointed to the drink as though it contained hemlock. "He's nought fraish!"

Antoine staged a full-fledged freak-out. As best as I could discern, his inspiration had been thwarted by frozen orange juice. Marilyn and I had to lower him into a chair to calm his hysterics. The upholstered chairs in my bedroom and the matching cover on our bed were the one complete luxury I had permitted myself when decorating the apartment the prior winter. The fabric was an off-white linen imported from France and patterned with interspersed green raindrop designs. I had also purchased a complementary cloth in turquoise, light blue and the same clear green depicting young birds in their nests. This was hand-painted and quilted to form a motif on the chairbacks, the seat covers and the pillow shams on the bed. Now I saw that the chairs were ruined, each with oddly placed, tannish-orange marks covering the backs and the seats.

When Jay and Milton Greene arrived, expecting to find Amy and me coiffed, clothed and ready to go, they found Amy almost prepared. I was covered in grime, on my hands and knees in the bottom drawer of the pantry searching for cleaning fluid. Milton and Jay simultaneously shook their heads as though you just couldn't trust a woman to be on time—and headed for the nursery shower.

A few moments later the doorman rang to say the limo was in the driveway and Milton, Jay, Amy and Marilyn filed past me in the foyer on their way out the door. En passant, Antoine of Paris mentioned that his assistants would drop by in the morning to unwire my bedroom. You could tell from the way he kept gulping his fourth drink as he left that a hairdresser's life is hell. He took the glass. It was Steuben.

Though the whole apartment looked like a hurricane had hit it, I ran back to the bedroom to study the tannish-orange stains on the chairs and those running down nearly the length of the bedspread. Near the tops of the chairbacks, the stains were wide, narrowing noticeably as they progressed downward toward the seats. On the seats themselves, the stains grew wide again, and two narrow stains ran down the chair bases to the floor. I thought of Marilyn's white legs. I looked at the tannish-orange stains, suddenly realizing what they were. I was the proud owner of two chairs and a bedspread bearing the body makeup imprint of Marilyn Monroe. For a cheap thrill, I told Grace, you could sit on her in my seats and lie on her on my bedspread. I should have sold tickets.

Telling all this to Grace seemed strange. We were not used to complaining to each other. Complaining was not graceful. It was even less attractive as I was complaining about one of Jay's clients to another client. Grace and I talked about how emotionally unbalanced people can suck up all the space, spend all the patience of the people around them, make you resentful. I was unaccustomed to this approach. I was supposed to love everybody. If I were well and they were sick, I was to provide round-the-clock nursing services with joy in the love of giving. Once again, Grace knew more than I did. At the end she came over and put her face very close to mine. "What can you do about it?" she inquired sensibly.

"Nothing," I answered. Without saying it in so many words, Grace had reminded me of something we both knew about ourselves. We were not confrontational, so it was best to move along. We went to pack.

I watched Gracie sort out tweed skirts, tailored blouses, cashmere sweaters and sensible shoes. She tossed chinos, jeans and warmer trousers off their hangers and onto the bed. Next came a couple of suits and dressy blouses, three cocktail dresses and one long gown for emergency. As we folded clothes and stuffed sleeves, Grace told me what was on her mind.

"I'm happy to be doing this film," she noted. "It's a lovely property, a good script, and I think there are new things I can bring to the role since I first played it. I'm looking forward to being in Asheville, North Carolina. We're going to shoot there at the Biltmore House." But then her smile faded and her eyes grew sad.

"I don't really want to go," she said. "Well, part of me does, but another part doesn't want this summer to end."

"Gracie," I noted with surprise, "you're crying." I put down the sweater I was folding and went over to hug her. We sat on the edge of the bed together.

"Lizzie and Don's wedding was so sweet. That's just the trouble. The whole summer was so sweet. My family and all those sweet children at the shore. My friends, staying up until all hours talking and walking through the city. Patting all those sweet baby bottoms. Everything was just so sweet." The summer's sweetness, the early September breeze and the open suitcases overcame her. She cried for a moment. "I want all of that," she admitted.

"I know, Gracie," I assured her, "and you'll have it."

She looked at me long and hard, as though wondering whether she could tell me a deep secret about herself. Then she confessed, "But I want more."

I nodded. "I know, Gracie," I answered, "and you'll keep on getting that, too."

"What I thought I could do, but what I'm not sure about now, is fitting it all together." There was a life of sweetness and a life of more. None of us was sure that anyone was entitled to both, could blend the two together.

"If anybody can do it, Gracie, you can," I said. And I meant it. "When you do fall in love for good, there is nothing you could make but a sweet life for yourself and your husband. Nothing you could be but a good wife and mother. But you can go on working. You've already achieved enough success to be able to pick and choose when you go to work and where. You're in a position where you can turn down jobs when they don't mesh with your family life. That's why I abandoned the notion of a career when Jay and I got engaged," I told her. "I was just starting out and, if I'd wanted to build my career, I would have had to take any good job offered to me. I used to say, 'If I were as successful as Elizabeth Taylor, I could pick and choose.'"

Grace pointed out that Elizabeth, who was only twenty-three, was already divorced from Nicky Hilton and rumored to be having problems with her second husband, Michael Wilding. "I didn't mean to use her as an example for your life, Gracie. It's only that you're as successful as she is, so you could decide when to work and when not to. Anyway," I concluded, "maybe Elizabeth just hasn't married the right man."

Grace nodded reflectively. "You're probably right," she concurred. I detected irony in her voice. "It's a question of the right man."

Many years later I would still recall that conversation and the months that followed it. The questions about the right man were one thing, the answer about where to find him another.

CHAPTER 5

Charmed Lives

$\mathcal{I}$n New York during the winter of 1955–56, everyone who was not already spoken for was falling in love. The rest of us were having babies.

Blair Richardson was born to Sally and John, confirming Sally's instinct that marriage and motherhood were the best of all worlds. Carolyn Reybold, with her two children and Malcolm's career in advertising blooming, was still in great demand as a junior model. While Bettina and Frank Gray in Massachusetts wondered at their three-year-old Lizzie's fascination with the magic of books and ideas, they propped Sam up by hand so he would have the confidence to stand alone. I wheeled our Amy back and forth from Central Park, as did her nurse Miss Mack, stopping at lunch hour in front of the MCA offices at Fifty-seventh and Madison so her father and all his co-workers could run a daily check on the progress of his progeny. Rita Gam and Tom Guinzburg looked serious about each other. And Grace called from her Asheville location to say that her younger sister, Lizanne, and her husband Donald were expecting their first child in the late spring. "L'il Lizzie's pregos," is what she said. When Grace used the word "little" she often pronounced it "l'il," swallowing the last "l" so it sounded almost like baby talk. Then with mock tears she added, "You're all dropping them like calves. Before you know it I'll be everyone's spinster Aunt Grace." The next day I sent her a pack of playing cards after pasting a small photo of her face over that of the Old Maid Queen of Spades.

As the long Thanksgiving weekend approached, Jay and I took an overnight train ride to visit Grace in Asheville. She met us at the station with a driver from the movie and a station wagon for our luggage. Gant had come down for the holiday as well, and on our first morning in North Carolina, Gracie conducted us on a personal tour of Biltmore House, the Vanderbilt estate where the *Swan* company was shooting on location.

"It's like a palace," Grace said enthusiastically. "I love it!" Considering what was about to happen in her life, it was fortunate she felt that way. But we knew nothing yet of her future.

We drove high up into the Smoky Mountains with Grace, who knew exactly where to stop along the route for the best view of the sweeping vistas beneath us. We rendezvoused at an inn atop a ridge, where we were joined for lunch by Alec Guinness, Brian Aherne and Roycie. Jessie Royce Landis had played Grace's mother the year before in *To Catch a Thief*. She was repeating this role in *The Swan* and would remain friendly with Grace all her life. We ate ourselves silly, played dozens of word games, and laughed so hard we almost fell off the undersized, stiff, small wooden chairs on which we were seated. There was no sense, at all, that this was a table of movie stars from New York, London and Hollywood.

The same was true at the Manor House, where we stayed with Grace and the rest of the company. It was there that Alec Guinness initiated what was to become a lifelong joke between himself and Grace. Jessie Royce Landis had bought Guinness a heavy, ugly tomahawk as a souvenir from her trip to an Indian reservation. Just the kind of gift you could live nicely without. When it came time for him to leave Asheville, Alec instructed the bellman to place the tomahawk between the sheets of Miss Kelly's bed. Many years later Grace found a way to have the same tomahawk placed between the sheets at Alec's country house in England. Another decade after that, when Grace left Monaco to do her early poetry readings in the United States, Alec got someone to secret the tomahawk between her sheets in a Minneapolis hotel suite. Again more years passed, and Grace shipped the tomahawk to Rupert Allan in California. Sir Alec was in Beverly Hills to accept an Academy Award. Grace wanted Rupert to be sure the tomahawk was placed inside his bed while he was out at the ceremonies. By some error, the Academy had neglected to see that Sir Alec was taken to the Governor's Ball at the end of the Oscar ceremony. He felt a bit let down as he returned alone to his hotel suite. When he climbed into bed and found again, after all those years, the familiar tomahawk, he felt that an old friend had come to cheer him.

At dusk on Sunday, Jay and I left Asheville in a small private plane piloted by Jack Seabrook, a longtime Kelly family friend who had joined us over the holiday weekend. It was going to be a tricky takeoff as the local airport was ringed by mountains swathed in fog. Saying goodbye at the door to the plane, Grace considered the minimal visibility and worried whether we should attempt the flight. The day before she had driven us along some of the circuitous roads lacing the mountains we could now hardly see. "Sweetie," I told her, "I would rather fly over those mountains in pea soup with Jack than drive on them in broad daylight with you."

Neither by phone from Los Angeles nor in person in Asheville did Grace ever mention Prince Rainier to me. But it was while she was filming *The Swan* that the plan for their next meeting evolved. During the previous summer, when Grace returned from the Cannes Film Festival, she had gone home for her sister Lizanne's wedding. Among the family and friends who had come was a couple known to the Kelly children as "Aunt Edie" and "Uncle Russ" Austin. They mentioned to Grace that they were traveling to Europe later, and that one of their stops would be Monte Carlo. Grace told Aunt Edie and Uncle Russ about her meeting with the Prince at his palace during the *Paris Match* shoot.

When the Austins arrived in Monaco, they tried to secure tickets for the most prestigious event of its summer season, the Red Cross Gala held yearly at the Summer Sporting Club. They learned the event was sold out. Not exactly shrinking violets, Aunt Edie and Uncle Russ hightailed it to the telephone to use the only connection they had. Placing a call to the Prince, Russ Austin informed His Highness that he was Grace Kelly's Uncle Russ, that Grace had told him to call the Prince if he had any problems, and that he needed pull to get his Gala tickets. The Prince said he would take care of the matter, and he did.

The next morning Prince Rainier's spiritual adviser, Father Francis Tucker, called the Austins at their hotel. He wondered if they might like to visit the Palace, as their niece Grace had done. During the visit Father Tucker confirmed the Austins' close relationship with the Kelly family and inquired if they might be able to arrange another meeting between His Highness and Grace if he came to the United States. The Austins were sure they could. They were becoming key backstage figures in a romance of considerable proportion.

In the autumn of 1955, while the Prince's plans for his American visit were being set, the original idea was to have him visit Grace during the shooting of *The Swan*. But those plans changed. Instead, the Austins, the Kellys, Prince Rainier and Father Tucker arranged a Christmas Eve dinner to be held at the Kellys' Henry Avenue home. Aunt Edie and Uncle Ross had known Grace long enough to have seen her turn away suitors and would-be friends whom she did not care for. They asked Margaret Kelly to see if this holiday reunion with the Prince was acceptable to her daughter. Grace had told them she would be pleased to see him again.

While Grace completed *The Swan*, I was in New York trying to organize a pre-Christmas celebration, the biggest party Jay and I had ever given. The party was scheduled to begin at ten at night. We invited many more people than our apartment could hold and began to worry when nearly every invited person accepted. I sent a bottle of champagne to the only other tenants on our floor, apologizing in advance for any inconvenience, and began to lay in supplies.

The night before our party was the night of the annual MCA Christmas party, a raucous affair to which only employees were invited. I cherished the opportunity to put the baby to bed quietly and spend a few hours adding final touches to the flowers, the bar setup and the food I had cooked. I would also have time for last-minute dusting before Jay got home around midnight.

At three I heard Jay's key in the lock. He was home. So were the last thirty or so people who had been left at the MCA celebration. When they departed at sunrise there was not a clean fork, dish, glass or napkin in the house. Half the liquor and all the mixes were gone, along with the food I had cooked for the party that was due to begin sixteen hours hence.

In those days there were three ways in which a woman's worth was measured: by the men who loved her, the popularity of her children and the way she entertained. I had already planned that my headstone would say, "She gave a great party." I was not about to trip over my own feet here. I sent the baby to my parents and tried to reconstitute the apartment, food and beverages for the hundred and fifty guests who would arrive at around ten.

Revelers trickled in slowly until just after eleven, when the theatre broke that night. Then the crunch occurred. I was summoned to the phone to speak with Adolph Green. "I'm with Betty and Steve [Betty Comden and her husband Steve Kyle] and we're on our way from the theatre," he said. "But we've got Lenny and Felicia with us, and since they weren't invited I wondered if it would be okay to bring them." My heart sank. I had asked Lenny Bernstein to select my new piano, prevailed upon him to guarantee its delivery for this night, and forgotten to ask him and his wife to the party! Mortified with embarrassment, I explained to Adolph, made him promise to get the Bernsteins to our apartment, and pledged to throw myself under the wheels of a passing truck when they arrived to show my contrition. All was fine. I was graciously forgiven.

Just as the Comden/Kyle/Green/Bernstein group arrived, so did Grace. She had flown in from California that evening, stopped at her apartment to change, and would leave for Philadelphia in the morning. You could tell she adored being back in New York among friends. Rita Gam and Tom Guinzburg were there. She and Grace enjoyed a wonderful reunion. As I swirled around playing hostess, I repeatedly caught sight of Grace. She radiated happiness. Soon, Jule Styne sat down at the piano and we began to sing. In addition to Leonard Bernstein, Harold Rome, Harold Arlen, Frank Loesser and Stephen Sondheim were at the party. One or the other sidled up to Jule, slid him across the piano bench, and played their own songs.

Then it was time for Christmas carols. Voices swelled convivially. We sang every carol we could remember. I had been standing with Marlon and our mutual friends DD and John Barry Ryan III, but I noticed Grace sitting on the floor directly in front of the fireplace. As I wound my way over, she made a space next to her on the carpet. I sat down as we continued to sing "Gloria in excelsis Deo" with more than a hundred friends of goodwill.

We were all New Yorkers at a time when that was the most wonderful thing in the world to be. Many of us were in our twenties or thirties, but those who were older were not separated from us. Most of us were theatre

my back on them, any more than you could. But the older I get and the more I achieve, the more I've worried that there would never be a right person for me to marry, at least not one I would fall in love with. All of this is wonderful," she indicated her surroundings as though her success was a cocoon in which she'd been contained, "but the more I get, the harder it is to find a man I could marry and spend my life with." I wasn't entirely sure what she meant. I had married at twenty, Grace was twenty-six and had amassed a lifetime of personal accomplishments that I had not.

"I don't want to be married to someone who feels belittled by my success. I don't want a husband who feels guilty because I can earn more money than he can. I don't want a husband who can only stay close to me by running around after me, managing my career. I couldn't bear walking into a restaurant and hearing the maître d' refer to my husband as Mr. Kelly, and you know that happens all the time to couples in this business." I did know that, had squirmed uncomfortably when it happened to friends of mine.

"Falling in love at twenty-six isn't as easy as it was a few years ago," Grace went on. "I'm able to see more of what the person really is than who I want him to be. The Prince is not going to be 'Mr. Kelly.' What he does is far more important than what I do. I want to help him in his work. I hope I can. That's the way it should be." Then her feelings took hold of her again. "And I love him," she concluded.

I was amazed that Grace could be so romantic and so pragmatic all at once. I believed she was in love, had never seen her quite this way before. I understood her wish to put herself in her proper place, as an adjunct to her husband. Neither of us questioned that this was the natural order of things. "I'm so happy for you, Gracie," I said. "I hope you and the Prince have a wonderful life together. Now let's get down to business: When do we meet the guy and when do you ankle this joint?"

Both questions were answered the following evening when Grace's lawyer Henry Jaffe, Jay, John Foreman and I were invited to have dinner at her apartment to meet the Prince and his chaplain, Father Francis Tucker. The chaplain was a jolly fellow from Wilmington, Delaware, who had been appointed by the Vatican as the priest of the parish of St. Charles in Monaco. He was part of the triumvirate that had shot its powerful bows and arrows at the hearts of the newly betrothed couple. It was not an easy evening for most of us. A priest and a prince sounded like dinner with a jury rather than a meal with a friend and her new fiancé.

Grace made introductions all around. During cocktails, polite, if stiff, conversation was made, congratulations offered, obvious questions asked tentatively so as not to appear intrusive. At the dinner table things loosened up a bit. Father Tucker told a joke, reminding the Prince of another one, reminding me of a third. Laughter, once again, was the great leveler. Grace began to relax, relaxing the rest of us. This wasn't so bad after all. It improved immeasurably when, walking into the living room for coffee, I addressed the Prince as "Your Highness" and he invited me to call him "Rainier."

While we were together, Grace wanted to discuss the planning for the forthcoming announcement of their engagement. Father Tucker began to outline the schedule as it had been set to date. Monseigneur (the Prince) and Grace would return with him to the Kelly family home in Philadelphia to make their formal announcement, which would be released to the press. The sole photographer recording this event was to be privately hired. One photo of the bride and groom, another of them with the bride's family would be released with the announcement. It would be brief and simple. The press would be there and gone within a few minutes.

It sounded neat as a pin and as realistic as Snow White and the Seven Dwarfs. Henry Jaffe, Jay and John tried to explain that the plan just would not work for the American press. They elaborated on the media's appetite for even insignificant news about Grace. Respectfully and accurately they foretold that this would be exacerbated by the person and status of her future groom, the Prince. They proposed additional availability as a means of allaying the near-riot they felt would ensue under the envisioned plan. They carefully explained that a starved press is an angry press, and that as a means for their own self-protection, the couple and Father Tucker might give them more of what they'd want in order to make them less aggressive.

The Prince would not be moved. As his resolve hardened, Father Tucker became less jovial. Grace sat farther back as though wishing she could disappear into the sofa pillows. Voices on both sides became more tense. More impassioned on the one side. More commanding on the other. Things were not going well. A battle was clearly in progress from which no true winners could possibly emerge. I couldn't stand it any longer.

"This conversation is making all of us terribly uncomfortable," I blurted out. I turned to the Prince. "It's quite clear, Your Highness, that you and Grace want to avoid as much chaos as possible, to have the most personal day you can." I turned to Father Tucker. "It's also clear that you are trying to represent the Prince's wishes." I looked at nobody in particular. "But it's not fair that you've asked three of Grace's advisers here, all of whom understand the press in this country, to help you achieve your goals, and when they speak with your best intention in mind you behave as though they are 'crossing' you in some way. They're giving you their best, most considered opinion that the only way to protect yourselves is to acknowledge what's going to happen and plan for it accordingly. They're advising you that if you ignore the reality of what this announcement will mean to the press, you're going to have all the chaos you're trying to avoid." The room was utterly silent. I was on a roll. "If you think that your plan is best and you're sure you are right, then this conversation can end now. If you think that Jay, John and Henry might have a point, then I beg you to listen to them."

Everyone looked at the floor. The silence lasted long enough for me to envision myself being convicted before the Sovereign Throne, marched up an outdoor wooden platform, bent over, and guillotined.

Quietly, but with thoughtful determination in his voice, the Prince spoke first. "I believe you all know what Grace and I hope to avoid. Perhaps you can offer us some specific suggestions on how we might accomplish our wish without making our private day more public than is absolutely necessary." He looked neither angry, conciliatory nor pleased, just princely. I was overcome with terror. Oh, well, I thought, at least John, Jay and Henry were all still *persona grata,* and Grace had other girlfriends.

A plan was established that allowed the young couple a private luncheon at the Philadelphia Country Club with Grace's family, Father Tucker, the Prince's physician, who was traveling with them, and a few close friends. Afterwards, at the family home on Henry Avenue, the press would converge. Other details would be worked out over the next few days. The planning session was over. At the door, saying our good nights, Grace gave me a kiss on the cheek. The Prince and the priest were polite but unsmiling, confirming my fears that Grace's expression of affection toward me might be the last one permitted her before her new status became formalized.

I was not in Philadelphia for the engagement announcement. Like everyone else, I read everything about it I could get my hands on. Grace and Rainier sat on the Kellys' sofa, their arms intertwined. Reporters and photographers were everywhere, popping questions and flashbulbs with blinding rapidity. There was no doubt it had been chaotic, but I felt vindicated, knowing it would have been worse had the press not been with them for the time allowed. Sometime later I learned that the Prince had been patient up to a point, but had finally put a stop to the session by muttering to Father Tucker, "After all, *I* don't belong to MGM."

Before the public announcement was made on January 5, 1956, Grace made special dates with each of her New York girlfriends to tell them, in her own way, about her betrothal. She did the same thing with each of her close male friends, again on a one-on-one basis. Grace was accustomed to doing things her own way, the right way. There were three other people she needed to tell. She had to tell them personally, but not in person as that was no longer appropriate. She wrote three letters—one to Gene Lyons, one to Oleg Cassini and one to Jean-Pierre Aumont. In each, she said goodbye. For each, she shed tears. Grace did not like losing anyone she had ever loved.

Immediately after their formal announcement, and before their first scheduled public appearance on January 10, Grace gave a cocktail party to introduce her fiancé to her close friends. When Jay called to tell me the time for this party, I was positive the only reason we had been invited was because of Jay. Surely the Prince had brooded over my rudeness at our first meeting. Surely, by now, the reserve I had felt from him at Grace's front door had hardened.

As we got off the elevator, we could see that Grace and the Prince were receiving just inside the living room doors. I remembered being told that as an American I did not have to curtsy. This was fortunate, as I could hardly stand. I concentrated on Grace's face. She looked like Sleeping Beauty and Cinderella all rolled up in one. I felt like the ugly stepsister.

When I reached Grace, ignoring my outstretched hand, she leaned across and kissed me on both cheeks. Her graciousness comforted me but the worst was yet to come. Turning to the Prince she said, "You remember Judy," dashing my one slim hope that he would not. Prince Rainier extended his hand. I extended mine. No flicker of recognition crossed his eyes. No smile of acknowledgment moved his mouth. Then he put one foot ever so slightly behind the other and, bobbing down and up in a tiny curtsy, grinned mischievously. My eyes opened wide. My mouth fell open. I was so grateful for the humor and warmth of the gesture that I would have offered myself to his cause for a lifetime, had I only known what it was. His curtsy was to become a running joke almost until our children grew up. At that time I still had not learned a commoner was *permitted* to have a running joke with a prince.

The next days were a whirlwind. Grace and Rainier made their first public appearance together at a January 6 charity ball appropriately titled A Night in Monte Carlo. He wore uniform, orders and medals. She wore white strapless, orchids and pearls. In groups of four or more, all of Grace's friends spent one or more evenings with the happy couple. Each of these concluded with a stop at The Harwyn Club in the East Fifties, where Grace and Rainier danced the most dreamy romantic dances to what had become their song, "Your Eyes Are the Eyes of a Woman in Love" from *Guys and Dolls.* On each of these occasions Malcolm or Carolyn Reybold, Sally or John Richardson, or Jay and I made long ceremonious toasts to their future and ours.

The press followed Rainier and Grace, separately or together, wherever they went. Grace was beatific but besieged. She was due within days in Hollywood to start filming *High Society.* She needed to sort clothes and pack, continue her singing lessons for the movie, start studying French for her next role, her future life. Plans for the wedding had to be made. She would not be married at home. The groom required that the wedding be held in Monaco. As Grace left for California, it was just beginning to dawn on me that she was going to be a princess, a real princess.

In Los Angeles, Grace's life grew even more complicated. She had to memorize lines, fit wardrobe, pose for stills, have hair and makeup designed, and shoot the musical remake of *The Philadelphia Story* in which she starred with two old friends, Frank Sinatra and Bing Crosby, and one new one, Celeste Holm. In addition, she continued her French lessons and entertained the Prince and his father, Prince Pierre, who came to California to spend several weeks with her during filming. She and the Prince needed to solidify the plans for their wedding. Grace had to select her wedding wardrobe and have it executed, make her personal guest lists for each event, and decide what she would take from her apartment, what she would leave behind. She was not only going to be married in April in a far country. She was moving away for good.

Between the young lovers, things went exceedingly well. Around them, some things jarred. Rainier was neither familiar nor comfortable with American ways. He'd had little contact with Americans except for the ones who visited Monaco and other European countries. He was a little put off because Americans are much more open and direct than Europeans. If Rainier felt this in New York, being in Hollywood made it even more startling.

In Hollywood, he spent time on the set of Grace's movie. If you have not ever been around a harmonious company shooting a happy film, it is impossible to comprehend the depth of the camaraderie that prevails. A common mission transcends the boundaries that normally separate people. This was especially true in those times, when everyone took intense pride in doing his work well. For the duration of the filming, the entire crew became a family. Years later, when I asked Robert Mitchum what he loved best about making movies, he answered, "The way the people feel about each other. It's the best."

This intimacy must have been intimidating for the shy, lonely, aloof ruler from the distant land. During childhood his family life had not been warm. His isolation from friends had been that which inevitably surrounds the monarchy. In Hollywood, his bride-to-be was no longer the delicate, removed beauty who floated through a crowd. Here she was one of the gang. He was her prince on a white charger and he was going to rescue her from all this. He could not possibly have known that what he was taking her from made her the very person he loved. She did not know it either.

Both Grace and Rainier found much of the talk surrounding them in Hollywood distasteful. No announcements about the future of her career had been made, but one presumed that a young woman marrying the Prince of Monaco was not going to continue as a movie actress. In Hollywood, some people were obviously intimidated, surprised, annoyed, aggravated. Gossip abounded. Rainier knew what the morning line said. Even though it wasn't spoken openly, he could feel it. "What's she going to do now? Why should she give up her career for *that?*" There was a kind of contempt in the questions. Rainier was proud of Grace's answers, which spoke of marriage, of family and of her hope that she could make a contribution to the Principality that was to become her home.

While Grace finished her last film in Hollywood in February 1956, Sir Laurence Olivier came to New York to attend a onetime NBC airing of his recently completed production of *Richard III,* and to solidify his co-starring, joint production with Marilyn Monroe in the movie adaptation of Terence Rattigan's play *The Sleeping Prince.* When I heard he would be in town, all I could think of was how wonderful it would be for Marilyn to work with Olivier. But when Jay told me to block a week for his visit, I realized that I, too, was going to meet him.

To this day I do not understand the adolescent self-consciousness that overcame me at the thought of this prospect. I had met or become friendly with nearly every well-known person in the arts, sports and commerce. I had visited at the White House with the three men who had been President of the United States since I was born twenty-three years earlier. I had even survived the Prince of Monaco in my friend's living room. Sir Laurence, though, was more than a girl could bear.

Jay went to pick Olivier up at the airport and I was to meet them at NBC. When I looked in the mirror over my sink, I saw a freckle-faced twelve-year-old girl. When I moved to the full-length mirror things worsened. I had learned to live with the fact that I have a long torso and short legs, but what was looking back at me in the glass was Toulouse-Lautrec in drag. My nylons bagged at the ankles like my crushed-down bobby sox had in the seventh grade. While praying that some magical transformations would take place before I reached NBC, I heard a key turn in our apartment lock and found Jay entering—with Olivier behind him. They had decided to pick me up on the way.

In the limo I buttoned and unbuttoned my jacket so many times that two of its five buttons fell off by the time we reached Rockefeller Center. I couldn't be sure what I thought of *Richard III* until I saw it again many months later. In the special viewing room, I sat next to its director and star, praying my stomach wouldn't grumble during the key scenes.

The only way I got through the week with Larry was to tell him how I was feeling. He was adorable about it, and even teased me from time to time about my "crush." One night, at a formal supper party at Nedda and Josh Logan's River House apartment, the straps of my dress kept slipping down from my shoulders. It happened every time he stood next to me. I told him it was on cue, just to embarrass me. One dropped. "See?" I whispered under my breath to him. "Sloppy."

He shook his head from side to side, letting his eyelids fall to half-mast over those wondrous eyes. Then in the voice of all my dreams he corrected, "Not sloppy. Sexy."

For a few months Marilyn had been living in an apartment in the other wing of our building. On the first day she met Olivier, Jay and Larry arrived on time and waited in the living room of her flat while she applied the finishing touches of her makeup. Three hours later she emerged from her bedroom. It was a bad beginning, a harbinger of things to come. Marilyn's anxiety over her initial meeting with Larry would fester into plague proportions during the filming of their joint production. Her internal self-destruct mechanism was so pervasive it guaranteed she would destroy any personal or professional relationship that had special meaning for her. Marilyn could always find a way to prove to you that she was as unworthy as she deemed herself. Tragic to watch, difficult to tolerate and impossible to cure, Marilyn made sure that most of her friends, lovers and idols ended up either pitying or loathing her.

The extraordinary contrast between Grace and Marilyn astounded me. Grace's parents may not have loved her as she wished to be loved, but they loved her the best they could. Her mother's sternness, her father's insensitivity hurt her. But her parents were there for her. Her brother and sisters may have taken unfair advantage of their meeker sister, but they were with her. Grace had been a part of a family unit. Even if its bonds were too tightly wrapped or wrapped in the wrong places, she knew such bonds existed. She believed she could replicate them in her own time and in her own way, improving on the original example.

Marilyn, however, had never had enough proof that such bonds were truly possible. No family unit had embraced her for long. No blustery group of competitive siblings had shared her battles and her blessings. She did not even know how to be a friend. She was filled only with her unfulfilled longing. She longed for something she had no proof existed.

I thought then that Grace had everything, because if you had as much as she did, the Eleventh Commandment was Thou Shalt Be Happy. It would be years before I would come to realize all she had was a chance at happiness. Though I was only twenty-three years old in 1956, I knew that was exactly what Marilyn did not have.

Only once in all the years I knew her did Grace speak harshly about one of her parents to me. When "My Daughter Grace Kelly—Her Life and Romances" became a ten-part serial syndicated by King Features in newspapers across the country, Grace broke the Eleventh Commandment. She called me from California, where *High Society* was filming, crushed and angry. Having spent the few years of her career saying nothing about her private life, she was appalled to learn that her mother had sold her story to the press. She had spoken with her mother, whose defense was that the money had been raised for her favorite charity. "Couldn't she have given a damn benefit?" Grace snapped into the phone. "Or written a check or baked cookies, instead of selling me to the highest bidder?" Grace had been used badly, and she knew it.

The deed was out of character for Margaret Kelly. She had been a woman who cared much for appearances, a woman who fought, often behind the scenes, to see that the Kelly family's reputation was upheld. She was used to this from her years as Jack's wife, from the time when he had run for office. She had made several trips or phone calls to Grace over the years to criticize her activities and the spoken or printed gossip they had engendered. Ma Kelly had wheedled, manipulated, coerced, threatened and intimidated her daughter in order to see that she married "the right man." Now that Grace was going to settle down and marry him, why would Margaret Kelly publicly rehash the very romances she had tried to veil over the past five years? Could she not see that her gaffe might also jeopardize the engagement that had just been announced? The last thing the future Princess of Monaco and her betrothed Highness needed was this type of exploitation. Something began to obliterate Margaret Kelly's judgment when her daughter became engaged to the Prince of Monaco, just as it clouded the perceptions of a great many others who knew Grace. At the time none of this was understood. When Grace concluded the call telling me about her mother's indiscretion with the press, she moaned, "First I had to fight the studio to avoid being a commodity. Now my own family trades me on the open market. Doesn't it ever end? When do I get to be just a person?"

Both of us should have known it was only beginning. L'il Gracie had wanted to be more than "just a person" and she had succeeded. One of the hardest balancing acts in life is to be "just a person" and more than just a person at the same time. Neither of us realized that the wire Grace had walked on as an actress had now been extended around the world. The publicly smiling little flower of Grace's poem—star of her own production "The Grace Kelly Story"—would fight her battles in the darkness of her nights until all her extraordinary stamina was finally consumed.

Grace called a few days later, happy again. "Judybird, Rainier and I are getting married in Monaco in April and I want you to be one of my bridesmaids." She was bubbling over and so was I.

Within the same twenty-four-hour period, Grace called five other friends. The oldest and dearest, Maree Pamp, got the call in Philadelphia. She was thrilled and said yes immediately. Bettina Gray was astounded when Grace asked her. She was sure their friendship had waned with time and distance, but was not so overwhelmed that she didn't accept on the spot. Rita Gam, in New York, was planning her own wedding to Tom Guinzburg for about the same period, but once she and Grace compared dates and figured out how the April calendar would work, Rita accepted happily. Sally Parrish Richardson said she would have to talk with John about seeing if they could manage the trip and the time away from his work. She was very happy to be asked and would be there if things could be worked out. Carolyn Reybold was also delighted with Grace's request and accepted, providing Malcolm's new employer would permit his absence. Every one of us was deeply touched by Grace's loyalty. She wanted her best friends as her bridal attendants.

None of us realized we would be the subject of a press release. Here's what happened in one day to Bettina Gray in a little town in Massachusetts when her name was among those given to the press as a Grace Kelly bridesmaid. It is copied directly from yellow lined paper on which messages and notes were left for her in the days immediately following the bridesmaids announcement.

Feb. 19th.

6:45 Dave Wilson and the photographer Ernest McLean sent by "some executive of the [Boston Herald]." Took photos and wrote article.

Feb. 20th.

1:00 A.M. Post called. Wanted to know if story in the *Herald* was
true.

3:00 A.M. A reporter called.

7:45 A.M. Hank Fontaine of WJDA in Quincy called.

7:55 A.M. Globe on front doorstep wanting Family photo. Put off
until 11:00 A.M.

2 men, A.M. from *American* wanted Bettina and Elizabeth [her
daughter] to pose in front of blown-up photo of Grace—gave
coffee while she dressed. Interview & pictures—Bettina showing Elizabeth photo of Grace. Wire services call to check
accuracy.

London *Daily Express* called.

Philadelphia (paper) called—who were the other bridesmaids?

11:00 A.M. Globe (Mr. O'Connor) asked for pictures. Grace Da-
vidson from *Post* (called).

11:45 A.M. Acorn (?) Television wanted 1 min. tel. appearance.
WBZ-TV film.

MGM newsreel. Newsreel film.

2 men *Globe*—Mr. George Croft.

Outdoor shots—snowballs for Willie [Bettina's dog].

1:45 P.M. Tina left.

For those of us in New York, it was pretty much the same. February
20, 1956, marked the first of forty-five days when I would take the elevator
down from my eighteenth-floor apartment to find a herd of reporters and
photographers in the driveway of my building and milling about near its
corner entrance on Fifty-seventh and Sutton Place.

Before I went out that day Rita Gam called. She had already seen the
media gathered outside her apartment. She suggested we get together and
agree to pose once, at my place, for the various accredited photographers
who were waiting outside or would call throughout the first day. We
scheduled such a "photo opportunity" in my living room for three o'clock
that afternoon. Jay and I had to catch a five-thirty train to attend a sneak
preview in Philadelphia.

The photographers were lined up into the public hallways of my
building. They came into and out of my living room in shifts, elbowing

one another for space, entry and egress. Rita and I made a brief statement to each shift of the press. Then my baby Amy woke up and cried. The journalists clamored for her to be brought out, and she appeared in a fluffy peach cotton dress with smocking across the top. I sat Amy on my lap while the cameras clicked away. She was quite delighted with all the fuss, unlike Rita, who was uncomfortable, and her mother, who was numb. When the mob cleared out, Rita left for home, Amy left for Central Park, and I left for Penn Station.

At one the next morning, taxiing up from our return train ride, Jay and I stopped, as usual, to buy the papers at a corner newsstand. Rita, Amy and I were blown up to fill the front page of the *Daily News.* Amy Kanter, like her mother and maternal grandparents before her, was a redhead. Though she would later grow a voluminous head of auburn hair, at one she had only a few wisps of peach-colored fuzz atop her pate. In real life, her blond eyebrows were undistinguishable. She photographed absolutely bald. But the *News* retouchers, accustomed to doctoring celebrities, had not been able to resist doing the same for Amy. They had given my seemingly bald baby bushy black eyebrows from labor leader John L. Lewis or Groucho Marx!

In the coming weeks the frenzy accelerated. When Carolyn Reybold got her first Associated Press call, she told the reporter she wasn't sure she could go to Monaco as her husband Malcolm had recently started a new job with McCann-Erickson Advertising. The next morning, when Malcolm got to his office, his secretary informed him he had an urgent summons to appear before the head of the company. Malcolm was worried. He had to rush to an outside meeting and by the time he got back found another three messages from his boss waiting for him. "Sounds like trouble," his secretary warned him as he fled down the corridor.

"What in the hell have you been telling the press?" his boss demanded. Malcolm was baffled. "My God, we've got calls coming in from all over," his boss exclaimed. "A girl is invited to be a bridesmaid for Grace Kelly and Prince Rainier, and McCann-Erickson won't let her husband go 'cause he just started a new job? For God's sake, you're making us look terrible. Straighten this thing out. Of course you're going!"

Carolyn got calls from every fashion house in New York offering her their suits, day dresses, evening clothes, accessories and jewelry if only she would wear them on her trip to the wedding. Malcolm did not have unlimited time to be gone from the office, and the cost of the trip was of some concern to the Reybolds, but in return for photographs of the marriage and an appearance by Carolyn the day she returned from the wedding, NBC's *Home* show provided the couple with free round-trip airline tickets on KLM.

Along the way each of the six of us, as well as Grace's older sister, Peggy, who was matron of honor, received calls from a Neiman-Marcus representative. Grace had ordered our dresses from the store, which was having them custom-made by a noted bridal design firm in Boston. We were each asked to block time for appointments when fitters would come to our home armed with the muslins. We were to buy our own shoes and gloves, but were asked to select wrist-length white kid gloves for our hands and dyed yellow satin pumps for our feet. Our custom-made hats were being done by a milliner in the East Fifties in New York. We were each given the phone number and asked to call directly to set our own fitting appointments. Our personal wardrobes for the trip needed to be assembled. Those of us with children were trying to make arrangements for their care while we were gone.

Within days of their Christmas Eve dinner, Rainier had given Grace a friendship ring, a band circled on top with large rubies and diamonds. Once their formal announcement had been made, the Prince told Grace that a proper engagement ring was being set especially for her.

In *High Society* Grace needed to wear a prominent diamond ring. She had selected a huge, square paste version from those submitted to her. When she arrived in Hollywood to make the movie, everyone asked to see her engagement ring. What she flashed was what she had, the friendship ring the Prince had given her in Philadelphia. To most people, she made no additional comments. But she did tell her hairdresser and friend Virginia Darcy about the single stone the Prince was readying for her. For several days Virginia watched Grace admire the first piece of jewelry the Prince had given her, while ignoring the enormous prop solitaire on her other hand.

One morning, though, Grace came laughing into her dressing room. She started to get hysterical, the way only she could laugh, with tears running down her face. "Look at this!" she howled, holding her left hand up to Virginia's face. Virginia thought it was the same prop diamond and informed Grace that as she saw it daily, she didn't get the joke. But it was no prop. As though the Prince had seen the prop and had it duplicated, this was the real McCoy. Grace told Virginia that she wanted to substitute it for the prop ring and wear it through the remainder of the movie. But Virginia reminded Grace that studio insurance would require guards on the set if she told. Together, they decided to make the switch but tell no one. Now, when people on the set asked Grace when her engagement ring was coming, she would reply mischievously, "This *is* my engagement ring," flashing the real one, which was mistaken for the prop.

MGM offered Helen Rose's services to design and supervise the making of Grace's wedding dress as part of their gift to their star. But the matter of who would do Grace's hair during the wedding festivities became a cause célèbre in Hollywood. Grace originally asked Lenore Weaver, who had worked with her on her Hitchcock films, to accompany her on the trip. But Lenore had another assignment and her studio would not release her. A number of people in town, including Lenore herself, Virginia and Hitch, thought this was extremely unfair.

Grace told Virginia that Lenore was not able to go, but she said nothing specific to Virginia about making the trip. One morning as they were riding to the studio in a limousine, Grace asked vaguely, "Is your passport active?" Virginia told Grace it was. Grace said nothing about taking Virginia to Monaco. She casually noted, "I have to get mine renewed because it's expired."

Each day, while Virginia dressed her hair for *High Society,* Grace studied her lines, her Berlitz French lesson book or a book on Monégasque history. And each day Sidney Guillaroff, MGM's hair design maven, would stop in for a visit, checking with Grace to see if his personal invitation to the wedding had been confirmed. Upon each inquiry, Grace told Sidney that she and her family had sent their lists on to the Prince and that this was all she could do.

One morning while Grace was checking on bead samples for her wedding dress, Sidney Guillaroff stopped by again. Virginia Darcy was outside the dressing room waiting to do Grace's hair. Sidney went in. Then Sidney stormed out. "How dare you do this," he barked at Virginia, his eyes as cold as stones.

"Do what?" Virginia asked.

"You're going to Monaco!" Sidney replied.

"I am?" Virginia inquired.

white one of Monaco and the red, white and blue of Gracie's homeland. The pennants and banners of the yachts furled and unfurled in the stiff spring wind.

The *Deo Juvante II* slowed into the harbor, with expert crews of uniformed, able-bodied seamen guiding it ever so smoothly to its mooring at the quay. A varnished wooden gangplank was ceremoniously laid between the deck and the shore. Soldiers stood crisply at attention, saluting as the world watched the shy young girl in a big white hat carry her poodle across the wobbly walkway.

Grace carried Oliver, but she carried a weightier, unseen load as well. She bore our myth and our expectations. We, your wives, would be your princess. You, our husbands, would be our prince. Together, we would raise the happiest children in the universe. This was a promise worthy of a great celebration. How easy she made it look! How easy we all thought it would be!

On cue, a barrage of fireworks thundered skyward off the decks of the colossal Onassis pleasure boat, the *Christina.* As our launch crossed the entrance to the harbor, Maree turned to me. "My God," she exclaimed, "these people really know how to say 'hello'!"

Jay called our attention to a single small airplane that had come into view. Crossing the port, we gasped as an enormous, artificial sun parachuted out of the plane accompanied by thousands of U.S. and Monégasque flags. The flags and the imitation sun floated high above our heads, danced gaily in an upward air current, then hovered tremulously before gliding off in a downdraft like tipsy kites. Looking toward land produced the odd sensation that Monaco had no windows. Each opening of every building was filled with open-mouthed faces calling "welcome" in a dozen languages. We turned back out to the bay to see the last wedding guests disembarking into their launches. Then the liner's engines stirred into action again. As the *Constitution's* bow pointed toward open sea, the roar of a twenty-one-gun salute issued from Fort Antoine in the Principality.

Straining our eyes against the sun's glare, we saw three men being ceremoniously led aboard the *Deo Juvante* in port. The first, we were told, was His Excellency Monsieur Henri Soum. As Minister of State, he had come to welcome Miss Kelly and tender the official respects of the Monégasque government. Next came Maître Louis Aureglia, President of the National Council, bearing welcome from the parliament. The last man was Maître Robert Boisson, Mayor of Monaco, who carried the sentiments of the city.

A half hour later we saw Grace, Rainier, the Kellys and the dignitaries leaving the yacht. Around her neck Gracie now featured a lei of orchids, a gift of welcome sent by the U.S. residents of Monaco. Two little girls of about six were brought to her as she stepped on land. They were dressed in the beautiful Monégasque national costume and bashfully presented her with a bouquet of lilies of the valley and forget-me-nots. Then Grace and Rainier entered a green Chrysler Imperial bearing the standard of the Prince and took off on a procession winding through the streets.

It was finally our turn to dock. Stepping onto the quay, we were led to special chauffeur-driven limousines meant to take us to our hotel. But first we had to start our own tour through Monaco. On an earlier trip to Europe I had arrived as a tourist, but nothing prepared me for that ride on our first morning in Monaco. We had to be sheltered by six guards for five minutes just to get into our cars and have them start forward.

Thousands of faces wreathed in smiles along the narrow streets shouted welcome to us. Clusters of spectators jovially danced jigs resembling Provençal versions of the Virginia reel. German college students raised steins and even whole beer kegs to salute us, knocking one another over in their own hilarity. French schoolchildren waved flags in one hand and banners of their own institution in the other. Old ladies dressed all in black, like mourning Portuguese fishwives, raised their withered hands in prayerful supplication. When traffic prevented us from moving, one of them came forward to lay a blossom and a psalm on the fender of our car. A toothless retiree from the Italian navy, still in uniform, dropped to his knees grinning wildly in front of a postal box. Four Arabic teenage boys ran to lift him up by his elbows and swung him back and forth like a salami over the curbstone while he tried to blow kisses to the American visitors. A pair of bleached blond twins, wearing hula skirts over their trench coats, undulated their hips from side to side while a pimpish-looking South American roué accompanist strummed his toy ukelele.

By the time we pulled up in front of the Hôtel de Paris, more than eleven hundred journalists had arrived in Monaco, nearly twice the number that had covered the earlier Geneva Peace Conference. Within the next twelve hours that number would grow to fourteen hundred, swelling again before the week ended to nearly two thousand. Curious tourists poured into the Principality, coming by land across three of its borders and by sea across the fourth.

The Hôtel de Paris was ready for us. Its lobby had an amazingly high ceiling. A massive crystal chandelier hovered over a circular red plush banquette with gilded arms and feet in the center of the room. In front of the round banquette, low gold cocktail tables were set at convenient intervals. To the left, double glass doors revealed the bar, set up with six rows of round tables and chairs that (oddly, I thought) all faced front as though waiting for a performance in the great hall. Outside the bar doors, other banquettes were wrapped around great marble columns, again with carefully arranged and highly polished cocktail tables set in front of them at knee height.

The reservations manager who signed us in and took our passports seemed familiar with each of our names, knew exactly how each of us was to be placed. He summoned the porter to escort us to our rooms, but not before the smiling concierge came out from behind his marble-topped mahogany desk to welcome us. Then we climbed the lovely marble stairway that led to the vestibule of the hotel and its rear rooms overlooking the harbor.

In our quarters we were greeted by a huge basket of fruits, crackers and biscuits, along with a bottle of the best champagne. When we threw open our double doors, we found a tiny, shallow balcony and a wondrous view of the port, where luncheon parties were in full swing on the decks of the yachts below.

Raising our eyes from the port, we looked up toward the ancient city of Monaco-Ville and its exquisite capstone, the Palais Princier, Palace of the Prince. Though it had been newly painted pink for Grace's arrival and the wedding, it, too, had the subtlety of all Monaco's pastel buildings, which seem washed with the beauty of time and history into the hues of dusky tea roses. Jay and I stood silently admiring the exquisite view for fully ten minutes, each with our own private thoughts. Then Jay shrugged his shoulders and, with his eyes on the Palace and his voice close to breaking, said, ever so softly, "Gracie's over there now."

In the Palace Court of Honor, Grace was, for the first time, meeting her new family. She had told me she had loved the informal time she and

Rainier spent with his father, Prince Pierre, during *High Society.* Born into a less affluent branch of a distinguished French family, originally as the Count de Polignac, Pierre had charmed Grace with his wit and ready acceptance of her. She had also been heartened, she told me, by the warmth and affection she saw pass between this dashing man and his son. But Pierre was the only member of her new family she had met.

Rainier's father had become a prince, under Monégasque custom, when he married Charlotte, Rainier's mother and a Grimaldi by blood. Princess Charlotte was the daughter of Monaco's Prince Louis II and a French-Algerian laundress named Juliette Louvet. Charlotte's parents had fallen in love, married in the Church, and welcomed their baby daughter during Louis's extended tour of duty with the French Foreign Legion in Africa. (Louis's father, Prince Albert I, had given much of substance to Monaco, but had little affection for his son. For this reason, Louis had left to join the army and remained away from home until he was thirty-eight.) When Louis and Juliette were wed, neither their marriage nor the birth of Charlotte was recognized by Albert I. He had forbidden the union and believed he had no obligation to accept its offspring as an heir to his throne. Louis and Juliette did not remain together.

Thus Rainier's mother, Charlotte, grew to maturity as the child of divorced parents and as a bastard—if not in the eyes of the Church, most assuredly in the hearts and minds of her all-powerful forebears. Hers cannot have been a joyous childhood. But in 1919, when Prince Albert realized that he was past seventy and that his son Louis would never marry again, he pragmatically swallowed his pride. A recently signed treaty with France stipulated that if the House of Grimaldi failed to produce an heir, Monaco would lose its independent status as a Principality and be annexed to the Republic of France. Overnight the bastard outcast became both a princess of the blood and a savior of the nation. Charlotte was twenty-one when her life was thus transformed.

Not long afterwards, Charlotte and Rainier's father, Count Pierre de Polignac, were married. Neither Charlotte nor Pierre was ever meant to rule Monaco, but they did deliver it two heirs, Antoinette and Rainier, both born within the first four years of the marriage. The family heaved a great sigh of relief. By then, Albert I had died and Louis took the throne. He held it until abdicating power to his grandson, Rainier, in 1949, when the latter turned twenty-six. Rainier's parents had none of the true responsibility or power of royalty, only its perks and its burdens. Unhappy together, they divorced when Rainier was six and maintained no contact over the years except to battle over his custody.

Grace suspected that Princess Charlotte already resented her. But her own passion for family unity, her natural role as peacemaker and her intuitive maternal instinct made her wish to mend the torn family that had so deeply hurt her fiancé. Shortly before his abdication, Rainier's grandfather, Louis, had married an actress three decades his junior, now known as Princess Ghislaine. Officially, as Rainier's stepgrandmother, she, too, would be present.

One woman Grace met that day, the one she hoped would become a friend, was Rainier's older sister, Princess Antoinette. Like her brother, she had been raised by nannies and schoolteachers, and had little love or closeness with either of their parents, particularly with her mother, Charlotte. Because of her diminutive stature, Antoinette was nicknamed "Princess Tiny Pants" by the press. This became shortened to Tiny. Her relationship with Rainier had grown strained in the mid-Forties when she fell in love with a Monégasque tennis champion and lawyer, Aleco Noghes. Noghes was not yet officially divorced from a woman reported to be Tiny's friend. Nevertheless, they were married in a civil ceremony and had three children together. By the time of Grace's marriage, that union had dissolved and Tiny had taken up with Jean-Charles Rey, the outspoken leader of her brother's political opposition group, and was rumored to be affiliated with a planned coup d'état to topple Rainier. She and her brother had grown distrustful of each other, and he had stripped her of most of her formal involvements with sovereign family projects. Grace knew that Tiny's official duties might be further diminished by her own presence, yet she hoped to bring Rainier and his sister together and to make of Tiny a friend.

Princess Antoinette lived in a nearby villa; Prince Pierre, in a beautiful house just down the road from the Palace. Other Princely Family members were to stay at the Palace in guest quarters, along with Grace and her parents. Moving Grace into the Palace served a threefold purpose. It elevated her instantly to the position of Sovereign Princess. It removed her from the constant inspection and harassment of the press, and it gave her the opportunity to meet the household and other official staff members.

At her palace, Grace went off to lunch with twenty-three adult relatives, while her Philadelphia nieces, Meg and Mary Lee, lunched in the children's dining room with their new playmates—Bitsy (Elisabeth), Buddy (Christian) and Baby (Christine Alix), the offspring of Princess Antoinette. These five children were to be a part of the bridal party at the Cathedral.

In our rooms at the Hôtel de Paris, things were buzzing. A gigantic floral arrangement was delivered to each bridesmaid. The Monégasques could never be said to skimp on flowers! Magnificent peonies, roses, gladioli and tuberoses filled our rooms with a riot of color and heady aroma. A small envelope revealed a card, handwritten in English: "Welcome to Monaco" it said and was signed only "R," the single initial identifying the Prince. Within moments, other baskets and vases were delivered, one with red and white carnations from the government, another with two dozen red roses from the National Council.

Porters and maids rushed in at intervals to deliver gilded boxes of candies with the embossed initials "R" and "G." Similar boxes were filled with scarves, some depicting the double monogram, others bearing scenes of various sections or points of interest within the Principality.

While the chambermaid hung our clothes in closets and laid them into drawers, the message porter delivered the mail. Each envelope contained an exquisitely calligraphied invitation or set of tickets to one of the many wedding events planned for our week-long stay. Almost all were written in French on thick, vellum card stock. The script was often so elaborate that between it and the unfamiliar foreign words, we had difficulty guessing what we were being asked to attend, where it was being held, or what we were supposed to wear. I could figure out that *Tenue de smoking* meant black tie. For a number of other wingdings, Jay's tail suit was going to get quite a workout. "Good," he commented cheerily. "I bought it for our wedding and figured I'd never wear it again. This trip to Monaco makes good business sense. I can finally amortize the cost of the suit!"

Hearing an enormous commotion from across the harbor, we ran to our open balcony doors. We could not see, but the maid told us that the Prince and Miss Kelly must have made themselves visible to the thousands of people awaiting them in the Palace courtyard. Grace and Rainier

women mouthing *"Les Dames d'Honneur,"* waving, blowing kisses, and bowing ceremoniously in my direction.

It was late morning on Saturday, April 14, when Rainier drove back to Monaco from Cap Ferrat to collect Grace and her parents for a family luncheon at Tiny's villa. Grace had not been out of the Palace since her arrival in the Principality two days earlier, and press appetite for her was voracious. They had created stakeouts all along the Corniches and side streets. The Prince was driving Grace and her parents to Eze-Bord-de Mer when a whole gaggle of reporters and photographers spotted his car and darted out from behind the bushes where they had been hiding. Rainier tried to keep driving slowly, even cautiously, but one of the reporters threw himself into the street only inches from his front wheels. Screeching to a halt, Rainier jumped out of the car to find the reporter lying on the pavement. Photographers clicked away at the apparently lifeless body, at the Prince and at his passengers. Then, when everyone had snapped enough shots, the prone reporter jumped up from the street, unharmed and laughing. The Prince was instantly transformed from worried to enraged. When he took the wheel again, what transpired was like a typical family drive in the country. Nobody agreed on anything. Grace, knowing from the start that the reporter had never been hit, was mildly amused by the prank. Rainier, having thought for a moment that he had hurt someone, was not. Jack Kelly, on the Prince's side, wanted to get out of the car and duke it out with the pranksters. Margaret Kelly tried to restrain him.

Both Grace and the Prince would have preferred a quiet wedding at a small mountain church, but both had accepted the necessity of a state function. They had both hoped for dignity, but Grace was better than the Prince at accepting the fact that when the worldwide press is involved, a great many of your wishes go out the window. For Rainier, this was a bitter pill to swallow. He was accustomed to controlling events, shaping them the way he believed they should be shaped.

Back in the Principality things were seething. Everyone knew that Saturday night marked the first large social event of the wedding week, a party to be hosted by Grace's parents. Our original invitations had said the party would be held at seven-thirty in the Salon Privé of the Hôtel de Paris. The night before, though, we had found instructions in our mailboxes changing the time to eight-thirty and the place to the Cabaret, a nightclub at the far end of the Casino's ground floor which had its own separate entrance off the Sea Terrace. By midday, anticipation began mounting among the crowds and the press. They were ready for action.

Only Virginia Darcy among her friends had seen Grace during her first two days in Monaco. Virginia left for the Palace in an official car at eight each morning and did not return until eight at night, unless the schedule permitted a midday return for lunch. Each time she appeared in the hotel lobby, the press, fans, family and friends besieged her with questions about what was happening up on the Rock. Virginia was discreet, but to a few of us she spoke more freely. Though Grace had been happy to be settled in her new home upon arrival, she was already feeling a little disconnected from the familiar and slightly disconcerted by myriad formal and old-fashioned rules. For example, the Prince thought it inappropriate for any man to visit Grace in her private apartment. Thus, even the French perfume house that presented her with selections of their product had to replace their male representative with a female one.

This may sound archaic, but it was merely a function—one of many—of a larger code of forms and courtesies that began to color every aspect of Grace's life. It was called protocol and it weighed on her heavily. Grace was a person who knew how to conduct herself. She had extraordinary instincts for doing the right thing, intuitive common sense and a natural elegance. She had learned to trust these qualities to get her through almost any situation in her life. But now she was faced with an unwritten yet required system of ceremonial conduct. Developed over many centuries, royal protocol covers so many aspects of speech and behavior that, unless you know the code, it can make you feel as though you are being judged and rated on each move you make and every word you utter. Gracie didn't know the code. In time it would become automatic, but in April 1956 the protocol of the court made Grace feel, for the first time in years, as though she were inept, clumsy and stupid. It was not a comfortable feeling for a young woman like Grace. And there were those among the Palace staff who—disapproving of her as an American, a commoner and an actress— had no intention of helping to make things easier.

Rainier was deeply distressed by the circus that was engulfing Monaco and the tawdry, carping tone of much of the journalism that was circulating throughout the world. He wanted to save Grace from the pain he was feeling. For this reason, he decided that the papers should not be brought to her. This would, he believed, permit her to enjoy her privacy. It was meant to protect her, but what it did was to cut Grace off even further from the real world, a world she knew, sometimes loved, sometimes resented, but nonetheless understood and had learned to thrive in. For though part of Grace was extremely private, another part wanted to be in the midst of the action or at least to know everything that was happening there.

The demands on Grace to look perfect were escalating rapidly. Throughout the first two days, she and the Prince had to pose for a variety of official photos. For each shoot, Grace had to don a different dress and accessories, change her hairstyle if required for the proportion of the outfit, see that her makeup was flawlessly tasteful and appropriate for the color, the formality or informality of the wardrobe and the setting. Virginia Darcy helped her to assemble every aspect of her appearance for these sittings.

When Grace returned from lunch at Tiny's that Saturday afternoon, Virginia had stories to tell her from the real world. "Uncle Russ" Austin, who had himself played Cupid earlier for Grace and Rainier, had taken Virginia to lunch and propositioned her. The proposition involved photographic rather than sexual favors. Some journalists wanted to provide Virginia with a minuscule camera so that she could surreptitiously take pictures of Grace while her hair was in pin curls or her makeup was being applied. If Virginia did not want to take the pictures herself she could give the camera to the maid. These journalists, of course, wanted photos of Grace, but if that proved too difficult they would settle for shots of any dress she wore for a photo sitting or was planning to wear to any event, of her shoes, her gloves, hats, room, anything! Russ assured Virginia that nobody would ever know about the plot, then confidently pressed the tiny camera into Virginia's hand, saying, "It's a roll of twelve. Bring us a dozen pictures and we'll give you $100 each—a total of $1,200!"

Virginia put the camera in her purse, innocently looked up at Russ Austin, and responded, "Okay. I'll ask her."

"You'll what?" he gasped.

"I'll ask her," Virginia replied nonchalantly. Uncle Russ whipped out a roll of bills, reminding Virginia that she could make more than a thousand dollars and suggesting that she just take it and do the job. But Virginia pushed the money away and repeated, "I'll ask her. If she says okay I'll do it." Then she walked off to her room leaving Russ and his reporter friends with their mouths agape.

"Guess what happened today?" Virginia asked Grace rhetorically when they met again at the Palace.

Grace sat quietly while she listened to the story. Then she looked Virginia straight in the eye. "Do you need the money?" she asked very seriously.

"No, Grace," Virginia replied, "I just wanted you to know what a circus it's getting to be down there with everyone, not just the press."

Only one story Virginia carried to Grace that day was of real concern to her. The night before, when Rita Gam and Tom Guinzburg were waiting in the lobby of the hotel for their car, Rita had suddenly fainted. A doctor, hurriedly summoned, diagnosed fatigue. Rita and Tom had abandoned the notion of driving to La Réserve in Beaulieu and had instead ordered a quiet dinner in their room. Grace was concerned that Rita might be coming down with the flu, or discomfited by all the press and the frenzy.

Invitations to certain wedding functions had been mailed to us while we were still in the States. Among them was the invitation for the first official function, the Saturday-night dinner dance being hosted by Grace's parents. During one conversation in New York, Grace had told Carolyn Reybold that she and Rainier had their hands full deciding how to stagger the various guests from the bride's side and the groom's. Carolyn had asked Grace if there were any special instructions she should be aware of in this regard. Grace replied, "Oh, no. My bridesmaids will be going to everything." Thus, when the Kellys' invitation arrived, Carolyn presumed it was already known she and Malcolm would be attending. The invitation, she believed, was simply a courtesy—a formality for her own record—and she had not bothered to respond.

We were instructed to take the elevator down to an underground passage that connected the Hôtel de Paris to the Casino. It was raining, and this subterranean passageway offered protection both from the crowds and the wet streets that could soil our formal, floor-length gowns. Carolyn looked beautiful in an Oleg Cassini dress of delicate lace with an organdy turtleneck collar, a flat organdy bow, and scalloped sleeves and hem. We all stood waiting to be permitted entry to the Cabaret foyer, where tall, liveried footmen guarding huge mahogany doors checked our invitations. Watching Carolyn walk down the crimson-carpeted marble stairway, I admired her extraordinarily erect model's carriage, not realizing that she was holding her shoulders back to keep the bodice of a size 6 dress from drooping on her size 5 figure. At the foot of the stairs we were being given small calligraphied cards bearing our table numbers. Jay and I collected ours as Carolyn and Malcolm approached the small table for theirs. Unfortunately, there was no seating assignment for the Reybolds, neither by card nor on the master list. Those doing the seating had worked from the list of acceptance cards received in the mail, and Carolyn had not mailed hers in. A Palace staff member located Grace's secretary, and two places were added hastily to the table where Sally and John Richardson were sitting. This was a small miscommunication producing a minor incident, but in Monaco for this occasion such things made one feel unduly maladroit.

Wearing a golden headband and a champagne *peau-de-soie* dress, Grace was the color of Van Gogh's wheatfields as she stood in the receiving line patiently introducing Rainier to an endless stream of people he had met once on his earlier trip to the States. Wearing a fixed smile and a slightly dazed expression, Rainier was patiently welcoming slews of Americans who shook his hand so exuberantly you'd have thought they were Texans pumping for oil. Each time one of Grace's own friends approached the line, her eyes danced with joy. It was the first time she had seen us since the ship landed, and even here—in this formal environment—Grace leaned forward immediately to bestow spontaneous kisses on her chums. Now, however, it was a kiss on each cheek in the European fashion.

Dinner began with salmon quenelles—airy, delicate fish dumplings that had been poached in bouillon. An aromatic roast lamb followed, accompanied by mint sauce, tiny *haricots verts* and crisp roast potatoes. After the *salade caprice*, we were served a towering baked Alaska accompanied by a 1949 brut champagne. As we dined, a lovely string ensemble set the tone for our mealtime conversation.

Then, seamlessly, the Aimé Barelli orchestra stole into the bandstand chairs to begin the after-dinner dancing. As they struck up the first song, Grace and Rainier's "A Woman in Love," the royal couple rose and stepped onto the floor together. Grace and Rainier looked only into each other's eyes, laughing and talking intimately. You could almost feel the warmth of their cheeks as they gracefully swept around the floor holding each other closely.

When Barelli struck up the second song, Prince Pierre, Rainier's father, brought Mrs. Kelly to the floor while Mr. Kelly escorted Rainier's mother, Princess Charlotte. Peggy, Grace's sister, followed the lead of Count d'Aillières (Rainier's Chamberlain, who would soon become "Buddy" to us all). Grace's brother-in-law Gabby began to dance with Rainier's sister Tiny, completing the family circle on the floor. By the third song, we were all dancing, enmeshed in the romantic fantasy that was unfolding before our eyes.

Suddenly, we were jarred from our dreamy dancing. Someone had decided to fly over Stan Rubin and his Tigertown Five, a Dixieland jazz group from Princeton University, who were all the rage Stateside. The notion had been that Rubin and the gang would rouse us Americans into a joyous romp of jitterbugging and the Charleston. Instead, at this early hour of the evening, the raucous music drove the guests off the floor and back to their tables. Ma Kelly, though, was no slouch at hostessing. Sensing the disaster, she quickly had Rubin relinquish the bandstand to Barelli once again. The Tigertown Five were victims of what we now call bad programming. Everyone sighed with relief, the earlier mood was recaptured, and the party lasted well into the night.

Grace's father, surrounded by Americans and particularly his Philadelphia cronies, seemed to regain the comfortable authority he had lost during the two days since his landing in Monaco. If he had complained earlier (as it was widely rumored) about the autocratic attitude of his soon to be son-in-law, he appeared thrilled with him on this night. Margaret Kelly looked as relaxed and happy as any hostess who knows she's giving a great party; and on the floor, Rainier peppered Grace's friends with subtle, witty asides as they danced by, eliciting easy giggles and repartee as testimony to the warm affection permeating "Gracie's group." Protected as we were from the carnival-like atmosphere of the streets, we were enjoying the full sense that this was a wedding, a blending of families, a union of friends.

* * *

The next day, Sunday, April 15, Grace attended a quiet early-morning Mass in the tiny Palatine Chapel at the far end of the Palace's Court of Honor. There would be time later for her to familiarize herself with the special pleasure of Sunday mornings in Monaco, when families in their best clothes walk to services in one of the Principality's many lovely churches. But on this particular day, a solitary moment of worship and reflection was in order, and true privacy was becoming a premium.

Media attention had heated up to an even higher fever. Someone commented that NBC had sent only nine reporters to cover the North African invasion, but they now had thirteen present to cover "the invasion of Monaco." We also learned that at its New York headquarters the network had added a clock telling Monaco time to the series of clocks telling the time around the world.

By mid-Sunday afternoon, tempers were flaring at the hotel. The friction focused on that evening's white-tie Gala to be held at the International Sporting Club. In the lobby before we went up to dress, I saw a woman without an invitation crying as her husband sought to comfort her. In the elevator, one Philadelphia tycoon tried to mollify the anger of another magnate by explaining that he had been invited to the Gala only because his wife and Margaret Kelly worked closely together at their hometown hospital.

At the Palace, the tension centered on Virginia Darcy and one of Grace's secretaries. Grace had explained there were not enough tickets for both women to attend the two scheduled galas, the first one that night, at the International Sporting Club, and the second at the Opera House three nights later. Grace had suggested earlier they decide jointly who would attend which. The secretary did not like her options. She had bought a dress for each party and announced her intention to wear both of them. In order to restore calm, Virginia offered to give her both tickets but Grace wouldn't hear of it. That morning the secretary had decided on the Opera. But as the magic hour approached, she grew greedy. While Grace was dressing, one of her staff members mentioned that Virginia's Gala ticket had mysteriously disappeared. When Grace asked to see her secretary and was told she had just left for the Hôtel de Paris to dress for the evening, Grace knew exactly where to find Virginia's ticket.

Virginia was willing to let it pass; Grace was not. Though she usually tried to avoid confrontations, when dealing with injustice Grace could be ruthless. She phoned the Hôtel de Paris, where her secretary, dressed in her ball gown, was chatting in the lobby with others en route to the party. Grace gave orders that she was to remain there and relinquish the purloined ticket to a Palace emissary who was en route to collect it. Though her order was protested, Grace stood firm and Virginia got her ticket back.

The invitation instructed us to begin our departure for the Gala by eight-thirty. The ballroom doors would be closed exactly at nine. Many of us missed hearing that another underground passageway could be used in lieu of the sidewalk. Though the doors of the hotel and the Sporting Club were only a few hundred yards apart, we shoved and sloshed our way through the throngs and the torrential downpour for what seemed like an hour.

Inside, a long marble stairway rose ahead of us, guarded on each side by pairs of footmen wearing tall white wigs, gilt-braided scarlet velvet coats and brocade knee breeches. The ballroom was three stories high. Row upon row of long, slender, white Corinthian columns had been placed along both sides of the room. Above them, on the second-tier balconies, papier-mâché mannequins dressed in crimson eighteenth-century footmen's outfits held elaborate candelabra. Above that, on the third-story balconies, still more candelabra were carried by blackamoor mannequins in white togas. Enormous crystal chandeliers swung overhead, suspended on ruby-red cords from the ceiling, which had been covered with midnight-blue velvet and studded with thousands of twinkling lights like stars in a perfect heaven.

Twenty musicians in white powdered wigs and matching Louis XIV costumes occupied the bandstand at the far end of the room. At the opposite end, the Prince's box was elevated on a raised tier to survey the entire spectacle. Every inch of space, but particularly the front of the floor beneath the long table of honor, was massed with luminous white lilies and Monaco-red roses. Within moments, the several hundred guests were in place at their tables ready for the Gala to begin.

Because of the notice that the doors would close at nine, we knew that the schedule called for Grace and Rainier to arrive shortly after that. But nothing happened. Protocol dictates that no music plays, no drinks or food are served until the Prince enters. As the time passed, people began checking their watches. Everything seemed suspended as though the room were filled with dress extras awaiting an overdue cue. Then we began to hear low-murmured, grumbling speculations. We bridesmaids, seated directly in front of and below the family table, had seen the red carpet being rolled out for the Prince and Grace and could not imagine what was keeping them. Not until later did we hear the story of Virginia Darcy's missing Gala ticket and Grace's efforts to reclaim it. Though neither Grace nor Rainier wanted to detain their guests, they were both determined that justice would be served!

It was ten after ten before Grace and the Prince arrived. We rose as one while Grace led the Princely party into its raised seats. As she walked to her center chair, Grace smiled beatifically and indicated her welcome with slight bowings of her head. Once the honored guests were in place, we remained standing for the Monégasque national anthem. Throughout the dinner I watched Grace enjoying her new role. We all realized that even princesses have encumbrances, but it surely looked as though the benefits far outweighed the burdens. Grace was dressed in a billowing-skirted white ball gown, a soft, blue satin stole framing her shoulders. Her hair fell softly around her face. Several times during the meal I caught her looking down at me or her other friends, grimacing or winking subtly so that only we could see her. At the time I thought, "How sweet of Grace to assure us, in this way, that we are still connected to reality." Looking back, I recognize she was reassuring herself, too.

Dinner itself was another spectacle. It began with a large rolling service cart covered in white damask wheeled to us by a liveried waiter. A circular receptacle that could have doubled as a backyard inflatable swimming pool contained the world's finest caviar. After clear turtle soup and langouste pilaf, we dined on duck and the freshest asparagus I have ever tasted. By the time the ice cream dessert concoction arrived, we all wished we had worn muumuus. Rare vintage wines, the finest champagne, and after-dinner cognacs and liqueurs accompanied the meal. Between courses we inspected the magnificent program set at each place. In addition to listing the entertainment, it contained a short tale called "Compliment" written by Jean Cocteau especially for the wedding of "Prince Rainier III of Monaco and Miss Grace Kelly." It was, of course, a love story.

Before the show started I noticed Grace motioning me to accompany her to the ladies' room. In the hallway where we met, I rhapsodized about the evening. "Isn't it purrrrfect?" she asked rhetorically, savoring the last word as though she were licking icing off a cake. "And the flowers!" she added not unexpectedly—we all knew that Grace had a passion for flowers of every kind.

At the powder room mirror, applying light lipstick, Grace turned to me and said, "I wanted you to come to the ladies' room with me, Judy-bird, so I could wish you and Jay a happy anniversary, and you and me as well. I meant to send flowers today, but the time just ran away from me."

"Gracie, I can't believe you," I marveled. "If I were you going through all this, I wouldn't even know what day it was, much less what else it signified. You're so sweet to remember it's Jay's and my third anniversary . . ."

"And three years since we met," she added, giving me a hug.

"Don't worry about the flowers," I told her. "If they put one more in our room I'll have to lie down and fold my hands across my chest."

Gracie drew her shoulders up as though going me one better and said, "Wait until you come to the Palace for dinner tomorrow. My rooms look like an annex of Max Schling!" She referred to the New York florist where she and I often stopped, particularly in the spring, when we knew we'd find the only arbutus in New York, imported by Schling from the South with the perfect pinkish-white color on the world's most delicate flowers.

"Prezzies?" I asked.

She nodded as her eyes twinkled. "And I'll show you the display of wedding gifts, too," she added as we started back toward the ballroom.

"It must be, if you'll pardon the pun, a royal haul."

Gracie raised her eyebrows, shook her head and shoulders like Sophie Tucker, and sputtered in the Red Hot Mama's accent, "Mir-ac-u-lous, honey." Then, gathering her skirts in one hand, she remustered her dignity and sailed through the ballroom door for a regal reappearance.

To open the show, Tamara Toumanova, one of the world's great ballerinas, danced an original piece especially choreographed for the evening. This was followed by a selection of songs from Eddie Constantine, an American who was the rage in Paris then and, to this day, remains a French performing legend. A majestic woman appeared onstage swathed in a billowing costume of blue and green feathers. She read a

The press had readied itself for all-out assault. They went after whomever they could get, however they could get 'em. In my case, this meant that two hours later, sitting in a padded chair at Elizabeth Arden, my head pulled back for the comb-out and my feet raised in front of me to accommodate the pedicurist, I had the strange sensation that someone was looking up my skirts. Raising my head, I spotted three photographers snapping away through the salon's upper window from a branch high atop a tall tree. Swell, I reflected, lowering my legs. A universally distributed crotch shot! My only comfort came from the fact that it was 1956 and no U.S. publication but *Police Gazette* would have printed it.

By mid-afternoon, the press had something else to write about. Mrs. Matthew McCloskey from Philadelphia, a close Kelly family friend, had been robbed of nearly $50,000 worth of jewels. It appeared that the thieves had made their way into her hotel room while she and her husband were out the previous evening at the Sporting Club Gala. Within the hour, headlines flashed across the world, though we were all asked not to make any more fuss than necessary about the incident.

By the end of teatime, one of our own, bridesmaid Maree Pamp, had discovered a $10,000 gem heist from her room. Once again, the press made hay while the sun shone briefly. They capitalized on the two burglaries by likening them to those in the Hitchcock film *To Catch a Thief,* shot on the Riviera two years earlier with Grace and Cary Grant. In fact, Cary and his wife Betsy called us from Madrid that afternoon, where he was shooting *The Pride and the Passion.* They had been hoping Stanley Kramer would be able to release Cary from the production schedule so they could be in Monaco for the wedding, but they informed us that would not be the case. Word of the gem heists had reached Spain, and Cary wondered if "someone was trying to play my part" as the Riviera cat burglar.

Just as false rumors of yet a third robbery were circulating wildly through the throng outside the hotel, the Aga Khan arrived. By then somewhat infirm, the Aga was nonetheless an imposing figure as he was rolled into the lobby in his ever-present wheelchair. In addition to his staff, he was accompanied by his wife, the Begum, a magnificent woman of great beauty and dignified carriage. Though the Aga and the Begum had made many previous arrivals in Monaco, their presence that day created another chaotic response. Neither of them was a stranger to Riviera weddings combining royalty with Hollywood. The Aga's son, the Aly Khan, had married Rita Hayworth in the nearby French hills only a few years earlier. The Aga's party was ceremoniously led through the lobby en route to the second floor and a royal suite in the rotunda, where round-the-clock guards would protect them during their stay.

Meanwhile, Rita Gam was in her bathroom soaking in a hot tub to relax and prepare for the bridesmaids' dinner at the Palace that evening. A few moments later, covered only by a loosely wrapped towel, she stood at the sink to begin her makeup. Rita looked down for her rouge. When she looked up two strange Turkish men were in her bathroom. Only the fact that it was not yet dark kept her from fearing for her safety. "What are you doing here?" she began to ask, but a hastily produced camera and flash of bulbs gave her her answer. The reporter and photographer fled with Rita shrieking. Her life was intact, but any remaining hope of privacy had been shattered.

The Monday night dinner at the Palace had been planned for the bridesmaids and their husbands only, but earlier in the day both Grace and Rainier had decided it would be fun to add a few more of their contemporary friends, particularly those from the States. Rainier's aide had phoned the hotel to invite Gant Gaither, Donald Buka and a dozen of Grace's other American chums.

The other guests were invited for eight-thirty, but Palace limos came to collect the six bridesmaids early so we could spend an hour alone with Grace. We had been told to dress informally. In the 1950s an informal dinner at a palace meant dark suits and ties for the men, cocktail dresses for the women. One set of uniformed guards saluted us toward the Palace gates, where a second set saluted us through the portals. A third set of guards met our car to guide us to Grace in her private quarters.

She was dressed in a pale lemon-yellow, satin cheongsam, printed randomly with circular medallions of brushed golden threads. If we had not already realized how much weight Grace had lost in recent months, we certainly did upon seeing her in the close-fitting, sleeveless, mandarin-collared sheath traditionally worn by Chinese women. A discreet slit in the side of the skirt added just a touch of spice to the demure look. Her blond hair was pulled up and back from her face into a broad, circular braid set at the back of her head. She looked like a precious ivory figurine greeting us within the walls of her leafy-green brocaded apartment.

Napoleon's bed and other exquisite Empire antiques filled the bedroom, office and sitting room. Warm tones of pale-to-heartier green covered the upholstered pieces, while the same hues coordinated the pink marble bathroom with the rest of the suite. Oliver, the much publicized poodle, darted about from one plumpy sofa to another, but seemed to have decided that the Little General's bed was the most appropriate resting place for a creature of his note. When we had spoken about flowers the night before, Grace had not overstated. Every inch of her apartment was banked with unbelievably lush displays.

Though each of us had bought our own wedding gifts, as a group we had purchased another to serve as the bridesmaids' present to the bride. The New York members of our contingent had been elected to do the shopping, so we had met one midday in front of Tiffany, strolled down to Cartier, and picked out a dressing table set of mirror, brush and comb. It was antique silver embossed with hearts and flowers. Cartier suggested sending it on to their Monte Carlo store, where the intertwined initials "G" and "G" (though both in reality were just for Grace, we laughingly used to call her Gracie Grimaldi) could be engraved in the official type style. Carolyn Reybold had collected the package from the local Cartier branch, showed it to the other bridesmaids, and wrapped it for this occasion. We told Grace it was for "remembrance of past happiness and wishes for future joy" and that it was given in "everlasting love."

Grace, too, had gifts for her attendants. Tearfully she told us how much it meant to her to share her happiness with close friends during her wedding week. Then she handed each of us a small jeweler's box containing a large gold charm. It was circular, its center a small flat disc, engraved on one side with Grace and Rainier's intertwined initials. On the other side, the wedding date was engraved in block letters, 19 AVRIL 1956. From this disc, a motif of arched points in golden filigree was laid to the outer rim of the charm, which, like the center disc, was banded with delicate golden rope. A tiny gold replica of the Princely Crown, with a miniature golden cross perched on its summit, formed the top of the charm. That was attached to a sturdy oval eye through which we could fasten the charm to a necklace or a bracelet.

By the time we joined Rainier and our husbands in the Salle des Gardes, the relaxed and merry tone of the evening had been set. We were in the meeting hall of the Prince's honor guard, with an enormous open stone fireplace set at one end, immense logs crackling cozily away. One wall of the room was windowed, giving a grand vista to the east of the Palace, and another was hung with three tapestries of Monaco's crest. When Gant Gaither arrived there was intense speculation about the cumbersome box he toted under one arm. He brought the box directly to Grace and Rainier, who eyed it suspiciously. Undaunted, Grace tore at the wrappings, lifted the top, removed the gift, and began to laugh so hard she could barely stand up. Jessie Royce Landis had given the ugly tomahawk from *The Swan* location to Gant, and as Rainier had by now heard the tale of its traveling history, he joined our amusement.

When dinner was announced, we proceeded to the fourth wall of the salon, where a long, narrow refectory table was set for buffet with antique Meissen china dinner service and rare silver. Though we dined informally with plates on our laps or at a variety of small tables throughout the room, this was not just a casual night at home. The strangers in our midst were an entire battery of liveried waiters, butlers and footmen. There were as many of them as of us. They wore gilded scarlet coats, knee breeches and pumps with large buckles. So many medals decorated their coats that Gant commented, "They must have been given one for every meal they served." But the relaxed atmosphere of the evening was in no way impaired.

Just as Grace was about to take us for an inspection of the wedding gifts, Rainier came over and asked her to excuse herself. The two were gone for several minutes, and we began to worry that something was amiss. But when they reappeared we noticed Grace wearing a new necklace. It was a present from Rainier's father, Prince Pierre. The family heirloom, which originally belonged to Rainier's great-grandmother, was inspected carefully by each of us. Hung from a lovely golden chain was a pearl the size of a large grape. Small rubies encircled it and a diamond filigree crown attached it on top to its chain. Grace was, of course, pleased and touched. Rainier, who had asked her not to bring to Monaco any jewelry that had been previously given to her as a gift, was fast reconstituting her collection, and those jeweled presents that were family heirlooms held a special place in her heart.

We left to see Grace's parents' rooms, walking through the often darkened and chilled hallways of the ancient Palace. A great deal of remodeling had already been completed, but a vast amount of work still remained in order to modernize the building without destroying its historic authenticity. Rainier had initiated the huge restoration, but as it had been planned to take place over many years, Grace, too, would now become actively involved with it. The Kellys' suite was entered through a foyer trimmed with gold-leaf boiserie. An elegant Louis XV console table held a vase of magnificent roses. The salon had rich, gold brocade draperies and still more of the gilded carved wood detail. A lovely fireplace was surrounded on either side by shelves filled with antique porcelain *objets d'art,* lit indirectly from within the cabinets. Rare antique wood pieces filled this sitting room and the bedroom as well.

Near the end of dinner Rita Gam Guinzburg had felt slightly ill so Peggy had led her to Grace's boudoir to lie down. When we crossed to Grace's apartment to check on Rita we learned that a Palace staff member had found her lying on Grace's bed and was distressed at discovering her there. Not wanting to make a fuss, Peggy had summoned a car to take Rita back to the hotel. When we arrived we found her gone.

Resuming the tour, Grace stopped here and there to point out rooms, artworks and particular furniture she admired, or things of special historic interest. Though she had only been in residence for a few hectic days, she had already made herself familiar with the small section of the Palace we toured that night. There was a charming wooden cradle in which Napoleon's baby son had slept. Grace cooed over it, while we admonished her to get to work on its new occupant. Concluding the tour, Grace led us into a long rectangular room of white and gold. She had fallen in love with the room and its twin crystal chandeliers. It was, she told us, where she had decided her bridal pictures were to be taken, and where we would be photographed with her on Thursday.

Grace suggested she arrange for us to return another day, quietly, so that an aide could take us to see the wedding presents in a more leisurely way. When we rejoined Rainier and the others, Grace began to tell us of her and Rainier's schedules for the following day. She was hardly past the lunch hour when we realized this was likely a cue for the evening's conclusion. But protocol dictated we wait until Rainier left, and he gave no indication of being anxious or even willing to rise. We forgot about watching for further hints of departure, and just settled in for a long night of pleasure.

That's exactly what it turned out to be, hours on end of the kind of time together all of us had longed for. Each of us told stories we had gathered during the preceding days. The one that got the biggest laugh, especially from Grace, had Rainier telling Father Tucker how amazed he was to find that his American fiancée spoke French so fluently, to which Father Tucker supposedly had replied, "I knew love was blind. I didn't know it was deaf, too!" We played word games, taught some to Rainier that he had missed during his previous stay in the States, and following his lead, told endless rounds of jokes. Rainier loves jokes, particularly those you would associate with fast and funny borscht belt comics. I was in my element, summoning up every accent I had ever done, delivering in rapid-fire style every story I had ever heard, both those that could be told in public and those that could not. When Rainier told a slightly "dirty" joke, he always apologized in advance for being "rude." But after an hour or more of some of the best stuff to come down the pike since Milton Berle, we abandoned such politesse.

Finally it was time to go, with Grace and Rainier personally escorting us to the waiting limousines with their dozing chauffeurs. The good nights, or good mornings, all around were both joyous and tearful. It had been a perfect night for everyone, not the least for the Prince himself, who loves this sort of socializing but does not care much for larger, more formal events. As he kissed me on both cheeks, he noted, "This has been wonderful for Gracie and me, Judybird. I hope we'll have many more such times together." Seeing the first clear light of a sunny daybreak through the night sky, we all cheered it as an omen for our mutual happiness and parted in the glow of everlasting friendship.

Though on Tuesday, April 17, Grace and Rainier had a day ahead of them that would normally have required a preparatory eight hours of sleep, after we left they were unwilling to break the spell. Watching the hillsides lighten in the early sunrise, they decided to drive up to La Turbie, the ancient village above Monaco.

As they reached the Moyenne Corniche, the sky turned to a warm, clear blue. The rain had washed everything clean, and the sun reflected back from the rocks and the treetops. Rainier drove his Mercedes sports car first into Eze-Village. Its sister town, Eze-Bord-de-Mer, where Tiny had her villa, could be seen at the seaside a few thousand feet below. But

last, with one even doubting the marriage itself would ever take place! At the start Monaco itself had been written about glowingly and romantically, as "the true fairyland" or "the golden Kingdom of love." Now, with the sale of the commemorative postage stamps in full swing, it became "the postage stamp–sized realm," "smaller than Central Park," the "pinpoint" or "preshrunk" Principality.

That evening we whirled in and out of more doors, through more well-wishing crowds, across town more times than one can imagine. In fact, our itinerary was so packed that neither the next day nor now do any of us remember one specific place we stopped. Minister of State Henri Soum and his wife hosted a large reception at Government House for missions and representatives of other countries, members of the diplomatic corps, leading residents of the Principality and its surrounding regions, and captains of the foreign ships docked in its port. I cannot recall whether any of us went there or just heard about it, it's all such a blur. I do know, though, that Jay and I gave our driver a list of stops for cocktail parties being hosted by people and groups all over Monaco. We had no way to recognize our hosts, but they recognized us from news photos as soon as we arrived and, rushing to welcome us warmly, ushered us with great flourish through the apartment to meet every single person there. Every now and then we would run into Rita and Tom, Bettina and Frank, Maree, Sally and John, or Carolyn and Malcolm, usually the only familiar faces in the room.

I cannot remember exactly who, but someone we knew from the States had taken over the Château de Madrid restaurant in Eze and invited us to a dinner party to which we arrived unfashionably late. This was the same eagle-perched château near which Grace and Rainier had sat quietly that early morning, but there was no such pastoral atmosphere when we bopped in. It was a very gay gathering and a great fuss was made about our presence. As we were taken around the tables, everyone wanted to ask questions about Grace or Rainier, or Grace *and* Rainier, or the parties or the wedding or the wardrobe or the weather. When we finally got to our chairs, a waiter caught us up with the others by bringing our first course—an individual, deliciously aromatic cheese soufflé. As I stopped talking for a moment to eat, I was suddenly aware that my throat felt as if it were burning up and ripping apart all at once. When I turned my head to answer yet another question, I opened my mouth and no sound came out. It was clear that I was ill.

Making our apologies to our table mates and the hosts, we slipped out to a limousine someone was kind enough to loan us. By the time we reached the hotel, my forehead was on fire. I was panicked at the thought of being laid low at this point. The civil wedding ceremony was to be held the following morning with only a small selected group of guests, including us, attending. And the morning after that was the main event.

Jay took charge as I moaned my way into bed, shaking with fever. He phoned the concierge and asked him to summon a physician immediately. While we waited for the doctor, Jay ordered hot tea with honey and fresh orange juice. I shivered and filed my nails. It was only moments until we heard a knock at the door announcing a man who turned out to be the Inspector Clouseau of the French medical world.

Jay spoke no French and I couldn't speak at all. I grabbed a pencil and paper and wrote in French what was troubling me, then I did a sore throat/fever/laryngitis charade. The doctor nodded knowingly and proceeded to give me everything short of an internal, though he never looked at my throat. He said nothing but clucked forebodingly. Removing a thermometer from his bag with a flourish, he indicated I should part my lips wide enough to accept it. Within ten seconds he whisked it out of my clenched jaws, read it on the wrong side, clucked again, and began to pace. Jay caught the doctor by the sleeve so I could pantomime a frantic suggestion that he inspect the ailing area. He approached the bed, but once at my side he stopped, perplexed. Then he grabbed the emery board out of my hand, opened my mouth wide, and stuck the sandpapered stick down my throat. I gagged, sputtered, and tried with my fingers to extract the grains of emery paper that were clinging to the sides of my tongue.

The doctor whipped into his bag to procure medications. First he handed me a bottle of tonic. I read the label while he rummaged through his satchel. The elixir promised to cure my kidneys, calm my nerves, adjust my bladder, vent my spleen, cleanse my colon, settle my stomach, and prevent warts. Nothing about throats was mentioned. The doctor had another remedy for that. He handed me several packages and a prescription for more of what was in the packets. And that was lozenges the size of goosedown pillows. I wondered if I could open my mouth wide enough

filming. Grace smiled wanly, distractedly, while Virginia reminisced. A moment later, though, Grace grew rigid with fear when Rainier appeared unexpectedly at her doorway. His face was ashen. "Something terrible has happened," he declared slowly, somberly.

Grace's eyes darted fearfully from Rainier to Virginia. Then, finding her courage, she asked, "Oh, my God, what is it?" Rainier told her that Buddy d'Aillières, his Chamberlain, had collapsed and been taken to the hospital, where he had been placed in an oxygen tent. Buddy was safe, reported the Prince, but it was still unclear whether or not he would be able to be present the following morning for the religious ceremony in the Cathedral. The Count was the only person with complete knowledge of every detail for the next thirty hours of events, so the Prince, while relieved to hear that Buddy was all right, was dismayed to think of the chaos his absence might create. Grace commiserated with Rainier, then watched him depart again to attend to the problems at hand.

The minute he was gone Grace turned to Virginia and shrieked, "Oh, my God, Virginia, I thought he had come to tell me he'd changed his mind!" It broke the ice. The two women laughed so hard they couldn't stop. Only the day before Rainier had heard what he thought were sobs emanating from Grace's rooms. He had come in to find Grace and Virginia bent double with laughter. And here they were again.

Shortly before ten in the morning, the few selected wedding guests began to arrive at the Palace. I felt perfectly fine, my illness having disappeared as quickly as it had come. Again we were passed through several sets of Carabiniers in full dress uniform. The last pair led us up the magnificent stairway in the Court of Honor, through the Galerie d'Hercule, the Galerie des Bustes and the Salle des Officiers in order to reach the Salle du Trône.

The throne had been removed for this occasion, the room banked in glorious displays of Easter lilies and fluffy white lilacs. Overhead, above the spot where the throne normally stood, was the canopy bearing the Monégasque crown and crest. (In fact, the crown of Monaco, seen everywhere at the Palace and on our bridesmaids' charms, no longer exists. It was stolen during the French Revolution and has never been replaced. Throughout the years we've seen several photos of Grace wearing a tiara or coronet, but neither she nor the Prince ever had a crown to their names.)

About eighty guests found their name cards on the rows of small gilded chairs that were arranged against the sides of the room. Members of both the bride's and the groom's families were present. There were official representatives from twenty-four foreign countries, heads of delegations, government officers of Monaco and the bridesmaids together with their husbands. Monseigneur Paul Marella, the Apostolic Nuncio of Paris, was present, representing the Pope, while the Very Reverend Father Tucker, who had been instrumental in making this match, stood watch as it came to legal fruition. Grace had two witnesses, her sister Peggy and Princess Antoinette. The Prince's three witnesses were his cousin, Count Charles de Polignac; Lieutenant Colonel Jean-Marie Ardant, Commander of the Eighth Cavalry Regiment at Constantine and Rainier's good friend, and Grace's brother Kell, whose pregnant wife Mary had flown to Monaco the day before so she could be present for both ceremonies.

Two empty carved and gilded armchairs, each with magnificent tapestry backs and seats, stood waiting for their occupants. I remember Grace and Rainier both looking quite nervous as they entered the room. Grace, however, now appeared to be the more composed of the two. She was wearing a demure two-piece dress of champagne Alençon lace over blush pink taffeta with matching Cuban-heeled pumps and white kid gloves that stopped just above her wrists. Her rounded Peter Pan collar with its small string bow, her hair pulled back and tucked beneath a pleated chiffon turban with flowers at her right ear, and her demeanor all conspired to make Grace look constrained, as though she were trapped in her own flawless beauty. The Prince wore morning coat and striped trousers, a white waistcoat and a gray silk tie. Male guests were in dark suits, white shirts and ties, and the women all wore hats and covered silk dresses one might choose for a late-afternoon tea.

Monsieur Marcel Portanier, President of the State Council, Director of Legal Services and Civil Status Officer of the Princely Family, began to conduct the ceremony. Exactly at eleven, after making a short speech, Monsieur Portanier began to read the articles of Chapter VI of the Civil Code delineating the rights and obligations of the couple. Grace sat so still it was impossible to be sure she was breathing. I thought of the game of statues we all loved to play as children. It would be just like Gracie, with her talent for make-believe, to freeze herself so hard she would have difficulty getting unstuck. That's how she looked as she was legally being joined in civil matrimony to Rainier.

The vows took a long time to read. Even longer was Monsieur Portanier's recitation of Rainier's titles for which Grace would now hold the female counterparts. There were one hundred forty-two of them, including four dukedoms, one of which—Duc de Valentinois—had once belonged to Cesare Borgia. Later, when we stood together rereading the list, Grace would cry out in mock horror, "Oh, no!" but during the first reading she looked wired and frightened. The only way I was sure she had not been turned to stone was that I occasionally caught sight of her familiar nervous habit of her forefinger struggling imperceptibly through her kid gloves to scratch her thumb, like a baby desperately trying to reassure itself on the rim of its security blanket. Until I noticed this I had been almost as dazed as Grace. Now, watching her fingers in their subtle struggle, I wanted to cry. I prayed very hard that Gracie would be able to feel her own flesh through her white kid gloves. I was sure that only the touch of her own skin could help secure her desire to remain "just a person." It was never more clear to me than in this throne room, on this very day, that Grace's other desire—to be more than just a person—would be taken care of for the remainder of her days.

Monsieur Portanier concluded his recitation and asked the couple and their witnesses to sign the official register. Rainier signed first. Then Grace, whose hand was visibly trembling, affixed her signature—Grace Patricia Kelly—very slowly lest there be any question that the deed was done. We adjourned to the Salon Bleu, where Grace and Rainier patiently received congratulations from each of their guests. Grace and Rainier were then led to the loggia of the Palace, where, for the first time as Their Serene Highnesses the Prince and Princess of Monaco, they waved to the thousands of people waiting in the Palace Square shouting out chorus after chorus of joyous acclaim.

The fog and heavy clouds had lifted by the time Grace and Rainier met with reporters, who had been waiting for them since early morning. Two days before, Morgan Hudgins had instituted a plan that included giving the press daily briefings, advanced itineraries and schedules. The sought-after couple had even been posing once a day for photos. All this had done much to soothe the media. Most of the press was warm in greeting the civilly united couple. It is hard, after all, to be grumpy with two young newlyweds.

By the time we were summoned in for the one o'clock luncheon, Grace was relaxed and adorable, her own sweet self. This so relieved the rest of us that we all unwound and chattered endlessly. Just before coffee was served Grace rose and walked down the table to where I was seated to deliver the familiar summons, "Ladies' room, Judybird?" she whispered. I rose immediately to accompany her.

Grace wanted me to tell the others that she and Rainier would leave shortly after lunch, but that she had arranged for a lady-in-waiting to take us through the display of gifts. Also, she was concerned about something. "I'm worried about Rita," she said. "I know when things are not going well for her and I think this is one of those times. Please do me a favor and keep an eye on her. I wish I could spend some time with her, but it just isn't possible. Please help me, Judybird," she importuned. I promised Grace I would and we rejoined the luncheon.

What we were shown that afternoon at the Palace was dazzling. Card upon card identified the donors—Her Majesty, Elizabeth II of England and Prince Philip, their fellow countrymen Winston Churchill, Somerset Maugham, the Earl of Mountbatten and the Duchess of Westminster. The kings, queens, princes, princesses, rajahs, ranees, emirs, shahs and sultans of every foreign country that still had titled rulers had sent presents, as had those from countries where the titles remained but the jobs had been eliminated. President Eisenhower sent a gift, as did Conrad Hilton, who was in Monaco as his official representative to the wedding. Presidents of every TV network and film studio were represented in the display, along with nearly every movie star, director and producer who had worked with Grace or come to know her well. Queen Elizabeth's solid gold tray lay next to an elaborate antique silver service that bordered a small silver-plated silent butler and then an etched Steuben bowl large enough to double as a trough! Betsy and Cary Grant had sent a lovely antique desk, only one of many priceless pieces of furniture. There were endless complete sets of pure silver and gold serving trays and coffee and tea services, flatware, candelabra, platters, dishes, urns and epergnes. Magnificent etched and clear crystal pieces were displayed along with old master paintings and complete matched ensembles of precious jewels for

circles that trailed their yellow satin ribbons down the fronts of our skirts. Small pearl or pearl and diamond earrings were our only jewelry. Our wide-brimmed yellow organdy, custom-made hats had been stiffened lightly with buckram so the brims stood out wide on the tops and sides of our heads. We darted about the room, helping one another fasten buttons, fluff petticoats and set hats at exactly the right angle.

Of the six child attendants, the four girls all wore identical puff-sleeved, white Swiss *broderie anglaise,* midcalf dresses made by Neiman-Marcus. (But thrifty Aunt Grace had bought their little white socks and Mary Janes by mail order from the J. C. Penney catalogue!) Wreaths of small fresh flowers circled the heads of Peggy's two daughters and Tiny's two girls, and the four carried miniature versions of the bridesmaids' nosegays. The two little boys (Tiny's son Buddy and a distant cousin, Sebastian, Prince Von Furstenberg) wore white satin knee breeches, white ruffled long-sleeved blouses, white stockings and white shoes with large antique buckles. Buddy was to carry Grace's ring; Sebastian, Rainier's, each on a plump satin cushion. Buddy's nanny had come up with the sensible idea of basting the rings onto the cushions to prevent them from clattering down on the stone floor of the Cathedral during the long bridal procession.

Gathered in Grace's favorite gold and white salon, we all tried to remain calm. In the bride's quarters, Virginia Darcy was busy decoding Helen Rose's complicated instructions for getting Gracie into her wedding gown, not that the bride hadn't practiced several times before. The dress was constructed in the way they made ball gowns in the late nineteenth century. In order to secure it on Grace, Virginia had to tape and lace several sets of straps underneath in the back which created and supported the pouf and bustle effects.

None of this was made easier by the fact that Grace's wedding outfit contained twenty-five yards of silk *peau de soie,* another twenty-five of light silk taffeta, ninety-eight yards of silk tulle and nearly three hundred and twenty yards of Valenciennes lace. Though no news at all about the dress was to have been given out, somehow a sketch of it had gotten into the hands of the press two days earlier.

Still, no sketch could possibly describe how unbelievably beautiful Grace looked when she joined us for picture taking. The bodice of her dress was of the Val lace. A stiffened stand-up collar rose up the sides of

Grace's swanlike neck, dipping to a V just at the base of her throat. The sheer lace was fitted perfectly to her shoulders and slim arms, down the full length of the sleeves that ended below her wrists in scallops covering a small part of the backs of her hands. Underneath the bodice, one could vaguely distinguish the taffeta strapless underbodice. Grace's white lace-covered buttons led down to a high, pleated taffeta cummerbund. Her tiny waist was emphasized by her exquisitely full-belled white taffeta skirt. In the front, the skirt had side gathers and fell to a perfect circle at the floor. The back of Grace's dress was such a wonderment of poufs and bustles that it was hard to tell where those left off and the skirt divided to reveal masses of Val lace which, together with the taffeta, constituted her train. Again, Grace's hair was pulled straight back with a newly designed, curled chignon set low on the back of her head. A stiffened Val lace skullcap closely framed her head. Shaped like an inverted sweetheart neckline, with rounded points at the center and just above her ears, it was cut back into semicircles above each brow. Grace was carrying a small white Bible and a loosely arranged bunch of lilies of the valley. Her white tulle veil was bordered in Val lace. When the front veil was dropped over her face, it reached just to the middle of her cummerbund. More than ninety yards of tulle, tied with stiffened bows of lace and taffeta, trailed down the back of her headdress, coordinating to the same motif on the train of her skirts. Seed pearls adorned her Juliet cap as well as the bodice of her dress. The lobes of her ears were adorned with simple pearl and diamond earclips.

Her makeup was exactly the right balance of pale yet intense colors. Unlike on the morning of her civil marriage, she did not appear to have been flattened into a single solemn dimension. Though she was enormously composed on the outside, you could still feel the deep vibrancy of life within her. I have seen a great many beautiful women, but I have never seen anyone as beautiful as Grace that day. If our fantasies had led us to expect perfection, here it was before us—courtesy of genes, Helen Rose and the fact that Grace expected even more of herself than we did. As she came round to greet each of us, something beyond beauty warmed the corners of the room. It was Grace's magic, the true coin of her independent realm, her huge and endearing soul.

Still very much the Gracie who tried to keep major moments feeling like everyday life, when she got to me and I told her there could never again be such a wondrous bride, she answered, "Nor such a tired one! I intend to sleep endlessly once we are out to sea." I started to say something else, but became suddenly aware that Grace was preparing for her religious wedding the way an actor does before going onstage. I could see her keeping herself relaxed by her own controlled comments delivered to each of her friends, but staying very much in the mood of the moment, the heart of the character.

We posed for pictures. Grace alone, the bridesmaids without Grace, the bridesmaids with her. With the children and without the children. Lined up one way, then another. Grace smiled sweetly almost all the time, taking great pains to make sure she put the children at ease, whispering little compliments to each of them about how wonderful they looked, how proud she was of them, how proud they would make their parents feel, how sure she was they would each do their part perfectly.

While the cameras were being reloaded, I turned to Rita, who was standing next to me in our lineup, and asked her how she was faring this morning. "Just fine, darling," she answered without a moment's hesitation. "Everything is fine." Her answer and her reassuring smile were so believable that I was forced to remember that Grace was not the only professional trouper in the room.

Once the indoor photos had been taken, we were asked to follow Grace outside onto the Galerie d'Hercule overlooking the double stairway leading down into the Palace's Court of Honor. There we posed again in various groupings, for some of which Grace dropped her face veil, for others of which she kept her veil back. Now, standing beneath the exquisitely hand-painted, vaulted and arched Galerie ceiling, looking down onto the courtyard, we all stiffened a bit. This was the wedding of the world's favorite movie star, Grace Kelly, to the world's favorite Prince Charming, Rainier III of Monaco. For a moment I felt like an interloper. What was I doing here? Why did I belong standing where I was standing? Would I be found out and asked to leave?

Again Grace's infallible sensitivity, her instinct for knowing what needed to be done, rose to the fore. With all her own thoughts and feelings running through her head and heart at that moment, with all her anxiety about the fact that everyone in the world would be watching her for the next few hours as she experienced the most significant moment of her life to date, Grace sensed my feelings, and perhaps those of her other friends. While we waited for Howell Conant to set up the next shot, Grace smiled her warm, everyday smile and put us all at ease. "Having all of you here with me today makes all the difference in the world. It reminds me that Rainier and I are just two people who love each other and are getting married. Sometimes this week, it's been hard to remember that. But looking at each one of my friends at this moment makes everything very personal and very real." She had not only made us comfortable, she had done so by making it seem that it was we who were comforting her. Only later in life did I realize how much Grace needed support at that moment. Her comments were not gratuitous. Though each of us led our own lives and would continue to do so thousands of miles apart, we were—in some way that none of us yet understood—all bound together.

At the Cathedral by 10 A.M., a cordon of honor consisting of firemen in full uniform and a special section of armed Carabiniers had formed on the steps. Ten minutes later His Excellency the Most Reverend Marella, representing Pope Pius XII, arrived, accompanied by Count d'Aillières, the Prince's Chamberlain, who had happily been released from the hospital in time to attend. Monseigneur Gilles Barthe, Bishop of Monaco, greeted the Papal Emissary and accompanied him in procession to the episcopal throne.

At ten-fifteen, the procession of the families began. H.S.H. Princess Charlotte, Rainier's mother, arrived with her Lady-in-Waiting and proceeded down the red carpet to her place in the front of the Cathedral. Organ music swelled through the great stone house of worship. Next came Rainier's father, H.S.H. Prince Pierre, attended by his Cavalry Major aide, followed by Rainier's stepgrandmother. Bedecked in a gray feathered hat, she was accompanied by her Lady of Honor, as was H.S.H. Princess Antoinette, who followed. Mother-of-the-bride Margaret Kelly was escorted down the aisle by a Lady-in-Waiting assigned to her. She took her place in the front row, on the bride's side, next to Grace's pregnant sister-in-law, Kell's wife Mary.

Back on the Galerie we divided into small groupings, each with our own private thoughts. For a moment, Grace strayed away from the rest of us, from her bridesmaids, the children, even from her sister Peggy. She took the few steps to the balustrade of the Galerie d'Hercule and there, with her face half in shadow, stood completely still, looking out over her courtyard, her palace, her new land. Howell Conant snapped a picture, but even if I had never seen it, that moment would stay forever in my mind. She was as alone as I have ever seen anyone in my whole life. And in that aloneness she was everything I had come to know her to be. The complex paradox of Gracie in that moment was so powerful you felt you could reach out, touch and be awed by it forever.

Then, just as I thought I saw it all, I remembered another photo, taken less than a year before. It was of Grace standing at the identical spot at the same balustrade. She was wearing "the dreaded taffeta dress." It was the first day she had come to Monaco, to meet the Prince. But as the Prince was late, the *Paris Match* photographer had taken photos of Grace alone at various spots throughout the Palace. In my mind's eye, I recalled exactly how Grace had looked in that year-old photo, could see very clearly her strength, her vulnerability, her pliability, her determination, her vast aloneness. I gasped inwardly, wondering if Grace had stood there looking out at Monaco and the Palace, knowing that it would one day be hers. Had something in Grace's extraordinary sense of how to direct her life known a year ago that she would be at that same spot today, dressed in bridal finery, as the Princess of Monaco? Had Grace herself, by willing it, created this scene for "The Grace Kelly Story" and then projected it across the Atlantic Ocean to make the canvas of her life even more majestic, the tightrope she would need to walk even more precarious? Realizing I would never know the answers to these questions, I turned away, leaving her alone. It would be decades before Grace would ask these questions of herself.

We were summoned to a new position near the bottom of the double, curved marble stairway leading onto the courtyard, forming a guard for Grace, who took her place in front of a bank of flowers with the Monégasque coat of arms overhead. More photos were taken with Grace standing under the crown, the cross and the initials that, as of this day and this hour, would be intertwined throughout her life—the "R" and then the "G," in that order, for Rainier's sovereignty mandated that not the wife's but the husband's identity was to take precedence.

Pairing off, waving our goodbyes to Grace, we began our long procession down the narrow ancient streets of Monaco-Ville toward the Cathedral. It was ten-thirty when we reached the Cathedral steps, exactly as scheduled. We mounted the red-carpeted stairs under the billowing silk canopy and approached the doors to enter. We had only an instant to take in the magnificence of the Cathedral. Huge golden baskets of white snapdragons hung from every high, glistening chandelier all the way to the altar along the center aisle and down each side. The altar itself, lit by tall white candles and banked in masses of white hydrangeas, lilacs and lilies, seemed as though it were six hundred miles away. Exquisite music reverberated throughout the great stone Cathedral. Behind it, sounding like a swarm of bees that had nested in the rafters and could not be routed, droned the incessant whir of the TV and newsreel cameras.

Once we were inside the Cathedral and on our way down the aisle with every eye upon us, we knew we were in trouble. We had expected to make our walk in perfect unison, running on automatic pilot. But the ecclesiastic music accompanying our procession was not the familiar selection we had anticipated. As we could not stop to discuss how to do our Rockette bit in tandem, we tried instinctively to feel the steps of the person walking next to us, watch the pair in front, and pray that the pair behind came out even.

Relieved to reach the altar, we filed into our pew slightly to the right of where the service was to be performed. The junior attendants followed, filing into their places directly in front of us.

Every head turned to see Grace enter the Cathedral on the arm of her father, the man who was sure little Gracie would never amount to much. As Grace and her father passed each row, the guests' mouths dropped open at the sight of her. Gloria Swanson's was so agape, I remember hoping there were no flies in the Cathedral. Ava Gardner, who was sitting with Rupert Allan, smiled so gently and beatifically at her friend that she herself looked as though she could be recommended for sainthood. Beyond Rupert there was, believe it or not, an empty chair. Frank Sinatra had planned to come and had gone on to London to equip himself with all the finest of the required finery. But on hearing how the press was lying in wait to capture shots of him and Ava at the same functions, he had decided it would be best to stay away and called Gracie to let her know he did not want to be accused of trying to upstage her and Rainier on their big day. Grace accepted this decision, by now used to the fact that nearly every aspect of her wedding had been altered by the presence and the perseverance of the press.

Watching Grace come down the aisle, I wondered how many hours she had spent rehearsing in her dress. As an actress, Grace would have known how important it was to see how the dress worked as she walked, stood, sat, kneeled and rose again. As a princess bride, she had probably practiced extensively. In any case, she carried the more than four hundred yards of cloth as though it were her second skin. Nearing the altar, Grace was joined by Father John Cartin, parish priest of her hometown St. Bridget's Church, who led her to her prie-dieu, where she awaited the Prince.

At ten-thirty-five, all of the troops positioned outside the Cathedral presented arms to His Serene Highness. Rainier wore a black tunic elaborately decorated with thick gold-leaf embellishments on its cuffs and epaulets. Gold stripes ran down the sides of his sky blue trousers and he carried a midnight blue bicorne plumed with white ostrich feathers. He himself had designed his wedding uniform, basing it on that of Napoleon's marshals. During his own procession down the aisle, the Prince was followed by his witnesses, Count Charles de Polignac, Lieutenant Colonel Ardant and Grace's brother Kell. Nearing the altar, the Prince was joined by his personal Chaplain, Father Tucker, Chamberlain Count d'Aillières and Monseigneur Barthe. He took his place at his prie-dieu to Grace's right, with his witnesses and spiritual counselors on that side. Grace's two witnesses, her sister and Rainier's, stood to her left.

Father Tucker had been assigned the role of choreographer/director for this production. He was bilingual and many of the participants were not. At his first instruction the witnesses drew closer to the couple at the altar. Throughout the ceremony it was Father Tucker who, in the best theatrical tradition, gave the bridal party their cues. "Sit" . . . "stand" . . . "kneel," he repeatedly uttered in a stage whisper we could hear but which could not be heard by the guests, nor by the microphones that peeped through the flower-bedecked altar.

It was ten-forty-one when Monseigneur Barthe began to speak. Seventeen minutes later he asked the big question: "Rainier Louis Henri Maxence Bertrand, will you take Grace Patricia here present for your lawful wife, according to the rite of our Holy Mother the Church?" Though the cameras rolled incessantly, and the floodlights glared, the Prince answered shyly yet surely, "Yes, Monseigneur."

Grace had hardly moved a muscle of her tranquil, erect posture in the seventeen minutes since the service began. Turning to her, Monseigneur Barthe intoned: "Grace Patricia, will you take Rainier Louis Henri Maxence Bertrand here present for your lawful husband, according to the rite of our Holy Mother the Church?" Very solemnly, for she was taking a vow from which she would never extricate herself, Grace announced her decision and her intention for the rest of her life. "Yes, Monseigneur," she replied, softly but firmly.

When it came time for the exchange of the rings, things did not go as smoothly. Sebastian, the little Prince Von Furstenberg charged with carrying Rainier's ring, dropped it. But Father Tucker swooped down so quickly and unobtrusively to retrieve it that no one behind us noticed. We few were also the only ones who could see Rainier struggling in vain to slide Grace's ring onto her finger. Almost imperceptibly, she lent a helping hand, twisting the ring over her knuckle without a ripple of effort showing in her composure.

Father Cartin from Philadelphia delivered a brief speech, offering good wishes for the future and fatherly advice to the couple. Then Monseigneur Barthe celebrated low Mass before the several impressively titled members of Church hierarchy gathered in our midst. The Choir School of the Cathedral offered a program of inspirational music, assisted by selections from the Monte Carlo Philharmonic Orchestra under the direction of Nadia Boulanger and M. A. Locatelli. Intermittently, three organists filled the Cathedral with their rich chords and, finally, the sound of bugles trumpeted forth a selection from the Prince's Carabiniers entitled "Aux Champs pour les Clairons."

Following the Mass and rendering of another hymn, the Most Reverend Father Marella read Grace and Rainier the paternal wishes of His Holiness Pope Pius XII. With some of the earlier tension draining away as the time passed, each of us could feel ourselves beginning to wilt. Grace, though, still looked as fresh as at the beginning, ever so intently focused as the Papal Emissary began his formal address. I believe she listened with all her mind, all her heart and all her soul to the words of the apostolic benediction. I believe that after every sentence, inside of herself, she replied "Yes," addressing not the speaker of the words, not even the Pope, but her own private God.

The wedding ceremony the world had waited for and talked about for four months was over. Grace's cousin Jean Goit had fainted during the ceremony, but a hastily summoned physician had removed her from the Cathedral without anyone but those sitting closest to her realizing what had happened. And when the Monseigneur had urged the happy couple to become "one in mind, one in heart and one in affection," and the Papal Emissary had declared that their beneficiaries would include the entire nation entrusted to their care, Grace had gotten a new marriage, a new husband, a message from the Pope containing blessings of the Lord, a new country, a new people and a new job. Much of the world had watched her sign her lifetime contract.

Leaving the altar, Their Serene Highnesses the Prince and Princess of Monaco proceeded slowly toward the immense Cathedral doors. Smiling in the perfect sunshine of this glorious day, Grace and Rainier took their places in their new open cream-and-black Rolls-Royce, the gift of Monaco's people, Rainier's people, Grace's people. Though the other guests were made to wait inside the Cathedral, we bridesmaids followed Grace and Rainier out into the warming sunlight, where we were divided into three Palace limousines. Then, with Grace and Rainier leading us, our motorcade set forth into the streets of old Monaco to greet thousands upon thousands of smiling men, women and children who were waiting to see it pass.

For these few moments as we drove through the Principality, Grace and Rainier got what they had hoped for, planned for, prayed for. Gone was the carnival-like whistling and screeching that had accompanied their earlier rides that week. In its place were thousands of people expressing affection, consideration, respect and hope, many of them openly weeping with joy. As we followed the newlyweds in our limousines, a Lady-in-Waiting advised us to acknowledge the crowds with more than smiles. Bending her arm at the elbow and raising her slightly cupped hand near her temple, she moved her hand slowly to the right side then to the left, in that familiar gesture of regal greeting we had all seen in newsreels since childhood, and suggested we do the same.

Before returning to the Palace, we stopped at the tiny Church of Sainte Dévote. The new Princess of Monaco left her car to lay her spray of lilies of the valley on the altar as an offering to the martyred, virgin patron saint of her new homeland. As the procession proceeded onward to Grace's new house, we bridesmaids continued to turn and wave slowly to her adoring countrymen. And for thirty years thereafter, each of us would recall those as the dearest public moments of the week, in some ways the most bittersweet, but nonetheless the dearest and truest.

In the Palace Court of Honor, seven hundred wedding guests milled about, unable to eat, drink or sit until the Sovereign couple joined them. It had been a long church service, a long wait while we drove through Monaco, and now it would be even longer until everyone could relax and enjoy the party. Grace and Rainier, we bridesmaids and the immediate families of the bride and the groom gathered once again in the white and gold salon for more picture taking. Then the families and attendants preceded them into the courtyard while the newlyweds appeared at the Palace windows for an ovation from the huge crowd in the square below. We waited just outside the special enclosure at the foot of the double staircase. Then a murmur that rippled through the guests made us turn our eyes upward to see Grace and Rainier on the Galerie d'Hercule, pausing at the top of the stairway. The applause began softly, then with each downward step they took it swelled to ever greater cadences. They smiled happily as they descended to the Aubusson rug that had been laid across the stones at the foot of the stairs to carpet their enclosure.

Tables for four had been set for the bridal party and immediate family members, all clothed in priceless lace-trimmed linen. Most of the chairs were gilded, carved, beveled and armless; but magnificent antique arm-chairs, their seats and backs covered in flowered brocade, were in place at the head table. The rear of the enclosure was dominated by the six-tier wedding cake, its enormous base embossed with carved three-dimensional sugar replicas of the turreted Princely Palace. Small scenes commemorating Monégasque history were sculpted into every tier. Between the fourth and fifth layers, a red and white duplication of the Monégasque crest had been woven out of spun sugar. At the top of the cake, their feet embedded in clouds of filigreed icing, stood two cherubs. A wavy platform above their small heads held a replica of the golden (if actually nonexistent) crown of Monaco.

Behind the cake, lace-clothed service tables had been set up from which the several butlers and footmen could attend to those dining in the enclosure. Throughout the luncheon Grace invited members of both families and her bridesmaids to take individual turns joining her and Rainier at their small head table. It was so like her to remember details that kept the day feeling personal. But then it was also getting closer to the hour when Grace would have to say goodbye to her American family and friends, and she intended to treasure every last moment of their presence, even though she was longing to be off with Rainier on their honeymoon, away from all the chaos of the past week.

In the Court of Honor, seven hundred guests made their way to the buffet tables that had been set across from our enclosure. For the most part, guests were required to stand and eat after making their selection from the sumptuous repast laid out for them. When I looked out, I could see people struggling with top hats, purses, plates, glasses and napkins, and though nobody appeared to be finding this easy, every face was smiling.

When the luncheon was nearly over, Grace and Rainier rose from their table, a pathway was cleared, and they walked out into the Court of Honor to greet their guests. They had hoped to be able to share a few personal words with their many close friends who were present. I could see that my mother and father were able to get near them, and saw Grace lean forward to kiss my mother's cheeks, first one side, then the other. But it wasn't long before it became clear that too many people were trying too hard to reach them and that the idea of their wending their way through the crowd was an impractical one.

When they returned to the enclosure, a coterie of guards was positioned along the balustrade, and Grace and Rainier proceeded to one side, where the cake had been rolled out and forward. In the traditional way, they clasped their right hands one on top of the other and made the first lucky cut with the Prince's sword. After those in the enclosure were served, the cake was wheeled out into the Court of Honor, where it was distributed to the hundreds of guests. Footmen made the rounds at our tables, presenting each of us with a small, white faille box. Trimmed in gold and white rope, tied with a golden cord and initialed with the intertwined "R" and "G," each box contained a tiny square of wedding cake for us to keep as a souvenir.

The luncheon had begun at 1 P.M. When an hour and a half had passed, Buddy d'Aillières leaned discreetly toward Rainier's ear and notified him of the time. Rainier whispered to Grace, and seeing them rise, we rose. We had been told earlier to wait for a few minutes after the newlyweds had gone to change before following Grace to the sitting room of her private quarters.

Arriving at Grace's suite, we found the door to her bedroom open. Virginia was making last-minute adjustments to her hair and going-away outfit. Grace reminded Virginia that after she stopped in England, she could stay in Grace's New York apartment until June, when Peggy's children got out of school and they were all coming to stay in the flat. Virginia reminded Grace about a particular hairstyle she had done for her on the *Constitution.* "Don't wear a braid again at that angle we had it at in the picture I showed you. You got away with it because you're so thin now," Virginia cautioned, "but you're gonna gain some weight, and then it'll be very unbecoming—a real German hausfrau look," she concluded. When Grace looked at her inquiringly, Virginia added, "A German hausfrau, you know. A person with no voice of her own. Promise?" Grace promised, knowing all too well about German hausfraus.

Grace came out of her bedroom to join us, still buttoning the jacket of her discreet light gray dressmaker suit. Virginia, who had already placed Grace's small white hat at exactly the right angle on her head, entered behind her, jovially suggesting, "Come on, girls. Let's all curtsy to the new princess." Everyone including Grace stood mesmerized, every eye in the room fighting back tears. Then someone joked, "I hope you don't get seasick. We're counting on your cruise for a little plumping up here and there!" During the crossing and the wedding week, Grace had lost ten pounds. It worked wonderfully for photographs, but when we saw her like this, in normal street clothes, she was too thin. After a few minutes of group chattering and giggling, and a few stories of amusing things that had happened during the day, everyone grew quiet. Then Grace started to come around, saying goodbyes to each of us individually. When she got to me, she scratched her ear, then looked up startled.

"Oh, my word," she cried. "I've forgotten my earrings and everything's been packed and taken."

"Will these do?" I asked, unclipping mine and offering them to her. They were small pearl and diamond clips I'd had made from some of my mother's jewelry.

"Nicely, thank you," said Grace sounding smug and playful. Then turning to the others, she giggled triumphantly, "Hey, you all," she called out, "Judy fell for it!" We all laughed as she pulled down first one lobe, then the other, attaching my earrings for her trip.

During the preceding week the press had been speculating daily about the route for Grace and Rainier's honeymoon, trying to extract information from us as well as every other possible source. Knowing that they desperately wanted to be alone, we had decided not to inquire as to their specific plans. One widely heeded rumor held that the couple would cruise near Rome in response to an invitation for an audience with the Pope. "Shoot up an Ave for me, Gracie," I said. "And see if you can get my earrings back by June!"

All at once, for no known reason, we all began to cry, Grace, too. Her sister Peggy, wanting to help Grace avoid running mascara, gave her the old college wave and cracked, "See ya later, alligator."

Then a male voice added, "In a while, crocodile!" We looked up to see Rainier, our tears now turning to laughter. He circled the room as, one by one, each of us extended our thanks and offered blessings of joy. Grace walked slowly over to pick up her white coat. Then in a flash Rainier put his arm around her, whisked her through the door, and they were gone. We stood mostly in shadow. A single ray of light illuminated a small empty circle in the center of the carpet. Nobody spoke. The smell of lilacs was overwhelming and the cooing of two pearl gray lovebirds in their corner cage seemed to grow louder by the second. But for that, the room and every living thing in it was stopped in stillness.

Countess d'Aillières appeared along with another Lady-in-Waiting. "Come with us!" they called, motioning us to follow them quickly. We fairly flew up and down the long corridors, in one salon and out the other, up small stairways, then down again, across and over, weaving our way throughout the Palace to a turret high atop it where we would be afforded the best view of the sailing. Bursting through the doors to a sort of widow's walk enclosure on the tallest tower, we took places along the balustrades so we could watch the harbor. Countess d'Aillières left us there and ran to fetch a few more of Grace's close American friends.

We six bridesmaids stood next to one another at the railing, watching for Grace and Rainier to arrive on the crowded quay. Overhead, a cluster of smoky gray clouds had blotted out the sunlight, casting us in shadow. Someone called out, "There they are!" and we watched as Grace, Rainier and the ever-present Oliver, now transported in sovereign arms, boarded the *Deo Juvante*. A stiff breeze blew our skirts wide, forcing us to hold our floppy hats firmly to our heads. Then the *Deo Juvante*'s crew freed its ropes from the dock, and the boat began making its way out toward sea. The wind blew the last gray cloud to the west and once again, "Grace Kelly weather" appeared to launch the honeymoon of our friends.

The streets and windows of Monaco were packed, as they had been when Grace arrived, with thousands of cheering, flag-waving admirers. Dozens of small craft guided the *Deo Juvante* out of the harbor as boat sirens bleated acclaim for the young travelers.

Seeing the *Deo Juvante* pass the breakwater, we ran quickly to the other side of the tower. Someone had brought a small box of rice from home, and we all tossed little handfuls of it into the gathering winds. Grace and Rainier stood on the bridge of their yacht as it glided out to sea. We alternately waved and blew kisses directly at them. They waved and blew kisses back, at least I'm sure Grace did, until she and we were all out of view.

We were just six American girls of the Fifties, like our friend Grace. But as she sailed off from view in her polite little going-away suit and we stood high on the tall turret, the wind whipping our organdy skirts the color of spring daffodils against the ancient creamy walls of the Palace parapet, I felt something very strong and very deep. Something for each of us, separately, and for all of us together. Something that would bind me to these women for life. Perhaps it was merely our love for Gracie and her love for us. If so, that seemed enough. That and the fact that we had lived through this week together, a week no other six young American women of our time would ever be a part of again.

Did I think at all about the future? Not at all. Not a bit about ours nor even Grace's. I was still young enough to think that all you had to do about life was to let it happen. Besides, it was the Fifties. From where we stood, we were pretty sure that as long as we looked the right way, married the right man, and did and said the right things, life would unfold before us as easily and enjoyably as it always had.

CHAPTER 7

Entr'acte

By the time Jay and I returned home from our extended continental trip, Grace had already sent three post-cards: the first telling me that once they left Monaco she and Rainier had been forced to moor less than an hour away in Villefranche when the Mediterranean grew unduly turbulent; the second saying that she and Rainier had enjoyed a reunion with Sally and John in Spain; the third describing the beauty of hidden bays and beaches in Corsica, where she and Rainier found, at last, the tranquility and privacy they had longed for on their honeymoon.

In early June, I got my first long letter from Grace. In it she bemoaned the fact that she had been repeatedly seasick while on her honeymoon cruise. Rainier, she said, adored the sea, and they hoped to make the boat a retreat for themselves and their future children. Determined to be a great wife, and thus a great sailor, Grace wrote off her first bouts with nausea to exhaustion, insisting to me that "I never had the problem on the *Judith R.,*" though she had only cruised Long Island Sound on my parents' boat and not the Mediterranean.

I wrote back immediately. Knowing of her passion for Olivier, I described in detail our visits with him and his wife Vivien Leigh in England. I also told her about Marilyn Monroe's wedding to Arthur Miller before their departure for *The Prince and the Showgirl.* (Over the years it has been written that I was a bridesmaid for Marilyn as well, but I do not recall any such designation. Perhaps the story grew from the fact that Marilyn had only four women friends and we all stood next to her during the ceremony. Perhaps it was the beginning of the truth that the designation "bridesmaid" was to follow me for the rest of my days.) I also told Grace that when I saw an East Indian actress named Anna Kashfi on screen for the first time in *The Mountain,* I had nudged Jay to inform him that, "Marlon is going to marry that girl!"

Phoning overseas still seemed, in those days, tantamount to scaling the Himalayas, and the cost of the two were about the same. So it wasn't until late July that I placed my first call to Grace in Monaco. I called with Betsy Drake Grant at my side, in order to let Grace know that Betsy was safe and alive after the *Andrea Doria,* the ship on which she'd returned from Spain, had sunk in the Atlantic Ocean off Nantucket.

One week later a letter with my friend's picture on the stamp told me I had another message from Grace. It was a brief note, written in her large rounded writing.

Darling Judybird,

    We're preggos! Ecstatic!! Rainier will make the announcement soon but wanted to share our joy with you and Jaybird first. Keep our secret and tell Amybird we'll have a good playmate for her when you all come to visit.

Lots of love,
Gracie

I barely had time to write her a congratulatory note in return, suggesting that her seasickness might have been early pregnancy nausea, before Rainier made his August 2 announcement to the Monégasques and the world. It was not yet four months after the wedding.

Her Serene Highness Princess Grace expects a child whose birth should take place in February. It gives great joy to the Princess and myself to share this new happiness with you.

That part sounded like a prospective father. He went on:

> The significance of this awaited event is clear to all of you. How-
> ever, I find it indispensable to link this guarantee of the Principal-
> ity's surviving in its independence and privileges, to the absolute
> necessity of establishing an era of total trust and confidence.

If Daddy was going to give them continuing independence, he was going
to ask for something in return.

> The projects for economical and technological development
> which have received my approval are neither unreasonable, impru-
> dent, nor opposed to the true interests of our country. They answer
> new needs which stem from a normal and desirable evolution of
> our general economy.

There had been a great deal of local speculation that Rainier, who was
all but single-handedly dragging his country into the twentieth century,
was proposing growth and change that would disrupt his people and their
way of life. Today he was letting his citizens know that new life meant
not only a baby in the cradle, but also a grown-up on the throne.

> In light of this news, so important for me and for yourselves, it
> seems impossible that we should not strengthen our trust in the
> future. The future does not build itself. It has to be molded
> according to the characteristics of every country, large or small,
> just as it has to be shaped according to every individual.

> One chooses one's future and then starts building it. I ask you to
> trust in the choice I have made for Monaco's future, and, also, to
> remember that the Principality has endured, and will only endure,
> as long as its Sovereign Prince has full and complete exercise of
> his power.

The content of Grace's and Rainier's respective birth announcements
made clear the separate agendas under which the newlyweds intended to
operate. They were the separate agendas of every young couple of the day.
He was going to do his job; she was going to do hers. For the earliest years
of their marriage, that is very much the way their lives unfolded.

Rainier was dedicated to modernizing nearly every aspect of his languorous, provincial and slightly medieval country. He was going to mold the future and build it, just as he said, forging ahead with projects to ensure economic and technological development. He was aware that local forces were gathering in opposition, but he was intent upon retaining and exercising his full and complete power, a power greater than that held by any other sovereign in Europe.

As her husband so accurately stated, "One chooses one's future and then starts building it." But what future had Grace chosen? And how had she determined to start building it? She selected the occupations of every woman she knew who was "just a person." She was going to run the house, have babies and raise children, entertain for social and business purposes, do a little volunteer activity, and be the perfect complement to her husband's life in every way. It was woman's work, and it was the job Grace cut out for herself in her effort to redirect her vast personal resources.

Throughout the summer Gracie wrote long letters to all of us. Some were filled with talk of the forthcoming baby, the fact that she had experienced some morning sickness but that it, along with her early months of exhaustion, now appeared to have passed. In other letters she chatted about trying to organize the Palace as a home without letting on that this was any more difficult than it would be for a suburban bride in Scarsdale or the owner of a small co-op in New York.

In terms of space and building location, when Grace moved out of her roomy Fifth Avenue high-rise-for-one into her family quarters at the Palace, it was a step down—literally. Many of her friends referred for years to the small west-wing Palace apartment that she, Rainier, the children and the nanny first shared as "the basement apartment." One actually did have to descend a few steps below ground level to enter its front door. Once inside, though the apartment was beautifully decorated, it was somewhat cramped.

No reigning family had lived in the Palace in Monaco for more than two hundred years. Grimaldi history had been riddled with divorce, liaisons, defections, peculiarities and rulers who preferred life in Paris or on the Riviera to their vast official residence. But Grace and Rainier intended to use the Palace as a home and augment the quarters there with a nearby country house for more casual living, along with Rainier's bachelor apartment in Paris. (His villa in Cap Ferrat, where he and Gisèle Pascal had lived together, was sold immediately.) Grace's early months at the Palace were absorbed with managing her household and the people, goods and services required to keep it running smoothly.

In New York, if her faucet leaked or her lamp refused to light, all Grace had to do was call the building maintenance man or the local plumber or electrician, who disappeared quickly after the job was done. At her new house, an entire maintenance staff worked every day and often lived there with her. Teams of electricians, plumbers, handymen and upholsterers were available at her beck and call. The housewife's dream! And while Grace had formerly made do with a once-a-week laundress, she now had a full-time laundry room staffed by thirty women who specialized in washing, starching, pressing, mending, embroidering and dressmaking. Liaisoning through a full-time staff director, Grace oversaw the cooks, butlers, maids and other domestic contributors who constituted her working staff. But her house was not only a home. It was peopled with the clerks, secretaries, aides and officials who made up the government of her new country. The cost of the convenience ran high. Bit by bit Grace paid for it. Her long-cherished privacy was slowly chipped away until, like her fading Stevens yearbook, it was nothing more than a nostalgic remnant of her American past.

As a twenty-six-year-old movie star, all Grace needed to manage was herself. In Monaco, she took on the management of an enterprise resembling a combination of the Ritz, the White House and General Motors, learning on the job with amazing alacrity.

The establishment Grace ran during her early years in Monaco was not a modern miracle. A relic of the sixteenth and seventeenth centuries, the Palais Princier had been built by her husband's forefathers in their heyday before the French Revolution. Long dank halls connected formal rooms filled with slightly faded brocade walls and masses of gilded furniture or ebony Venetian pieces. The lighting was, to put it politely, dim. An ancient cistern under the Court of Honor had originally been created to furnish water in the event the Grimaldis were besieged. But as the only people besieging them in the mid-twentieth century were foreign tourists and the international press, the thousands of gallons of stored water now served only to assure the pervading dampness that clung to the Palace walls like a feverish, clammy sweat. This did not appear to affect the alternately smiling or angry countenances of Grimaldi ancestors whose portraits occupied wall after wall. The depth of discontent visible among certain of the deceased Grimaldis told you that better lighting, a dry cistern and a little chintz would not have helped. And while Grace struggled to whip the place into acceptable shape, living antiquities frowned upon her every bit as persistently as did her husband's more distant relatives.

Grace never mentioned it in her cheery letters, and only casually referred to it on her first visit to the States that fall, but during her early months as a new bride she was devastated by the constant, cutting disapproval of her mother-in-law. Far from her own home and country, newly married and pregnant for the first time, Grace needed to feel embraced by her new family. Separated from her girlfriends, her sisters and her mother, she craved a woman's shoulder.

Princess Charlotte, however, had never acquired such talents, even for the comfort of her own children, Rainier and Antoinette. Throughout Rainier's childhood, his mother used him as a pawn on the chessboard of her unhappy life. So while Grace yearned deeply for Charlotte's approval, what she got was a series of slurs and rebuffs.

Certain elderly members of Grace's household staff were nearly as hostile as Charlotte. One old majordomo who had, for years, supervised the ten footmen, the wine cellars, the silver, the crystal and the table settings had a fixed way of doing things and would not be moved by his new mistress. To every new suggestion Grace made, he patronizingly responded, "Oh, we don't do things that way here." Grace was an enormously tactful young woman, and she offered her ideas for change subtly, but the old man rejected them with skillful subterfuge, implying that he was helping to keep Grace along the well-established Palace lines to which she should hew. On rare occasions, he would comply with her direct requests, but his compliance was a onetime affair. The next day he would go back to doing things his way, exactly the way he had done them before Grace's arrival.

Grace had adored flowers since childhood. Now she was mistress of a home with exquisite space, soil and climate to grow everything imaginable. Talented professional gardeners guaranteed her a supply of all her favorite varieties to arrange as she wished. But the ancient Palace employee responsible for table flowers was unmovable. He, too, had a way of doing things to which he expected Grace to conform.

At the Palace, Grace had a lot more help and a lot less freedom than any one of her American friends. Then, too, it quickly became apparent to her that even the most trivial of her acts, statements or expressions within her household reverberated throughout the Principality. Thus, while Grace learned to manage a household on the grand scale, she was also learning to play the approval game on an especially vast playing field. It was not merely Rainier's approval she needed to win (and we all thought it was our job to earn our merit badges, rather than have them automatically awarded), nor that of her household employees. Grace had to earn the approval of every last one of the thousands of citizens of Monaco.

In the context of those times, it is not hard to explain the skepticism Monégasques felt about their new Princess. In the 1950s, throughout Europe and even among certain classes in America, being a movie star implied you were a kept cutie from *The Follies*. "A lost woman, a lowlife," as Rainier recalls. Movie stars—and Grace was one of them—were merely rich and famous white trash.

The supremely privileged European class into which Grace had married did not abide interlopers. That, coupled with the eccentricities of earlier Grimaldi sovereigns, explained why no high-ranking royalty from foreign countries had attended her wedding to the Prince. Aristocrats knew that if they opened their exclusive club doors, their ranks would swell to unmanageable proportions. The only way to arrest this distasteful expansion was to maintain that something you could not control predetermined your future—birth. Only if you were born well, into the right family, the right name, the right line of succession, were you guaranteed admittance to the club.

Grace had the wrong bloodlines and no protectorate at the start of her marriage. Everyone in Monaco was watching her tightrope act the way some people watch them at the circus—overtly hoping she would keep her balance and reach the other side, but secretly waiting for her to trip badly.

Because Rainier knew too well that being wellborn carried no entitlement to love, because he wanted to love and be loved in a loving family, because he fell in love with Grace, and because he was smarter than most, Rainier had put Grace's name on the club's roster. But the aristocrats of Europe and the people of Monaco were going to make her work herself to the bone to deserve the listing.

Inside the humble and willing Grace, however, there lived the self-willed, autonomous Grace who had not married as a teenager and had scored a string of upset victories as a young adult. As the approval-seeking Grace smiled and cajoled and sighed and tried again with the Palace staff, her hostile mother-in-law and her suspicious subjects, her second self must have cautioned, "Hey, Gracie, wake up! What kind of deal is this? You worked hard to get yourself to a place where you called almost all the shots and now everyone but you has the right to call them. Blow the whistle. Put your foot down. Get some control!" Yet at that time in her life, like most dedicated new brides of the era, Grace seemed anxious to pass control along to anybody who wanted, needed or felt entitled to it.

By autumn, distractions came to her rescue. She and Rainier returned to New York, where they intended to see friends and family and dispose of her apartment there. Upon their arrival it was immediately clear to all of us that the expectant pair hoped to be ignored by the press and the public as much as possible. With Sally and John, Carolyn and Malcolm, Rita and Tom, Jay and me, Maree (when she came up from Philadelphia), and Bettina and Frank (when they came down from Dedham), as well as with a host of other friends, Grace and Rainier spent their New York holiday evenings exactly like any other comfortable young couple.

Grace gave dinners for six or eight people at her apartment, sometimes aided by a cook and a maid, sometimes not, but always served in the dining room. She and Rainier visited her friends' apartments, where they took off their shoes and ate sitting on the floor around the coffee table. On one such evening at the Reybolds', Grace was determined to initiate Rainier into our charades game. He took to it immediately, initially only brave enough to guess at others' pantomimes, then hurling himself into performing them for his teammates with such skill that he was forced to admit to us his childhood ambition to be on the stage.

At the start of the trip, many of Grace's daytime hours were absorbed with a job she regretted having to undertake—deciding how to dismantle her New York apartment. Some of her things were to be shipped to Europe, others sold, and a few "undecideds" stored at her parents' home in Germantown. Her friend Rupert Allan had left *Look* magazine and was working for our old friend Arthur Jacobs's public relations firm. Together, Rupert and Arthur were developing a proposal by which Arthur's company would represent the interests of the Sovereign Family and the Principality of Monaco. When Rupert saw how burdened Grace was with her tasks at the apartment, he suggested that she hire Phyllis Blum, a rangy Vassar graduate from Purchase, New York, who was working for Arthur, spoke fluent French, and was both bright and capable. Grace liked Phyllis the instant they met, engaged her immediately, and was freed to spend more of her afternoons with her friends.

Grace had lunch with each of us, alone and in small groups. Most of the lunches consisted of chicken sandwiches at home or at watering holes like the drugstore on the corner of Madison Avenue at Fifty-sixth Street, where you could see so many familiar faces grabbing a bite between meetings or errands that we had dubbed the place "little '21.' "

In early summer MCA told Jay and me that we were to move to California in the fall. A month later, when we learned we were expecting our second child, we decided to keep it a secret until our things were packed and on the trucks to the West Coast. On the day Bekins pulled away from our Sutton Place driveway, I was set to have lunch with Grace and Rita at Quo Vadis in the East Sixties. Later that evening we were all going to gather at MCA for a large going-away party being given for Jay and me. Before lunch Jay and I called our families (his parents in California, mine in Paris) to tell them they would be grandparents again early in 1957. Knowing Grace was pregnant, and having just heard from Rita that she was, too, I hurried off to meet my friends.

Once the three of us were seated, drinks in hand, Rita proposed a toast, "Here's to all of us being together often."

As we sipped our drinks Grace added, "And to one of us a mother already, and two of us about to be." I held up three fingers, but nothing registered. Then Grace's face lit up. "You're pregnant, too!" she exclaimed. When I said yes and told her I was due only a week or so after she was, Grace protested, "Oh, no, it's not possible. I popped in the middle months ago and you're not even wearing maternity clothes yet!"

Having opened up the subject, Grace, Rita and I bemoaned the dreadful selection of clothes for pregnant women available on both sides of the Atlantic. En route to New York, Grace and Rainier had stopped in Paris for a maternity wardrobe, but those things she bought she considered merely the least of several evils. Almost every maternity dress of the Fifties was a two-piece number featuring a straight skirt that expanded as you did because it had a front-and-center hole cut out of its middle large enough to accommodate a major melon. These skirts were tied to the waist by two strings that pulled together in opposite directions through a large cloth eye. In an era when even moderately priced clothing was quite well made, maternity outfits always looked as though they had been whipped up at home by a first-time student from the Singer Sewing Machine Center. Over the cutaway skirts, maternity designers hung tent-like tops in drab, serviceable colors made of fabrics that inevitably scratched.

Grace did tell Rita and me immediately about two dresses she had found at Lord & Taylor, one made of simple gray flannel, the other a black dress with good lines that worked well for dinner. Both, she told us, cost $39.95! I noted that, as ugly as they were, I was relieved that I could start wearing maternity clothes at my party that night and thankfully mentioned that I had found one really nice cocktail outfit. Grace added that she was planning to wear her "one good one" to the party, too.

When night fell, one hundred and fifty friends of Jay's and mine gathered in MCA's Georgian, salon-like conference room. A sudden hush among the guests signaled the arrival of Grace and Rainier, a hush followed by stunned murmurs as the guests whispered to one another under their breaths. Grace's hair fell loosely from a snug headband, making her look about fourteen years old. She wore a lovely (if two-piece) maternity dress made of pale cocoa lace over white taffeta. Her off-the-shoulder collar left her pale neck bared, and was trimmed with a four-inch-deep fichu of matching material. Grace looked like an angel. Her dress was perfect in every way except one. It was identical to mine! As everyone watched to see our reactions, Rainier, Jay, Grace and I collapsed with laughter. Leaning toward Gracie, I whispered, "The Bobbsey Twins Get Knocked Up!"

"What's fair's fair," countered Grace. "Since you wore *my* coat when *I* arrived in Monaco, I thought I'd wear *your* dress when *you* left New York!"

On one of those days before I left, Rita, Grace and I decided to run a few errands at Saks Fifth Avenue. We strolled down Madison Avenue almost without notice. Grace's hair was in a loose bob with no turban or scarf concealing it, but nobody stopped her or even gawked as we walked along chatting. Occasionally heads turned to look at Rita, but if they recognized Grace they left her in peace and walked briskly on.

Our final stop at Saks was the lingerie department. As the saleslady laid out selections for us on the counter, I could feel a small clump of people gathering behind us. Alone for a few moments while the saleswoman disappeared, we chatted on obliviously. When she returned, the clerk asked us to lean forward, cocking her finger as though she needed to share a secret. "Your Highness," she said to Grace, "I have to ask you and your friends to follow me into the stockroom, where you can complete your orders. By then we'll have a path cleared and some guards who can escort you down to a waiting taxi so you can get out without any problem." Our three heads spun around to see a crowd of about four hundred Saks shoppers who packed the floor on every side all the way back to the elevators. "It's worse downstairs," the clerk added, "and worse still on both of our side streets and along Fifth Avenue, too." By the time we were led to the cab, with a half-dozen guards protecting us, several thousand New Yorkers had stopped what they were doing at four in the afternoon to run to Saks for a peek at the Princess. Grace looked disappointed and not a little frightened, but it was Rita who spoke first about how uncomfortable she was in such situations.

"I'm usually all right about it," Grace chimed in. "I don't like it, but I guess I've gotten used to it. It's just that I so hoped none of this would happen here." She was silent for a moment, then she added, "Maybe it's being pregnant that makes it seem frightening. I want so to protect our baby from all that." This was the 1950s. We did not worry about maniacs in crowds with knives or guns; it wasn't physical safety that worried Grace for herself or her child. What she wanted to protect her baby from was an unnatural focus of public attention, a distortion of reality or of values, a skewed sense of self.

For the most part, though, Grace's trip to New York continued private and undisturbed. She and Rainier dined without interruption with friends at neighborhood restaurants all over the city. With the Reybolds, they enjoyed a thirty-two-course Chinese feast at the Pagoda in Chinatown, where forty-eight hours' notice was required for preparation and where Rainier was intrigued by his first exposure to melon soup. The following night Grace and Rainier told Jay, John Foreman and me all about it when we tried out a new Viennese restaurant on the Upper East Side. As we studied the menus and Grace asked her ever-present question, "A l'il chickie, Judybird?" Rainier, noting the amount of poultry she and

I had been consuming, cautioned, "When the two of you deliver your newborns, the babies won't cry, they'll cluck!"

During our dinner, when Grace was asked how her work with the apartment was coming, her eyes grew misty. It was clear that giving up 988 Fifth was a wrenching experience for Grace, though she never spoke openly about it. Rainier had mentioned earlier in their visit that they had thought about keeping the place for the annual trips they planned to make to New York. He had also alternatively proposed that they buy a townhouse. This would mean moving the Consulate of Monaco from its Rockefeller Center offices to the lower floors of the house, while the upper floors were used as their home-away-from-home. But at dinner, as Grace described which things were being shipped to the Palace, which could be used in Rainier's Paris apartment, and which would be placed in the new country home they hoped to acquire near the Principality, I realized for the first time that more than sentimentality was at work inside Grace. Grace had earned her Fifth Avenue apartment, working for it herself and earning everything in it. 988 Fifth represented Grace's independence, her professional accomplishment, her Americanism, her transition from being her parents' daughter in Philadelphia to her own woman in New York. That apartment was hers and hers alone. I wonder now if Grace had any idea that far back that almost nothing ever would be again.

On the last Sunday before Jay and I were to leave for California, we spent a long, lazy day with Grace, Rainier and the Reybolds at the Long Island home of Monaco's New York Consul, Marcel Palmero. Since we had sold our car before going west, Grace suggested we drive to the country together to meet the Reybolds, who were already on the Island. I expected to see a limousine, but when we arrived at Grace's building, the four of us piled into a rented green Chevy with Rainier driving.

In mid-afternoon, Grace, Carolyn and I took off for a long stroll around Marcel and Lucille's property, kicking at the russet- and mustard-colored leaves that had fallen to the ground so we could hear the sounds of them swooshing and crunching underfoot. We found a small pool of rainwater underneath a tree and stopped to toss pebbles into it. Grace had on her $39.95 Lord & Taylor gray flannel dress; mine was of the same material. The late-afternoon dampness pervaded both. Grace inhaled through her nose deeply. "There's something about the smell of gray flannel when it's this time of year, the smell of the leaves and the wet dirt, the colors and feeling of biting air that will remind me all my life of autumn and my childhood here on the East Coast. Oh, how I love it."

We stood listening as the pebbles we tossed clinked over rocks hidden in the khaki brown water. "It reminds me of the start of school," Carolyn noted.

"And of new school clothes and lunchboxes and pencil cases," I added.

"And of football games and dates with new boys and first kisses," Grace reflected sentimentally. "I'm going to miss autumn in New York," she added, and then realized she had just let us know—for the first time—that not everything in her life was perfect. After a moment of silence she asked, "Won't you miss it, too, Judybird?" I nodded, swallowing deeply. We started to walk again, occasionally stopping to pick up a leaf or a fallen twig. Though two of us were mothers already and two pregnant, we looked at that moment no older than we had been when we had rhapsodized, in three different states, about our first Tangee Natural lipsticks, sweater sets, dickeys and penny loafers, about who had asked us to the big game, or the Halloween carnival, or how early we would get our first invitation for New Year's Eve. Awash in the nostalgia of the paths we had already traveled, and the mystery of what might await us in new homes and new places, the three of us quietly rejoined the others.

On the drive back to town singing camp songs in the rented Chevy, I could not stop thinking about the transition so many of us were making. Changes had never seemed significant to me before. Like Grace, as a child I had grown accustomed to making friends, then having them move away or go off to boarding schools, colleges or jobs that separated us from one another. We accepted the fact that marriage often changed things, too. A husband's work dictated a couple's social life. My own life as an MCA company wife made that patently clear. I thought about how all our lives were taking shape. We would be living away from one another, and some of us away from New York, that wonderful town which had swept us all up together in its swirling vortex of dizzy distractions, hurtling us on to our next errands and our next dinners, promising us that just keeping up with the race was the route to eternal satisfaction.

We had all parted once before, only a few months ago in Monaco. And see how easily we had come together again? Surely it would be that easy the following year, or the year after that, or—perhaps—even before a whole year passed. In any case, we each had lives to get on with. And if Grace had time for us in her future, we would surely have time for her in ours.

Rita, Sally and Carolyn would be in New York when Grace and Rainier returned there with their firstborn the following summer. It had taken Rita only a few weeks to pull herself together after her wedding and Grace's so she could join her in-laws at their Long Island estate for the summer. Her winter would be spent in the city, apartment hunting, shopping for the baby, decorating the nursery, and delivering the newest scion for her husband's dynasty. By the following summer, Rita would be splashing in the Sound with her firstborn and hostessing luncheons on the terrace of the Guinzburg country home for her husband's friends and associates. I was sure she and Grace would see each other often.

Sally and Carolyn seemed like a package deal of Grace's—"The Barbizon Girls." Sally was remaining in the city and Carolyn was moving only a few miles away to suburban Lloyd Neck. From what I could see, there was to be no significant change in either of their lives that would interrupt their friendships with Grace.

There was not a doubt in my mind that Maree, Grace's oldest friend, would always be a part of Grace's life. They would see each other in Philadelphia on Grace's visits to her family there, and in the summer months at the Jersey shore, where Grace and Rainier had already promised to spend annual vacations with their child. Maree had not yet remarried, but I was certain that when she did it would be to someone who lived in Philadelphia. By then Maree seemed to me as indigenous to the City of Brotherly Love as the Liberty Bell.

Bettina's future relationship with Grace was less clear. I had first met Bettina as we were about to sail to Monaco. If she had not come to New York to see Grace in those pre-wedding years, would she make the trip more often when Grace came home from across the Atlantic? I had no idea of the answer, but suspected that Bettina would be the one of us who would have the least contact with Grace as time went on.

I was moving the farthest distance away. I could see no reason Grace would come to California. She had not liked Hollywood when she worked there and would now have no obligations forcing her to make the trip. But I fully expected to see her in New York, intending to time my trips with hers for this purpose. Having been bicoastal since the days of the *Super Chief* and the *Twentieth Century Limited,* I considered New York Hollywood-on-the-Atlantic and Beverly Hills Manhattan-on-the-Pacific. At the time the distance of my move seemed inconsequential. I was busy thinking about the baby I had, the one on the way, the rented home we had to settle into, the househunting for the one we would buy, and all the California friends I was looking forward to being with.

Had you asked me in those days to predict what would happen to us all in the coming decades, I would have guessed we would go on exactly as we were, only getting more settled, having more babies and more houses, and growing older. Most of us had been aching since our teenage years for premature matronhood, and we had gotten what we longed for.

Being so much more enlightened than our mothers and having married modern men, we were going to make happy marriages and be fulfilled wives. Like our mothers before us, we would be sure to entertain well and to quietly act out the role as the good woman behind the great man. With the perfect balance of humility and self-esteem, we would raise beautiful, healthy children. We would put something back into the world which had given us so much by working, without pay, for those less fortunate than we. We would keep old friends and make new ones, being sure to give more than we got. If life gave us the chance to be together again from time to time, that would make all of us happy. But as it was not polite to be greedy, we would learn to live without that if required. We were good girls growing into good women, so life would be good to us.

In this comforting spirit of bonhomie, I said goodbye to the other bridesmaids on the East Coast, wept buckets at my final embrace with Grace, and boarded a prop plane with Jay, Amy and our nanny for the eight-hour journey west, where I would begin life in a celluloid orange grove.

As a displaced New Yorker, I awoke to my first Beverly Hills Christmas morning thinking I had gone to Mars. Twenty-two-month-old Amy was tugging at my nightgown, impatient to open packages so we could rush to the swimming pool and frolic in the eighty-two-degree sunshine. While Amy rocked furiously on her new wooden horse, Jay placed a call to Grace.

She and Rainier had sent us a large pink and blue mohair blanket for our bed, and Amy a yellow smocked batiste dress. After thanks were exchanged, I apologized for not having answered her last two or three letters and promised to write soon.

As Grace was again complaining of fatigue, I expected that she would be taking it easy for Christmas, but not our Gracie! Every Monégasque child between the ages of three and twelve had received a personal invitation to a Christmas party at the Palace. The only adults present were Grace and Rainier. In four shifts, more than six hundred children were led to the Salle du Trône, where they were shown a movie, entertained by clowns and magicians, served refreshments, and handed an individual surprise gift. "They're so sweet," Grace exclaimed. "I look into every little face and try to figure out how to make each of them feel at ease and glad they came." I was later told it was the unhappy mission of a Palace cleaning crew to spend three hours washing the traces of sticky fingers off the antique furniture and the brocaded walls.

Before we hung up, Grace wanted to know where we were going to spend New Year's Eve. We told her about Annie and Charlie Lederer's biennial party just up the street from us. "Annie Lederer," Grace reflected. "Isn't she Anne Shirley, the actress?" When I said she was, Grace asked, "And I know Charlie Lederer is a wonderful screenwriter, but isn't he also someone's relative?" When we explained that he was, indeed, Marion Davies's nephew, Grace wanted to know all the details of the party. Though she was incredibly thrifty, Grace waited patiently on the costly overseas line while I fetched the Lederers' droll invitation in rhymed verse. Before we said goodbye, Grace made me promise to write her about every detail of the celebration.

Supporting Amy by the stomach as she kicked her little legs in the pool, I wondered about Grace's sudden avid interest in New Year's Eve in Hollywood. On her California visits, Grace had declined almost every invitation for this kind of socializing, so I thought she might have just

CHAPTER 8

Period of Adjustment

*W*hile Grace finished packing u
New York apartment, I unpacked in California away from my family,
reunions with old friends, and met new ones. Arriving in early Noven
I had almost three months to get our rented Bedford Drive home run
smoothly before my new baby was due.

With less than two months to go until their heir arrived, Grace
Rainier returned home to Monaco to find that the renovation and dec
tion of their nursery had hardly begun. Grace wrote me a hastily scribl
letter describing the disaster and bemoaning the fact that she had no
where to turn for help as she would have in New York. A few days l
another letter came. With great relief Grace wrote that she had loca
George Stacey (who had decorated her New York apartment and si
become a friend) in France, where he was doing a major renovation
an old castle for another American client. George had agreed to come
the rescue, and as Christmas neared, Grace wrote again and again,
scribing his innovative designs for shelving and toy storage space, and t
final selection of the perfect yellow, a color Grace adored, which wou
accommodate either the boy or the girl she expected within a month

been making small talk. Then it dawned on me that though Grace was the Princess of Monaco and had everything every young woman dreamed of having, she was just plain homesick at holiday time.

At three in the morning on January 1, 1957, rotating orchestras at the Lederers' kept the dance floor crowded and the party in full swing. My obstetrician and pediatrician both approached me to tell me they were going home, should I need them. And though my due date was still five to six weeks away, I was told that I had done more than enough lindying and Charlestoning to burn off the mounds of caviar I had devoured at the Wassermans' pre-Lederer gathering earlier that evening.

At the piano in the living room, I found Sol Chaplin playing while Danny Kaye and Groucho Marx tried to outdo each other recalling lyrics to old vaudeville songs. Danny invited me into the game, and with his arm around me we shouted out phrases, hoping to beat Groucho to the punch. A large snifter on the piano held rounded pretzels, in the shape of sour balls. I popped one into my mouth and before I could start to chew, felt it slide straight down into my windpipe. Danny saw I was choking and tried every way he knew to get me to cough. I continued to gasp for air in vain. Heimlich maneuvers were unknown in those days, and when I pointed to the powder room, Danny and Groucho supported me to its door. Once inside, with my finger down my throat, I retched violently, loosened the ball-shaped pretzel, and breathed just in the nick of time.

Someone went to get Jay, and as it was nearing four o'clock, we decided to leave. At our house, before I was completely undressed, I felt my throat still blocked and went to the bathroom to gag again. The retching was dry, but when I looked down I realized that was the only thing that was. The entire gray bathroom carpet was drenched with blood. I had torn the placenta loose when I choked and was hemorrhaging everywhere.

Jay called our obstetrician, who called an ambulance. On the ride to the hospital, I heard a medic tell Jay, "We may be able to save your wife, but there's little hope for the baby."

As Dr. Leon "Red" Krohn performed the emergency Caesarian, I watched the whole procedure mirrored on the glass of an overhead lighting fixture, praying hard until I heard someone say, "It's a girl," and redoubling my prayers until I heard the first tiny wail of life issue from her. Some hours later, when I woke again, I was told that my baby was born with hyaline membrane. In term births, this tissue automatically tears itself away from the lung, permitting the baby to shift smoothly from a liquid to an air environment. But in babies as premature as mine, the membrane often would not come dislodged. Victoria Kanter weighed four pounds twelve ounces and was being closely monitored in an incubator. Either she would pass the membrane within thirty-six hours and live with no residual effects, or she would die. I lost consciousness again but awoke in only two hours' time to be told the God-sent news that the membrane was a thing of the past.

Within a few hours, flowers and a telegram arrived from Grace and Rainier, and the following morning I woke to Grace's sweet voice on the phone. Though she jokingly complained that her first baby was supposed to have been older than my second one, I realized that the story of Vicki's birth might have scared her, with her own delivery so near at hand. Reassuringly I noted, "I tell you, Gracie, we're lucky to be having children in this era. If they can save the baby and the mother in a situation like mine, it's proof that modern obstetrics can do anything!"

"Yes," replied Grace, rather unconvincingly. And for a moment, I remembered that she was having her first child in a country where a physician had stuck an emery board down my throat nine months earlier. She was to give birth in the library of the Palace apartment, which was being converted for the occasion into a temporary delivery room. Perhaps because I was so vulnerable myself, it was one of the few times in those early years when I realized deeply that Grace had left every significant familiar and reassuring thing behind on the day she moved to Monaco.

Grace's mother flew to the Principality after the New Year. Ma Kelly was not the only foreigner to arrive for the event. Once again, the press descended on Monaco. As with the wedding, it was not society reporters who came, but top-rated journalists from the world's major publications and broadcast media. More than two hundred and fifty of them gathered.

This time, though, unlike the wedding, the attention did not disturb Grace and Rainier's happy hour. Rainier busied himself with the complex and pressing matters of government, while Grace shared the last days of her confinement with her mother. On January 23, 1957, without anesthetic, Grace went into normal labor. She gave birth to a beautiful eight-pound eleven-ounce daughter named Caroline Louise Marguerite—and to the continuing rule of her husband's sovereignty. Within the week she was flooding the transatlantic mail with thick envelopes containing elaborate descriptions of her *Wunderkind* and dozens of snapshots.

Within the next two years Rita gave birth to Kate Guinzburg (July 1957) and Mike Guinzburg (September 1958); Sally delivered her second son, Hunt Richardson (January 1959); Carolyn had her third daughter, Nyna (November 1959); and Grace had another eight-pound eleven-ounce baby, who, because he was a beautiful blond boy named Albert Alexandre Louis Pierre, Marquis des Beaux, immediately assumed his fourteen-month-old sister's right to sit upon their family throne.

The bride and her bridesmaids had gone from a count totaling seven children at the time of the 1956 wedding to fourteen, or double, by the end of 1959. A few months later Maree, who had married Philadelphia stockbroker Joseph ("Bud") Rambo in 1958, brought the count up by one more when she gave birth to Louise, her second daughter, in 1960. It ought to tell you a lot about what we were doing in those years, and in some ways it does, but in other ways it misses things—things we might have been missing ourselves.

Rita and Tom and their two children spent the winters in their spacious new East Sixty-fourth Street apartment. When the warm June weather came and the senior Guinzburgs departed for Europe, they left their Locust Valley estate in what Rita felt were her most incapable hands. Rita's kindly stepfather, Ben Gam, died of cancer (a disease we did not mention out loud) in 1957, leaving Rita once again fatherless as she had been when Milton McKay plummeted from an uptown hotel window so many years earlier.

Rita's marriage to Tom was stagnating. She was no longer certain what she had seen in Tom, and couldn't figure out why he had married her. If it was for her beauty and her fame, she would keep them intact, in spite of the fact that, in her opinion, movie stardom had derailed her ability to grow in any real way. Wondering what she really knew how to do besides act, Rita decided to bring some of her theatrical talent to her marriage. She had a knack, she knew, for casting. So she began to throw parties, casting them as she would plays, and developed a reputation as a successful young hostess in Manhattan literary, artistic and social circles. She never let that talent go dead on her, but barged ahead, performing vigorously for the outside world while inside wondering if Tom could not just as easily have hired a social secretary as married a wife.

In those early years after Grace got married, the only times Rita felt fulfilled were when she was carrying Kate and Mike. But Mrs. Guinzburg had a busy social schedule and a career as well as two children, so she hired a full-time governess the way others in her group were doing. Kate and Mike were now someone else's charges. When a day came without an acting job, volunteer work or a party to plan, Rita Gam Guinzburg felt that she was nobody.

Unaware of actually missing Grace, Rita found herself treasuring the long letters they wrote back and forth. Neither of them complained, but Rita got used to reading between the lines of Grace's offhand comments and hoping Grace was able to do the same with her. It gradually dawned on Rita, when she visited with Grace on her early New York trips, that her friend felt very isolated in Monaco. Grace did not speak of problems, only of her challenges and the methods she had chosen to meet and conquer them. Rita began to feel that Grace needed an audience for her life and Rita was glad to serve as a claque of one.

Knowing that New York represented the glamour Grace had sought when she fled from the more provincial Philadelphia, Rita resolved to keep New York alive for Grace by sending little Manhattan memory gifts to Monaco. From a midtown Madison Avenue hosiery store, she'd ship a half-dozen pairs of size 9½ nylons in Grace's favorite go-with-everything neutral shade. Farther uptown, Rita would see a particularly pretty needle-point canvas and send it along for Grace to stitch with a note and suggestions for color changes.

If Rita had questions that she tried hard to keep inside, such was not the problem for Sally. Though she had live-in help, Sally spent most of her children's waking pre-school hours with them. She and John had established a pattern for their lives, and Sally had no wish to see it interrupted. She questioned little and readily accepted that the answers to anything she might ask had already been provided for her in her developing years. Grace and Sally wrote regularly, and spent time together whenever Grace was in New York.

The other one of the New York Barbizon Girls, Carolyn, aware from the start of the discrepancy in their backgrounds, was not that secure in her relationship with Grace. Even their early careers had seemed skewed to Carolyn. As an actress Grace spoke lines and expressed herself, and as her success grew, so did the spread of her name. Carolyn, though, felt herself to be the uncredited silent rack on which they hung the clothes, the shelf on which they rested the soap flakes, the prop in a product sale.

As Grace's stardom grew, Carolyn came more and more to idolize her. In Carolyn's eyes, as in many of ours, Grace was the master at doing the right thing. The better Grace got at this, the more Carolyn believed that she herself was an inadequate reflection of her friend. Carolyn believed it was her responsibility not to embarrass Grace in any way. To be honest, by the time Grace won the Academy Award and became a princess, several of Grace's friends shared some of this feeling. Part of it came from our own sense of inadequacy, but another part came from a look we all knew, a look that every now and then passed across Grace's face. It was a look that suggested Grace disapproved of you. As time went by, no matter how often Grace reaffirmed her close feeling to her, Carolyn became convinced she had somehow betrayed Grace's trust by her own social ineptitude. She had seen *the look* too many times.

There had been a night years earlier, in Grace's pre-Oscar days, when Carolyn and Malcolm had accompanied Grace and Oleg Cassini to the theatre. Both young women wore off-the-shoulder, Ceil Chapman cocktail dresses and small fur stoles. Before curtain time, photographers had spotted Grace standing under the marquee chatting with Oleg and Carolyn, and had swept in to capture the young group for the morning papers. The following day Grace got the pictures, and that night she brought two or three shots to the Reybolds' apartment when she came for dinner. As Carolyn studied them, she thought she heard Grace mutter, "They take all the bows without making the pictures." Even though they were friends, Carolyn neither asked Grace to repeat her comment nor requested an explanation. She just presumed Grace was telling her that she did not belong in the photo, that Grace had made the movies and Carolyn was taking the bows. Nothing more was said, but Carolyn began to feel the white hot stab of guilt. She told herself she should have gotten out of the way so it would be Grace's publicity alone. She accused herself of trying to upstage Grace, even though a part of her knew it was her model's reflex to stand still and smile when a flashbulb went off. Carolyn resolved, in the future, to walk behind Grace and out of her limelight—to know her place.

Once she had relegated herself to second-class citizenship with Grace, things grew worse. Several years earlier on her first visit to El Morocco,

Carolyn had seen a girl wearing a forest green strapless dress with a wide cuff across the chest. She had always wanted to find a dress in that style. During the height of Grace's stardom, Carolyn found just such a dress in maroon. She also found antique maroon glass jewelry to go with it.

On the night Carolyn planned to wear the dress, for the premiere of one of Grace's movies, Grace came by her apartment to see the children. Excitedly, Carolyn showed her the dress. Grace said nothing, but Carolyn was suddenly sure she had seen *the look*. Again she was inflamed with guilt, realizing that her maroon dress had the same strapless neckline as the pale blue satin dress that Edith Head had designed for Grace to wear when she won her Oscar. "I don't blame her for being annoyed," Carolyn thought. "It was her dress for the most special occasion of her life—the Academy Awards. And here I've gone and gotten a cheap copy without thinking of what that would mean to her."

With clothes and parties seeming so significant to us, Carolyn's self-perceived gaffes compounded themselves on the night before we all left for Monaco. Grace had bought Chinese brocaded fabric and had two or three cheongsams made around the time that she filmed *Bridges at Toko-Ri*. Many other young and fashionable women in New York had added one or two similar dresses to their cocktail party wardrobes. And Carolyn had found one for herself in pale beige with embroidered turquoise threads.

On the afternoon of the Palmeros' pre-sailing party, Carolyn and Sally were on the phone and Sally asked, "What time are you going to the Palmeros'?"

Trying to work, care for her children, and get ready for her trip, Carolyn was confused by the welter of plans and receptions. "I don't think we've been invited," she told Sally. But Sally insisted they must have been and told Carolyn she and Malcolm had better go. She hastily decided to wear her ivory and turquoise cheongsam.

Arriving at the Palmeros' early, for a small private pre-reception drink, Carolyn noticed that every single woman in the room but her was wearing black. Shaken to feel that she alone was standing out in her pale Chinese dress, she thought she heard Grace say, "*Well,* I see the *Reybolds* got here." And at that moment Carolyn felt sure that she and Malcolm had not been invited and were crashers at the party. She wanted to flee, removing both her wrong dress and her uninvited self from Grace's vision.

But she decided it was more embarrassing to leave and forced herself to stay. It grew only worse when the throng of other guests arrived, and the room filled with more women, all in black dresses.

If these incidents were not already proof to Carolyn that she had destroyed her friendship with Grace, her agreement to be flown to the wedding in exchange for an appearance on the *Home* show cemented the conviction. The Kellys were only paying for our bridesmaids' dresses and hats. So when Grace asked us to attend her, each of us had to find a way to finance the cost of travel, hotel and other expenses. Some of us borrowed from our parents; others simply wrote out the necessary checks. But the Reybolds—with two children, Malcolm's long illness, medical bills and a new job—had nowhere to turn. Carolyn thought Grace might understand this and realize that without the NBC trade-off, Carolyn could not have gone to Monaco or been in the wedding.

When Carolyn asked Grace to approve her *Home* show dates, she felt Grace was annoyed. NBC wanted Carolyn to appear in her bridesmaids' dress. Grace said no. About the appearance itself, Grace was cool. And though it was clear to Carolyn that Grace didn't like the idea, when she finally gave her consent Carolyn had no choice but to go ahead. By the time of the wedding, Carolyn felt she had damaged the friendship.

I cannot imagine any of this was as Carolyn perceived it, except for the *Home* show incident. The instant Grace had become engaged to Rainier, she was obsessed with fear that those close to her might be capitalizing on them and the fame of their union. Her mother's indiscreet pre-wedding syndicated newspaper interview had proved to her that the enemy could be anywhere. Carolyn's appearance on the *Home* show commercialized the wedding even more, and it embarrassed and displeased Grace. We never discussed it but I'm sure that's true, sure because of what happened with her old and very dear friend Gant Gaither's book.

Gant told Grace that he was going to write a book about the crossing to Monaco and the wedding—a chronicle that would give some background on Grace before she met Rainier and describe the days from the time of their meeting until their honeymoon trip. Grace was usually very supportive of her friends and any projects they initiated. It was a facet of her unshakable loyalty. But she was nervous about Gant's book. She made him promise to send her and Rainier a manuscript so they could make deletions, additions or other changes. When Gant sent the material, it arrived in galley form close to Christmas and Caroline's birth. Grace and Rainier were given only a short time to read it, and extensive corrections were no longer possible.

Published in mid-1957, *Princess of Monaco* was a sweet book, filled with nice stories and anecdotes from a friend who had been present during the period he wrote about. There were a few errors, but they were the kind that come from misguided hearsay or the inability to find people with whom to check facts. Not one sentence in Gant's tribute should have offended anyone, yet the newlyweds were extremely distressed by it. Rumor held that Rainier was the angrier of the two, but it fell to Grace to lower the boom on Gant, and lower it she did. He who had been so close was stricken summarily from Grace's list. It is hard to say how it was possible for a person as loyal as Grace to have taken such a course of action with a friend over so inconsequential a matter. To be fair, I should add that, after some years, Gant and Grace were reconciled, and that the reconciliation was so strong and so complete that Gant became like a member of Grace's Monégasque family; that her children grew up close to him; that for years he visited twice annually at the Palace and continues to make those trips even now, long after Grace's death; and that it would be impossible—if you had seen them all together—to believe that Gant had ever been banished. But banished he was. And banished by Grace. Unlike the subtle comments or grimaces Carolyn thought she heard or felt, Gant's fall from Grace resounded on both sides of the ocean.

It was the first visible symptom of a disease Grace caught almost the moment she got to Monaco. It was called royalism. And though it accredited her stature, it unsettled her friends, angered her detractors, and annexed her time. As a world-renowned movie star, she had already learned to live in the limelight. As a princess, appearances became even more important. Grace felt an obligation to control not only herself but those close to her in order to avoid embarrassments.

Prince Michael of Greece once said, " . . . learning to be a prince isn't something you get taught in a class. You learn it every day, drop by drop, like getting an injection." Grace realized she had not been given daily injections of monarchy since childhood. Anxious to please and be accepted in her roles as wife, mother and princess, she began to overcompensate for her lack of formal training. Contracting royalism did not make her snobbish. It made her nervous and, for the first time since she had become an adult, not entirely true to herself. Carolyn could see none of this, though. To her, as to the rest of us, Grace made her life as a princess seem like the fairy tale we wanted and needed it to be.

In 1958 Carolyn wrote Grace to tell her that she and Malcolm had moved to Rose Cottage, the guesthouse on the Long Island Colgate estate. This would allow them to supervise, at close range, the building of their home, which was near to Sherman Fairchild, on the water and up a lovely, long six-hundred-foot driveway. In the country, away from the daily bustle and distractions of the city pace and the city streets, Carolyn began to grow more introspective. She had planned to commute to the city to model, meet friends or join Malcolm in the evenings, but the house, the children and the logistics of suburban living made this impossible. On weekends she accompanied Malcolm to the customary gatherings at Sherman's place, but during the week she found herself isolated and friendless. As she thought more about Grace and the presumed perfection of her current life, Carolyn grew to feel less and less worthy of their original bond.

Bettina, who had written Grace off once before, immediately after her own marriage to Frank and her move to Massachusetts, wrote her off again. Having moved every two years during her childhood, Bettina wrote people off easily and got on with things. She could see absolutely nothing in her life which bore any similarity to the life Grace was leading. Bettina knew that when they had separated earlier, Grace had maintained the friendship. She remembered Grace coming up to Belmont with Oleg Cassini for her goddaughter Lizzie's christening, and a later visit Grace had made when the two chatted late into the night on Bettina's bed until Frank had interrupted them by announcing, "I'm probably the only man who ever kicked Grace Kelly out of his bedroom, but I've got to get some sleep!" Bettina now assumed that such intimacy had come to an end.

Bettina was wonderfully happy with her own life. With no territory of her own, she slid joyously into her husband's milieu. She joined her sister-in-law Dinnie Gray on the Patient Care Committee at the Cox Center for cancer treatment. Though they were not her strong suits, at work Bettina was obligated to use a great deal of patience and diplomacy. At home, it was Bettina who blew up fast and Frank who kept things inside.

Bettina herself had always been curious and encouraged her daughter

Lizzie's relentless curiosity when it became evident at a young age. Sam was Mr. Mellow, but Lizzie was enough to keep a dozen of the world's best mothers hopping. Lizzie devoured books and ideas like a high-speed Electrolux. First it was the pre-school books that Bettina read to her, but Lizzie learned to read to herself before school, and that only increased her appetite for ideas. If there was ever an elementary school child being tailor-made for the Sixties, Lizzie Gray was that child.

Grace wrote regularly to Bettina, but Bettina rarely wrote back. When she did, her letters were perfunctory. Grace kept writing about future visits Bettina might make to Monaco, but Bettina recoiled at the thought. Why subject herself to anything so uncomfortable? "I'd do something gauche," she told herself, "wear the wrong clothes, won't have the right shoes."

Married to Bud, Maree settled into a life in Philadelphia that was exactly what life in Philadelphia had always been for her. When the two had met, Bud was a widower, a devastated man who had lost not only his wife, but the year before that an adored daughter to leukemia. Left alone with his surviving fifteen-year-old, Wendy, Bud was exactly the kind of cause a girl like Maree (or any of us for that matter) could really sink her teeth into. Maree fell in love, put on her white cap, climbed onto her cross, and dutifully joined the rest of us in the dual lifetime career to which we had all pledged ourselves: nurse/savior.

We were, every last one of us, firm in our shared belief that our job in life was to make some man happy. We accepted this as the mission of marriage. We realized that men, raised by fathers not unlike our own, did not show their feelings much. Certain that this deprived them of life's greatest moments, we had all duly registered for round-the-clock shifts in which we could cure them of this ill. We would pry from our husbands, albeit gently, their innermost thoughts and feelings, proving that we could be trusted as the vessels that would privately and lovingly contain the doubts, fears, hopes and dreams they had never been able to share with one another.

As wives, we would not only be sexy, romantic and efficient, we would also be the mothers and fathers their own parents had been unable to be. We would not demand their respect; we would earn it. We would allow our husbands to fail and love them nonetheless. We would never take credit for their successes, not even when we had played a significant part in their achievement. Under no circumstances would we betray our husbands, neither to themselves nor to anyone else. We would gratefully accept their financial support, inevitably supporting their own self-acceptance. We would not harbor secret yens, much less public ones, for any other man because when we had said "I do" what we had meant was "I do hereby dedicate the sum total of my sexuality to you for the remainder of my days on earth." We had all seen too many Grace Kelly movies.

The only thing that we were vehemently unwilling to do was to name what we expected in return. In an era of secrets, the best-kept secret in town—whether in New York, Lloyd Neck, Dedham, Philadelphia, Beverly Hills or Monaco-Ville—was that we expected our husbands to give back to us exactly what we were giving to them.

It was the ultimate fantasy to believe that we, who could not even truly be intimate with one another, would be able to be intimate with our husbands. We posed constantly for one another, wearing our bravery and selflessness like medals on our cocktail dresses, while deep in our hearts we entertained the notion that not other women, but our very own husbands, would one day become our best friends. To set the stage for this scenario, we began doing what you do when you buy war bonds or give blood—we gave until it hurt.

Maree gave at home and at her version of "the office," Chestnut Hill Hospital and the ASPCA. And while her husband, like ours, did real work in a real office, Maree, like the rest of us, found in her ever-increasing number of children infinite opportunities to perfect her skills for "Giving 101."

Grace wrote Maree often. From these communications and the hours they spent together on Grace's trips to the States, Maree found Grace engulfed in motherhood. To her, it seemed that Grace wanted more children, and then more again.

Letters, phone calls and trips, however, were not enough to fill the gaping hole in Grace's life. Parted from her closest friends, her mother and her sisters, Grace sought and found replacements in Monaco. Two of the women to whom she grew close were already in Monaco when she married Rainier; the third was an import.

Tall, heavyset and handsome, Milica (pronounced "Militza") Banek was the widow of a Yugoslavian shipping magnate so powerful that the economic fortunes of his country rose and fell, dependent upon the affairs of his various companies. During her husband's life Milica had run both their Dubrovnic townhouse and their glorious seaside home, giving huge and grand parties but remaining an unknown and not terribly interesting quantity to their friends. But Milica had emerged from her shroud of mourning like a butterfly emerging from a cocoon. Almost immediately after her husband died she became known as "the outgoing Milica," "the amusing Milica," "the charismatic Milica," a woman of enormous presence.

During World War II, Milica had whisked her family out of Europe to the safety of New York, where she lived for nine and a half years. She fully expected to become a U.S. citizen when she completed the required ten-year stay, but at war's end, on what was supposed to be a brief trip to the Côte d'Azur, she fell in love with Monaco and settled there instead. Almost immediately after her arrival, she met Rainier's father, Prince Pierre, and fell promptly and madly in love with him, too. Though he did not return the compliment, Pierre, Milica and Rainier became fast friends.

Milica and Grace clicked instantly, beginning a relationship in which Milica played the roles of friend, mother, social mentor and confidante. Milica was nearly seventy when they met. Grace immediately recognized her loyalty to Rainier and Pierre, and her sophisticated comprehension of Monégasque and other European ways of life. In these difficult years of adjustment, Grace entrusted Milica with the thoughts and feelings she could not even share with her longtime American friends. Being wiser and older, Milica did not need Grace to be as perfect as so many of us needed her to be.

A second older woman, the exiled Russian Princess Ania Chervachidze, became Grace's friend, confidante and party playmate. Her personal history was sprinkled with names of czars and other Russian aristocrats, revered artists such as Vladimir Horowitz, and famous, titled, talented and accomplished friends from one corner of the world to the other. Like Milica, Ania was sweet, supportive and trustworthy. But if Milica was the port, a safe harbor for Grace, then Ania was the unexpected wind that blew across it. In her lovely home high above the Monte Carlo Beach Club, Ania hosted luncheons, dinners and all manner of entertainments to keep her friend, the American-born Princess, amused.

The youngest member of Grace's new triumvirate, and the only import, was Phyllis Blum, who had helped Grace dismantle her New York apartment. In 1958 Grace found herself in need of a good secretary. Rupert Allan mentioned that Phyllis was eager to return to Europe, where she had worked for a while after college, and Grace immediately contacted her to make the necessary arrangements. Though Grace had a marvelous ear and thus a fine French accent, Phyllis had a far better command of the language, which would stand her in good stead in her new position.

Very soon after Phyllis's arrival in Monaco, it became clear that she and Grace would be friends. They were, after all, two young, contemporary American women. Phyllis was bright and witty, a nonstop talker. And Phyllis had no axe to grind, neither wanting nor expecting any other job at the Palais Princier than the one she had signed on for. For a time, Phyllis kept a respectful distance from Grace. Her humor and her penchant for practical jokes were shared first with Maureen King, the children's governess.

Maureen ("Killer") King had come to the Palace as governess for Caroline at the time Albert was born. Over the years she became a Grimaldi family fixture. The very humor that drew her and Phyllis together also brought her close to Grace and to Rainier, who had named her "Killer" in reference to her hardy appetite. Grace and Rainier had both determined that younger women, rather than older spinster ladies, would be better able to help them raise their children, and Maureen's fun-loving, affectionate yet disciplined approach to life was exactly the combination they'd hoped for. Then, too, Maureen's English childhood and amazing command of French made her able to assure that the children would be raised bilingually.

Grace and Phyllis immediately fell in step with each other, but their American stride made them, at times, seem out of step with the Palace and the Principality. Grace now sat as Vice President of Monaco's Red Cross. When a meeting was called, she and Phyllis would arm themselves with pads, files and memos, expecting to launch into the business at hand at the start of the meeting. But the Monégasques anticipated a more social and perfunctory role for their Princess. Together, Grace and Phyllis gradually taught themselves to curtail their efficiency, realizing they could only become more productive by appearing to be less adept. It was not an unfamiliar game to us, the women of that time, but the rules under which it was played were worse for Grace than for the rest of us.

In early years, Grace did some of her holiday shopping in the States. To the real presents she and Rainier gave to key staff members, she added amusing or whimsical little extras she believed would be fun to open and own. One personal maid who received a comically shaped cake of soap fled in tears, thinking Grace was implying she had body odor. And when Madge Tivey Faucon, Grace's Lady-in-Waiting, opened a zany-looking, multicolored feather duster, its humor escaped her completely. Enraged, Tiv decided Grace had embarrassed her by sending a message to the whole staff that her status was no more elevated than that of a chambermaid.

The President of France, Charles de Gaulle, held much of Monaco's future in his enormous hands. In order to prepare for her and Rainier's first state visit with him, Grace studied every detail of his recently published war memoirs, and reviewed hundreds of years of French and Monégasque history. Like a senior in high school, she stayed up nights cramming as if for a critical exam, plagued by anxiety about the coming trip and one of her frequent head colds.

When she and Rainier arrived at the Elysée Palace, so many flashbulbs popped that Grace was temporarily blinded. She feared this and her nearsightedness would result in her walking into a wall. Writing about her panic, she said she could only think, "Thanks, Grace. There go Franco-Monégasque relations!" But she headed for the tallest outline she could see ahead of her, praying it would be De Gaulle, and her prayers were answered. Like many a lesser man, the General was enchanted by Grace. When the trip concluded, *France-Dimanche* paid her the perfect compliment by reporting, ". . . the victory of a wife who has succeeded . . . in raising her husband ever higher, the victory of a princess who had contributed to reaffirm the prestige of her prince." At that point in her life, Grace wanted no attention paid to her accomplishments on her own behalf. The only tributes she hoped to attract were those for a good wife, a good mother and—because it came with the territory—a good princess. After De Gaulle, Grace felt as proud as a child who has performed well at her first recital.

When it came to the children, though Grace read all the books on child care, she and Rainier put them away in order to play parenthood

1937, Ocean City, New Jersey. Little Gracie, the middle daughter, practices her balancing act between her dad and Lizanne (left) and her mom and Peggy (right).

1951, New York City. The youngest of three, I get all the goodies . . . here with Montgomery Clift at the premiere of A *Place in the Sun.*

1949, Palisades Park, New Jersey. Carolyn Scott, leaving her teens, gets a new family: older husband, Malcolm, and twelve-year-old stepdaughter, Patricia.

Stills from some of Grace's films:

1952. With Gary Cooper in *High Noon*.

1953. With Clark Gable in *Mogambo*.

1954. With Ray Milland
in *Dial M for Murder*.

1954. With James Stewart
in *Rear Window*.

1954. With William Holden
in *The Country Girl*.

1955. With Cary Grant in *To Catch a Thief*.

1956. With Frank Sinatra in *High Society*.

1956. With Bing Crosby in *High Society*.

1955, Hollywood, Academy Awards night. They won! Jay's clients and our best friends, Gracie and Marlon: Best Actress and Best Actor of the Year.

April 15, 1953, New York City. Lifelong friendships. I meet Grace and marry Jay Kanter, all on the same night.

1954, New York City. Malcolm Reybold, Oleg Cassini and Carolyn Reybold share Grace's lime-light at a Broadway opening night.

1954, Hollywood cocktail party. Rita Gam and Grace, movie star room-mates holding the wolves at bay.

May 6, 1955, the Princely Palace of Monaco. Your Highness, may I present Miss Kelly in the dreaded taffeta dress?

June 1955, Philadelphia. Standing between her sisters, Peggy Kelly Davis and Lizanne, the younger bride, Gracie wonders if she'll be "always a bridesmaid, never the bride."

January 5, 1956, Philadelphia. Rainier looks on modestly as Grace's parents admire her ruby and diamond engagement ring, which was replaced soon after by an enormous emerald-cut solitaire.

Same day, same place. Even with the press present, a little nuzzle from Gracie cheers the Prince.

Later Rainier joins the Kelly clan for a press announcement of his engagement to Grace.

January 6, 1956, New York City. Grace and Rainier make their first public appearance as fiancés at a charity ball at the Waldorf Astoria.

Aboard the U.S.S. *Constitution:*

April 4, 1956, New York City. Grace smiles happily at a pre-sailing press conference, a moment before photographers stampede her.

Peggy, Gracie, Bettina and I take a morning "constitutional."

Top: Clockwise, Bettina Gray and Gant
Gaither (backs to camera), Morgan Hudgins
(standing), Peggy, Grace, Frank Gray, me.

Center: Gracie and Oliver hold lifeboat drill
with the press.

Pa Kelly with Grace's older sister, Peggy, his
adored "Ba."

Nighttime, below decks on the *Constitution:*

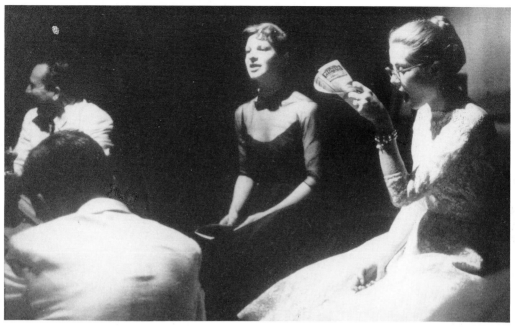

Grace and I lead a sing-along.

Maree lounges languorously.

Dottie Sitley, Donald Buka, Gant,
Gracie, Bettina, Ralph Sitley and I tell
jokes in the bar.

Gant and Gracie laugh at my Louella Parsons impersonation.

Gracie (next to her dad) demands quiet in order to concentrate on her teammate's charade.

Gracie pleads with Jay for a better clue—she really wants to win.

April 12, 1956, the *Deo Juvante*, outside Monte Carlo's harbor. Gracie waves as Rainier guides his yacht and his fiancée toward her new homeland.

Same day, thirty minutes later. Attention please! Grace, Oliver and the infamous white hat land in Monaco.

April 16, 1956, the Cathedral, Monaco. Grace holds her wedding rehearsal notes as she, Rainier and the rest of us await instructions.

April 17, 1956, afternoon, Palace Court of Honor. Grace and Rainier at a reception to thank Monaco's citizens and its elected officials for the gifts of diamond jewelry to Grace and a Rolls-Royce to Grace and Rainier.

April 18, 1956, Palace Throne Room. Halfway married at the civil ceremony.

Did Grace know in 1955 (above) that she'd be back in 1956 (below), mistress of all she surveyed?

The bride holds Sally's hand . . .

. . . and adjusts Carolyn's hat.

Hail, hail, the gang's all here! Back row, left to right: Peggy, Carolyn, Maree, Grace, Sally, Bettina, Rita, me. Front row, left to right: Peggy's daughters, Meg and Mary Lee, Sebastian Von Furstenberg, and Tiny's kids, Christine, Elisabeth and Christian (Baby, Bitsy and Buddy).

Here comes the bride, with her father and *"Les Dames d'Honneur,"* heading on foot to the Cathedral.

And here comes the groom.

April 19, 1956, the Cathedral of St. Nicholas. A solemn moment of love and dedication at the altar.

Same day, outside the Cathedral. The newlyweds en route to their car and the post-wedding motorcade through the Principality. The rest of us follow.

Same day, the Palace balcony. The bride and groom acknowledge the congratulatory cheers of thousands waiting in the Palace square below.

Kellys and Grimaldis united. Left to right: Kell, Pa Kelly, Ma, Grace, Rainier, Princess Charlotte, Prince Pierre, Princess Antoinette (Rainier's sister Tiny).

We take turns at the bridal table—here it's Carolyn and Sally with Rita, Bettina, Maree and me awaiting our turns.

The wedding luncheon. The bride and groom with his father and her mother.

Rushing off to change for their honeymoon—at last!

Same day, boarding the *Deo Juvante*. Grace, Rainier and Oliver leave on their honeymoon cruise.

1957, the Palace. Rainier, Grace and even baby Caroline dress up for an official portrait.

October 13, 1959, Elysée Palace, Paris. Grace has just conquered President Charles de Gaulle at a dinner he hosted to honor her and Rainier.

1960s. Rainier checks out Grace's gown, amusing her as well as President and Mrs. Giovanni Gronchi of Italy.

For Monaco's first family, family comes first:

November 1958, Philadelphia. Three generations of Kellys share Thanksgiving Day at the house on Henry Avenue. Grace and Rainier are at the right.

1958, Monaco. Albie wears a stocking cap, Grace one of her many hair-concealing hats, Rainier his uniform, and Caroline the traditional costume as they pose for photos on the Monégasque national holiday.

1960, at sea. A little filial affection between Albert and Caroline goes a long way, especially in grass skirts on a cruise.

August 15, 1963, London airport. To protect their children and Monaco, Grace flies with Albie while Rainier and Caroline travel on a separate plane when the family spends a sentimental holiday in Ireland.

February 1965, Monaco. Albert checks out newborn sister Stephanie as Caroline checks him out and their parents watch lovingly over all three kids.

1977, Roc Agel. My how you've grown— Albert, Stephanie and Caroline on a haystack at the family's country home.

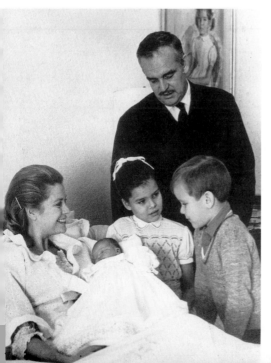

Where did the time go?

1969, the Palace. Only yesterday, it was easy to assemble the kids for family photos.

December 24, 1971. Or for the annual passing out of Christmas gifts to Monaco's children.

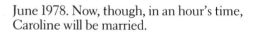
June 1978. Now, though, in an hour's time, Caroline will be married.

1968, Monaco. Ari Onassis and Grace at one of many galas.

1969, Monaco. Sophia Loren and Grace at a costume ball, with Sophia's husband, Carlo Ponti, in the background.

August 1969, Monaco. At the Red Cross Gala, Grace is joined by (left to right) pals David Niven, Maria Callas and Rainier's cousin Prince Louis de Polignac.

December 7, 1978, Monaco. Grace chats with Cary Grant, who visited annually for the Circus Festival (Cary's and Rainier's favorite event).

1977, the Palace. Don photographs Grace "scrying" into her crystal ball as we visit by the pool.

Mid-1970s. Carolyn, Robin and Jyl Reybold sharing Christmas on Long Island.

1970s. Rita Gam, actress/author/ documentary filmmaker.

1981. Don and I on a rare beach weekend in Europe.

1980s. Maree Rambo grabs a few quiet moments by herself.

August 1982, the Palace. Grace with Bettina (left) and Vera Maxwell, one month before the accident.

1981, London. Lady Di, on her first night out after her engagement was announced, visits with Grace and Prince Charles at one of Grace's poetry readings.

February 1980, Gstaad, Switzerland. Grace and Caroline catch some sun at the family chalet, where all have gathered to celebrate Stephanie's fifteenth birthday.

January 3, 1982, Gstaad. The day after Grace wrote me the last letter I ever got from her, she, Rainier and Stephanie (now almost seventeen) walk the dog in snow country.

August 1982. Grace beams, Albert "mugs" as they dance on a cruise ship in Scandinavian waters.

July 1982, Monaco. In the gardens she loved so well, Grace joins Rainier for the last official photo ever taken of them.

September 18, 1982, the Cathedral, Monaco. A day of infinite sadness. Grace's beloved Caroline, Rainier and Albert at her funeral Mass.

October 14, 1982, Monaco. One month after the accident, her neck still in a brace, Stephanie joins her father, sister and brother for a memorial service at the Cathedral.

January 1983, Chateau Marchais, France. One month after their official mourning period has ended, Steph, Albie, Caroline and Rainier try to lighten their loss with shared laughter.

October 19, 1988, Beverly Hilton Hotel. Don and I at the Princess Grace Foundation-U.S.A. Special Gala Tribute to Cary Grant.

Same night, same place. Back row, left to right: Michael Caine, Eva Marie Saint, Robert J. Hausman, Gregory Peck, Barbara (Mrs. Cary) Grant, me, Liza Minnelli, Dina Merrill, Roger Moore. Front row, left to right: Frank Sinatra, Merv Griffin, Robert J. Wagner, Shirley Temple Black, Quincy Jones, Albert, Stephanie, Rainier and Henry Mancini.

November 2, 1985, the Bistro Garden, Beverly Hills. Sally and Carolyn are in New York, but our reunion includes (standing, left to right) Rita Gam, my Amy Kanter Thiele, Marée's Linda Pamp Farnum, Bettina Gray, Rita's Kate Guinzburg, Lizanne Kelly LeVine, and (seated, left to right) my Nina Franciosa, Vicki LeVine (Lizanne's daughter-in-law), Maree Rambo, my Victoria Kanter Colombetti, Caroline, me and Lizanne's Gracie LeVine Packer.

by ear. Jointly they committed themselves to raising children who would be both seen and heard, an uncommon notion among Europeans in that era, and even less common among royal families. Grace and Rainier encouraged a great deal more rambunctious curiosity and freedom than might have been anticipated inside the Palace walls. Grace quickly convinced Rainier to build a modern swimming pool and cabanas in the Palace Gardens. When summers came, the sounds of children shrieking and splashing in the custom-designed, turquoise, Italian mosaic pool were the familiar noises of Grace's own childhood summers in Ocean City.

Longing for a family getaway site close to Monaco, Grace and Rainier bought the exquisitely situated Roc Agel in 1957. High atop the old La Turbie Road, sixty acres of land contained an ancient farmhouse, outbuildings and enough room for the goats, rabbits, pigs, chickens and cows that roamed about freely unless Oliver the poodle was after them. Grace set about to redecorate, completing the work in 1959. Retaining and augmenting the tiled roof, huge beams, Moorish arches and thick stone walls, she made the house livable with the addition of modern kitchens and bathrooms, generous closet space and the vibrant but soft colors with which Grace had always surrounded herself. Paul the driver had his own separate quarters, as did the Italian couple who tended the house while the family was at the Palace. But on weekends, and during the long summer weeks when they stayed at Roc Agel to escape the heat and the season's social madness, it was Grace, Rainier and Maureen who seemed to run the place. Like any decent suburban husband and father, Rainier puttered for hours in his machine shop and toolshed, while Grace, who had never exactly been the Julia Child type, took to experimenting in the kitchen. When her children napped she usually went for long solitary walks on the mountainside, where the abundance of wildflowers delighted her.

In these earliest years of her marriage, national publications carried sporadic articles on Grace. They, like her letters, portrayed an earnest young woman whose only desire was to remain close to hearth, home and country. While the citizenry of Monaco applauded her dedication and her local triumphs, the scope of her life as well as her fame seemed sure to dwindle as it shrank into her self-elected domesticity.

In Hollywood, Jay continued to receive scripts and movie offers for Grace. When the projects were interesting he called her about them, even sending the scripts on. She was always delighted to hear of the offers, particularly if they came attached to directors she admired, but her refusals became increasingly more automatic. In an age when appearances counted for everything, an important part of our friendship was to accept the appearance a friend wanted to portray. Neither Jay nor I probed to learn whether Grace rejected these movie roles easily. It was enough for us that she rejected them. Perhaps we detected a bit of wistfulness in her voice when she did, but that was to be expected from a young woman who had risen to such heights in so short a time and then moved along to a new life.

Never once did it dawn upon me to equate what my move away from New York meant to me with what Grace's move from that most compelling of cities meant to her. But Grace in Monaco, like Carolyn on Long Island and me in Beverly Hills, was a displaced person. We had always thought that we were above being affected by things like which town or city we lived in. Most of us had moved into Manhattan from other places and had adjusted so easily and happily to New York itself that we were sure we could move out of it again with similar equanimity. But that was not the case. For New York in the Fifties was much more than just a place where we lived. It was food for our souls.

In that muggerless city we could walk alone day or night, anywhere we chose. Within the course of five minutes, we could be famous at an opening or anonymous in our apartments. We could walk our dogs with our hair in pin curls under a scarf or run our errands within three blocks of where we lived, greeting by name a dozen familiar owners of small shops we patronized. Nobody noticed how we were dressed or coiffed. But forty-five minutes later, we could lunch at a chic East Side restaurant where everyone who saw us believed we were born well-groomed.

No matter where we went, the city carried us along with an energy of its own. If we woke in the morning with nowhere to go and nothing to do, merely planting our feet down on a New York sidewalk gave us a sense of purpose. We marveled at the number of clothing stores run by people who could actually make a business out of selling what was in their windows, but it confirmed our belief that if a difference of opinion made the world go round, there was nowhere better to prove that than right where we were.

Then, in a matter of months, Gracie, Carolyn and I all moved to the suburbs. We walked only for air or exercise. Grace had to summon a car and prepare herself to be seen in public. Carolyn and I had to own one, be sure we had gas, that the children's bubble gum wrappers and crushed potato chips were not strewn all over the floor. We all lived in places where people saw us leave our houses, knew where we went and when we came back. We did not just "go out" anymore. We had to have reasons. If friends came to visit us, they did not arrive or leave anonymously. Their cars, parked out front—whether at the Palace, on a Lloyd Neck driveway or on a street in the Beverly Hills flats—told anyone who drove or walked by who was visiting. We stayed home more than we ever had before.

In Beverly Hills, I knew I had gone Hollywood when I found myself one bright and sunny day moving my car from the parking lot of Saks to the parking lot of Magnin's, a distance of one whole block! With no one to see on the streets and, outside the small triangle comprising Beverly Hills, not a store window to look into, I could no longer count on walking aimlessly through town to absorb my energies. Unconsciously I determined that if my social life in New York had helped to keep me distracted and happy, I'd have to have even more of one in Beverly Hills. It was also clear that Jay and I were expected to absorb a great deal of the MCA entertaining borne by the Wassermans before we moved. Outgoing and adaptable, I entered a phase of my life that can best be described as socio-manic-elative.

Véronique Peck, whom I'd met in New York with Greg, was responsible for admitting me as the only American regularly included in midday repasts with a group I named "the French lunch bunch." It consisted of Véronique; Anne Douglas, who had recently married Kirk; and Quique Jourdan, Louis's wife. We all had children of the same age, and when it was time for the older ones to go to pre-school, Anne and I—along with Janet Leigh Curtis—formed a car pool heading to John Thomas Dye in Bel Air. When school fairs came in the spring, we joined Nancy Reagan and other JTD mothers running food and game booths while our husbands manned elephant rides and cleared dart boards. The Douglases and the Reagans always had the hot dog booth. Kirk recalls the first year when Mr. R. decided to work the forward counter instead of the back burner as the time he told Anne on the drive home, "I think Ronnie's planning to run for office!"

Janet and I spent numberless afternoons gabbing as my Amy and

Vicki and her Kelly and Jamie Lee entertained one another with their antique china tea sets and elaborate dollhouses, all *de rigueur* in their group. When we were not together, our nannies met, with our offspring, in the local parks.

I had never been a big cocktails maven in New York, but in Beverly Hills, nearly every afternoon at five, dressed in the mandatory tight-crotched Jax slacks and crop tops, one group or another of us met at Edie and Lew Wasserman's, at Jeanne and Dean Martin's, or at our house for drinks. A new and instant close friend was the young British actress Joan Collins. She was living with my childhood acquaintance Arthur Loew, Jr. (grandson of both Marcus Loew, who founded MGM, and Adolph Zukor, who founded Paramount), and delighted me when we first met by referring to the picture she and Robert Wagner had just completed in Japan as "Stop Overacting" rather than *Stopover Tokyo,* as the studio preferred it to be called.

Within a few months after we moved to California, John Foreman came out from the east and lived over our garage until he got a job in public relations at Rogers and Cowan and a place of his own. Gene Kelly lived across from our newly bought home on Rodeo Drive, and only the alley where our garbage cans were discreetly placed separated us from Natalie Wood and R. J. Wagner. Other New York friends, Judy and Dick Shepherd and Julie and John Forsythe, had children at John Thomas Dye, and were pals we saw often; and we were delighted when Ruth and Milton Berle moved west.

Our daily cocktail gatherings were followed by dinners out at Chasen's, Romanoff's, the Villa Capri, the Luau and La Scala in groups of four, six, eight, ten or more; by sneak previews at theatres in various parts of the city; by screenings at the studios or in home projection rooms; or by premieres and parties of all sizes.

We gave or went to parties in one another's backyards, which were covered with tents and warmed by heaters after our swimming pools had been drained and filled with scaffolding and boarded over to make room. (I once asked a hostess what kind of party she was giving so I'd know how to dress. The answer "drained, tented, heated and catered" told me all I needed to know—a big one.) We danced on rented portable dance floors laid over rented fake grass to the music of Bernie Richards's rented orchestra and mambo groups. I was in heaven when both Marlon and

Tony Curtis were present, as I'd do all the North American dances with Marlon, then alternate the South American ones with him and Tony as they took turns on the bongos and congas. We ate cracked crab, chili and New York strip steaks provided by Maude and Dave Chasens' place, drank vodka tonics and vodka gimlets, and remembered to keep our flowing sleeves away from the gargantuan ice sculptures that graced the buffet tables, melting slowly as the night wore on.

On weekdays, when we weren't playing with our kids, we ate #11's at the Bedford Drive Hamburger Hamlet, tunafish sandwiches with Cokes at home or with pineapple sodas at the Beverly Hills branch of Schwabs. Occasionally, we poked our forks into the rubbery, air-filled California omelets at Frascati's on Wilshire.

After lunch we shopped for the extensive wardrobes we needed for the casual-to-formal, never-ending round of dates, dos and events at which we were sure to see one another over and over again. We bought every conceivable version of their stiletto-heeled pumps as fast as Ferragamo could ship them, disregarding the fact that our feet would be irreparably damaged by being squeezed into their narrow toes. We liked them because they had a low vamp, and "low vamp" was a designation many of us harbored in our secret hearts. We shopped at Saks, Magnin's and— when we were ready to splurge—Amelia Gray.

When we weren't shopping, lunching, partying or premiering, we swam in one another's heated pools or played tennis on one another's courts. I took seven lessons with Barbara Rush on Jeanne and Dean's court, but quit when the cabana mirror told me my left arm looked atrophied in comparison with my right arm, which was ballooning with muscles.

It wasn't that we never stayed home at night. We did, and often, because Beverly Hills was still a place in those days—like most suburban enclaves—where a lot more entertaining was done in the home than outside it. It's just that we never stayed home alone. There were always friends for dinner at the table, on TV trays, for a barbecue or a game of charades. Joan Collins and I engaged in furious wars over the enactment of British versus American pronunciations, and because we made a great fuss telling everyone we were only six months apart in age, I always got to act first on the basis of the long-standing imperative "age before beauty." While Joanie and I argued, John Foreman, Arthur Loew and

Bob Wagner sneaked our team's folded charades off the coffee table, subtly playing off early victories to our repeated dismay before we finally caught them at their ruse red-handed.

When we left town we went to one of two places—Las Vegas or Palm Springs. On the afternoon before any one of our group was set to open in Vegas, you could see us, en masse, wending our way to the airport, where we departed for one- or two-day stays of sleepless, three-shows-a-night nights, 4 A.M. Chinese dinners at the Sands and 8 A.M. chuckwagon breakfasts. Most of us had our gambling under control. For those we knew who did not, we formed a cajoling team, jockeying them away from the tables when things looked as if they were getting out of hand. In Palm Springs, we stayed at the Racquet Club or divided up into groups at the homes of friends like Mary and Jack Benny, the Martins, the Sammy Cahns, Frank Sinatra or Betsy and Cary Grant.

One particular Vegas jaunt was for the carefully planned, highly secretive elopement of Joanne Woodward and Paul Newman. All the arrangements had been made through Beldon Kattleman, who owned the El Rancho Vegas, a low-slung hacienda-style hotel that featured luxuriously equipped adobe bungalows with one or more bedrooms. When the wedding day came, Joanne, Ina Bernstein (Joanne's MCA agent and close friend) and I went to the airport at noon, with Paul, Jay, John Foreman and writer Stewart Stern set to follow later. Our tickets had been booked under false names, and Joanne was wearing a scarf and dark glasses to conceal her identity. At the ticket counter, we were informed there was a flight delay. The attendant took our tickets and suggested we have coffee or lunch and listen to the public address that would call all passengers by name when the flight was ready. After lunch we seated ourselves near the counter; Joanne did some needlework and Ina and I read. Apparently, two flights to Vegas had been delayed. When the p.a. system began to broadcast, it called one set of names to one gate for one Vegas flight and a second set to another. Panic struck as we three realized not one of us knew either our flight number or our assumed names! We approached the small counter. The ticket agent leaned discreetly across it to say, "You're on Flight #63, Miss Woodward, and it's boarding now at Gate 5." So much for secrecy at the airport.

On several occasions, I started letters to Grace, always filled with stories of what we were doing and with whom. Most of the letters were put aside so I could dash off to one appointment or another. I would begin again, only to be interrupted before completing the newer effort. Realizing I had almost stopped writing her, I took to reducing the scope of my letters to small notes containing only perfunctory news that we were all well and occasionally a bit more elaboration on the growth and activities of my children. Undaunted by my lack of response, Grace wrote ever onward as though I were her most consistent pen pal.

Was I bored? No! Was I having fun? Yes! Was I satisfied? I did not know. Small underpinnings of my assuredness were coming slowly loosened like warning tremors before a major quake, but I neither recognized the signs nor addressed myself to repairing them. My first "off" day came very early after my daughter Vicki was born at the start of 1957.

On a day that was both warm and cold, overcast and sunny, a day that seemed suspended in its progress for not knowing what it was supposed to be, Paul Newman called at noon to say that he was out from New York for a fast trip, had finished his meetings at Warner Brothers, and would like to come by to see the baby and me. Arriving before Vicki's two o'clock feeding, he stayed on afterwards for sandwiches and a beer. I had known Paul and Joanne since they had been in *Picnic* on the New York stage. Though we all considered ourselves friends, I could not remember ever exchanging intimacies with them. That was hardly unusual, considering the times. But on this afternoon Paul and I just lay on the floor in front of my unlit fireplace, propped on pillows, talking about whatever came into our heads.

After a while Paul asked, "Do you ride?" and I told him that I had ridden horses regularly until I was nine and then never done it again. "Let's go riding," he suggested, bounding to the telephone to arrange horses for us at a stable on Riverside Drive in the Valley. When he said he had his favorite mount, but I had a choice between two labeled "spirited" or "exhausted," thinking of my recent C-section and my years of inexperience, I chose the latter.

Once astride, and out on the ring under the gray suede sky, "exhausted" proved to be an understatement. "Exhumed for this occasion" was a more apt description. Paul did about four turns around the course, while my horse slow-motioned himself all of ten yards away from our original point of departure. Coming to a broad mound of ants, my nag wheezed as though climbing an Alp. What the stable hands had neglected to mention was that my horse had been pried away from his dinner for this booking. By the time he finally made it four-fifths of the way around the oval, I had stopped holding his reins.

When I finally got to a distance thirty feet away from the stable, my horse must have smelled his abandoned oats. Suddenly the nag, reins flopping around his rickety neck, took off like a bolt of lightning. Into the stable doors he galloped, through the stable and out the other side, across the driveway and smack into rush-hour traffic on Riverside Drive. Cars screeched to a Walt Disney halt on all sides as I, doing a half nelson around his neck, tried to retrieve the reins. Finally the nag skidded to a stop. Paul galloped up to join me, followed by the grooms, and because neither I nor my mount was crushed between cars, we collapsed with laughter.

The day was so satisfying and comfortable that we both wanted more of it. I called Jay at the office to tell him where I was and ask what time he'd be home for dinner. He was working late and getting a bite out with some co-workers. Paul called and canceled an appointment he'd made to join a group of other friends. We sat in a horsey, wood-walled café in the Valley, at the bar with some dusty studio wranglers who'd just gotten off work, had some drinks and munched some dry hamburgers. And we talked. We talked about how we felt being the son and daughter of our mothers and fathers. What we loved and resented about being the brother and sister of our respective siblings. What excited us when we were in every single grade in school and what tortured us as we had reached adolescence. We talked about what our parents wanted us to be and what we wanted to become. About what our friends, mates and children needed from us and what we needed for ourselves.

I told Paul that in the back of my mind something told me I should be working, but that the work I'd want to do—producing films I thought then—was neither appropriate for a woman who was the daughter of a movie mogul and wife of an agent, nor possible for a mother of two. Paul told me that he doubted his own talent would ever be large enough to please him, and we wondered together what made Marlon's artistry so far beyond the reaches of the ordinary imagination. We conjectured that ordinary imagination might plague us both, that we both had too much demand for safety regulated into our souls to let them expand, or too much propriety inbred to ever take chances like others we admired. The evening ended around nine when we questioned why we had never talked like this before, neither together nor with others we were closer to, and whether we would ever talk like this again. There had been nothing sexual about our time together, not the least bit of flirtatiousness nor any hint of longing for anything but what we shared. It would be a long time before I knew what to call it, but it left me shaken and unsure.

By summertime, a large group of us had taken to gathering for endless afternoons-into-evenings at Arthur Loew's house on Miller Drive. We sat around his bar, cha-chaed to the newest albums, and took dips in the pool as Arthur cautioned us to "beware of the piranhas." I don't remember eating much, except an occasional barbecued steak, but I do recall drinking. We drank a lot. And we laughed at everything, including ourselves. Arthur said we reminded him of Hemingway's expatriates in *The Sun Also Rises.* Looking back, I think we, along with many other groups I belonged to in the city at that time, were like a ship of fools, dancing and drinking our way out of the Fifties, trying to anticipate the dangers that were yet to come to see if we could survive them when the world changed. It had been too much of a good thing.

By October 1957, I knew that no little angel rode on the shoulders of the beautiful and the famed. Larry Olivier called from London to say that Vivien had lost her baby. Marilyn Monroe and Arthur Miller lost theirs soon afterwards. Though Marlon was set to marry Anna Kashfi, I had already become close enough to her to see her in what appeared to me to be vitriolic fits of rage, auguring ill, I suspected, for a long and contented union. Arthur Loew decided that, for my twenty-fifth birthday, he would give me a solid week of commemorative parties. It began to make me sound as though, reaching a quarter of a century, I belonged in the Smithsonian.

Arthur's first party for me was to be held at his house the weekend before my birthday. Jay called from the office to say he'd be home just in time to shower and change, and to tell me that Marlon and Anna had been secretly married at Marlon's aunt's house in Pasadena that afternoon. I got into a tub, had my left arm raised and was about to shave under it when my bathroom door flew open to reveal the newlyweds, dripping with rice and confetti. "We heard on the radio," Marlon said, "that the press is out in force at every highway into and out of the city, looking for us. We were going to head toward the Springs, but I figured we'd better come here instead." Taking Anna by the hand, he came in and sat on the edge of the tub. I asked, ever so politely, if they wouldn't mind waiting in another room while I finished my bath, and when I did rejoin them, clothed, found them helping Miss Mack feed the children in the kitchen.

Once I learned they planned to stay the night, I offered our bedroom. "We can stay at Arthur and Joanie's," I volunteered. "There's another birthday party tomorrow at lunchtime there, and I'm sure they won't mind our using the guest room." I darted outside to pick fresh roses, put my best Porthault linens on the bed, arranged most of the roses in vases, and sprinkled petals of the remaining ones across the sheets.

At six-thirty the next morning, we were awakened at Arthur and Joanie's house by a London call from a reporter who'd gotten the number from Miss Mack and wanted to know what Marlon thought about his wife turning out to be Joanne O'Callaghan, daughter of a Welsh factory worker, rather than Anna Kashfi, the lifetime resident of exotic Calcutta, India. It was certainly news to Marlon! By the last of my week-long birthday celebrations in the private room at Chasen's the following Saturday night, Marlon and Anna were one week married and light-years apart.

Since every restaurant or club in California closed early, Jay and I began entertaining at home, late at night, on a near-regular basis. If our front porch light was on and our cars were in the driveway, you could be sure the Kanters were open for business. Jay had to go to the office so he retired as early as he could slip away, but I took to ordering eggs in restaurant-sized packages to accommodate the guests who dropped by and stayed until the hours when scrambled-with-bacon sounded just right. We gave parties for everything—a party for Joanne Woodward on the night she won her Oscar for *Three Faces of Eve,* a party for Joan Collins's birthday, and parties for people who did not want to go home when other people's parties ended.

Responding to a request from a New York MCA agent, Jay went to the airport to pick up Warren Beatty, a young actor who was coming out west to test for movies. Warren had no place special to stay, so he hung out at our house. We took him to a party at Debbie Powers's, where he met the now-free Joan Collins, and the two of them fell in love. John Foreman and I, deciding Warren had a unique charm, bet someone else that we could make a star of him in the industry within a month, just by talking him up at parties. Nobody had seen him act, and though he appeared only in one *Dobie Gillis* episode after his arrival, our plan worked even better than we'd dreamed.

There was an immense amount of flirting going on. Some of it was the wise European brand, the kind that never goes anywhere but makes an evening more amusing. But then there were sardine games and the itchy sexuality that accompanied them when you found yourself in too-tight quarters with someone attractive on the shelf of the blanket closet. It was all right to flirt, or even to go further. Sometimes the wives arranged it so their husbands would find themselves in compromising positions with the wives of their friends who had expressed an attraction. The main thing was never to flirt, or go further, with a ringer—someone outside the group. Your husband's buddy, golfing partner, tennis mate, director, producer, star, agent or client was acceptable. That was *en famille* and no one would end up any the worse for the wear. But "don't go to strangers" was the unwritten law on which the culture survived. I was not exempt from the message.

Life careened on like this. Joan Collins got pregnant by Warren and needed an illegal abortion, just as all the rumored available establishments below the border shut down after a raid. I called New York and found the name of a New Jersey place; then she, Warren and I took off for the east, staying together in one room at the Hotel Beverly on Lexington and Fifty-first. Joan was heavily bewigged and nervous. On a cold spring morning, with sleety rain pummeling the top of our tinny rented car, we drove across the Hudson and found a nameless, faceless complex of identical postwar apartment buildings. Our instructions were to drop Joan in front of the complex. She was to turn left into the second building inside the courtyard. Once she disappeared from our sight, we were to drive away immediately, returning an hour later to fetch her on the sidewalk. She was not going to be aborted in the building she turned into, but in another building that none of us was to know about.

Frightened to death that Joanie would be maimed and we would not know how to find her, Warren and I parked our car on a side street in the New Jersey town, walked in the rain to a coffee shop, and waited at the counter. A slovenly waitress in a torn hairnet and a faded pea-green dress poured us cup after cup of cloudy, lukewarm coffee. The cream floated on the top like mildew, but we drank it anyway while the only other patron played "Love Is a Many Splendored Thing" over and over again on the countertop jukebox. When we finally collected the ashen-faced Joanie, we drove back to Manhattan for a two-day stay in our one double room at the Beverly, where both Warren and I could watch over Joanie but where the dust on the windowsills was thick enough to grow plants.

Could I have written to Grace about all this? I did not think so. Nor could I tell her that as the days passed I grew further and further estranged from Jay, as our lives became like those of two friendly acquaintances who changed clothes at the same locker and did not care enough to have an argument. We were the peace-at-all-costs twins. When things happened in our marriage we thought were too dangerous, Jay would simply announce, "It won't happen again," and I would nod obediently, knowing I was the most at fault, but not knowing how the trouble would just go away because we said it would. I began to feel compelled to stay in perpetual motion, as though I could not afford to stop for fear of what I would find in stillness. It became difficult for me to spend quiet time with my children. They reminded me too much of who they were, which reminded me to wonder who I was.

Jay and I began living two separate lives but in the same house. For the outside world, of course, we kept up appearances. On a Sunday morning when Eddie Fisher and Elizabeth Taylor arrived at our house on one of their first disguised outings after their much-publicized union at Grossinger's, we celebrated their togetherness and ours with a happy brunch of bagels, lox and cream cheese from Nate 'n Al's delicatessen. But the notion of anyone's togetherness being as blissful as it appeared to be was beginning to smell more fishy to me than the Nova Scotia.

During a party at Chasen's and another one shortly afterwards at a friend's house, I began talking with the young actor I'd met years before on his first Broadway opening night, when I'd told him "I'm sure we'll be seeing more of you." Tony Franciosa had by then married Shelley Winters. Though Jay and I had known both of them casually over the years, even before they knew each other, they were not part of our gang. My attraction to Tony was dangerous, because it was not on home ground and because Tony himself had a dangerously compelling energy that did not seem to have been contained by the mores of the movie mob. I was attracted to that raw energy, and by his voice, which rose like compressed steam from somewhere that was missing in most of the people I hung around with. Aware that I was cha-chaing too close to the edge of the floor, I determined it was time for therapy.

Cary Grant and Betsy were living apart, but both were in treatment with a Dr. Mortimer Hartman in Beverly Hills. Hartman was one of several doctors in the city using the experimental drug lysergic acid on patients in a variety of therapeutic and study programs. Some were designed to assess creativity with artists under LSD, some to treat anxieties of terminal cancer patients, and others to rehabilitate the psyches of shell-shocked war veterans. Hartman and two other doctors were using the drug as an augmentation to more standardized psychotherapy. I had been uninspired by my brief, earlier Freudian analysis in New York, found the concept of treatment with LSD fascinating, and decided that if it was good enough for Cary Grant it must be good enough for me.

I had never smoked a marijuana joint; taken a diet, sleeping or wake-up pill; nor had any attraction to drugs of any kind. The intriguing notion was that LSD, an enzyme, opened the unconscious mind. We were not allowed to drive to sessions. Betsy Grant delivered me for my first morning date to a small, dark office on Lasky Drive in Beverly Hills, where I had visited earlier for psychological testing and to sign a release.

I was first asked what kind of music I would like to hear. After selecting Rachmaninoff's Rhapsody on a Theme of Paganini, I was handed three small blue pills to swallow. I would have to wait until a few years into the next decade to realize they were the "Baby Blues" Bob Dylan sang about. At the time, all I knew was that they were made by the Sandoz Laboratories in Switzerland, and when I told other people I was taking LSD, they thought I was speaking about landing boats used in World War II.

I donned the mandated eyeshades and, within moments, reexperienced birth, fusing ever more deeply and over and over again with everything in the universe and all the wonders of creation. When Betsy came to collect me more than five hours later, she took me back to her Mandeville Canyon house, where I did my Henry VIII imitation by devouring two chickens and told her I'd found God. As I had experienced birth feet first on Lasky Drive, I called my mother in New York to learn I had indeed been a breach baby. I announced to Betsy that we were all alike in that we were all infinite and called Cary to tell him I now understood the profundity of his earlier statement, "The only way out is through." After sailing away euphorically on two pills for my second session with Hartman, I simply put on the blinders and Rachmaninoff for my third one and fused off into the stratosphere.

For eight months, once a week, I swallowed little blue pills that sent me into the wild blue yonder in ever more profound states of bliss, while on earth I maneuvered my life into a state of limbo that came close to approximating hell. Trying to read my acid-induced revelations the way a gypsy reads soggy tea leaves, I looked for a sign to tell me whether it was Jay or Tony whom I loved. The answer kept coming back, "both of them," until I was praying that one or the other of them—both if necessary—would opt out of the triangle.

While floating about in my consistently euphoric fusion state during a session in my eighth month of treatment, I crossed a line into uncharted territory, entering—without warning—into a vast, unending sea of dysphoric panic. Not once in any earlier session had I experienced even the most remote unpleasantness. Almost too scared to speak, I finally dared ask my doctor what was the matter. When no satisfactory or comforting answer was forthcoming, I began drowning. I tried to unfuse myself without success. My mind and body would simply not get back together again, nor even approach each other. The harder I tried to get my mind out of the infinite and into the physical person I could see lying there on a couch on Lasky Drive, the more my mind swam away from the heart that was beating so hard it felt it would explode.

My friend Marion Donen came to pick me up, but I could not leave. The effects of the drug were not wearing off. My panic mounted to even greater heights. Hartman kept me in his office for two or three extra hours, but I was convinced I was in a state of separation that had never been experienced before by any other human being and would never end. I prayed to get back into myself so I could just go insane, whatever that meant. At least they took crazy people to hospitals where someone knew what to do with them. Hartman gave me Compazine, a drug meant to bring me down. For a while no relief came. Then, gradually, my mind began to rejoin my body, first touching it only for an instant before skittering off again, and finally uniting enough so that I slept for a moment or two. When real sleep ultimately came, I stayed another two hours in a side office. And when Marion returned a second time to collect me, responding to Mort Hartman's call, I had been on Lasky Drive for more than ten hours.

I was left with residual panic that dogged me day and night for the next two weeks. Dr. Hartman saw me every two or three days, but I had no wish to take any more "baby blues." I had lost confidence in him as well, but could not exactly expect help from my general practitioner, and so turned to Dr. Hartman in desperation. I begged him to make the panic attacks go away, but had no relief until the second week after my "bad trip." On that visit Hartman threw me a pillow before walking out to take a phone call for a minute. "Here," he said. "Take it out on this." Within an instant after he closed the door, I was beating up on the pillow with both fists, as though trying to smash it to smithereens. There was one brief instant of relief, during which I suspected that it was my anger I'd been unwilling to face which had sent me into the tailspin in the first place. Then I pulled myself together and left the office on Lasky Drive for the last time.

Sporadic panic attacks continued to come upon me without warning. I'd be driving my car and have to pull over to the side of the road and lie on the floor until they subsided. Or they would come in the night when it was hard to tell whether I was asleep or awake until I could hear myself talking myself back to sleep again and see myself whole and returned to undisturbed breathing. One night in La Scala, an attack came upon me so suddenly and alarmingly, I prayed with all my strength that this illness in my mind would transfer itself into a physical illness so I could be treated by regular doctors in regular hospitals.

One month later, Jay and I were at a friend's house, preparing to join Simone Signoret at the Huntington Hartford Theatre for her husband Yves Montand's opening. I was handed a double old-fashioned glass filled with vodka and tonic, took one sip, felt a pain in my left shoulder, dropped the glass, and doubled over in excruciating pain.

An hour later I was at Cedars of Lebanon, and shortly after that was diagnosed as having acute peritonitis, brought about when an ovarian infection had spread to the peritoneum, the membrane that lines the abdominal cavity. For several weeks I remained at Cedars with nobody able to understand why the massive IV doses of antibiotics I was being given round-the-clock relieved neither my symptoms nor my disease. My shoulder pain remained unbearable, though it was only referred from my abdomen, where the peritonitis raged on. Tubes were placed down my throat, through my nose, and up my urethra and rectum. My overused veins throbbed and turned blue-red from phlebitis, and my fever continued to mount. I, who detested drugs, begged in tears for my next morphine shot only halfway through the cycle of four hours that was to have separated them. Peritonitis was a fatal disease before the advent of miracle drugs, its final stage being the formation and ultimate bursting of an internal abscess. Though doctors could find no other cause for my illness, their medicines just did not work on me.

In a last-ditch attempt to save me, my doctors emptied out most of my blood (its white count now reading leukemic), replacing it with a clean supply. They were going to see, during the night, if my fever broke. If not, they planned to cut me abdominally the following morning to see if they could locate the killer abscess that was not visible in the X rays. When dawn came, my temperature had dropped a full point to 105 degrees, and by evening of that day I had regained complete consciousness for the first time in four weeks. After being discharged from the hospital a week later, I spent an additional three bedridden weeks at home recuperating.

Not long after that, I decided to get a divorce. It was a fairly ugly business, as mostly everyone knew by then about Tony and me. One-third of my friends commiserated with me that there had to be more to life and love than what I felt I had with Jay. Another third treated me like a pariah. And the final third counseled me to do what they had done—stay married, have affairs with whomever I wanted, and remain discreet. The advice of the last group fell on deaf ears. As a woman who fell in love with one man while she was married to another she loved, it may sound self-serving to say that I was too much of a prude for this course, but that is the truth. This was not about sex, it was about love—falling in love, and finding myself in the fall. I could no more have settled for a union in which I was the repeatedly unfaithful partner than for one in which my husband was. I was still in search of "the right man."

Even though I was the one seeking it, divorce left me with an overwhelming sense of failure. How could I, dedicated like Grace and my other friends to calming waves, have made some of such tidal proportions? How could I be dissolving the family in which my beloved daughters were to have grown and flowered? How could I have betrayed a good man like

Jay, separating him from the little girls he loved so dearly? I had betrayed his trust, the trust of his company, the trust of our friends and, worst of all, my trust in myself. Yet I could not do otherwise. I would make it all right again by building a good marriage with Tony, providing a happy home for the children, and doing my best. But how could I, the girl who always expected to do the right thing, write my friend Grace, the girl who always did the right thing, the beatific wife/mother/princess in Monaco, to explain what I did not even understand myself? I was not even sure that once Grace heard I was divorcing Jay she would remain my friend. Had I put pen to paper, how would my letter have begun?

> Dear Graciebird,
> After my LSD panics, my assignations and Shelley Winters screaming on my front lawn in broad daylight to stay away from her husband, I wanted to drop you a note to say we are all fine.

Or might I have tried this?

> Gracie dear,
> Jay is now going with a very nice divorcée named Kit Bernard, who has three children. Trouble-making friends urge me to protest my girls spending weekends with him because they think he and Kit are living together without being married while I am too worried about his criticism to let Tony spend the night here. I have decided, though, that I ought to teach my children what I believe—that if Jay and Kit and her kids are happy together unmarried, and if they are good to my kids, I don't give a hoot whether they're married or not.

If that wouldn't play, I could try this approach.

> Dear Grace,
> My father was in town yesterday and came by to visit the girls and me. In front of the kids, he began yelling that if I did not stay married to Jay he would disown me and have "one of those operations" performed on my brain. The girls don't know from lobotomies, but they were terrified and are having nightmares. I've told

Dad he can see them on future trips, but only at his hotel, not at my house, where he might be tempted to lash out in another such eruption.

I could have told Grace that my father threatening to disown me was like hearing an old LP. For a generation of men who made money to buy freedom, men of my father's era were masters at using it in attempts to confine their wives and children. Grace knew about these men who had grown accustomed to control at their offices and on the daises where their charities honored them. She knew that when they could not control their families as quickly or easily as they wished, they threatened with money, believing that was their only true worth or all their families wanted from them. I once told my father that it was he who mattered to me, not his money. His eyes grew fearful. When I further suggested he give to charity or flush down the toilet whatever money he kept giving and taking away so we could just talk together like two people who cared deeply for each other, he froze in terror and left the room.

I might have told Grace that, in truth, I did not believe any third party could destroy a marriage of substance. Tony and Shelley had been living on separate coasts and having serious problems for a long time. Jay and I had been living together, but on different wavelengths for a similar period.

In honesty, I could have told Grace I would rather teach my children, even if by painful example for us all, that life gives you another chance if you make a mistake. Or that I did not want to be one of those mothers who served up guilt with her children's dinners by telling them I had spent my life in an unhappy marriage for their sake.

I wrote nothing to Grace, not even a perfunctory note, just nothing. But she continued writing me regularly and never mentioned hearing a single word about the dissolution of Jay's and my marriage nor about the scandal surrounding it.

As soon as we filed for divorce, some of our friends chose sides, though neither Jay nor I asked for such allegiances. If friends had liked us both before, when we lived together, we expected they might continue to like us both living apart. It was our marriage that had failed, not our friendships with others, nor even—in the long run—our friendship with each other.

While waiting for my divorce to become final, Tony and I made plans to go to Europe for the Venice Film Festival and for his pre-production work on a film that was to shoot in Italy. It was my first trip across the Atlantic since Grace's 1956 wedding, and I longed to visit her in Monaco. But I wasn't sure whether I would be welcome.

When I called Grace and heard her voice at the other end of the phone, the only change in it was a slightly more exaggerated English accent, a bit like a foreigner who had learned to speak the language at a European finishing school. I told her of my forthcoming trip and heard her gleefully insist, "You will be coming here to visit with us, won't you?"

"Grace," I asked, "have you heard about Jay's and my divorce?"

"Yes, dear," she answered softly, "and I'm very sorry about it for both of you. It can't be easy, regardless of the circumstances." In one sentence, she had told me she knew what had happened and condemned no one.

"I'll be coming to Europe with Tony," I went on, "and I don't know if you would be comfortable with us both visiting you there." I thought I owed Grace an out if she wanted one.

"We look forward very much to seeing you and getting the chance to meet Tony," came her unhesitating response. "When will you be coming?" I promised to ring back when I knew the exact August dates, and before we hung up, Grace suggested that we aim for the weekend of the Red Cross Gala. "We'll be a bit hectic, but you might enjoy the evening, and if you can stay a bit after the weekend, we can still have some quiet time together."

Perhaps, more than anything else, that explains what it was like to be Grace's friend. No admonitions for not writing, though letters from her pals were very important to her. No questions asked. No explanations required. No judgments passed. Forthcoming expressions of sympathy and unity when most appropriate. Instant invitations to visit when most feasible. Offers of fun and friendship when both were most needed. Though Grace's position had become more elevated since first we met, the gifts of her friendship were no less exalted than they had always been. We did not use the expression "unconditional love" in those days, but that's what Grace was good at giving. At the time, I could not even admit to myself how much I needed it, but looking back I know that Grace's unfailing loyalty touched me so deeply that it helped me to restore my faith in myself.

CHAPTER 9

Shake, Rattle and Roll

*L*ife with the Grimaldis was very *gemütlich*, Graustarkian and giggly when I visited them in the early Sixties. Rainier was forging ahead with courageous projects for the growth and development of Monaco, encountering opposition from powerful adversaries like Aristotle Onassis and would-be powers like his sister and her second husband, Jean-Charles Rey.

The Greek shipping magnate had primed the boom in the Principality with huge investments, appearing at first to be an angel of mercy. But the power Onassis had garnered with his money soon proved a double-edged sword. It was said that if Rainier allowed him to continue pouring cash into Monaco, he could wind up owning the place. On the other hand, if a halt were called to the Greek's infusion of capital, the foundation of Monaco's boom might crack.

Rey was another matter, a problem complicated by the emotional entanglement between Tiny and him. As a leader of the opposition group in the National Council, he had been a constant thorn in Rainier's side. As a prospective brother-in-law, he would be a snake in the family garden. Rainier had already lived through his sister's original revolt, when her political ambition became clear to him. But after his marriage to Grace, all that appeared to have dissipated. Tiny had been forgiven, and she, together with her brother and sister-in-law and their respective children, presented a happy family face to the outside world. Behind the scenes, though, Princess Antoinette and Jean-Charles Rey were actually plotting to wrest control of the Principality from the Prince.

One might have expected to find Grace and Rainier testy and on edge. To the contrary, they seemed exceptionally energetic, filled with an appetite for more adventure, more progress and more joy. They were the young, wonderful-looking and healthy parents of two very young, wonderful-looking and healthy children and—despite the burdens and crises of their political struggles—life seemed good.

I never visited them in their first Paris apartment. Rainier's cramped bachelor quarters had been converted to house the master and mistress, their two children, nanny Maureen King, Phyllis Blum and whichever aides accompanied Rainier on his forays to the French capital. Travel for the family, whether there or elsewhere, always resembled a troop movement. In their case, though, the cadre looked more like a troupe of traveling players than a well-oiled government machine. With little Caroline and Albie in tow, there were always loads of toys, games, stuffed animals and cutout dolls spilling out of carry-on bags and makeshift cases for plane and train trips. When the gang finally settled into the Paris flat, normal household chores had to be attended to. These included the personal laundry of the Sovereign Family, but the apartment had no space designated for hanging out the wash to dry. Phyllis and Maureen made the best of things, rigging clotheslines indoors that ran, like an overhead maze, through the hallways connecting the back rooms to the foyer and salon. Grace always laughed about having to duck the wet wash as she raced through the Paris apartment trying to accomplish her day's responsibilities.

This same kind of quick and easy transformation between their formal and informal selves was exactly what I experienced in Monaco both at the Palace and at their country home, Roc Agel. Grace and her family were entirely capable of comporting themselves with appropriate gracious formality at one instant, and then speedily shifting into a mode of casual comfort. It was great fun to watch them do it, and I loved the way they made everyone feel at home in surroundings that most suited them, whether stately or cozy.

In late July 1961, before Tony and I left for Europe, Grace warned me by phone that I needed to bring a long gown for the Red Cross Gala. The new Summer Sporting Club had not yet been built, and the old one housed the splendid festivities on its large outdoor terrace. The sound of Mediterranean waves lapped at the pilings while the star-filled sky was rivaled by the jewel-laden necks, earlobes, wrists and fingers of the super-coiffed, designer-clad female guests. The men, young and old alike, were all impossibly tanned. It was another of those evenings when the titles of Count, Earl, Baron and Prince obliterated the names that went with the actual person at hand. In Italy, I had learned to introduce Tony with the "c" in Franciosa sounding like "ch" rather than with the soft "c" popularized in America. As we moved in and out of the Hôtel de Paris and the Sporting Club, cameras flashed like fireworks and the crowds roared his name. The European paparazzi had, by now, been immortalized by Federico Fellini in *La Dolce Vita,* and had grown consistently more aggressive. Tony had become a huge target for them on the Via Veneto during earlier Roman filming of *The Naked Maja,* which co-starred him in a steamy romance with Grace's friend Ava Gardner, both on and off screen.

The day after the Gala, Grace and Rainier hosted an al fresco lunch in the Palace Gardens. In addition to several titled guests, they invited Sammy Davis, Jr., who had received a standing ovation at the prior night's Gala; Hjordis and David Niven, who were neighbors and close friends from their nearby Cap Ferrat villa; and Tony and me. After a half hour of cocktails, tail-coated, white-gloved butlers informed us that luncheon was being served. We found our calligraphied place cards at various flower-clothed tables that were set in the shade of the tall pine, palm and magnolia trees to shield us from the sun. Grace had mixed the guests, which made for reintroductions and lots of "getting-to-know-you" luncheon chitchat. Once or twice during the meal, I caught Tony's eye and winked conspiratorially. I remembered how out of place I felt on my first visit to the Palace, and could still feel the slight edge of concern that I would be found outré in some way. I presumed, correctly, that Tony was having a mild case of culture shock as he thought back to his East Harlem origins.

Following coffee, most of the guests prepared to leave. We took our lead from them and started to say our goodbyes, but Grace insisted we linger on along with Sammy and the Nivens.

When only the show biz contingent remained, we pulled a small group of garden chairs and chaises into a homey circle at the west end of the garden. Flopping down, everyone breathed a sigh of relief. It was a perfect summer afternoon, the sun's rays dappling the intensely hued petals of the camellias, roses and bird-of-paradise bordering the lawn. Albert and Caroline had gone in for naps, and the only sound was that of soft leaves on immense hundred-year-old trees that murmured in the breeze overhead. If each of us had dreams of what the perfect palace gardens would look like, this paradise would surely have equaled them.

David Niven broke the silence first. Turning to Sammy and then to Tony, he remarked wistfully, "In all this luxury, it doesn't seem possible that when we fellows were starving young performers we engaged in elaborate plots to wangle free meals out of unsuspecting cafeterias all over the city of New York!" The contradiction in circumstances got to each of us until we were all laughing out loud. One by one, David, Sammy and Tony told the tales of their early scuffles for survival. The delicious incongruity of hearing these stories in such a lush, palatial setting kept us all in high spirits.

Rainier was as hungry for details of their schemes as David, Tony and Sammy had been when they scammed Child's out of free meals. Watching the ascoted, blazered Prince, I could see the adventurous young boy who had longed to go on the stage while he was learning to hold his tears back during flogging sessions at the British boarding school where his regal, divorced parents had sent him to be shaped into a leader of men. His servants might call this thirty-fivish, mustachioed monarch "Monseigneur," but he looked to me like every boy who yearned to run away from home to join the circus. I knew what I was seeing—the Rainier with whom my friend Gracie had fallen in love.

When the last of the titled weekend guests left, Tony and I joined Grace, Rainier and the children at Roc Agel. The La Turbie Road was tortuously curved and extremely narrow. The driveway to Roc Agel itself could barely accommodate the large American-made car we had rented. "You look stunned," Grace noted as we alit from the car.

"I remember driving on those high narrow roads with you in the

to do a smashing job of it. And if we believed ourselves to be more enlightened than our parents before us, like them we expected to be in control.

So at Roc Agel, Rainier, Grace, Tony and I danced to the new music, trying to look as pretty as we could or as graceful, doing steps that made us feel a little foolish because they were the forerunners of an era when looking pretty or graceful and being in control were not the point at all.

Rainier and Tony begged off rather early, leaving Grace and me to chat alone. After they had gone I felt obligated to talk a bit about Jay and our divorce. I began by telling Grace I thought it was barbaric that the court required one of the divorcing parties to publicly present grounds against the other. "What happened between Jay and me was our own business," I insisted. "The last thing I wanted to do, especially in a court filled with strange onlookers and reporters, was to discuss our private problems. Yet in order to be divorced, I had to give a legally acceptable charge against him.

"I asked my lawyer," I told Grace, "what the most innocuous grounds were which would be accepted in a California court. And he told me 'mental cruelty.' " Grace and I both giggled for a moment imagining Jay inflicting real cruelty of any kind on anyone. "Then I asked my lawyer what specific form of mental cruelty was the least defamatory, and I was told I could say that Jay worked too hard, never came home for dinner parties on time, and thus caused me to become ill and distraught. So that's the charge I used in court, having to lie and find a witness who would lie to corroborate my testimony."

"It also makes you sound very dumb!" Grace chimed in, immediately getting the point of this foolish charade.

"Exactly," I concurred, "because, of course, I admired Jay for his devotion to his work and was quite capable of starting dinner without him if he was held up, but it seemed the least offensive way out."

"You're right, Judybird," Grace concluded, "I don't believe in divorce, but that's for me, not everyone. I quite agree that if the law makes divorce legal, it might require counseling as a deterrent, but it should not conduct . . . ," she paused, so I completed the sentence.

". . . a public inquisition on people's private lives." Grace nodded her assent.

We stayed up until three in the morning, at one point stopping to raid the refrigerator so that Grace could make us sandwiches out of "a l'il chickie," tomatoes and freshly grown basil, my first taste of the difference between the real thing and the dried variety. Grace described a bit more about her life in Monaco, though she was careful not to appear complaining. On this summer trip, I had witnessed the highest season of them all. It looked sunny, warm, hospitable, merry and endlessly festive, my idea of a great time, if not Rainier's. Grace, too, seemed to roll with the endless round of parties, international visitors and touring royalty to be entertained, except for the fact that it took more of her time from her children than she liked. But it was Grace's intention, even in those early years of her marriage, to see that the calendar in Monaco expanded to make "seasons" out of other cultural events. In between seasons, there were still her trips to Paris, to the East Coast of the States to see family and friends, yachting jaunts, and trips for winter sports that she and Rainier planned with the children. I perceived that her life was busy with current obligations and a wealth of plans for the future. I did not ask, nor did she offer, information about how it felt to be in Monaco out of season, on a dank, gray winter day when one's mind and heart might be filled with memories of life in New York City.

When I returned to California, I rented a small house on Bedford Drive where my girls, Miss Mack and I shared quarters with a tiny, aged and sprightly maid who came with the house and entered regular polka contests on her Sundays off.

Joan Collins had returned a past favor by accompanying Tony and me to Mexico the prior summer for my first and only abortion. Aside from being terrified that I would be mutilated in the filthy lean-to of the Tijuana shack where the surgery was performed, I wanted a baby by the man I loved with whom I had conceived this child, and the fact that "society" made it more advantageous to abort it than to let it live infuriated me. It also showed me how afraid I was to risk ultimate disapproval, even though I appeared to have broken all the rules. I had been a "bad" girl who now felt compelled to be "good." A child out of wedlock could not be worked into the self-portrait I needed to paint. And in early November of that same year, while in New York on an advance trip planning my wedding, I found out I was pregnant again when I had an early miscarriage. I only prayed I would be as fertile after my upcoming vows.

When Christmas vacation came, I left California with Miss Mack and the girls for my wedding in New York. We all set up residence at the Navarro (now the Ritz Carlton), next door to my parents' apartment at the Hampshire House. Tony was in the middle of rehearsing for the out-of-town tryouts of a new play called *The Umbrella,* in which he co-starred with Geraldine Page and Franchot Tone. New Year's Eve was his only night off from rehearsal. We were married by a judge in a lovely, paneled, library-type room on the second floor of the St. Regis. The man officiating seemed more intent upon auditioning his snappy repertoire for our best man, comedian Mort Sahl, than upon joining us in holy matrimony; but we soon forgot his disappointing performance and proceeded to welcome our one hundred twenty-five guests to an adjacent forsythia-bedecked ballroom for a black-tie dinner dance celebrating our union and the New Year while the snows fell heavily outside tall, elaborately mullioned windows.

My parents did not come to my second wedding. My father had forbidden anyone in my family to attend, and had taken my mother to Florida so their presence in New York would not be even more embarrassing. My brothers and their wives defied their paternal instructions, but we had all been through this before, when we had been disowned for attending brother Burt's wedding to his first wife, a convert to Judaism whose only flaw was that she had neglected to have been born into the faith.

The morning after our wedding, Tony rose early to attend rehearsal and I arranged a birthday party for Vicki in our hotel suite. Rita brought Kate and Mike Guinzburg.

The early 1960s were not great years for Rita. In spite of her status as Mrs. Thomas Guinzburg, she was steadily losing the very quality that had propelled her out of her parents' home as a girl and allowed her to function in the real world—bravery, an underlying belief that she could conquer the unconquerable. Armed with that bravura, which in one way or another each of us had possessed at the time of Grace's wedding, life had seemed simple. Or if it was to present difficulties and complexities we had not foreseen, we had promised ourselves we could surmount those with direct applications of courage. Rita, though, became flooded with the very self-doubt our era had promised would never afflict us.

Though she and Tom still took winter vacations to St. Johns in Caneel Bay with Elaine and John Steinbeck and continued to summer at the Guinzburgs' Locust Valley estate with the children, Rita's marriage was slowly falling from under her. No closeness had developed between Tom and her. Rita felt she wasn't a real artist, a real woman—which by our definition meant a female whose identity was forged by devotion to the right man—or a real mother. Having brought little to her marriage in the first place, she eroded that contribution even further.

Two weeks before Christmas, when Mike and Kate Guinzburg were five and six, respectively, their father Tom walked out of the family's huge Sixty-fourth Street flat. Though she had done little to keep their marriage vital, Rita felt totally and irrevocably abandoned. In the legal harangue over property and custody rights that followed, it was symbolically important to Rita's self-esteem and to her protective concern for her children to remain—legally—Mrs. Rita Guinzburg. She would have to live without the physical presence of the second man who had, however briefly, given her an identity. She would not agree to live without his name if she or her lawyers could help it.

With a healthy sense of selfhood apparently beyond her reach, Rita directed her energy to her talents as an actress. She took her children out of their Manhattan nursery school and moved to Minnesota to become a member of Sir Tyrone Guthrie's classical repertory theatre.

Once in Minneapolis, Rita opened a big house where she, her children and their nanny set up residence. Attempting to enroll the kids in a neighborhood nursery program, Rita came up hard against a midwestern wall of anti-Semitism. Undaunted, she checked further and ultimately enrolled Kate and Mike in day classes some twenty miles from home, where she found a nonrestricted pre-school connected to the university.

The enforced boundaries of Guthrie's British theatre philosophy were salutary for Rita. There was no room at the Guthrie for scattered, self-indulgent conduct. With an unwritten motto of "Don't complain, don't explain, and, certainly, don't apologize; be a professional, do your job as best you can, and get on with it," Rita found life there as demanding as the British army. She recognized, though, that it was good for her and resolved never to have any further emotional scenes in front of anyone but her druggist! While her year in Minnesota gave Rita the opportunity to explore and fulfill her creative gifts and helped her grow immeasurably as an artist, her assessment of herself still depended upon an attachment to a male figure. Now, instead of a lover to guide her, she had Sir Tyrone stirring her artistic objectives to more meaningful heights. Though she wrote to Grace at length about the theatre, she, like the rest of us, left out any truly personal revelations.

Bettina, tucked away in Dedham, was a young woman who believed she was not entitled to upheavals or revelations. As a child she had been taught not to blow her own horn. Tactfully, Bettina had acquired that self-deprecating humor by which many of us learned to undersell ourselves, or at least to minimize any appearance of self-importance.

What Bettina thought was important was her daughter Lizzie's curiosity and the development of the important ideas in Lizzie's head. In the early Sixties, Lizzie Gray came home from the Beaver School toting a guitar and singing "We Shall Overcome." Only the attempt to answer her child's socially upheaving questions and sharing the magic of Lizzie's love for Tolkien's *The Hobbit* relieved the boredom that was beginning to overwhelm Bettina in Dedham. Through Lizzie, Bettina vented her own stultified intellectual curiosity. Her emotional curiosity was as dormant as ever. Bettina, the young woman, was the girl who had moved every two years and learned to accept the way things were. Under this preordained reality, she valiantly tried to make the best of being the wife and mother she was meant to be.

Maree was busy building her second family, tending to her large Chestnut Hill home and her girls while Bud went off daily to his stock brokerage firm. Grace, who had known Arvid Pamp, Maree's first husband, was pleased to learn from Maree that he kept in contact with his daughter Linda, even though he had remained in Colombia.

Maree continued to do volunteer work, always looking forward in the winter to Christmas Eve, when she held a large open house for friends of all ages who had nobody with whom to share the holidays. During spring vacations Bud, Maree and the children took off for a holiday in St. Croix. It was a homogeneous family group. Linda was at an age when dolls were still important in her life. Louise, eight years her junior, seemed like a real version of a plaything. Their trips together were not colored by sibling rivalry, but gave Linda the chance to play more hours with her baby sister, dressing her up, fixing her hair, and, mostly, as Maree recalls, dropping her.

In America we avidly read all the coverage the international press had just started to give to "the Beautiful People." Grace and Rainier were reported to be at the hub of the opulent glitter, and though we knew from Grace that they turned down more invitations than they accepted, the photographs of Grace in her elaborate dresses and her letters telling of particular parties made us aware that ol' Gracie could not quite be called a stay-at-home.

In Philadelphia, Maree studied the photos of Grace in her lavish ball gowns, all created by leading French couturiers, and read of her school chum's rise on the various lists of the World's Ten Best-Dressed Women. And Maree giggled. As a teenager, she remembered Grace as having the ultimate worst taste in clothes. Ma Kelly gave her middle daughter a $35-a-month clothing allowance, which sufficed, even in their circle, only because Grace's mother had always had her dressed in clothes left over from her sister's cast-off wardrobe. Peggy's rejects would go directly to their mother's sewing machine for adjustments and then right onto Grace's back. Fordy, the Kelly's chauffeur, was fond of noting, "Ma Kelly has money to burn, but she doesn't like to smell the smoke!"

Now the hand-me-down kid was being lionized as one of the world's greatest paragons of fashion. While that pleased both Maree and Grace, it only reinforced the way Grace was about clothes. As a young girl in Philadelphia, as a movie star, and now as Princess of Monaco, she had sudden flurries of bad taste which I used to call her "Ma Kelly throw-backs." Grace, who had a great eye for beauty, also had a dowdy streak in her. We can all look back over pictures of ourselves in which the clothing we wore has gone out of style, but there are pictures of Grace over the years in which she looks like an unstylish frump. Inheriting her mother's practicality, she kept almost all her clothing, the good along with the bad, as faithfully as a squirrel storing nuts for winter.

The acclaim that the Princess garnered had little effect on Fordy, her family's chauffeur. When Princess Grace was visiting her parents at their Henry Avenue house in the early 1960s and Maree came by to visit, Fordy would answer the door, ask perkily, "You want to see Grace?" and then go to the stairs to announce the visitor by yelling up, "Gracie, you've got company." Between those visits and the summer ones that Grace, Rainier and their children made to the Ocean City Kelly family home, Maree was among the two of her bridesmaids who saw Grace most.

Next to Maree it was Sally who visited with Grace most often, either in New York or at the Jersey shore. Like Maree's, Sally's life seemed to be the most balanced and familiar. She and John were married, and their boys were proceeding calmly through elementary school, unagitated by any of the changes that America, and particularly its youth, were beginning to experience.

Sally still made it a practice to be home from errands or volunteer work by the time her boys returned from school in the late afternoon. She had begun to assist with benefits and other fund-raising activities in support of the George Junior Republic, a supervised community for young people who had had brushes with the law. During the summer Sally and the boys settled into a rented home for a three-month stay in one of two associated house complexes in upstate New York. The boys attended day camp during the week and frolicked with their parents on the weekends when John regularly came up from the city.

Not so far away on Long Island, Malcolm Reybold thought of his newly built house as a "nice little family nest." He was apparently unaware that his wife Carolyn was beginning to feel more and more like a bird trapped in a suburban cage. Carolyn's trips to the city became increasingly rarer. In order to go to town, she had to drive fifteen miles to pick up the sitter and deliver her to the children, then drive to the station, take the commuter train in, and—at the end of the evening—take the commuter train home, drive to the house, and pick up the sitter for another fifteen-mile jaunt to get her home before retiring with her alarm set for the crack of dawn so she could get up to feed her children, dress them, and get them off to school. Malcolm began staying in the city overnight more frequently than he had before, while Carolyn turned every bit of her focus and her energy inward on herself and their three daughters. The bleak winter months were the worst for her. She agreed with a visiting friend who noted, "Winter on Long Island is like something out of a Russian novel."

Some relief did come when Grace called to say she was in New York and set a date for them and their daughters to go to the ballet and to tea. Carolyn took only her eldest, Jyl, Grace's ten-year-old godchild, who became instantly mesmerized by the beauty and warmth of her illustrious godparent, as well as awestruck by the recognition and adulation the crowds heaped upon her.

Carolyn was impressed by the independence she saw Grace nurturing in her oldest child. At the ballet, although little Caroline was only four, Grace encouraged her to purchase her own program and count out her own change in American coins. And at the Palm Court of the Plaza, where Sally and other friends joined them for tea, Carolyn thought of the small Princess as a mini-reporter as she watched her walking around the table or the room, thinking of questions and returning to her mother to have them answered on the spot.

When Grace returned to Monaco and Carolyn's life settled back into its usual pattern, Carolyn found herself feeling terribly isolated. Even those cocktail parties she could have attended with Malcolm held no attraction for her. Not only was much of the conversation superficial, but Malcolm made her uncomfortable by telling what he called "amusing family stories" in which he usually got his laugh at the expense of Carolyn or their children. Though she was only ten, Jyl Reybold, too, knew something in the family household was wrong. Like many other children, she prayed at night before retiring, starting with the words, "Now I lay me down to sleep." But unlike other children, Jyl often ended her prayers by politely asking the Lord to let her die before morning came.

With no other focus for her energies, Carolyn began to develop what sounded to me like an almost obsessive concern with her own health, Malcolm's and that of their three children. Malcolm himself was a hypochondriac. In addition to several real ailments, there were frequent references to other mysterious problems he would not discuss.

Carolyn must have sounded confused or unhappy when an old friend from California visited her on Long Island and suggested she find a psychiatrist. "Everyone in California is in analysis," her friend urged. Carolyn was at first resistant to the idea, knowing that Malcolm disapproved of psychiatry and the expense connected with it. Finally, without telling her husband, Carolyn began making periodic withdrawals from her household account and sporadic trips to Manhattan, where she secretly began analysis.

At exactly the same time that Carolyn began her self-investigation, I abandoned mine. Following my near-disastrous treatment with LSD, my decision to divorce, and my embarkation on a new marriage, I was sure I would have my life under perfect control once again. Tony had always lived in rented quarters or in places Shelley owned. He wanted to buy his own "dream house," and now seemed to be the time. In the fall of 1962 we moved into a large house on Arden Drive in Beverly Hills and began slowly to redecorate it.

I was still driving car pools, taking the girls to ballet and other classes, and working with various charities. Tony and I shared a strong social conscience, though his seemed more activist than mine had been to date. We had been part of a large group in Hollywood that attended parties and worked for Jack Kennedy. After his inauguration we had seen the President and the First Lady at the home of various California friends and co-workers who entertained them. Occasionally, the President's sister and brother-in-law Pat and Peter Lawford invited us to their Santa Monica home at the beach for parties in Jack's honor. But this proximity did not make me more than one of the millions of other Americans who were stirred by the young President. At twenty-eight, I decided that if my generation was indeed going to shape the world to its liking, it was time to get on with it. The recognition that I was actually responsible for a great deal more than I had originally acknowledged was both comforting and stimulating. I had always been generous with dollars in accordance with my means, but the sense that I could go to work and spend my time and energy shaping the society, molding the community we shared on this planet with our fellow human beings, was new to me. I learned quickly that I was motivated to work for causes more difficult to espouse than for those that had already won widespread popularity.

By the mid-Sixties I was involved with everything from policy-making and fund-raising to office and field work, serving on boards such as the United Nations Association, West Los Angeles Chapter of UNICEF (then a target of the John Birch Society), the Constitutional Rights Foundation and the American Civil Liberties Union Foundation of Southern California (which I have remained deeply committed to). I co-chaired a drive for fair housing legislation, and was appointed to the Women's Advisory Council for the California Fair Employment Practices Commission and to the Advisory Committee for the California Board of Education charged with developing new Bill of Rights curricula for vari-ous grade levels of the state's public school system.

Though Tony continued to get regular top-level job offers in television and on the stage, he received fewer and fewer scripts for movies. Eventu-ally, his agents told us they thought he was being blackballed by the major studios. They believed that my father—who had never accepted our marriage, still was not speaking to me, and remained close to Jay—had seen to it that Tony's career in pictures should be slowed to a halt. According to the rumors, the current West Coast Paramount studio head was the man carrying this message to his peers on behalf of my father.

If Hollywood often seems like a battleground of competitive major corporations, it is first and foremost a company town. No industry presidents or vice presidents (and, as the saying goes, "there are more of them than us") wanted to be identified as a quotable source. Privately, many of them abhorred what was going on, but saw it as a family squabble.

After Tony and I had been married just over a year, I flew to New York and called my father, telling him I wanted to come to Greenwich, Connecticut, where he and my mother had moved after selling their large house in Rye. My mother was in Florida, and perhaps because I caught him off guard, my father invited me to the country at lunchtime on Saturday. This was first and foremost a business meeting, a form of human communication my father could tolerate. When we retired to the living room with coffee, in a businesslike and unemotional way I told him why I had come. I also demanded that the industry blackballing of my husband be put to an end.

My father denied he'd had anything to do with initiating the campaign I described. I said that just wasn't good enough. I gave him the names of three people who had finally had sufficient courage to allow me to repeat what they had told us—that my father's studio head vice president was implying to his counterparts at the other major studios that Mr. Balaban would be just as happy if they neglected to hire his daughter's husband for a role. "Since I didn't ask anyone to do it in the first place," my father asked, "why or how can I ask them to stop?"

"I'll tell you why you have to do it," I told my father. "You've spent a good part of your life working for causes and issues which are meant to give a fair shake to everyone in this society who deserves one. You are the great proponent of equal opportunities for all, the great man who bought the Bill of Rights and gave it to the Library of Congress, who purchased the Emancipation Proclamation and gave it to the church at which President Lincoln worshiped. Even if you have not been behind this blackball, your name is being used as its creator, and that belies every single thing you have stood for in your adult life. As a board member of the National Conference of Christians and Jews, you ought to abhor the fact that my non-Jewish husband is a victim of the very kind of persecution you loathe, and that the only 'crimes' he has committed are three: he was born Catholic, he's been divorced, and he fell in love with your daughter, who fell in love with him. Are you willing to stake your reputation for fairness on those accusations?"

My father would have made a great poker player, though the only time I had ever seen him deal a pack of cards he dealt faceup to validate his statement that cards weren't his forte. He still needed to know how serious I was about the matter at hand. "If you are unwilling to both make a call and write a letter about this, with a blind copy to me and proof of delivery, I'm going to court."

"My God!" my father exclaimed. "Why would you do a thing like that?"

"Because I am unwilling, after all these years, to betray all the ideals you taught me growing up!" I had no more ammunition. But I didn't need any. My father promised to send me a copy of the letter for approval the following week before mailing the final draft.

"There's another thing I need to ask you," I continued. "It has to do with what is going on in our lives together at this stage."

"What's that?" my father asked somewhat warily.

"I'm only about thirty years old, and I don't think I have any time to waste loving the people I love and spending time with them in ways that make us all feel better. How can you, in your seventies, think you have such a luxury of time that you can waste it the way you do with us when things don't go exactly the way you think they should? If you ever feel you can explain it to me, I'm always available for the answer."

There is something wonderful about letting go of the hook a parent has in you. But there is something awful, too. My father looked at me rather helplessly and said, "I can't talk to you about this. You make too much sense." Then he got up to leave and turned back only to ask hopefully, "Can you stay for dinner and overnight?" and in that single moment the balance of need had shifted. The myth of his omnipotence died as I recognized that he wanted my approval as much as I wanted his. If that made me sad, it also made me pray we had enough years left to learn to be close as adults.

Grace, though, did not have enough time. Maybe that was always the case in her life. In 1960, Jack Kelly, the handsome, swaggering, all-powerful father of Grace's reticent childhood, contracted cancer. During the four years after her marriage, Pa Kelly had persisted in flinging the little digs and darts his daughter Grace had become accustomed to since childhood. But she was aware that in those days he did it more to remind her and others that they should not be inordinately impressed with her new status. For in truth, before he died, Jack learned to harbor deep—if undeclared—respect for his middle daughter.

There was not as much time for them to enjoy this relationship as there would have been had he lived for another few years, another decade or longer. But there was just enough time for Grace to be reminded of how many years it had taken them to come to this mutually respectful, even affectionate truce. Not long enough for Grace to bask in Jack's long-withheld approval that she had craved since childhood. Not long enough to heal the wounds in her soul, but long enough to show the other Kelly children, especially Peggy, who for years had been the apple of her father's eye, that in his final vision it was little worthless Gracie who had won the family competition for its patriarch's admiration. Perhaps, for his children's sake, Jack Kelly should have died either later or sooner. But for all of his power to dominate, it was for him—as with us all—the one subject over which he had no say.

CHAPTER 10

Show Me a Hero

Gracie lost a lot in the early Sixties. A lot of us did. Consumed with the desire for a large family with many children, Grace became pregnant twice, only to see her pregnancies end in early miscarriages. Her view of herself as an indomitable child-bearer was shaken to its core. So was her dream, usually held deep within herself, that she would be able to act professionally again in her lifetime. Her early years as "just a person" who happened to be the wife of a prince, mother to their children, and benefactor to a group of regional charities came to a resounding conclusion as public opinion, local and international politics, and the will of her subjects conspired to show her what price she was expected to pay for her princessdom.

During the first five years of their marriage, Grace had subtly let Rainier know how much she missed working as an actress. With her usual solicitude, Grace pled her case with neither complaint nor implication that the life Rainier was providing for her was less than wonderful. "I want" was a hard thing for all of us to say. But Grace communicated to Rainier the importance of doing something that was her very own. Rainier was aware of the melancholy that pervaded Grace when her father died, her pregnancies came to untimely ends, and her career began fading more distantly into the past. And because he truly wanted Grace to be happy, he began to consider the possibility that she might make an occasional film appearance if the proper situation arose. It was a generous way of Rainier backing Grace's faith in herself, a fair exchange for the ways she had been backing his faith in himself during the political crises that had been brewing since their wedding.

During the early years of their marriage, there had been trouble between Rainier and the National Council of Monaco. Each side had rejected the other's proposed constitutional reforms. The Council's opposition bloc chafed at its inability to initiate legislation and felt hamstrung by having no line-item veto over the national budget, which was, by law, always submitted by the Prince. Intransigent and traditional, the bloc vehemently opposed Rainier's innovative plan for the future development of the Principality. This included a creative program for expanding Monaco's terrain through a series of land reclamation projects.

In 1959 the Council had made a brash end run by vetoing the Prince's entire annual budget. He countered with a divine right touchdown, taking to the airwaves to announce that he was suspending the Constitution, dissolving the Council, and abolishing the right to demonstrate for political purposes. Though his tactics were labeled "undemocratic" and "dictatorial," even the liberal U.S. press took no stand against him. Perhaps the media recognized that in moving decisively against the entrenched, short-sighted provinciality that plagued many of his countrymen, Rainier was finally and firmly establishing the true commencement of what was to become his long, dynamic, popular and extremely successful rule of Monaco.

Three years later, though, Grace and Rainier found themselves up against a heavyweight, one who literally threatened the Grimaldi rule and the independence of all Monaco—France's President, Charles de Gaulle. Nearly half of the individuals and entities that had recently been attracted to Monaco's tax-free haven were of French origin. Newly situated in Monaco, they made vast contributions to the revenues of the Principality. But when they left France, they seriously depleted its tax rolls. In the spring of 1962, when Rainier decided to halt further French investment in his country's far-reaching television enterprise, De Gaulle decided to remind the Prince that his rights were not as divine in some quarters as they were in others. The General demanded that Rainier rescind the order regarding French investors in Monaco's TV operations. Rainier refused. Through an emissary, De Gaulle sent word that France would abolish the tariff agreement between the two countries that autumn. This would effectively end Monaco's right to provide its liberal tax advantages and force the Principality to draft new economic policies in concert with those of France.

For Grace, the timing could not have been worse. It was just at this juncture that the personal opportunity she had waited for so patiently presented itself. Earlier in the year Alfred Hitchcock had offered her the starring role in his upcoming film *Marnie*. Grace and Rainier discussed the project in detail. They both reasoned that she had proved to their Monégasque subjects and the world that she was a dedicated princess, a devoted mother and an exemplary wife. Surely no one would question her loyalty and commitment to her life in Monaco if she returned to make this one movie. Together, Grace and Rainier decided that it could be done.

On March 18, 1962, a carefully worded communiqué was issued from the Palais Princier. Their Serene Highnesses, accompanied by their children, would vacation in the United States that autumn. While on this holiday, the Princess would play the leading role in *Marnie*, to be directed by Alfred Hitchcock. To reinforce the brevity of their absence, the announcement concluded with the statement that "Her Highness will return to Monaco with her family in November." It was probably the worst-timed announcement in show business history, though looking back, I think there never was a right time for it.

All of Grace's Stateside friends were happy for her. But our pleasure was overshadowed by the buoyant enthusiasm Grace herself expressed to us. When I called the Palace her voice bubbled like that of a teenager. I realized that being a working actress, even a returning star, would be quite a change in Grace's daily life, if only for the brief period of the shooting schedule. "Don't you think that going back to work," I hypothesized, "might feel strange to you after having been away from it, the way you have been, for five years?"

The first part of Grace's answer came slowly, reflectively and cautiously. "Yesss," she responded, "likely it will feel strange." There was a moment's gap in our conversation while she sorted out her feelings. "But won . . . der . . . ful!" she erupted, unable to contain her delight any longer.

We talked about the possibility that we might be able to celebrate our birthdays together, either in Los Angeles or on location in October. I said I wasn't sure if I wanted to be away from my family on this day, but Grace suggested that if she were out of town I might have one celebration at home and another on the weekend with her, Rainier and the Hitchcocks. When we hung up I remember wondering why acting again meant so much to Grace. On the one hand, she seemed to have everything anyone could want as Princess of Monaco, wife to her husband and mother to her children. Was it just the lark of it all, the notion of having the fun of the work on top of everything else? That was the way she had tried to make it sound, but I had come away with my first suspicion that there was a great deal more at stake. There was something about Grace that I had missed, and therefore simply did not comprehend.

It was not only Grace's friends, but also her fans around the world who were thrilled to know she was going to make another movie. As it turned out, however, we were to be overridden by a small but vocal minority— Grace's Monégasque subjects.

The Princess of Monaco belonged in Monaco, not in Hollywood. The Princess of Monaco should not cheapen herself by working as a common actress. The Princess of Monaco must not be seen kissing another man on the screen. The Princess of Monaco, a reserved Catholic woman, should not play the role of a frigid, neurotic thief, nor should she appear in a film that contained a rape. Once back in Hollywood, the Princess of Monaco would surely turn her back on her family and the community obligations of her Principality. She would abandon her dedication to her role as Princess just as quickly as she had picked it up in the first place.

The Palace tried to counter these charges with a series of reassuring and reasonable responses. Nothing stemmed the tide of disapproval. It mounted daily, feeding on itself, in every shop, restaurant and living room, across every telephone and wash line threaded throughout the Principality.

Rainier stood firm against his subjects' provinciality to forward his plans for the country's development, but his wife acceded to their will.

Grace gave a short interview to *Nice-Matin* in which she stated that she would not be appearing in Hitchcock's production of *Marnie* because its shooting schedule had to be moved to early 1963, when her family would not be able to accompany her to the States. And, she added, "I have been very influenced by the reaction which the announcement provoked in Monaco." From a master at the art of understatement, it was the understatement of a lifetime.

I had not written to Grace in quite a while, but after reading her decision I decided to call again. I realized something of vast importance had just happened to my friend. At that point in my life I didn't know quite what. It had not yet dawned upon me that we had selves that might operate separately from the needs of husband and family. By phone, Grace sounded so reassuringly brave that it enforced my belief that she had taken the only action possible. Besides, we were both still too young to think about life in terms of "forever." In the back of my mind—maybe hers as well—there was the thought that circumstances would present Grace with another opportunity to act again at a later date. But underneath I heard something in Gracie's voice I had never heard before. It was the sound of hope dying.

By autumn of that year, when De Gaulle's six-month ultimatum had expired, though we heard that France was readying to attack Monaco or at least cripple it by cutting off its utilities and transportation systems, no such disasters occurred. Instead, the two leaders reached an agreement under which Rainier was allowed to retain the independence of his country simply by giving the Frenchmen back to France, specifically those who had established residency in the Principality during the past five years. For De Gaulle and Rainier, a face-saving negotiation resulted in a compromise. So there was no war in Monaco during 1962 except for the one Grace lost.

Between the Prince and Princess, though, there had grown the strong bonds of camaraderie under fire, and a shared sense of humor that attested to the comfort of their union. One morning that year, Rainier presented Grace with a cartoon from *New Yorker* magazine which he had cut out and had framed for her. It depicted a king and queen in the privacy of their bedroom, with the wife announcing to her husband, "Don't pull those divine rights on me, Buster!"

* * *

In the spring of 1963 my father called from the Beverly Hills Hotel. I presumed he was going to ask me to drop the children off for breakfast with him the following morning, before they went to school and he went to the office. Instead, with no fanfare, he asked simply, "Can I come over to have breakfast with you, Tony and the girls?" It was a good day, the first one on which my father and my second husband had ever met. Tony had night shooting that evening and I was to go to the Coconut Grove, where Nat "King" Cole was opening, in order to present Nat with an award from the United Nations Association. I invited my father to go with me, and by the time we drove to the Ambassador Hotel, I was able to tell him what I had confirmed to Tony a few hours earlier—that we were expecting a baby in December.

By that time I had begun to live a double, though not surreptitious, life. A year earlier Al Lowenstein had called me on a trip to California. He was becoming ever more widely respected for his work in a variety of humanitarian causes both at home and abroad. The first outsider ever permitted to make a presentation to the United Nations Security Council, Al had exposed the reality of South African apartheid to that body. His U.N. presentation had grown into a book, published under the title *Brutal Mandate*. By the time Al and I had our early 1960s reunion, he was already working closely with Dr. Martin Luther King, Jr., and the Southern Christian Leadership Conference. Al had enlisted my support early on, and the work was growing to new and feverish heights.

On the one hand, I was a Hollywood wife—lunching, gabbing, dining with all the same friends I had enjoyed for years and with new ones whom Tony and I had come to know together. A lot of the women in our group were pregnant at that time, and we resembled, en masse, the makings of a fat ladies' convention. The other half of my life was consumed with day and night meetings and phone calls enlisting support of every kind for Dr. King's movement and his upcoming Civil Rights March in Washington.

It was a wonderful summer and, at least for the first part of it, a marvelous fall. I felt pregnant in every possible way and I was loving it. I shared long hours with new friends, working on events, fund-raising and political mobilization. I had Al Lowenstein back in my life, inspiring me to believe that what each one of us did mattered. Oh, there were crazies out there. We knew that because we could see them and hear them. But there were more of us than of them, and we were most assuredly going to change things, make them better for ourselves, for the children we had, for those who were on the way and for our children's children.

Then—way too quickly—a fuse blew. A major fuse. I had been up late working on budgets for a campaign to feed the hungry in the South, and had arisen early to drive car pool and make calls about pre-planning for a 1964 voter registration drive. After ordering my Thanksgiving turkey for the following week, I leaned against my pillows and fell back to sleep. A half hour later I awoke sharply with Tony shaking me. And when I did, the world had turned upside down. Tony was pointing to the television screen. Camera shots jumped from streets I could not recognize to other streets, to the studio and back onto the streets again, where cars, ambulances and motorcycle policemen raced about or stood stone still in terror. A voice so choked with tears and incredulity as to be unidentifiable was telling us that President John F. Kennedy had been shot in the head while riding in a Dallas motorcade. Within minutes we knew that he was being treated in the Parkland Hospital Emergency Room. And not much longer after that, we discovered that though there were more of us than of them, we were powerless.

Even now, the weekend of November 22–24, 1963, remains kaleidoscopically unfathomable for most of us who were alive then. My little girls in their navy blue John Thomas Dye jumpers, crisp white blouses and red sweaters were ushered out of their classrooms at the lovely, whitewashed schoolhouse where we and the Reagans and a lot of other secure families had sent our children to be prepared for the world as we knew it. They were taken to the well-manicured school lawn, overlooking the lush gardens of protected Bel Air mansions, and they were told to stand at attention. Then an adult voice, devoid of any ability to sound reassuring, informed them that President John F. Kennedy had been shot in Dallas and lay dead there; and the flag was lowered to half-mast.

We mothers drove immediately up the hill to collect our children. It made no difference if we were liberals or conservatives, Republicans or Democrats, we had been equalized by the sudden and terrible realization that our children would not grow up as we had.

The President's death fell hard upon Gracie, in more ways than one. She had admired Jack Kennedy enormously for his energy and his strong Irish-American drive, the same drive she had learned to respect and emulate during her childhood years. She admired his leadership and his ability to arouse us to be positive and active reflections of our beliefs, regardless of what she—or any of us for that matter—might have felt about the political positions he had taken on the individual problems of the day. Grace and Rainier had visited Jack and Jackie Kennedy at the White House. A photo had been taken in which Grace, wearing a white hat that looked as if it were made of torn feathers, was looking up at President Kennedy, who towered above her. She was smiling, and the angle from which the photo was shot made her smile look impish and flirtatious. For a time afterwards, rumors had circulated that Jackie Kennedy hated the picture, believing it showed Grace admiring her husband in a less than official way. The whole uproar had embarrassed Grace terribly.

On the day President Kennedy died, Grace was in Monaco. Because it was eight hours earlier in Texas, Jack Kennedy was still asleep when Grace rose to join her people in celebrating a national holiday. She donned a pastel wool suit with a boxy, hiplength jacket and straight skirt, pale hose and low-heeled, pointed calf pumps. Keeping her softly waved and bobbed hair uncovered, she set forth with her children and their nanny to attend the traditional Monégasque carnival. Her day was spent happily, touring the various games and exhibitions with her subjects. At one point, in order to show her good sportsmanship, Grace accepted a boothkeeper's invitation to stop and play at his stand. She lifted one of the rifles from the felt-covered counter, and without taking off her prescription sunglasses, aimed and fired at the shooting gallery. A photographer snapped her picture in the act, and she continued on her way. Not until she returned to the Palace at the end of the day did Grace and the rest of Monaco learn of the Kennedy assassination.

When she did, she was shattered. So was Rainier. The Consul who advised them on American matters was, at that time, on an ocean liner crossing the Atlantic. Placing a ship-to-shore call, the Consul and their Highnesses discussed the advisability of making plans to attend the Kennedy funeral. No announcement of burial plans had reached Monaco yet, and the Consul had not spoken with anyone in Washington. Grace was in such a state of shock herself that she imagined the Kennedy family would be consumed with grief and unable to function. She reflected that it might appear invasive if she and Rainier flew to Washington. Grace and Rainier made plans to honor the President at a special Requiem Mass in their own Cathedral.

That is not, however, how it all came out in the international press. First, without ever bothering to mention the time difference and the fact that the Kennedy motorcade was hours from starting when the photo was taken, newspapers carried the picture of Grace with a rifle pointed toward an automated gallery of ducks and pinwheels (the target off camera, of course). Under the photo, stories around the world accused Grace of being heartless, insensitive and devoid of all taste. Here was a young woman, American and of Irish lineage just like the fallen President, who went out on the day of this heinous shooting to shoot for fun and pleasure. Every bit of dirt that could be imagined blossomed from that inaccurate representation: Grace was pro-handguns and against gun control. Grace had joined a legion of hunters and elitists who advocated shooting laws so permissive that they—and perhaps Grace herself—were responsible for the society in which the Lee Oswalds and Jack Rubys could grow to manhood and then destroy. Then came the stories about Grace's failure to attend the Kennedy funeral. These insisted her absence attested to her callousness, that she had turned her back on her own country and its slain hero. Other journalists revived rumors circulated at the time of the old photo with the Kennedys, Grace and Rainier. They speculated that Jackie had issued orders that Grace was not to attend, or that Grace feared she would be expelled if she tried to enter Washington.

Grace was emotionally distraught. She issued clarifying statements both about the carnival photograph and her decision not to attend the presidential funeral. They were, of course, totally ignored by the rabble-rousing press. But Grace was so deeply affected by these criticisms at such a painful time that for the rest of her life she went to every funeral to which she was invited and even sought out funerals of anybody she had known, lest her failure to attend them might elicit unwelcomed gossip. The incident turned Grace into a funeral junkie, against her better wishes if not her better judgment.

On the night of the day that Ruby shot Oswald, Tony and I sat with Amy and Vicki in the den watching the British *That Was the Week That*

Was episode that had been produced on the Kennedy assassination and sent hastily to America for TV airing. Our baby was not due for another four weeks, but I began to feel the steadily strengthening pinch of labor contractions. Miss Mack and our housekeeper were off, so I asked Tony to go next door to see if the neighbors' teenage children could come and baby-sit while we went to the hospital.

Though Dr. Krohn had been prepared to let me deliver normally, at the hospital he began to hear a slowing in the baby's heartbeat, indicating another placenta separation. Not wanting to risk a prolonged labor, he delivered my third daughter, Nina Franciosa, on November 24, 1963, by Caesarian section. No incubation was required as the baby was not as premature as Vicki had been. I began to nurse, but had to shift Nina to a bottle when severe pains in my abdomen proved to be a recurrence of peritonitis, contracted while in the delivery room. Three nights later, on Thanksgiving Eve, alone in my hospital room waiting for Nina to be brought in, I read and reread the telegram Grace had sent two days earlier. It said, "THANK YOU SO MUCH FOR REAFFIRMING OUR BELIEF IN LIFE JUST AT THE TIME WHEN WE ALL NEED IT SO BADLY. LOVE FROM ALL OF US TO ALL OF YOU. GRACE."

By the end of the year, though I did not yet know what to call it, I knew "The Sixties" had arrived. In many ways it was a different revolution from the one we had been expecting. "Moon/June/Croon/Tune" songs were gradually disappearing from our airwaves. Our children were singing songs called "If I Had a Hammer" and "Puff the Magic Dragon." As a mother of three girls, I had never expected them to have a hammer unless it was for shop class in elementary school. As for Puff, I myself was crazy about Peter, Paul and Mary, and thought it was an adorable song until the rumor spread that it was actually a paean to the joys of smoking marijuana. Some scrawny-looking boys from England with unkempt hair were chanting away about all their lovin', and we were no longer gliding around our dance floors like gazelles, but learning to crack our necks, press our palms downward, and climb our vines while we did dances called the Watusi, the Mashed Potato and the Monkey. Mary McCarthy had blown our cover, and perhaps the cover of some of our mothers, by writing *The Group*, which informed anyone who cared to know that not every girl born before the end of World War II had remained pure as the driven snow until her nuptial night. I wasn't sure whether that made the ravaged

had never played with our own children. It took a long time for most of us, but the body count of strangers in our bedrooms on nightly television finally convinced us that, declared or not, Vietnam was a real war and we were in it up to our ears. Once we understood that fact, it began to divide not only our national estate but also the very homes we lived in.

Bettina and Lizzie Gray had long shared their intellectual interests. Reading books and comparing ideas, they had grown to have a healthy respect for each other's views. But one afternoon in the mid-1960s, the adolescent Lizzie brought home a photograph that was being circulated widely in Harvard Square. It showed a group of napalm-sprayed Vietnamese children running in fear down a long dirt road. "Mummy," Lizzie inquired, "what do you think of Lyndon Johnson's escalation of this war?"

"I think the government knows more about what's going on than I do," Bettina answered. "But your grandfather always said our armed forces would never win a war fought on an Asian mainland." It was a 1940s answer to a 1960s question—a World War II answer to a war that could not be defined simply by what our government knew because, as we later learned, from the opening volley there was way too much our government did not know. In matters of national or international significance, we had been raised to think that we were the followers and "they" our leaders. Our children, though, were not content with these roles, nor pleased with the way the roles were being played. Their new questions and our pre-programmed answers widened the schism that came to be known as "the generation gap."

Armed with the seemingly bizarre notion that they were entitled to take independent stances on matters of substance, our children followed examples that had only recently been set for them. Years later the fledglings' revolutionary behavior would be attributed to disrespectful "liberals" or "radicals" who were supposed to have set the tone for the times. I recall it differently. The first "youth movement" began in Little Rock, Arkansas, in 1957 and raged on through 1962, when it relocated to the campus of Old Miss, the University of Mississippi. During those five years, tens of thousands of middle American school-age children—under the guidance of Governor Orville Faubus, Governor Ross Barnett and their huge cadres of U.S. law-enforcement officers—taught our children everything they needed to know, and then some, about rioting, civil disobedience and allegedly justifiable anarchy.

We watched our TV sets to see white Americans shooting down their black neighbors, and sympathetic white ones as well. Defying the law of the land, which had declared segregation unconstitutional, and invoking the name of the Lord, Governors Faubus and Barnett were showing us their version of "doing your own thing." And "Two-Four-Six-Eight We Don't Want to Integrate" became the first actual protest song we or our own kids had ever heard.

Some of us were unaffected by the troubles of the day. Our children were too young or we did not watch the news with them. Sally Richardson did not think that the causes, movements and demonstrations of the Sixties were of much value. Time, she believed, would ultimately cure our national ills. If we all just exercised a bit more patience, things that needed to be changed would be. It was the sort of faith in society that we had been raised with, the comfortable notion that we were led by an enlightened elite who would do the right thing. I did not share Sally's views.

At that period a personal ill and divisive wind was blowing across the Reybolds' suburban dream house on the north shore of Long Island. Malcolm was obsessed with his health. He had also kept to himself a diagnosis of skin cancer and another malignancy, never telling either his friends or his wife of this concern. And by the middle of the 1960s, Malcolm started to worry that he had a bad heart.

Still secretly seeing her psychiatrist, Carolyn, too, was becoming obsessed with physical ailments, her own as well as those of her three daughters. She began seeing a homeopathic doctor and put her children under his care as well.

Not too many years before, Jyl Reybold had been a little girl who sat at her mother's side watching Liberace on television and writing "candelabra" at the top of her Christmas wish list for Santa Claus. Now, as she reached her high school years in the mid-1960s, she was a chronically sick teenager. Jyl did not feel sick, except for those minor aches and pains and an occasional flu for which her father once took her to a traditional local doctor. But her mother and the homeopath she was seeing thought she was sick. Gradually the litany of "diseases" Jyl became afflicted with mounted. If she complained of an upset stomach she was taken out of school, rushed to the doctor, diagnosed as having diphtheria from swimming, and kept out of school for a protracted period during which she lived like an invalid. Jyl had two thoughts: one, that there was not much point in trying to go to school because it wouldn't be possible for her to attend with any regularity; the other, that there was something highly abnormal going on in her household. She did not feel sick, only confused. In desperation, Jyl turned to Sherman Fairchild, her family's friend. Sherman agreed that something was wrong and promised to talk to Malcolm, but for all his influence over his neighbor, even Sherman could not get Malcolm to focus on the problem or its magnitude.

It was a period when Malcolm's testiness grew into rages. At home, he refused to talk about his problems and simply closed his eyes to those things he did not want to make time for, including the household checkbook, where he would have found evidence of the thousands of dollars of money withdrawn for his wife's secret visits to her New York City psychiatrist. To cement the division in their family, Malcolm took to living by himself in one wing of the house.

Nothing, though, divided the families of Maree or Sally, nor did anything separate them from the constant sense of continuity they shared with Grace.

While the girls were at Springside in school, Maree filled her days with lunching, shopping, a bit of volunteer work, running her home, and planning vacations. The world outside her own sphere in Philadelphia had little effect on Maree's family. Nor was there any disruption in Maree's friendship with Grace. The two continued seeing each other in Philadelphia and at the shore. Now, with her daughters more grown, Maree was also able to sandwich in solo jaunts to Monaco, where she would stay at the Palace or Roc Agel with her friend.

Like Maree, Sally was a person who never felt herself enslaved by the times, nor to some extent even affected by them. Fads did not send her rushing to the nearest clothing store. She was simply developing in her own way and on her own schedule. And in the Sixties not too much was happening that would alter that course. With the boys spending a full day at the Browning School in Manhattan, Sally decided to take a four-hour-a-day job doing benefit planning to raise funds for cancer care.

Sally and John saw mostly other couples who had never been divorced. But divorces and other marital adjustments she had observed around her led Sally to realize that life was not exactly the bed of roses she had believed it to be. The myth of getting married and living happily ever after was being modified by her increasing awareness of reality. In her thirties,

Sally felt she was at last growing up. Though she remained comfortable in her own skin, she began to question some things, among them the value that our generation had placed on appearances. Sally began to realize there was not one right way to look, dress or even live, yet she became firmer in her own resolve to live by her and John's rules rather than by anyone else's. And Sally had a lot of rules that worked for her.

When Grace came to New York, she and Sally spent time together. They had lunch, they did errands, and Grace had Sally and John included in many evening festivities planned for her. The nature of their relationship remained very much as it had always been—easy, comforting and good.

Life was not that comfortable for Bettina, and the worse it got, the less she had any inclination to maintain contact with Grace. Bettina had grown bored and unhappy—bored with her life and bored with Frank, who was also growing bored with her. Their son Sam was still a calming influence. It was Lizzie who brought the turmoil of the outside world home.

Bettina lost interest in everything, and so everything annoyed her. She was still doing volunteer work at the hospital, but that had grown stale. Coming home to the ever-challenging Lizzie exhausted her further. When her daughter, her husband and her son retired for the night, Bettina began curling up in an armchair, hoping that comforting references to her past would soothe or inspire her. "Into each life some rain must fall," sang Ella Fitzgerald over and over again on the phonograph. "But too much is falling in mine," Ella warbled. Bettina sat up all night listening as Ella sang out about the discontent she herself could not express.

Feeling the way she did, Bettina simply had nothing to say to Grace. It never dawned upon her to say how she was feeling, because how we were really feeling was still not something we talked about easily, if at all. When Grace's letters continued to suggest that Bettina meet her in New York on her next visit to America, Bettina rejected the possibility without further thought.

By 1967, Lizzie Gray, a classic incipient revolutionary, was enrolled at the very proper St. Timothy's boarding school. She had a boyfriend, but that wasn't serious. What was serious was her vision of a career in the revolution that she thought about during most of her waking hours. Her mother had other plans for her. That year *The Graduate* started playing to rave reviews in the local movie houses. Lizzie, the budding revolutionary, was not allowed to see it. It depicted hard-drinking overachieving fathers, hard-drinking oversexed and unfulfilled mothers, and children who defied their parents' conventions and emerged as heroes. Not for our precious darlings, such exposure, thought many of us. Nor for their tender eyes the explicit sex scenes that were just erupting across the nation's movie screens. We were from the days of the Hays Office censors, when even fully clothed married couples were not allowed to be seen on film in the same bed unless one of them kept at least one foot on the floor!

Rita's children were a bit too young for *The Graduate* in 1967. Perhaps Rita was, too. Nearly obsessive about having her kids keep a clear picture of Tom as their father, Rita nonetheless retained a desperate interest in forming a relationship with another man. In her imagination she still saw herself as Audrey Hepburn in *Roman Holiday* or *Sabrina.* She met "the" man. She kissed. She fell in love, the very picture of wide-eyed adoration. Her voice rose. She became "adorable." The guy went back to his wife. A romantic adrift in a sea full of liberated married men, Rita believed all of them.

Whenever Grace came to New York, she and Rita played. Rita viewed their time together as very giggly, girls-on-the-town stuff—one girl married and very settled, the other single and with a certain amount of theatrical visibility. Winning the Best Actress Award in Berlin took Rita to Europe. On the way home she stopped in London. Grace phoned New York to speak with her, tracked down first one number in London, which Rita had already left, and finally located her at a second number. With no husband waiting for her at home, Rita decided to accept Grace's invitation to spend a few days in Monaco and accompany her to a gala. She had a dress made at Jean Muir and flew over to join her pal. She presumed that Grace comfortably accepted her status as a single, working actress and expected it would be only a matter of time before Rita and another Mr. Right marched down the aisle. In the middle to late Sixties, Rita found Grace to be very British and continental, both in voice and in attitude. She felt Grace was totally embracing her surroundings.

During this period Grace increased her dedication to binding her Monégasque family together. She was intent upon having more children, but it was just at this time that she suffered a second miscarriage, making her question whether this ever would truly be possible.

From the start of her marriage, Grace had determined to remain in the reflection of her husband's light. During their first years together, it had been Rainier who pushed Grace forward to a more visible participation in the Principality. In the early Sixties, though, with resumption of her acting career now impossible, Grace found it necessary to create a new role for herself. Many women would have been content with a self-image such as the one Grace had already built—a great wife, marvelous mother, retired screen star, loyal friend and dedicated Princess/benefactor. Most women would have reveled in the beautiful and luxurious surroundings of her Palace and her life in the Principality, punctuated by official visits and family holidays to the most renowned cities and resorts in the Western world. They would have been sufficiently challenged by tending to her children, running her enormous staff, fitting her elaborate wardrobe, and relishing her collection of royal jewels. Grace, though, was not most women. What she needed, she realized, was a career—something that would make her less emotionally dependent on Rainier, whose own energies were being swallowed whole by the goals he had set himself for Monaco.

What Grace sought was an appropriate career for a European wife, because being a European wife was the talent Grace had perfected in her early years in Monaco. When people talk about what a European wife really is, they say such a woman is eternally supportive and compliant with the needs of her husband and family. Many who still insist that Grace's transformation was the greatest triumph of her life explain that European wives are "women who service their husbands in every sense" . . . "women who are completely submissive" . . . "nonconfrontational women" . . . "not even like American Southern wives who seem submissive but in fact are terribly strong, just totally submissive and supportive women."

I would agree that Grace became a European wife, especially in the mid-Sixties, when she realized a resumption of her acting career was impossible. At the time I'm sure that I, too, regarded that as a triumph. Shortly afterwards, though, I gained a perspective that forced me to a different conclusion. To become a European wife, Grace picked up the brush and carefully painted herself backward into a corner. What she did

The movie went over schedule. It turned out not to be worth all that time and money. The only thing about the film that attracted the public's affection was its theme song, which became Frank Sinatra's "Strangers in the Night." Realizing we would not be able to finish our continental stay with the planned week in Monaco and still get home in time, Tony urged me to take the children and the nanny to Monaco by train so I would not miss the chance to be with Grace and her family.

An enormous display of exquisite flowers awaited us in our suite at the Hôtel de Paris. The card from Grace regretted Tony's absence, welcomed our presence, and informed me that she and Rainier would collect me for dinner around nine o'clock. When the hour came I was waiting outside the hotel as my hosts arrived in their favored runabout, the Austin Mini Cooper S, its sides painted like straw caning, with Rainier at the wheel.

We dined high in the mountains at Ferme St. Michel, and I was delighted to see Grace and Rainier both looking so well. She had lost most of her weight from Stephanie's birth and was aglow with new mother-hood. Fashion was less restrictive than in the previous decade. Clothes looked younger, softer and shorter, and Grace had adapted her hairdos and wardrobe to the new styles. Both of us were wearing long loose falls, pieces of false hair attached at the crown either by being woven into our own front hair or anchored with headbands. And both our falls fell down near to our shoulder blades, where they were turned under with just a suggestion of a pageboy. Grace and I gabbed so long about the problems of matching the quality of false hair to our own, and, in my case, the problem in trying to match my own natural red color, that Rainier finally interjected in his most comically mincing accent, "And, darlings, it's been almost impossible for me to find a fall that picks up the highlights in my eyes!"

Grace wore a pale pink, sleeveless linen dress, its Empire waistline tied with a soft satin bow. Like mine, her skirts had been shortened to reveal her knees, a prelude to the mini-skirt craze that was fast approaching. She wore her enormous engagement ring, a two-stranded pearl choker, gold hoop earrings and no other jewelry. Her mid-heeled pink kid pumps kept her from appearing taller than the Prince. She carried a pink envelope bag and an off-white cashmere cardigan to throw across her shoulders when the Mediterranean breezes chilled the night.

The three of us talked without end about our children and children in general. Grace and Rainier confirmed Caroline's independence and self-reliance, yet they also admitted that she was a most demanding child. According to them, Caroline alternated between adoring her baby sister and wishing to dispose of her. About Albert, she was not so equivocal. There her sibling rivalry raged. Grace insisted, "I've bent over backward not to favor the younger child, hoping to avoid just such jealousies, even though Albie's much cuddlier than she is, or at least more consistently cuddly." But we all agreed that children get their competitive urge from some source we cannot entirely control or mold. Years later Caroline herself would remind me of the time in their childhood when her jealousy of Albie was so intense that she tore her favorite cutout book into shreds upon seeing that he had touched it!

Grace had secured us a tent next to hers when we two mothers and our six children met late the next morning to spend the day at the Beach Club. The Monte Carlo Beach Club, called simply "the Beach," is a private oceanside enclave east of the city. It is open for admission only on a daily basis to the public, with membership reserved for residents of nearby villas and guests at facilities run by the Société des Bains de Mer (SBM), which oversees all the casinos and the finest hotels in Monaco. At street level are a group of permanent cabanas, more like small apartments, where the utmost in privacy is offered, if not the closest proximity to the sea. Grace and her family retained one of these, but had also selected a canvas cabana location right in the center of things. There they could change clothes behind the curtain, store bathing suits, and loll in the chaises provided for sunning. Though Grace disliked the throng that passed by this spot and often gawked, it allowed her to remain at her tent while she watched the children swimming in the small pool directly below it. It also placed her just behind a hedge from the larger, Olympic-sized, saltwater pool where the children swam as they grew older. In her bathing suit, Grace retained very much the body she'd had when we met. Nursing three children had increased the size of her breasts, but her upper arms remained slender and firm. Her waist was not as infinitesimal as when she had married, but she had been excessively thin then anyway. Though her hips and thighs were a bit fuller, I was still envious of her long, lean American athlete's legs and marveled out loud about what good shape she was in. "It's not easy," she replied, "not around here. The caviar alone is enough to be my undoing."

Bikinis were getting smaller that year, and while Grace herself wore a more classic one-piece suit, she did not seem offended by the brevity of the male and female bathing attire around her, nor even by the popular habit of shedding bra tops. For all its social conservatism, Europe took a natural view of nudity, and it was clear that Grace had adapted her more puritanical Philadelphia references on bared bodies to those of her current homeland.

At lunchtime we gathered our children and headed for two tables at the railing of the Terrace restaurant overlooking the big pool. The children and their nannies sat at one table while Grace and I joined Ari Onassis and Maria Callas at the other. The relationship among them and Rainier had begun to cool, but Grace obviously still adored Maria. Ari always struck me—and Grace as well—as somewhat crude, if witty, exuberant and brilliant at commerce. Grace's connection with Maria, though, was thick and deep from the start. She adored Maria's voice and respected her rise to the very apex of her chosen field. But Grace was, in addition, extremely attuned to Maria's soul and would remain so until Callas died. Speaking about my "Uncle" Spyros Skouras when we first sat down, the threesome told me a story about a cruise they and Rainier had taken together some years earlier on the *Christina*, not too long after Grace had come to Monaco.

It seems that Spyros Skouras, who was president of Twentieth Century Fox, had gotten a brainstorm upon hearing that Grace and Maria were cruising with Rainier and Ari on Ari's yacht. Calling Ari on the ship-to-shore phone, he begged him to see if Grace and Maria would appear together in Fox's upcoming religious extravaganza *The Greatest Story Ever Told*. Ari agreed to transmit Spyros's offer. At dinner that night in the dining salon, he informed Grace and Maria that Skouras would pay each of them $1 million to appear in the film, with Maria to play Magdalene and Grace to portray the Virgin Mary. For a moment, they told me, everyone had remained silent. Then Grace exploded, "No way! She gets to play Magdalene and I get stuck with the Virgin Mary? I want *her* part or I'll stay home!" Of course, neither woman appeared in the movie.

Everyone ordered lunch and I still couldn't decide what to have. Maria gave me a suggestion that Grace and Ari roundly endorsed. Even as I agreed to try it and gave my order to the captain, I reflected on the fact that the word *tête* on the menu made the dish sound ominous. I put the mental picture out of my mind and decided I should be gastronomically adventuresome.

Luncheon was served. A covered platter was set before me, and when the cover was whisked away I wished I could have been, too. For on my plate was the completely intact head of some small animal *en gelée*. While my astonished eyes looked down to see it wiggle in its molded aspic, its astonished eyes looked up at me with no greater pleasure. Its nostrils were slightly flared. Its mouth opened to reveal a slightly hairy tongue that had been stretched across the plate. "Beautiful!" everyone exclaimed in assorted languages. I was literally tongue-tied. My instincts told me to beg off and ask for something else, but everyone was so delighted with the presentation of the dish that I determined to brave it out. Trying to wipe all preconceived notions from my mind, I tackled the head that lay before me. I made the first and only cut without looking. The instant I got the courage to pop the morsel into my mouth, everyone wanted to know if I didn't think it was splendid. I didn't, but was too stunned to express any true feeling. Instead, while I chewed, I concentrated very hard on not being sick. For the remainder of the lunch, I did what kids do when they hate what has been served to them. I cut up pieces of the head and pushed them around the plate with the jelly and the parsley, hoping nobody would notice.

Before lunch ended Ari reissued an invitation he had offered once before, insisting I make time to take his boat for a cruise to the Grecian Islands. He and Maria also asked me to join them that night at a small dinner party at the Château de Madrid high atop Eze, where I had briefly dined during "wedding week" the night my laryngitis hit. Likely I was destined never to finish a meal at the Château, because along with my first bite of my favored cheese soufflé that night came the mental picture of my heady lunch. I raced to the ladies' room, and left early. I had a dream later in which I had lost a contest and was tied to a seat at a long refectory table until I consumed the heads of a group of small farm animals, each one of which was winking at me.

On Saturday night I joined Grace, Rainier and their other guests at the Palace for a cocktail and then in the caravan of limousines transporting us to the Red Cross Gala. Grace had an exquisite tiara woven through the coils of her soft blond hair, another loose fall trailing down the back of her neck past her shoulders. Diamond and sapphire jewelry reflected the clear blue of her eyes. Her dress was made of white organza trimmed with lace, and when she walked it floated behind her as though aided by a wind machine on a movie set. Among the weekend guests who were seated at the Princely table were members of the Royal Families of Spain, Greece and Denmark. Trini Lopez, whose recording of "Lemon Tree" was a huge hit at the time, provided the entertainment.

The next day at the Palace, Grace and Rainier hosted one of their customary lunches for their Gala guests. I was invited to bring all three of my children as Caroline, Albert and Stephanie would be present for swimming in their magnificent Italian mosaic pool. After lunch at round tables under the trees, the children began to play together while the adults adjourned for coffee to a small white canopied area set up at the north side of the pool. An elderly King of an ancient European ruling family began to tell stories.

The King began to talk as Grace, Rainier and I shot subtle glances at one another. At various times his story seemed to be winding to a close, but just as it did, the King would find a new facet of it he wished to expand upon. As he droned on, my littlest child, Nina, not yet two, informed her sisters that she needed to "go potty." They told her to ask me for assistance which she did, waddling over to the canopied area where the King was holding forth. She came directly to me, smiling at everyone else, and proceeded to tug at my skirt. Thinking she just wanted to talk, I put my index finger up to my closed lips and nodded in the King's direction so she would understand not to interrupt. She leaned against my knees and waited. Once again it seemed as though the King was concluding, and Nina took that opportunity to try again, but the King resumed with gusto.

While he continued to talk, a footman came around to each of the adult guests with a silver platter of fresh fruit. When he reached me, though I did not want anything, I selected a banana for Nina, who pointed at it longingly. I peeled the banana partway down, handed it to Nina and resumed listening to the King. Once or twice more, Nina started to speak and then realized the King was not stopping. Rainier winked at me, and Grace later told me that though I couldn't see it Nina was by then twisting her legs together tightly. Finally the King made a flourish that guaranteed he had come to the end of his tale. Nearly everyone, including Nina, started to talk, but the elderly gentleman, unphased, took another deep breath and continued. It was too much for Nina. She marched over to where the King was seated and shoved her banana into his face.

There was a moment's shock when everyone realized that the baby had actually done what all of us secretly felt like doing. Napkins were furnished, while I offered profuse apologies, not made easier by the fact that I could detect both Grace and Rainier were trying to hold back their laughter. Finally, Grace was biting her lip so hard that she insisted on showing me where I could take Nina, though I knew perfectly well how to get there myself. The instant we closed the door to the bathroom in the poolside dressing room, we collapsed in laughter.

After we had finally pulled ourselves together sufficiently to rejoin the others, we decided to deposit Nina with her older sisters, Amy and Vicki, and with Albert and Caroline. We found only Albie playing at the shallow end of the pool. "Where are Amy, Vicki and your sisters?" Grace inquired. Wordlessly, Albie pointed to another poolside bathroom, so we set out for it with Nina in tow. Nearing the door, we heard the most amazing clamor. Amy, the oldest at ten, was trying to dissuade Vicki and Caroline, both aged eight, from whatever they were doing. Opening the door, we found the two younger girls trying to lower baby Princess Stephanie upside down, headfirst, into the toilet bowl. Amy gave us an "I tried" look while Grace and I ran to rescue the baby. "Vicki!" I huffed, just as Grace huffed, "Caroline!" But before any question could arise as to who the culprit was, Caroline put her hands on her hips and, in the very image of self-justification, indignantly announced, *"She* was *an-noy-ing* us!" It was, of course, an inadequate justification for sticking a baby headfirst into a toilet bowl, but as we had just come from fifteen minutes of laughter, and likely had occasionally felt the same way about each of our own babies, Grace and I collapsed with laughter again, making disciplining or lecturing the girls out of the question. The merriment was so contagious that it made Amy, Vicki, Caroline, Nina and even the nearly drowned Stephanie laugh. And there we stood, the two mothers and their five daughters collapsed in howls.

That night, after getting the girls settled in, I dressed for a party at a magnificent Cap Ferrat hillside villa to which Grace and Rainier were taking me. I had been told to wear dinner pajamas, so I donned a brand-new pair I had purchased in Rome at Emilio Pucci, and headed for the lobby to await Grace and Rainier, who, once again, arrived in the Mini

Cooper to collect me. The doorman signaled me that Their Highnesses had arrived and I walked out onto the hotel's front steps. As I did, Grace's eyes opened wide and she pointed her finger at me. I heard her shout, "Rainier, look!" and the two of them began to laugh so loudly that all heads turned. In a panic, I looked down quickly, expecting to find I'd forgotten my pajama bottoms. Grace opened the passenger door and alighted from the car. She was wearing off-white pajamas, they were Pucci's, and they were identical to mine! The paparazzi and fan cameras had begun to pop the instant Grace and Rainier's car was spotted. Now they went off in a continuous explosive round. Grace assured me she did not mind doing our Bobbsey Twin act once again. Then she whispered mischievously, "Let's hit our marks!" We turned to the crowd and the cameras, and struck a variety of mocking Bobbsey Twin poses.

In accordance with protocol, we were the last to arrive at the villa. Cocktails were served while everyone came to say hello to Grace and Rainier, pay their respects, and be introduced to me. When Trini Lopez approached, Grace was warmly enthusiastic about the success of his performance the night before. Rainier suggested that perhaps we could get him to pick some good numbers for Grace and me so we could go out on the road as a duo.

It wasn't until after dinner that the party really took off. A small combo played the music of the day, and every one of the guests began to dance, dance, dance. It was just at the start of the 1960s disco craze, and we monkeyed, watusied and frugged our hearts out as the night wore on. When the action really heated up, people began to shout out requests for Trini Lopez to sing. He obliged first with one of his favorites to resounding applause. Then he asked Rainier to join him on drums. The hired musician left his seat. Rainier, in his blue blazer, ascot and white trousers, positioned himself at the drum set. He gave off a couple of riffs, just to test the equipment and get his wrists limbered. Then, with Trini singing, and the rest of us clapping, he and the combo ran through a highly energized version of "Lemon Tree." It was so good, we made them encore the entire number, and Rainier was—by the second time around— playing with great freedom and precision. When he came off, Grace was his greatest admirer—among many.

The party ultimately began to thin out, even though the Prince and Princess had not yet gone. Rainier wanted to call it a night, but Grace was bent upon staying to the very end. We were sitting on the sofa in a brief break from dancing when she told me, "I never want to go home. I always like being the last to leave a good party. Rainier likes to leave early, and everyone around me is always telling me I should not stay up so late. To be truthful, I do get tired with my schedule and all, and probably should take their advice, but it's only on evenings like this when I really feel relaxed." I nodded, sipping my champagne. "There's so much to do and never enough time," Grace added. She paused, sighed and concluded almost in a whisper, "And so many restrictions."

We had been nearly the last to leave the party, but rejoined each other late the following morning at Roc Agel, where I'd been invited to bring my children for the day. When the time came for lunch I helped Grace bring plates of sliced tomatoes and raw vegetables down to the patio area from the kitchen on the upper floor. Rainier was nowhere in sight as Grace stoked the coals on an American-style black iron barbecue. But then I heard him. As the kids darted back and forth around us in a game of tag and Grace stoked her coals, Rainier "hit it" on his drums from the garden-level room where they'd been set up. He played through a selection of swing band pieces recorded in the United States back in the Forties and early Fifties. When the coals were ready, Rainier abandoned his music to assist Grace with barbecuing hamburgers. The kids lined up with their plates to get the first ones hot off the flame, together with an assortment of salads, condiments and the homemade potato chips for which Grace had now become famous in her circle of friends. I realized how much this retreat at Roc Agel meant to all of them.

After lunch the nannies took the babies off for naps while the older children played nearby. Of Amy, Vicki, Caroline and Albie, it was clearly Caroline who was the most demanding—demanding of Grace's and my attention, and of the right to organize the other children as she saw fit. She enjoyed managing the others and was fairly cross when Grace cautioned her to allow her guests to pick the games or the running order for a change.

"She *is* a very demanding little girl," I said. Grace nodded, raising her eyebrows to confirm what I'd noted. "But I also see a self-reliance in her," I added, "that's amazing in one so young."

"That part's to the good, I think," Grace said. "She certainly doesn't remind me of myself as a child. But then the times are different now, and

Rainier and I are trying to raise them without making the same mistakes our own parents did."

At that moment Rainier came out from the tool room, cursing about something that had been misplaced. He was in a foul mood, and though Grace tried to placate him and put his anger in perspective, he was in the kind of mood to let someone have it, and he barked at Grace. I felt embarrassed, as she did for me, at being an observer to this moment of discord. When her husband turned to go inside again Grace simply said, "I'm sorry. He's just frustrated, so many things pressing on him that even up here, some of them get brought along to unnerve him." Telling her I understood, I decided it was not my business to pry nor to tell Grace that I understood all too well about men who erupted in anger and lashed out at the nearest target with increasing frequency. We were still very busy playacting for each other, our loyalties committed to elevating our husbands. And we were both still sure that, in time, as we made our men happier, their anger would subside.

Trying to compose a thank-you note that night on the Rome-bound train that hurtled me side to side in my berth, I thought about our friendship. It seemed obvious to me by then that it would be lifelong, not destroyed by the gaps of time when we shared no visits, nor even by my decreasing written communications. I was going to be thirty-three that autumn, Grace thirty-six. I wondered whether turning forty would seem as big a deal to us as it had been to the generation before us. I suspected that we would be young forever.

CHAPTER 12

Available Options

*T*he presumption of immortality that had comforted me into my third decade was shaken to its core when my brother Burt, only forty-three, died of cancer that fall the day before my thirty-third birthday. As I sat by his hospital bedside, Burt had taken my hand in his and told me, "I know I'm going to die, and soon. Mother doesn't want me to say that and won't let the doctors say it either. But that's what's going to happen." Not only because he was my brother whom I loved, but also because he was my contemporary, I found this unbearable to digest. "I don't want to die," Burt told me. Every sentence was a burden for him. "I don't want to die," he repeated, looking at me imploringly. But three days later, when he did, my big brother had no more lessons to teach me, save for his example of a pain-ridden yet graceful death.

Tony finished the Sinatra movie just before Burt's October funeral. He accompanied me on the train to Chicago for the burial, where I remember trying to hold my mother and my father (Burt's stepfather) together. I had spent a good part of my adult life as the road company manager for other people and the role came naturally to me—so naturally, in fact, that I neglected to grieve for myself, except in those uncontrolled moments when I could not find a task that helped me to avoid it.

Not too long after Christmas, John Foreman suddenly appeared at our door in the middle of the afternoon. When he insisted I accompany him for a drive, I went, believing it was to discuss something about Tony's career (John was now his agent). In the car John tried to get me to see that I had not allowed myself to recognize my own feelings about my brother's death. He told me that I was way too busy taking care of everyone else's emotional needs and denying my own. He urged me to give myself the space in which to mourn. Though I was grateful for John's friendship and concern, I defensively insisted I was doing just fine.

By spring I was getting depressed easily, though I was always able to snap out of it. Tony had started filming a television series called *Valentine's Day,* and he thought my mood might be caused by the restrictive nature of our new schedule. When friends repeatedly invited us out I would decline and stay home to have an early dinner with my husband and our kids. The rest of the night I read while Tony studied lines, or watched television after he had gone to sleep. For a few months the only other adult I saw socially in the evening hours was my ex-husband, Jay, who came to our house every night at dinnertime after he finished at his office to visit with Amy and Vicki. By June my only nighttime activities had become an occasional political meeting in preparation for the upcoming California primaries.

Then friends began taking me out to dinner and dancing at The Daisy. It was an amazing phenomenon at that time, the first disco where you could see young and middle-aged Hollywood at play, frolicking at their own private membership club.

It was at The Daisy that I met a young actor whom I shall call "Sam." He flirted with me outrageously and led me while dancing by some unwired electrical impulse I had never felt before. In August, Tony and I gave a huge backyard party for his mother and two aunts, who were out from New York and staying with us. The night was an odd one for many reasons. Perfect balmy breezes blew through the hanging garden lights and flickered the hundreds of votive candles on the tables. The men were dressed casually and the women wore either pajamas or the new sliplike mini dresses that had wafted across the Atlantic with the British revolution. Our friends Alex North and his then-wife Shirl had asked if they could bring their son Steven. He brought with him a breathtakingly beautiful young British actress who had just arrived in America. She was overwhelmed by the crowd and the party, and I took Jacqueline Bisset to the powder room to assure her that nobody would bite. Steve McQueen, Tony and a group of pals shot pool in our lanai, which opened into the backyard through sliding glass doors, making the inside and outside feel like one big room. I danced with everyone, particularly with "Sam," once again mesmerized by the fact that I, as follower, could be so completely attuned to him, as leader, without any pressure applied.

When Tony left for Europe to make the movie *Fathom* with Raquel Welch, I went to a party at the rented Bel Air home of Joan Collins and Tony Newley, and found "Sam" again. And so began what I had put off for way too long, the grieving for my brother and my own process of growth. Like most people, though, when they decide to grow up, I had to take two steps backward for each forward step.

Before Tony left, I had tried to explain to him that I was entering a strange stage of my life—that I had finally let myself feel about my brother's death, and that this had made me suspect there must be more to life than the way I was living it. "I've grieved for myself," I explained, "but when I really feel for Burt and what he lost, it makes me realize that what is lost for him is the gift of life. If I'm lucky enough to have that gift still, I feel that I must somehow discover how to use it better than I have." I did not know what I meant by that. I suppose I just wanted to talk about it, about life, about Tony and me and our children—who we were, the way we felt about anything and everything.

To be fair, Tony was engulfed in work that distracted and absorbed him completely. He was racing about having fittings, learning lines, swamped with preparations for the movie he was to shoot in Spain. Here was this woman he had married who always had everything wired not only for herself but also for him and everyone else, and she suddenly wanted to address the meaning of life. He tried to hear me, but the only thing he could offer was, "I realize you never really had time to mourn your brother's death. If you want to just stay in bed for a month or so until you recover, that's fine with me." I couldn't make him understand that I did not want invalidism, I wanted to grow. To be honest, I did not understand much better than Tony what I really wanted.

When he left, though, I went backward, sideways and forward all at once. I started seeing "Sam." I reread Krishnamurti. I attributed every-thing in life to some mystical force that was compelling me to do what I did not want to do in order, allegedly, to be who I wanted to be. At the same time I began to look at my children differently, more slowly. I began to feel connected to them in a way I had only glimpsed earlier. I really heard them; they really heard me. I discovered that I'd been missing most of everything that mattered to me—missing it with misspent time, chang-ing the outside world rather than my inner life as I'd aged.

On my thirty-fourth birthday, I was taken out to dinner at the Luau by Joan Collins and Tony Newley and our writer friend Tom Mankiewicz. We returned home to find the house dark. I opened the door with my key, and as I entered my foyer more than one hundred people began coming down my stairway carrying candles and singing "Happy Birthday" in the darkness. Everyone yelled, "Surprise!" The lights went on and a miniature version of The Daisy, replete with Ted Neeley's live music, went into action. I had five very fast screwdrivers and do not recall much else about the evening except that we all converged at the real Daisy just before its two o'clock closing, where I sat out in the rear garden and told director Brian Hutton that I felt as if I'd died and nobody had told me.

A friend of mine had started seeing a therapist, Dr. Albert Duvall, in Westwood. Duvall practiced something called "medical orgonomy" and had been taught by Wilhelm Reich, who founded the treatment. I went to the bookstore and the library to read up on Reich's work. Everything he said on paper struck a chord of response in me. Just before Tony returned to America, I began a program of regular sessions with Dr. Duvall.

It was not in time to have avoided another mess, another scandal, another broken marriage and the resultant pain for everyone. The instant Tony returned home that December, alleged friends told him stories about "Sam" and me. I tried to explain what was happening and that the relationship was only a symptom rather than the disease, but Tony was a goner. I asked for a separation, not a divorce. I needed time, I said, to work with Dr. Duvall. Tony could not accept that, and I understood. I was not even able to tell him what had gone wrong with our marriage. I knew things about him that made me unhappy, but was convinced that my problem was no longer about "the right man" but about "the right me," whom I had never been able to identify. Long before I heard it elsewhere, I explained to Tony, "At twenty I went from being somebody's daughter to somebody's wife and somebody's mother. I don't have a clue who I am or what I want. It isn't fair to blame you, because I've certainly allowed you to believe that I was blissfully happy and could handle everything, not only for myself but for you."

Two decades later, when John Foreman and I were discussing marriages of our generation, he made a remarkable observation. If I'd heard it back then, I would likely have been better able to explain myself to Tony in December 1966, for what John said was:

> Most marriages of our day went like this. The guy rode up on a white horse, swept the girl off her feet and said, "Marry me and I'll give you everything you want."
>
> Years later the husband and wife would sit across from each other while the wife wrenched from herself the admission that she was miserably unhappy. "Why are you unhappy?" the husband asked. "What do you want?"
>
> "I don't know," the wife responded. "I thought you knew and were going to give it to me!"

I'd had two such marriages by the time I reached my mid-thirties. I believed that if I could not change the pattern, I'd be able to see myself lounging against some nightclub banquette forty years later proudly introducing all my friends to my twenty-sixth husband. It was not a pretty picture.

Tony and I negotiated the legal separation he wanted, and for the next several months I went to Dr. Duvall two or three times a week. In the spring of 1967 we put our large Arden Drive house in the Beverly Hills flats on the market, and I moved with my three daughters to a smaller rented home off Benedict Canyon. It was far less formal than the other California houses I had lived in, and was situated atop an almost two-acre knoll with no other houses around.

During the early part of that summer, Grace went to Montreal for the Expo, and I went to New York and to Monterey Pop. What I started doing that summer was unwinding, examining what I had already known and opening myself to what I did not know. I was asking myself what I did accept and what I could not. I liked a lot of the music at the festival, some of the people and none of the drugging. I liked most of the questions, fewer of the answers and all of the scenery. Though it is somewhat embarrassing to admit it, I was the almost-thirty-five-year-old mother of three and I felt—for the first time in my life—that I was making my own decisions, uninfluenced by anyone, not parents, husband or lover—nor even friends. I had only four people I was responsible for—myself and the three children I had brought into this world and wanted desperately to do right by.

While I mingled with the flower children in Monterey, Rupert Allan flew to Montreal to join Grace, Rainier, Albert and Caroline. Stephanie had been dropped at her grandmother's house in Ocean City as the Montreal Expo festivities and subsequent planned tour of Canada were a bit too hectic for her tender years.

Montreal was a madhouse. The city was more excited about Grace's appearance than about that of any other visiting celebrity or dignitary scheduled to attend. Grace was four months pregnant and ecstatic with her reception there. She had visited Quebec with her brother Kell for Winter Carnival when she was a girl, and coming back this way was wonderful for her.

The last two days at the Expo were the most heavily booked. In Grace and Rainier's honor, luncheons for both days were scheduled, along with a large cocktail reception, a dinner and a gala dinner dance. But on their second-to-last night in town, Rupert was hastily summoned by the Prince to the suite he and Grace were occupying. There he found the two young Canadian diplomats from Foreign Service who were assigned to the party throughout its stay, Grace's Lady-in-Waiting Madame Ardant and the Monégasque Chief of Police, who had been traveling with them. Everyone was solemn and still except for two doctors who were giving instructions and the ambulance personnel who were loading Grace onto a stretcher and carrying her out the door.

Rainier directed Rupert and one of the young diplomats to accompany Grace to the hospital. He insisted they not leave her alone, but wait with her on her gurney at the medical complex until she was taken into the operating room. She was having her third miscarriage. Rainier would stay with the children as Grace wished. With her group and local police guarding her, Grace was taken down the elevator and out to the ambulance. She was conscious, knew what was happening, and was trying to avoid the stares of the curious as she passed.

Grace's fourth child, a little boy, was born dead. Her doctors assured her she should consider herself fortunate as the child had died inside her more than a month earlier. It was small consolation to Grace. Two days later, when she was permitted to leave the hospital, taking Caroline and Madame Ardant with her, Grace flew to Ocean City to join Stephanie and recuperate. Rainier took Albert, Colonel Ardant, Rupert, the Canadian diplomat and his own security officer by train across Canada, but the trip was now private as their official visit had been thrown off schedule. It was the last time Grace would ever be pregnant. And that would color her relationship with her baby daughter Stephanie in ways we would not comprehend until many more years had passed.

Knowing how difficult her miscarriage had been for her, all of Grace's California friends were determined to make her August 1967 trip there with Rainier and the children an easy, relaxed one, full of congenial gatherings. Rupert Allan and Frank McCarthy hosted an al fresco Sunday luncheon to welcome them to California. It was clear that Grace badly needed to let her hair down, because when I first greeted her and asked what she had done earlier that morning, she replied in good humor, "I hit the rail at Good Shepherd in Beverly Hills."

One evening during their visit, Linda and John Foreman hosted an informal evening at home for about forty friends and acquaintances, all in show business. We had been hooked all year on a game we had invented called "Newton, U.S.A.," and the moment they heard about it Grace and Rainier wanted to play. The game had been born, we told them, on a night when we all began to wonder who we would be if we were not who we were, living where we did—if we were not part of the movie world but lived in the middle of the country instead of in the heart of screenland. Our imaginary town was called Newton, U.S.A., and we had had designated both the "real" name and the "real" job each of us would have as residents of that average community.

Identifying those Newtonites present, we explained that Linda and John were Vi and Art ("Skeets") Wilkins, he in ladies shoes. Natalie Wood was Mary Frances Peterman, usherette at the local movie house; Roddy McDowall was Homer Box, the town C.P.A., who had a crush on her. Shirlee and Henry Fonda were Wilma and Lloyd Potts, Lloyd our trusted mailman. Paul and Joanne Newman were Newton's Roger and Leona Henderson. He was the movie projectionist, while we always noted about Leona, "She went to Bennington." Bob and Marion Donen Wagner were Dwayne and Ada Clark. We never knew quite what he did, but noted in private, "His family had money." Steve and Neile McQueen were, respectively, our mechanic, Leon Brown, Jr., and his peppy little wife, Rosita.

Jason Robards and Lauren Bacall were Sven and Gretchen Heeholder. He worked at the airport, she ran the Mode O' Day shop. Cloris Leachman was our lady roofer, Rita Bascomb. Rosalind Russell and her husband, Freddie Brisson, were, respectively, our public stenographer and our Roto-Rooter man, Elsbeth and Carl Dugan; while Lee Remick and her then-husband Bill Colleran were, respectively, our town manicurist, Rayjean, and our mortician, F. Donald Hooper. Costume designer Donfeld was Roy-Earl Rickenbacker, who ran Roy's Record Botique featuring "The Pick O' The Platters."

Peter Sellers was Newton's optometrist, Lambert Cox. Joan Collins and Tony Newley were Harriet and Dwayne Smythe. He worked at the A&P, where she bought all the new hair products. Julie Andrews, Laverne Karnes in Newton, sold hosiery. Faye Dunaway was our beautician, Helen Smeader. Polly Bergen and then-husband Freddie Fields were Bootsie and Arnold Johnson, he in used cars. Rock Hudson was our dry farmer, Russell ("Moose") Burgess. My estranged husband, Tony, ran Newton's Red Cock Saloon as Manuel ("Bud") Fragazzi, and I was Bernadine Rasmussen, who wrote the weekly society column and worked at the Greyhound Bus Depot lunch counter.

Grace and Rainier instantly wanted to become Newtonites. He is still known in the group as Edgar Brooker—coal, lumber and charcoal briquets—she as Olga Brooker, Newton's beloved tap, toe and adagio teacher, who gave lessons to all our children for "practically nothing."

I had invited Grace to bring her children for lunch and the afternoon at the very start of her visit. My new housekeeper/*au pair,* twenty-year-old Cindy Hixon, had reported to work two days before the planned afternoon to find me knocked out by a twenty-four-hour flu. I sent Cindy to the market, made cookies, and arranged flowers on the morning before my guests arrived. Just as the doorbell rang I remembered to tell Cindy, "You may call the visiting children by their first names, but please address their mother as 'Your Highness' or 'Ma'am.' " Wide-eyed and amazed, Cindy watched me open the door to greet Grace and her brood.

After lunch and swimming, the children retreated inside with their games, while Grace and I settled ourselves into two poolside chaises to play catch-up. The one-story house I had rented after separating from Tony was high in the hills on an isolated knoll off one of the canyons where raccoons, deer and even coyotes roamed. It was very still; the only sound came from a small, recirculating waterfall that cascaded down tiers on the ivied hillside into the natural rock pool below.

After a few moments of silence Grace asked, "Are you all right, Judybird?" We had not really talked privately since I had separated from my second husband eight months earlier. I nodded.

"And you?" I asked, referring mostly to her recent miscarriage. Grace nodded, less convincingly. For another few moments there was nothing but the sound of the waterfall splashing across rocks and down into the deeper water. Grace seemed to be thinking of exactly what she wanted to say next.

"You've got to make some compromises, you know. No marriage works without them," she cautioned. Though her tone was affectionate, a suggestion of the stern schoolteacher crossed her face, tightening it just a trifle. For a moment I felt myself reacting to that admonishing aspect of what she'd said, resenting her assumption that I did not already realize the truth of it. I kept quiet, though, and thought about the fourteen years we'd known each other, and how I felt about this extraordinarily complex woman who had so extended herself to me in friendship throughout those years. What I wanted most was to be honest with Grace, at least as honest as I was learning to be with myself.

"Do you really want to talk about it, Gracie?" I queried. "Because we can still be friends the way we've always been if I just say 'thank you, sweetie, for your concern' and let it go at that."

"What would you prefer?" Grace countered, not unexpectedly.

"I would prefer to tell you something about how I'm becoming as the years pass. It's the kind of thing I cannot say easily in letters, and our chances to be alone together grow rarer as time goes by."

"I'd like to talk," Grace answered, quickly adding, "I'd like you to talk."

"This isn't a game of 'doctor,' " I reassured her, "where 'if I show you mine you have to show me yours.' To be honest, I think what you should know is that I've only recently discovered which compromises I'm willing to make and which I'm not. Unlike you, Gracie, I didn't marry at twenty-six after defining myself up to that time. I married at twenty and . . ."

"If you think I knew everything I needed to know about myself at twenty-six, you're wrong," Grace interjected. "I knew a lot more than I did at twenty. But you're almost thirty-five now. Have you learned any more about yourself or changed measurably since you were twenty-six?"

"Oh, my God, yes!" I replied. "I think I've discovered more that I need to know about life and changed more in the past ten months than in all the years that went before."

"Well, I'm nearly thirty-eight," Grace observed. "So do you imagine I've learned more and changed in the eleven years since Rainier and I were married?" Grace asked it as a very pointed question.

"I'm sure you have," I answered directly. "But I don't know what you can do about those elements of change, considering the circumstances of your particular life, and your particular commitment."

"Neither do I," Grace admitted. "I love Rainier, so I do my best to make things work." She was still for a moment, then inquired, "If you feel differently now than you used to, how do you think that would affect being married in the future?"

"Well, in the first place, I don't know that I'll ever get married again," I replied.

"Taking the veil, Judybird?" Grace exclaimed.

"Hardly," I assured her as we both laughed. "But it's only now, in my middle thirties, that I've been able to accept the fact that we are—each of us—really alone as we go through life. Trying to obscure that truth has, until now, succeeded only in obscuring me." Grace looked at me quizzically. "One day early this summer Tony came to pick up Nina and I watched them drive down the hill. Then Jay came to pick up Amy and Vicki and I watched them drive away. Just afterwards, my mother called to report that my father's doctors felt he had suffered a very minor stroke while fishing in Bimini, but that there were no aftereffects. I was outside, looking over the hills and listening to the birds chirping and a rattlesnake clicking in the distance, and I said to myself as it crashed over me like a gigantic wave, 'Judy, you are alone in this world. No matter who you love or who loves you, you are alone.' It was the first time in my life that I was ever able to accept that."

"How does it feel?" Grace inquired.

"Part of the feeling is incredibly joyous and liberating," I admitted. "But for a person like me who'd been trying desperately to avoid that truth for so long, the news fell hard. I cried a lot for the next two months, probably for the loss of the romantic, if infantile, notion that I—who had made such a career out of relationships—was not exempt from this truth. Probably, too, for the people whom I'd unintentionally hurt so badly in the process."

"I think I alternate," Grace interjected, "between accepting that truth and trying to deny it with every bone in my body." Reflecting upon that for a moment, she asked, "So do you intend to be alone—I mean not married—for the rest of your life?"

"No, I have no such intention, but recognizing that I am alone, whether married or not, does make me think very differently about what I want in a relationship with a man. And it's the first time I've ever known that, too. So it now becomes my responsibility to myself to be honest about that with any man I'd become involved with."

"How would that change what you'd do if you met someone you cared for?" Grace asked.

"In the first place, I don't think I'll ever 'fall in love' again the way I have in the past." We both grimaced sadly.

"Don't tell me, Judy, that you've given up on romance!" Grace exclaimed.

"I haven't given up on it," I assured her. "It's just that I think that romance, as I used to define it, is very short-lived. If it's to be long-term, it probably comes from something I've not yet experienced, because I've never hung in there long enough to develop it."

"I still don't understand what you'd do differently next time," Grace declared.

"Well, I've always gotten married before believing that the marriage was forever, that because I'd fallen in love and my husband had, too, that there was no way we'd ever part." It suddenly dawned upon me that Grace married that way, too, not only because of her and Rainier's love for each other and her convictions about marriage, but because she was raised in a religion that forbids divorce. "Maybe we shouldn't go into this part,

Grace," I proposed. "I know you don't believe in divorce, that it runs contrary to your religion, and that you would not, no matter what the circumstances, allow your marriage to fail."

"You're right," Grace nodded. "I would never be divorced from Rainier if it's within my power to prevent that. But are you saying you'd get married, recognizing the possibility that you might get divorced?"

"Considering my track record to date, don't you think that's a rational thing to recognize? What that buys me," I continued, "is the responsibility to confront problems as they arise instead of feeling I have to swallow everything that happens, no matter how it makes me feel, in the name of 'eternal bliss,' which doesn't exist anyway. It's denying how I felt as each of my marriages proceeded that finally made me feel so burdened that all I could do was cut and run. And no matter what the faults of either of my husbands, I'm the one who did that. I'm the one who kept my mouth shut, refused to confront unhappiness as I gradually felt it accumulating, and painted myself into a corner so painfully constricting that I'd do anything to get out of it. So it's my responsibility not to do that again, no matter who the man is or how he reacts to that, isn't it?"

After thinking a moment, Grace said, "You talk about confronting problems as they arise. In the years we've been friends, I've never known you to be confrontational."

"The only two people I know who are less confrontational than I've been are you and Jay," I agreed. We both laughed.

"So what do you do in a relationship such as the one you envision? Walk around all the time arguing? Because that doesn't strike me as any way to build a good marriage, nor much fun either!" Grace noted.

"The truth is, Grace, that there is only one main thing I want in a marriage which I've never had, nor ever even asked for until it was too late to explain it."

"And what's that?" Grace asked hastily.

"I'm not looking for some ideal fifty-fifty relationship. I do believe that there are both natural givers and takers in the world and I enjoy being a giver. But I anticipate everything about a man so that I can make him happy and we can be happy together."

"Surely you don't entertain the fantasy that some man is going to do that for you?" Grace asked.

"No, I don't think men are raised to do that the way women are. And if there is one who has been, I'd be too old to 'do it' with him by the time I found him!" Grace roared. "But I do think it's not too much to ask a man to learn to listen to me when I do talk about my feelings, my inner life or my growth in the same way that I really listen to him when he speaks about his. I want two-way intimacy. If I can't ultimately arrive at that point, I can't think of why I'd really want to be married. I recognize that if I did not have money of my own there might be other compelling reasons to be married. But as I do, it's rather like the old saying, 'First get an independent income. Then practice virtue.' I don't want to live with a man who isn't willing to do part of the emotional work to keep us together. He doesn't have to do as much of it as I will, but if we do confront a problem recognizing that one or the other of us really feels he or she can't go on living together without some mutual effort to change the problem, if he won't be party to that effort then I'd rather be alone."

"How would you ever know if you'd found such a man before you actually married him?" Grace asked.

"I would make a lousy Catholic," I admitted. "Because I'd never marry anyone again until I'd lived with him." Realizing Grace might react badly to this approach, I asked her, "Does that offend you?"

"No," she answered simply, "it doesn't offend me. But I don't know what it would mean to your children."

"That, of course, is the big question," I concurred. "I would certainly never move hot and cold running lovers into our house, so first I'm talking only about someone with whom I could seriously project living a life. Secondly, I'd be more concerned about how it really affected the children than how others thought it affected them. If their school friends' parents, for example, suddenly said their kids couldn't come for overnights to 'the house of sin,' that would be a problem. But as I would advocate that my own girls live with a man before marrying him when they grow up, depending on the right age to explain that as the way I feel, I wouldn't be believing in one set of standards on the one hand while preaching a different one on the other."

"I suppose if you believe that, then that is what you should teach your children," Grace acknowledged. "I'm not sure that in some part of me I don't believe it, too, only I could never take that position publicly nor advise my children that way. Apart from the obvious reason, it goes completely against the grain of my religion."

if it would be all right for him to help me change the sheets. It would, she nodded, so the three of us set out down the hall.

Nina watched from a bedroom chair while Don and I remade the bed. Then Don took her place on the chair while I tucked her in and read to her from *Goodnight Moon* and *Sam and the Firefly,* two of her favorites, with which Don seemed to be completely familiar. Every now and then Nina raised her head to see if Don was still there. She'd smile and wave with two fingers before falling back down on the pillows. On one such checkpoint, she signaled Don to come and lie across the foot of the bed. Every now and then I would look up to see him smiling the smile of a man who liked families and children best of anything.

It was not until a month later that Don and I began seeing each other. Once we did, neither of us saw anyone else. We made no great statements, no pledges and no promises. We simply enjoyed being together one day and then the next as well.

Amy and Vicki went to spend the Christmas holidays in London with Jay and Kit, who had moved there with Kit's three children from her first marriage. Don and I took my housekeeper Cindy and our four kids who were under the age of seven—Robert, James, Sean and Nina—to Lake Arrowhead for the snow. We had a vacation unlike any I'd ever had before. It was ten o'clock at night when we arrived and found the house we'd rented had been snowed in during a recent blizzard. The path to the front door was barely visible in the drifts. After driving around until we found a light on in a neighboring house, Don borrowed a shovel and dug us through to the entry. Then he unloaded the entire contents of our station wagon, including bedding, food, sleds, clothing and even firewood. When we went upstairs to see the bedroom, we discovered that the children's four bunk beds had no mattresses, just wires strung across the bed frames at distant intervals. Though they were exhausted, impatient and cranky, the kids laughed at our suggestion that we could string them through the wires like hot dogs on a spit and light some firewood on the floor beneath them to toast them up good!

Piling back into the car, we found a phone booth and called the rental agent, who said, "I don't do business past office hours," then cruised motels until we found one with a single large room the seven of us could camp in for the night. Fritos and Cokes from a nearby vending machine

constituted our midnight supper. After moving into the house the following morning, we played games, cooked and washed endless supplies of
soggy mittens, scarves, socks, underwear and ski clothes. On New Year's
Eve, Cindy, Don and I opened a bottle of Dom Pérignon while the kids
danced to Linda Ronstadt and the Stone Ponies singing "Different
Drum." We played in the snow for hours every day, and warmed ourselves
over the single living room vent that brought heat into the bottom floor of
the house until the furnace beneath it ignited and burned the floorboards
while we poured soft drinks and snow on the unexpected blaze to prevent
disaster. I wished very hard that Amy and Vicki could have been with us.
Although it may sound strange for a middle-aged woman who had sum-
mered at the best European resorts or cruised in her family's yacht along
the East Coast of this continent, who had wintered at leading ski resorts or
at the finest hotels in Palm Beach, it was the best vacation I'd ever had.

By the following spring, Don and I started living together with my
three daughters and—when they could be with us—his three sons. One
night, after we'd been living together for a time, we sat in the car in the
driveway of my hillside house after coming home from dinner, and
watched the full moon vibrating above us. "I really love being with you,"
Don began. "I have a great time with you, love the fact of all the kids
together, and everything about working at our relationship and our separate lives every day."

"But . . ." I said before he could.

"But there's something missing. I really feel I love you," Don insisted,
"but there's something missing. I had it with Carole. You probably had
it with Tony or Jay, or both. Do you know what I mean? Do you feel it,
too, that there's something missing?" I nodded. "What is that?" he asked,
and because he couldn't think of a word to describe it, he made a sound
like a big wrench coming from his stomach.

"I don't know whether it's the same thing for you as it is for me," I
offered, "but that 'ungh,' " I imitated the sound he had made, "is something I always did have before and do not have with you. I'm glad it's
missing," I added. "It's the hook." Don looked at me quizzically. "The
hook that it 'has to' work between us, that one of us would not be all right
without the other, the hook that makes each of us feel less than we are
instead of more of what we are when we're together."

Don nodded in assent. "That's what it is," he concurred. "I'm glad it's missing, too." He thought for a moment, then added, "The hard part is remembering that we're entitled to the pleasure of not having it." As the years progressed, that would prove harder for one of us than for the other.

CHAPTER 13

Il Est Interdit d'Interdire

(It Is Forbidden to Forbid)
—MOTTO OF THE 1968 STUDENT REVOLUTION IN PARIS

Just as the seventh decade of the century was ending, we bridesmaids and the bride were crossing the line into our forties. Many women of our mothers' generation had seemed old at forty, frumpy and plump. Though we had longed for instant matronhood in our late teens, as the big 4-0 approached, we still thought of ourselves as young women, not matrons. In the world at large as well as in the smaller universes of our homes and families, only the radical customs of the young reminded us of how much the times had changed and that we stood on an island between the older generation and our own children trying to make our lives manageable in both worlds.

Hippies had become a fact of our everyday lives. Though Sally's and Maree's children still dressed for school almost exactly as their parents had two decades earlier, some of our kids set forth in the morning dressed as rejects from an Indian reservation, a gypsy caravan or an army unit on latrine duty. Seeing many of their established hopes gunned down one by one, in 1969 a large segment of our country began to place its hope outside the establishment. For younger citizens that meant visions of salvation through the new middle-class version of summer camp, Woodstock, where 400,000 of them gathered together to make music and love, not war. Older citizens, getting closer to heaven themselves, looked skyward to watch Neil Armstrong take man's first steps on the moon.

By the time Paul Simon and Art Garfunkel sang to us in 1970 of their "Bridge Over Troubled Water," it seemed the appropriate theme song of the era. It was unclear any longer who filled the nation's jails, the Daniel Berrigans or the crooks—the good guys or the bad ones. While the generation gap was dividing families, the gap between the franchised and the disenfranchised was dividing the nation. At the movies *M*A*S*H* showed us the insanity of war in Vietnam while *Diary of a Mad Housewife* depicted lunacy on the domestic front. In Monaco, where Grace and Rainier screened motion pictures at the Palace in the projection room given to them by Grace's father as a wedding present, there were more and more films they did not choose to see and few they could run for their children.

On the rare occasions when Bettina did drop Grace a note, she mentioned nothing of what was happening in Dedham. She did not tell Grace that her boredom had grown to the point of exhaustion. Bettina, the coper, could cope no more. For the most part, she passed her days in numbness, without feelings. Only occasionally did her emotional engines rev up, and, when they did, it was inevitably her rage that provided the fuel. Himself bored and restless, Frank saw his wife sinking into an emotional and functional paralysis.

Grace knew that Lizzie Gray had been attending the Beaver School, but she did not know that Lizzie had originally enrolled there because its curriculum offered Russian. Convinced that nuclear war was approaching and that the Russians would be victorious, Lizzie—who had always been favorably inclined toward winners—had meant to study the language. She never did get around to doing that, but by the time she graduated, her parents' own battle royal was all too clearly a war from which no winners would emerge.

After her first year at Radcliffe, Lizzie joined her Harvard senior boyfriend on a summer trip to Kansas City. She wanted to be away from her parents and hurled herself headlong into her first "mature" relationship. In Bettina's day girls got married for such reasons. In Lizzie's, you simply split with the guy to K.C. To assure herself of not having to be anywhere near home, Lizzie next enrolled in the Experiment for International Living, which took her to Ireland for the summer of 1971. She also decided to call her godmother, whom she'd not seen since her christening. That call resulted in an immediate invitation to spend a week with the sovereign family at their retreat in Roc Agel.

Dressed in secondhand khaki green fatigues, with her knapsack strapped across her back, the hippie revolutionary disembarked from the plane that had carried her to Nice in the South of France. Wandering around looking for a familiar face, she heard her name called over the loudspeaker. "Will Miss Elizabeth Gray please make herself known to the flight crew?" the voice requested.

"My God," thought Lizzie, "they're going to search me for drugs!" Such was not the case. The crew simply wanted to escort her to curbside, where Aunt Grace was waiting in the corner of a large black limousine, wearing her omnipresent head scarf and dark glasses. While an attendant scampered to fetch Lizzie's luggage, Grace kissed her goddaughter on both cheeks and asked her if she had her return ticket to America. The Riviera was flooded with hippies who had no return transportation and no way to buy any, Grace explained. Once assured that Lizzie—despite her attire—was better prepared, the two women settled back for the drive up the mountain.

Other than the annual arrival of a Christmas gift sent through Neiman-Marcus and an occasional handwritten note, Lizzie did not know Grace. The rebel Lizzie harbored no condemnation of her godmother, who represented the very establishment Lizzie so opposed. Her only preconceived notion was of a woman who must be extremely competent to have done so splendidly every single thing she had set out to do.

Lizzie rose at nine o'clock on her first morning at Roc Agel, making her own bed as we'd all taught our children to do when they houseguested anywhere. Five hours passed before the clock struck one in the afternoon and members of the family began emerging from their rooms. Lizzie was baffled as to why they would all sleep so late. It wasn't until that night, when she joined them for the first of several evenings out, that she realized they often did not get to bed until the sun rose. Lizzie liked summer season life with the Grimaldis. She was nineteen and Caroline fourteen, but the two played tennis together and got along well. Lizzie was impressed with Caroline's sophistication in such matters as social poise, clothes and the ability to mix easily with adults at various gatherings.

Albert was away at camp in New Hampshire, but Lizzie found the six-year-old Stephanie to be a smoldering presence in the Grimaldi household. It was clear to Lizzie that the child had her father wrapped around her little finger. When a contest of wills arose between her two parents over something concerning Stephanie, Lizzie noted that Grace lost and lost badly. Caroline, being the oldest, had already gotten the lion's share of the children's publicity. Albert was the hereditary Prince. But Stephanie, Lizzie thought, was the one to watch out for.

Though some aspects of life at Roc Agel seemed normal to Lizzie, others seemed rarefied. In the morning, she'd see Rainier outside chatting with a donkey, then hear him grumble about the yogurt he was consigned to eat for the diet on which he had placed himself. When Grace started to list their evening plans, Lizzie protested that she hadn't brought the appropriate clothing. "Don't worry," chimed Aunt Grace, "we'll go right into my closet and find some things for you." Wearing her *de rigueur* brown thong sandals and her surplus Marine Corps tank T-shirt, Lizzie held up dozens of creations from French and Italian couture houses until she and Aunt Grace had pulled together a wardrobe for a week.

Quite a week it was. After the concert and supper party of the first night, they ate the following evening at a local restaurant and danced all night at Régine's. The third night saw them hosted on a magnificent yacht in the Monte Carlo harbor. One afternoon Grace suggested she drive herself and Lizzie into Monte Carlo to do some shopping. Lizzie needed new blue jeans, Grace had a few errands to run for herself and a list of records to pick up for Caroline. Realizing she had no cash, Grace called the bank from Roc Agel asking that they prepare a certain amount for her withdrawal. Arriving at the bank, Grace realized there had been a misunderstanding about the amount she'd requested. Instead of $300, a packet containing $30,000 worth of francs awaited her!

What Lizzie also began to distinguish was the difference between being very rich and being royal. She realized that anyone with a lot of money could have bought the best seats at the concert they had attended. What could not be paid for in francs or dollars was the row of plants placed in front of their seats so their view would not be blocked nor their privacy invaded. Even if you were a multimillionaire, Lizzie realized, policemen at every intersection would not clear all traffic to salute you through upon recognizing your license plates.

What interested Lizzie most was the power dynamic of the family. She found Rainier witty, relaxed, catty and not at all pious—a cross between strong ruler, warm father and wicked little boy. And though she herself found Grace to be available and loving, she knew that if she were Grace's child she'd want to leave home early! It would be hard, Lizzie suspected, to have a parent who was so powerfully clear and sure of herself. Years later, when she became a lawyer, Lizzie thought of Grace in terms of a word used in her legal practice—congruence. A plaintiff or defendant was incongruent when he or she waffled. When every aspect of their statement flowed together so tightly as to be unshakable, it was said the person had congruence, and that is what Lizzie saw in Grace. In her own mind, as Lizzie saw it, Grace was one hundred percent sure that what she said was right. "If I were her child," Lizzie reflected, "I'd either do as she said or not. What I wouldn't do was argue because there is nothing I could say that would sway her." It dawned upon Lizzie that such a mother, without meaning to, could stifle the creative discoveries her own children might need to make for themselves.

As a woman, when Lizzie looked at Grace she saw resolute commitment. And she saw trade-offs. One afternoon Grace pulled a movie script off the top of her desk and handed it to Lizzie. "A friend just sent this to me with an offer to play in it. It's a charming part," Grace told her. "Just a little streamlined thing toward the end of the movie where I walk in, say some wonderfully written things, and walk out again very quickly." After taking the script back, she thumbed through it, found the right pages, and read her lines aloud. "It would be so easy to do," Grace noted, "don't you think?" Lizzie agreed and said so. "Well, you know," Grace sighed as she placed the script neatly on a stack already piled on her bookshelf, "I made a deal when I got married that I wasn't going to do this anymore." Lizzie watched her godmother straighten the scripts on her shelf and wondered what the trade-offs truly had been, what this beautiful, perfect woman had to give up to be sitting here at Roc Agel, overlooking the Mediterranean and living this marvelous life where they give you all the money you want at the bank and wave you through the intersections. By the end of the week, Lizzie was incredibly impressed with Grace—and glad she did not have to live with her.

Lizzie hitchhiked from London to Nepal in 1972 while her parents were divorcing. Her mother, Bettina, stayed at home all the time, swal-

lowed entirely by her sense of inadequacy. She felt intellectually unworthy, emotionally depleted and sexually flawed. She even quit her
part-time volunteer work at the hospital, telling her director, "I have
nothing left to give. Nothing." Bettina spent the next two years in her
nothingness, still believing that men were "up there" somewhere—that
it was a man's right to say when you ate dinner and where, what you
should buy and when, whom you should see and why. Without a man to
direct her, Bettina felt nonexistent, except for her pain. She wrote to
Grace to thank her for the kindness shown to Lizzie, convinced they
would never see each other again and believing that was as it should be.

Maree's friendship with Grace grew steadier as the years passed. Grace
still made yearly trips to Philadelphia and the Jersey shore, and as Maree's
children grew older, this freed her to travel to Monaco more often.
Sometimes Bud would join her for some planned festivity that involved
a week-long round of parties, but often Maree just went to visit Grace.
She loved staying at Roc Agel, but was always slightly uncomfortable
houseguesting at the Palace. Grace's life was, by then, so enmeshed in
duties and obligations that she kept full-time office hours. While Grace
worked, Maree sat around feeling like a bump on a log, neither free to
leave the Palace nor wanting to stay. At night, after dinner, she'd be
walked to her room across the courtyard. There she'd remain for the
evening and often until lunchtime the following day, alone, without even
television for company. Though Rainier owned, at various times, a Rover,
an Austin Mini Cooper S, Rolls-Royces, Imperials, Citroëns, Jaguars,
Lancias, station wagons and a Mercedes-Benz, Maree was never invited
to use a car for sightseeing or shopping jaunts, and wasn't sure it was polite
to ask.

In America, Maree's family seemed to have missed the revolution
entirely. Her older daughter, Linda Pamp, went briefly to Pine Manor
Junior College before becoming engaged at eighteen to Peter Farnum, a
handsome young Penn graduate. They were a golden and glorious young
couple, one as beautiful as the other. Linda, who had always written to
her father Arv during the years when he lived in Colombia, had grown
closer to him since he'd been living in New York. She wrote him joyously
to tell him of her engagement. For reasons unknown to either Linda or
her mother, she has never—to this day—heard from him since.

By the late 1960s, Grace was receiving only tidbits of carefully edited news about the Reybold family, and, as Carolyn rarely wrote, those arrived in the cheerful, chatty notes Jyl sent off to her godmother every couple of months. Grace was not fond of Malcolm Reybold, and never had been. In the early Sixties, she'd learned he and Carolyn were separated when Cholly Knickerbocker's column reported, "Malcolm Reybold, who at one time was a big name in Grace Kelly's life (in fact, Princess Grace 'confessed' to his wife that there had been a romance), has now moved quarters to the elegant Colony Hotel in Palm Beach . . . to establish residence for a divorce from his pretty brunette wife, Carolyn, who was one of Grace's closest friends. . . ." Grace had met Malcolm before he and Carolyn knew each other, but she had never gone out with him. She couldn't imagine why he would prolong this fiction of a romance between them, especially at a time when it might so wound Carolyn. The gossip item convinced her that Malcolm cared more for his own publicity and shallow values than for friends or family.

Though Malcolm had frequently been staying in town, on one night when he was at home he inspected the family checkbooks. Spotting dozens of $75 checks written to a doctor he did not know, he erupted, "What the hell is going on? Who is this guy?" Carolyn admitted she had been seeing a psychiatrist. Malcolm immediately took charge. He insisted she see a new doctor of his choosing and made that a condition of his paying for further treatment. Though Carolyn did not protest, when Malcolm looked at the checkbooks again several months later, he found that his wife had continued to see her own original therapist.

The same summer that Lizzie Gray visited Grace, Carolyn took two of her daughters to Europe. She told no one of her plans in advance. Malcolm phoned from Texas, where he was traveling on business, and asked her if she would pick him up on his return to New York. Carolyn gave him a number to call on arrival. When he phoned, he merely received a message telling him that Carolyn had left his car in a Manhattan parking garage. In the car he found a note from Carolyn on the front seat. It said, "We need prayer. We need a miracle. I have taken Robin and Nyna and gone to Lourdes."

From the French shrine, Carolyn called the Palace. She wanted to arrange a visit and, as her money had run out, borrow enough to pay for return airfares for herself and her two daughters. Though Grace was just about to host a major local event and had a trip scheduled for the following morning, she did get the transportation money to her friend. A year later Malcolm stopped in Monaco on a European business trip to repay the loan. But the temporary relief Carolyn found in Lourdes was not to last long.

Sally's life seemed as calm as Carolyn's was turbulent. She and John shared a political conservatism. Blair and Hunt had gone through boarding school without giving their parents worries of any magnitude. Sally loathed sit-ins and other college demonstrations, and was glad her sons were not inclined to participate in any at Princeton, where they were both enrolled. She found the current vogue for swearing stupid and felt the same way about the loud rock music that emanated from the Princeton dorm windows. She was sure the eardrums of an entire generation were being destroyed. When her sons came home from college with a bit too much hair hanging over their collars, Sally simply got out the scissors and chopped away. The sexual revolution offended Sally, but as she had sons rather than daughters, she avoided the subject by not questioning the nocturnal activities of her offspring.

Until the boys went to college, Sally had centered her entire life on her home. Now, with the boys gone, she decided to get a full-time job. Joining the staff of the Beekman Downtown Hospital, she became Director of Volunteer Services. She took to this challenge with enormous energy, and her life began to revolve more around work than around home. Though Grace's own schedule took her farther from her immediate home life, she and Sally remained close friends. As Sally worked in the daytime, she could not have lunch or go shopping on Grace's trips to New York, but they dined together at night, and when Grace's other New York friends entertained her, Sally and John were always included.

Rita was living in a sprawling prewar apartment at 1095 Park Avenue, where she'd settled not long after returning from Minneapolis. Rita felt that Grace did not know what to make of her, a sometimes-employed repertory actress with two children, who was trying to hold things together. It's difficult to know whether Grace was really disapproving or even baffled about Rita, or whether Rita merely felt critical or confused about her own situation. At the time, she was seriously involved with a married man whom she'd been with for two years. Weighted heavily by guilt, she was convinced he was the only man in the world for her and could not find the strength to break off the relationship.

On Memorial Day weekend in the early 1970s, Rita found an identity of her own, and this one had nothing to do with a man. For three days before the holiday weekend, she'd been visiting doctors complaining of terrible stomach pains. She had been told that nothing was really wrong and that she should call after the holiday with a progress report. On Saturday morning, with nearly everyone she knew in the country for the weekend, Rita dialed her agent Dudley Malone. By the time he got to her apartment she'd struggled to put on a pair of jeans, though her abdomen was too tender to close the zipper. Dudley immediately took Rita to Lenox Hill Hospital, not far from where she lived. Rita was worried that there was nobody home to look after her children, so Dudley promised to stay with them until she was out of the hospital. With Dudley gone, Rita was forced to make her own decisions, to take over for herself. In the emergency room, she was asked to sign papers permitting the insertion of several tubes that, it was explained, would clear her "blockage." As no one would give her an actual diagnosis, she refused to sign. Instead, she called her friend Margaret Truman Daniel. Margaret and Rita had grown friendly when their children were small, and Margaret now volunteered to call Rita's doctor to get him in from the country for a second opinion.

On Memorial Day, having located a world-renowned surgeon in the Virgin Islands who was en route to New York, Betty Rea, whose husband had founded the Guthrie Theatre, moved Rita to St. Luke's Hospital. Women, it dawned upon Rita, made very good friends. It was a time when she needed friends because she had just been told she had cancer.

Strangely enough, Rita was not as frightened as she expected to be. All the good instincts that operate in a crisis came forward for her. Never for an instant did she think she was going to die. The moment she regained consciousness after surgery, finding herself hooked up to six tubes, Rita began to make decisions. "This is like opening night," she thought, "when there's nobody but you to do what needs to be done." Rita began ticking off instructions to herself. "I'm going to start breathing correctly" was the first thing she mandated. "I'm going to exercise. I have to learn how to hypnotize myself so I can get off painkillers as fast as possible and start a natural healing process." There was no man to encourage her or to stay by her side. Believing her children would be frightened of the truth, Rita did not even tell them how seriously ill she was.

After her illness, taking charge of her own healing process, Rita felt there was an enormous schism between her lifestyle and Grace's. They still saw each other and enjoyed each other's company, but Rita viewed herself as a Park Avenue farmer with five animals and two kids riding bikes and playing basketball in the dining room and the foyer. When Grace came to New York, her shoes looked perfect, her gloves matched, her clothes were impeccable. Grace's environment looked beautiful to Rita, who had always admired the perfection of appearances. She cherished the perfection she saw in Grace, took at face value the Grace that was being presented for world view. It was an easy thing to do in those days, for Grace was getting extremely proficient at not letting the chinks show.

By the early 1970s, Grace had turned forty. Over the years, we had continued to see photographs of her at international society events which told us she still looked amazingly young and beautiful. In April 1966, there were photos from Seville, where Grace opened the Feria, or Spring Fair. She looked radiant in a traditional Andalusian dress made of ruffled pink lace, outshining Jackie Kennedy, who had elected the somber, if stylish black costume of the local riders. She had written a letter to tell me that she had tried contact lenses in Seville. Nearsighted, Grace had always been accused of aloofness. In fact, she couldn't see anybody who was standing more than six feet away from her. Criticized for wearing her schoolmarmish tortoise-rimmed glasses, Grace decided contacts were "the answer to a matron's prayer." En route to one of the Feria's major events, the contact lenses had slipped from their case and were replaced too hastily, the left lens on the right side of the case, the right lens on the left. A few moments later when Grace put them in, her eyes ached and watered like faucets. Unable to bear the discomfort, with mascara running down her newly made-up cheeks in brown rivers, and nearly blinded by the mispositioned lenses, Grace had been forced to take them out and arrive at the event late, streaked and sightless. It was her first and last attempt with contacts.

She had become extremely friendly with Marc Bohan of Christian Dior and with Parisian hairdresser Alexandre, who coiffed Elizabeth Taylor and Jackie Kennedy. Grace admired and respected both men and, over the years, the various trusted assistants who took care of her needs. Her warmth, generosity and personal concern for the staffs at each salon made her revered there for life and afterwards as well. During Lizzie Gray's visit to Roc Agel, a huge box containing a layout of the entire Dior collection had arrived for Grace's fall wardrobe selection. Each design was sketched and swatches of fabric alternatives were attached. When it came to ball gowns, Grace inevitably selected dresses in pale or clear colors. As a blonde, she had long ago learned that apricots, pinks, yellows and blues complimented her fair hair, eyes and skin. Occasionally, though, Grace went wild with color. In preparation for a Venetian ball honoring Olympia Brandolini, she had Bohan make her a dress of bright fuchsia. Describing it to me in a letter, she recalled an Elizabeth Arden lipstick we had all tried as teenagers called "Sky Blue Pink." The Dior dress was a cross, she said, between that and the more exotic Chen Yu nail polish our mothers always thought looked trashy.

An astrology buff, Grace decided to use her fascination with the stars to buffer the shock she felt at turning forty. In the Belle Epoque dining room of the Hôtel Hermitage, where she herself had supervised the magnificent, historically accurate renovation, she gave her fortieth birthday party, ostensibly for herself and her Scorpio friends. Those included Maree Rambo, Hjordis Niven and Rupert Allan. Rock Hudson was a Scorpio. Grace and Rainier had helped us all celebrate his thirty-fifth birthday in Hollywood, and Rock planned to fly with Rupert Allan to Grace's fortieth in Monaco. Rupert, though, required open heart surgery and could not make the trip, so Rock, essentially shy and fearful of knowing few people there except Grace and Rainier, decided to stay home as well.

Many of us who were born under other signs were asked to share in the celebration. Bilingual invitations were mailed around the world. They read like horoscopes for those born under Grace's birth sign. Forecasting "Days for Travel . . . Journey to Monte Carlo indicated," we were invited by "H.S.H. Princess Grace of Monaco, High Scorpia" for dinner and dancing on November 15, 1969, at the Hermitage and for brunch the following day, poolside at the Hôtel de Paris. Our love forecast told us "Venus enters your sign. Romance is favored and may become highly inspirational by mid-November." Our health forecast promised that if we survived the two events we could be assured of living to a ripe old age. The invitation advised us to avail ourselves of our own private nests at the Hôtel de Paris, which was being wholly reserved for our occupancy. Bud and Maree Rambo did attend Grace's fortieth birthday festivities. Don and I did not. But we giggled over the descriptions Grace later sent of all the beautiful people. One told of Elizabeth Taylor in all her glory, sporting the huge diamond that her Scorpio husband Richard Burton had just bought for her. Grace said she'd found it hard to take her eyes off Elizabeth, whom she thought to be "almost unbearably beautiful." Next to this comment was an asterisk. At the bottom of the letter, under her signature, Grace had added, "*Forty . . . Ugh! I almost cannot bear that either!"

Her little joke turned out to be portentous, for what Grace bit off in her fifth decade was almost more than she could chew, let alone swallow. Her three miscarriages had made it clear to her she would never have another baby. Monégasque politics and the will of her subjects had made it equally clear that she would never act again either. Her commitment to becoming the total European wife deprived both her and Rainier of the chance to mold their relationship in accordance with the changing needs of each partner. What was left were her children and the only other creation she could build from scratch, the role of a perfect modern-day princess. Her predecessor, Princess Alice, might have set the tone for European reverence toward Monaco, but Grace believed her job to be of even greater scope. It had been more than a dozen years since she'd made her last film, but Grace was still a universally acclaimed celebrity. Her instincts toward the invention of "Grace Kelly, Movie Star" had been nearly infallible. Once she committed herself to it wholeheartedly, the invention of "Grace, Princess of Monaco" was a far more complex and taxing matter.

Being powerless to control the press, Grace decided to use it. It was not a new talent for her, but required a new application—the application of a princess whom Grace herself would define for the world as best she knew how. In creating that role, she would design a pattern for others, particularly her own daughters. She hoped to provide them with a map that would steer them clear of the rougher shoals of their disordered generation—a generation in which it was forbidden to forbid. Caroline was twelve when Grace turned forty, Albert eleven and Stephanie four. Perhaps it was even harder on them than on Rainier to find they were living with a perfect person—a person of such enormous ambition that she would not allow herself to be less than that, a person whose need to shape everything around her would, at times, absorb the very coziness, curiosity and sense of adventure that had helped to make her so special from the start.

I believe Grace was mortally terrified of raising her children in the world that raged about her. The notion of it being forbidden to forbid so threatened her that, for a time, it changed her in ways she could not even perceive. She wanted, more than anything, for her children to be happy and well. The idea of drugs and the dangers of teenage life without limits made her all the more anxious to control. Then, too, the press had just begun to write about Caroline and to hound her during her normal activities. It was clear to Grace that her children were going to be subjected to the very invasions of their youthful privacy that she and Rainier had tried to prevent. Women worldwide had come to look upon Grace as an exemplary mother, and it was taken for granted that she would direct her children down an exemplary path. All of the work she had invested in bringing glory to Monaco and to Rainier would fail if she could not accomplish this task. At stake were the things that mattered most to her—the safety and well-being of her three children, the reputations of herself, her husband and their country. The stakes were too high for anyone, even Grace.

She began to make decisions colored by fear, and in that process she reminded me of a statement Eleanor Roosevelt had made about herself. "I erected," Mrs. Roosevelt said, "someone a little outside of me who was the President's wife." In her forties, Grace erected someone a little outside herself who was the wife/mother/princess of Monaco. It was the only period during her lifetime when I thought of her, in the vernacular of the day, as uptight. She made countless public statements opposing the new sexual freedom, relaxed dress codes, and nudity and violence in films. Those were elements of the new world she opposed and had every right to speak about. But she also shrank her curiosity about the world of ideas. She lost her will to examine and clung closely to her will to condemn.

As Rainier grew more absorbed with the multiple facets of his country's revitalization, Grace dove headlong into her own spheres—culture, philanthropy and historical preservation. Watching the world grow uglier, Grace became a one-man band tub-thumping for beauty on both an esthetic and a spiritual plane. Using money she had inherited, in the Sixties, Grace had created the Princess Grace Foundation of Monaco.

Originally, she underwrote the operation of a new gift shop on the Rock where Monégasque artisans could exhibit and sell their work. In 1970, with the first shop doing well, she selected the interior design, the decor and even the window displays, and launched a second store in the downtown area.

Grace's initiation of Monaco's now-world-renowned Garden Club fulfilled three of her goals. It gave her a year-round and time-consuming commitment toward which she could formally direct her love for flowers. It allowed her to unify women from previously isolated segments of the Monégasque population. And it became yet another vehicle through which she could raise funds for worthy causes. The annual Concours de Bouquets each May has long been recognized as one of the most prestigious contests for master flower arrangers from around the world. Even Rainier submits his design to the international jury in the men's division. Never a dilettante, Grace became a walking encyclopedia about cultivated flowers, wildflowers and plants, able to discuss not only their Latin names, but everything that was known about their habitats, blooming seasons and care as well.

Because of her intense devotion to the young, Grace became President of Monaco's La Leche League and a vociferous worldwide advocate of breast-feeding. When AMADE (L'Association Mondiale des Amis de l'Enfance—World Association of Friends of Children) asked her to become its Honorary President, she accepted that job, too. The organization worked internationally for the abolition of poverty and deprivation, and sought to combat both mental and physical illness among the young. When Grace opened its Italian chapter she said, in a passionate speech, that the group was born ". . . in a spasm of anguish . . . with no other force than its founders' will to succeed . . . until the earth is bound with a network of the true friends of children."

Since childhood Grace had been especially passionate about the ballet. Knowing that Monte Carlo had long ago been acclaimed for its own Ballet Russe, Grace began dedicating herself to creating a new and respected ballet presence in Monaco. Caroline's teacher, Madame Marika Besobrasova, was the consummate ballet mistress, respected by her students in spite of the extraordinary demands she placed upon them, but unsupported by the community, many of whom found her vain, impatient and dictatorial. Trusting that Madame B. could train the caliber of dancers she envisioned, Grace began their cooperative effort by providing funds for scholarships to enhance enrollment at the École de Danse Classique.

In 1967 Grace helped fund a tour for a small company called The Ballet of Monte Carlo Opera under Madame B.'s direction. Rudolf Nureyev and Carla Fracci were company members. Then Madame B. arranged for Nureyev and Margot Fonteyn to appear at the Principality's centennial celebration. Next the two women saw to it that prominent dance companies returned to appear in Monte Carlo for Grace's newly inaugurated International Festival of Ballet. But still Grace was unable to wrest funds for a new national company from the National Council. When Grace found that Casa Mia, the three-story villa built by the Singer Sewing Machine heir, had come on the market, Rainier quietly purchased it and gave it to his wife. Her foundation undertook funding the renovations and decor. And once she had completed supervising both, Rainier dedicated the facility to the collaboration of the two women, naming it the Académie de Danse Classique Princesse Grace.

By the early 1970s, Grace's job was taking up as much of her time as Rainier's was his. Caroline was in a middling period of her teenage development. In the interests of removing her from the curious eyes of the press and public in Monaco, Grace and Rainier decided she would be better off having the camaraderie that could be found in an English girls' boarding school, where, Grace believed, Caroline would be protected from the dangers of the revolution. At St. Mary's Convent of the Sacred Heart, the top Catholic school in Great Britain, Caroline found herself surrounded by the daughters of socialites. The atmosphere there was one of passive acceptance of the status quo, an adherence to style that limited her exploration of substance. Had Grace not been so fearful in that era, she might have recognized that a stimulating intellectual environment could have stretched Caroline's active curiosity, enabled her to make interesting friends, and perhaps challenged her to set her sights on Oxford or Cambridge.

I had never before known Grace to opt for such narrow vision. Though her tastes had always run to the classical and traditional in esthetics and the arts, until then she had maintained an avid curiosity on a broad range of subjects. For the first time since we had met, I felt Grace's curiosity shrinking rather than expanding. She wanted desperately to protect herself, her marriage and her children from a world she perceived as increasingly hostile and dangerous. To accomplish that end, she began building walls around her life, walls that would in time separate her from the things she most cared about.

My own fortieth birthday was not due until 1972. By the time it came, aging in years meant little to me. Both of my parents had died during the previous year, my father first of a heart attack, my mother ten months later of cancer. On the trip to New York and Chicago to bury my mother, receive condolence calls and settle her affairs, I contracted pneumonia. Grace called to express her sympathies and I told her that the loss of my second parent so profoundly spelled the end of a cycle in my life that the notion of my fifth decade seemed of no consequence.

Don had stopped acting, since he had little interest in pursuing the profession as a lifetime career. Together we had started an independent company to develop motion picture properties for production. After two years of renting my house, Don and I had bought it, living there with my three daughters and—whenever they came to us—his three sons. Amy and Vicki usually spent their school holidays and part of their summer vacations with their father Jay and his wife and children in England. From there they made trips to ski in Switzerland or cruised through the Mediterranean on a chartered yacht.

Don and I spent an enormous amount of time with our children. With both of us working and so many kids to stay close to, we began to sacrifice much of our adult, nighttime social life. Though we did see some of my old Hollywood friends occasionally, our nights were often spent with the writers and other co-workers who were involved with our film projects. One of the projects we had first developed was a script written by Don's ex-wife, Carole, and her second husband, Jack Cole, a producer/director of commercials and title sequences. We had optioned Peter S. Beagle's novel *The Last Unicorn.* Steven Geller had already completed the script for the movie version of Kurt Vonnegut's *Slaughterhouse Five* when he joined us to write the screenplay for *Jesus Christs,* an innovative novel by the former *New York Times* journalist A. J. Langguth.

Hollywood was not much fun in those times. Drugs were everywhere. One of the most misused words of that era was "contact." With so much marijuana everywhere, expressions like "contact high" floated about on the social scene indiscriminately. I knew what was meant by it. I myself had been suspected of enormous marijuana consumption because I got the giggles so easily in rooms where others were smoking. When the real smokers would come down from their highs, I stayed happy, causing everyone to believe that I was the greatest user of them all. Actually, I tried grass once in its usual form, but even on my second puff, when Don had inserted a menthol filter into the tip of the joint, I thought it tasted and smelled like old gym socks. The myth of grass was that it brought everybody into this special contact zone. Like all drugs, though, what marijuana did was isolate. In my view there was no way it could do anything but spoil a party.

Don had experimented with a number of substances before we met, but had abandoned all of them except for marijuana. Even that he used in a manner we both thought of as recreational. He would smoke a joint the way people used to take a drink—at the end of the day, at a social gathering or on vacation. I drank only an occasional glass of wine or champagne, but Don also enjoyed a drink more frequently than I. When both of us were seeing Dr. Duvall for treatment, he had recommended that Don give up pot. The purpose of medical orgonomy, we knew, was to unify the energy in our systems so that mental and physical energy flowed freely through an unarmored structure as it did in other living creatures. Albert Duvall explained that marijuana pulled energy up into the brain and locked it there, producing a result antithetical to the purpose of therapy. For months at a time, Don used no grass. Then he'd lapse back into smoking, but always on the same recreational basis.

The people we entertained most often as the years progressed were my ex-husbands, his ex-wife, the new spouses and the children of all these unions. I did not have to join a commune, I simply married into one. We numbered twenty-three strong: Don and I and our six kids; Don's ex-wife, Carole, and her husband, Jack Cole, with their two children; Jay and Kit Kanter, Kit's three children from her first marriage and their two sons, Adam and Michael; and Tony and Rita Franciosa with their sons, Chris and Marco. When the Kanters moved back from England, we took to celebrating family birthdays together, usually also sharing Thanksgiving, Christmas, New Year's Day, Easter, Mother's Day, Father's Day, the Fourth of July and Labor Day. At one point I mentioned to Carole that if we began to celebrate Ground Hog Day ensemble, I intended to resign. "I know I've been a big perpetrator of all this family togetherness," I said, "but I'm not sure why we're all at my house so often."

"That's easy to figure out," Carole reasoned. "You were married to more of us than anyone else."

In an era when so many families were coming apart, I was enormously comforted by being able to bring our complicated one closer together. Friends were always congratulating me for having done that, saying that we had set the example for how to keep a family on close terms after divorce. I did work hard to keep us all together, but my efforts would have proved fruitless had not the other adults in the group been so family-oriented. We all had children together; none of us had left a previous wife or husband to marry the person we were now with. After a time, sharing the development of all our kids made the assorted ex-wives and ex-husbands in our family feel like brothers and sisters. The kids loved it, of course. In their youngest years they had probably fantasized that their own two parents would reunite and marry again. As this had not happened, having all of us together so often and enjoying such warm mutual friendships was extremely reassuring. Because it gave the children a sense of unity and lessened their conflict, we adults were gratified by our efforts.

By the time I got to my forties, I had learned to do many of the things I had originally detested. The little girl who had a math block at Ethical Culture now took care of the figures everywhere—at home, in our production company, for her family's estate. The magic of being a grown-up had finally set in. The privilege of meeting my responsibilities provided me with the freedom to enjoy my pleasures. My father had visited us in California a few years before he died. Don and I were not yet married, so when Dad came, Don went to sleep elsewhere at the end of each evening. One afternoon, sitting in my kitchen, my father told me he was comforted by seeing that I was a good adult and a wonderful mother. He had always been an extremely conservative man, the kind that had once said "S.O.B." at the dinner table and then apologized to my mother and me for the next twenty minutes. I was surprised when he offered, "If Don usually sleeps here when I'm not here, he doesn't have to leave at night on my account." Some people grow more rigid with age. Luckily, my father was not one of them. Losing my brother, I believe, made him reevaluate what mattered in life and what did not.

When my mother died, though, she was still on no better terms with life or death than she had ever been. Although madly in love with each other, my parents had never been able to grow together into the kind of companionship you hope will result in such a long-term marriage. My father enjoyed few relaxations—his boat, horseback riding, his philanthropies. My mother loved music, the opera and luxurious surroundings. Neither of them had ever found a way to blend these interests. Though they were lovers, they had never become friends, and thus had grown apart rather than together. It made me very sad to see them age, and finally die, without ever having made the connection that would have so comforted each of them. If it was my father who had made me strong, it was my mother who had given me the priceless gift of self-esteem. For my own sake, as well as to honor their memory, I was very clear that what I wanted most in life was to give those gifts to my own children and to build a marriage based on friendship by constant communication.

After living together for four years, Don and I decided to get legally married. I phrase it that way because when you have six kids all down with strep throat on the same weekend, stagger four-hour intervals through the night sticking pills down throats and thermometers up rear ends, you feel about as married as you can get. One day, though, we went to rewrite our wills. Our lawyer informed us that under present law neither of us had any legal standing with the other's children. If anything happened to me and Jay, for example, Don would have no legal position in Amy's or Vicki's life in spite of the fact that they had been living with him for years.

We were married under a yolky midday sun on a Saturday in May by a nondenominational woman minister from The Little Chapel of the Flowers in the Valley. Her name was Pierina Lo Piccolo and Don found her in the Yellow Pages. Only Pierina, Don and I, and our six children were present. Our youngest, Nina, demanded a touch of tradition in the otherwise informal setting under a spreading tree on our front lawn. She fitted out a basket that would qualify her as flower girl replete with pink roses, baby's breath and a giant Hershey bar.

"Why the Hershey bar?" we asked.

"I'm not sure how long these things take," came her response.

"I've never married a whole family before," Pierina opened perfectly. "So why don't each of you tell us what it's like to have become close and want to stay close together—being married, being a family." We had invited a small group of close friends for early dinner, and at sunset, when they arrived, we all kicked off our shoes, made a circle on the lawn, and danced the Greek, Israeli and middle European folk dances our children had learned at the Oakwood School. Only casually, much later in the evening, did we mention we had married earlier that day.

The next morning we took our six children to the Renaissance Pleasure Faire. We had lunch under the shade of a huge oak tree. "This is great," commented Vicki. "We had a great day yesterday at the wedding, but it's not like anything different has happened to any of us." It hadn't. We had simply declared for the state of California the commitment we had already made to God and to ourselves to be a family. The rest was up to us, just as it had been since the day we'd begun. Just as it would be for all the days to come.

CHAPTER 14

Middle-aged Spread

By the early 1970s, nearly twenty years had passed since we had all been together in Monaco at the wedding. In spite of that, it was still not uncommon to hear ourselves referred to as "the bridesmaids." There was something so powerful about Grace's legend that no matter what direction our individual paths had taken, our connection to her was like a nonremovable, indelible, lifetime name tag.

Though Grace continually updated us on one another, maintaining the sense that we were a cohesive group, the preoccupations of her own life began to separate Grace from a certain facet of herself as I had known her. From a distance, I read numerous quotes in the press that revealed a woman who was becoming increasingly more conservative. The statements I read in the newspapers or in articles or interviews with her began to reveal zealous criticism of nearly every facet of modern-day life. I wondered if I would find this same attitude when we next met privately.

The first such occasion arose in the spring of 1972 when Don and I decided to attend the Cannes Film Festival. I called Grace to tell her we were coming and would be staying in Cap d'Antibes. Don had never met her or Rainier. On arrival, we realized that most of our days and nights would be taken up with meetings, parties and screenings connected to the Festival. Grace had sent an invitation to us to attend both the Grand Prix, which was being held during the festival period, and a ball she and Rainier were hosting at the Palace. I phoned to tell her that we would have to miss the race as the day had already been scheduled with a series of meetings, but that we would love to attend the party. Grace said she had some errands to run in Nice and suggested, if it was possible for me to get away, that we have lunch alone at a restaurant there.

In an interview Grace had said she deplored the new trend for women to wear pants in public. Though it was being done everywhere and by nearly everyone, I decided to wear a skirt instead. When I arrived at the small local bistro in Nice, Grace was already there. She was wearing matching beige trousers and jacket with a pastel printed blouse. Though beautifully tailored, it was a pantsuit nonetheless. I laughed when I saw her and, when she didn't know why, explained, "Here I went and put on a skirt so you would not count me among those to be 'deplored' for wearing pants in public. Does that mean I get to deplore you instead?" I asked jokingly.

Grace remained quite serious. "I do," she answered, "think it's too bad that people no longer dress with any sense of what's appropriate for the occasion. I did say something about pants on women being overdone, but I didn't mean on a day like this when we're just having a casual lunch in a small restaurant."

I responded with equal seriousness. "Perhaps you're being quoted out of context," I offered. "You know far better than I how to protect yourself from the press, but the impression that's being left from certain interviews is that you've grown practically Victorian in your outlook. It makes you sound stiff in a way I've never known you to be."

"These days there are so many things that distress me," Grace admitted. "I have a hard enough time just trying to set standards for myself and my family, but when I am asked to speak out I do feel it's my responsibility to defend those values we all seem to be tossing aside."

"That's certainly your right," I concurred, "perhaps even your obligation, but values are values and pants are pants, and the way you are quoted often makes you sound as if you don't exactly understand the difference between the two. I've also read quotes in which you've spoken out against modern permissiveness . . ."

"Don't you find these dangerous times in which to raise our children?" Grace interjected.

"I do," I acknowledged. "The kinds of mistakes we could make when we were teenagers were, for the most part, not awfully significant, even though our parents thought they were a big deal. Now, though, whole lives are being wiped out by the dangers available to kids. I find that scary, but I also think it gives us an opportunity, maybe even an obligation, to educate our kids earlier and more honestly about the complexities of life."

At that point I took out photos of our six children, as Grace had not seen the girls in some time and had never met our sons. Passing them across the table, I realized that Robert, James and Sean all had rather long hair.

"I won't let Albie's hair get that long," Grace noted instantly, "though his hair does go below his collar in a way which I had never thought I'd tolerate. The part about long hair that really bothers me is the habit of keeping it unkempt and dirty." We talked for a moment about how the young people wanted to de-emphasize the value that our generation had placed on appearances.

"In the greater scheme of things," I commented, "I sort of feel the way Annie Sullivan did in *The Miracle Worker*. Remember where Helen Keller's father announces to her, 'Miss Sullivan, cleanliness is next to godliness,' and she answers, 'Captain Keller, cleanliness is next to nothing!' " Grace laughed, agreeing that in that context there were far more important issues at stake.

As we talked about our families, I told Grace how mine had expanded to include all the Kanters, Franciosas and Coles, our exes. "Judybird, how do you do that?" she exclaimed. "It must be so difficult."

"The hardest part," I confessed, "was when we were first together and the children tested how successful they'd be at playing one parent or one set of parents off against the other on matters of discipline. Don's boys would be staying with us, and if they had a cold we'd insist they stay out of the pool. Then they'd insist that their mother and Jack let them go swimming even when they were sick, and that she knew more about taking care of them than we did."

"You don't have to tell me about that!" Grace sighed. "I can tell you even with my own three that they play one parent against the other without any divorces or stepparents in the picture."

"It's really easier with stepparents when there's a difference of opinion," I told her. "All we say is, 'Your mother and Jack love you, and they do whatever they think is best for you when you're living at their house. Because we love you, too, when you're with us we do whatever we think is best for you. We all have your best interests at heart, but that doesn't mean we all agree on doing everything the same way.'"

"Would that we could settle conflicts between two parents living together as easily as that," Grace lamented.

I asked Grace to tell me about the thousand and one activities she had gotten into, and she began listing them and recounting her progress or lack of it with each organization. Though I lost count, I think she had become honorary chairman or president of more than thirty groups by then. "I don't know how you squeeze it all in," I observed, "what with your family, the Palace, entertaining, flying around to functions, moving between Monaco, Roc Agel, Paris, Switzerland and all your other pit stops. Your life sounds unbelievably hectic!"

"Too hectic," Grace sighed. "It's taking more and more time away from the children, even though the older ones are in school most of the day or away at school. I never seem to have time for myself any longer. Rainier has a similar schedule, and though we try to be with Stephanie and the other children when they're home, there never seems to be any time to relax together." She sneezed. And sneezed again. "I'm getting colds more often again, the way I used to when I was a child, and they last longer. I don't run temperatures and it's not the flu. I know it sounds silly—probably it's age—but I get tired so easily so much of the time."

"Isn't there any way you can free yourself of some of these duties?" I inquired.

"I keep promising myself I'll do that," Grace answered, "but instead it seems that I take on more each year." She paused for a moment. "Maybe that's the way I want it," she reflected, as we looked at each other pointedly while the waiter served us. Before digging into her *coq au vin* she added offhandedly, "Idle hands are the devil's playmate." I'd grown accustomed, over the years, to the throwaway lines Grace used in conversation or in letters which told me more about her than she was comfortable revealing, perhaps even told her more about herself than she wished to acknowledge. I knew it was always best to read into them as I pleased, but wisest never to focus on them or question her further. I observed that custom, but would remember the phrase often as the years passed.

"If you did have more time to yourself, what would you like to do with it? Among those things you *could* do in your position?"

"Sometimes I can think of a million things, sometimes none."

"A lot of my women friends in America," I told her, "talk about wanting to go to work or go back to work. Some feel there's nothing they're qualified to do except philanthropic work. Others feel that their talents and resources give them too many options. Likely," I conjectured, "they all envy you."

We smiled for a moment at the irony of Grace's life, the unreal fantasy of it that warmed the dreams of women all over the world and the reality of limitations her position placed upon her. Then Grace said what was very like her to say, "There are truly so many wonderful things about my life. I, of all people, have no right to complain."

"Speaking of complaints," I interjected, "I read an interview in which it sounded as if you were complaining—across the board—about women who work. They quoted you as saying that women who work 'only do it to get off the hook and avoid their family responsibilities.' Do you really feel that way, Gracie?"

"I know the interview you mean. It's the same one in which I said that being the underpinning of the family is a woman's physiological job." I nodded, remembering that statement as well. "Do you disagree?" Grace asked. "Do you question women's role as the pillar of the family in that way?" I said I did not. "Well, then, how do you equate that with every young mother thinking she can just traipse off after her baby is born and do whatever work amuses her?" Grace was becoming passionate and testy. "If they don't want to be mothers," she added, "they shouldn't have children. It's all this silly 'doing your own thing' business. Just have the baby, drop it off somewhere, or leave it at home with someone who'll take care of it, then put it to bed at night when you have time. Horrid!" she exclaimed. "Who nurtures the child, gives it its values, its sense of belonging and family, its base in life? Who watches for signs of trouble, who soothes, directs and loves the child? The strange lady at the day-care center? The baby-sitter?"

"Whoa, Grace," I interrupted, "you don't have to sell me on all that.

Of course I agree with what you're saying when we talk like this. I know that people have gotten careless about raising children, that the early years are the most formative. But when I hear that you've said 'women who work,' presumably meaning all women who work, 'only do it to get off the hook and avoid their family responsibilities' it makes you sound like a rarefied snob with no sense of what's happening in the real world. Forgive me for saying this, too, but there's also a part of it that strikes me as somewhat hypocritical."

"How rarefied, or snobby?" she asked, understandably wounded by my insinuations that she might be either of those things. "How hypocritical?"

"Well, for one thing," I explained, "don't you realize that the way inflation is going a lot of women are being forced to work regardless of their children's ages or their personal desires, just so they and their kids can have a decent home, some food on the table, a doctor when they're sick and a way to stay warm in winter? They're a lot of single mothers out there, Grace, with ex-husbands who can't or won't send child support and no parents of their own to turn to. I'm not talking about people who want more luxuries. I'm referring to women who do half or all of the breadwinning to support themselves and their families. Are you putting them down?"

"You know I wasn't referring to women who *have* to work!" Grace protested vehemently.

"*I* didn't presume you were, but there are a lot of women who don't know you personally who are reading your statements. What do *they* presume? God knows, Gracie, you're one of the least spoiled and most compassionate people I know, but perhaps living as you do where you do, you don't realize the number of women who fall into that category."

"I suppose you're right," Grace concurred. "I try to keep our life as normal as I can and to keep abreast of what's happening, but the circumstances often do separate me from the real world. I try to avoid it but . . ."

I chose my words carefully. "You yourself aren't among those women who have to work for a living, yet you just gave me a list of work you do that takes as much of your time as any paying job would. Are you just, in your own words, getting off the hook or avoiding your family responsibilities?"

"Oh, Judy, that's different," Grace countered. "The things I do are all for worthwhile causes. And they need to be served by people who can help in the way that I can. Many of them are actually among my duties. Others are things I feel so strongly about that I just could not turn my back on their needs. You can't be opposed to my volunteer work for charities and the arts?"

"Sweetie," I assured her, using one of her pet affectionate terms, "I'm not opposed to any work you do, nor any work at all, for that matter, with the possible exception of hooking, which is hard to blend with family life." Grace laughed. "It's you who publicly opposed women who work, not me. And your opposition would have to apply to me, because *I* don't have to work, but I've been working for a few years. Nina is only nine, and she's still around a lot."

"Oh, Judybird," Grace interjected, "I don't mean people like you. I know what a loving and conscientious mother you are, how deeply you involve yourself with all aspects of your children's development."

"Then what you object to," I tried sorting out, "is not women who work but women who don't have to work but do from the instant their kids are born, and women who think that because they work they don't have to put in the extra effort required to be a good mother."

"Well, of course," Grace agreed. "Every child is a maze of sensitivities. It's all I can do with my three to be aware of the changing moods and stages they go through, to do my job as a mother . . ."

"Especially since you work," I couldn't help interjecting. Grace gave me a look that said "touché." "That's the part that made you sound hypocritical," I said frankly. "If you really wanted to, couldn't you limit your own activities in some way? I've heard that you actually receive individual Monégasque citizens to listen to their private problems and offer counsel or support. I'm not suggesting you should curtail your activities, Lord knows I admire you for them. But if you really wanted to, you could rearrange your life, cutting out a lot of the work you do, and just stay at home, seeing your children when possible, planning parties, having fittings and manicures, and playing gin rummy with 'the girls,' as some of our mothers did."

"That would bore me," Grace admitted honestly.

"It bores a lot of other women, too," I said, "whether, like you, they had a career before marriage or whether, like me, they didn't. I thought girls like us weren't supposed to work, but the truth is that until I started working, nothing seemed very real to me, I could never sort my life out properly. It's only since I started working that I've been able to do most of the other things I wanted to do, for my husband, my children or myself. There's a lot that's awfully different about us, Grace. Those differences have always existed, and in a lot of ways they've become greater not smaller as the years go by. But my guess is that both of us have enormous energies. We both like challenges. We're both a little driven, and though we may complain about the results of those drives, neither one of us would be entirely ourselves without them. While my life is on a much lower economic scale than yours, neither one of us is forced to run the vacuum cleaner regularly, to hit the supermarket three times a week, or to sweat over a hot stove to whip up three meals a day for 'the mister and the little ones.' "

There was a long pause while Grace digested what we'd been talking about. I could see her pulling into herself in a way that was familiar to me by then. "Sometimes," she finally said, "I think it's better for me not to examine why I do what I do. Mostly, I'm better off when I just do what needs to be done and let it go at that."

"Sometimes," I said, "that's safer for all of us."

Moving a demitasse so she could take my hand in hers, Grace reached slowly across the table. "God," she said, "I wish we lived closer so we could talk more like this."

Part of me wished that, too. Another part wondered if the distance between us was not safer at this point in our lives. Her comment did, though, elicit the pang of guilt I felt about not writing the letters I continually had promised. "I'm sorry I'm such a lousy letter writer," I apologized.

"I confess that some time ago," Grace admitted, "I did count the letters you owed me, not to make you feel bad but because you're always so busy apologizing for the fact that you don't write often. I think it was somewhere past fifty." I winced, feeling terrible, and Grace knew it. "I don't want you to apologize anymore about it, sweetie. I didn't mean to rub it in."

"I've gotten awful about keeping in touch with friends, all friends," I admitted, "maybe because, other than having children, for so many years all I did was socialize, almost to the point of becoming a professional 'best friend.' Sometimes when I get a letter from you and think about how good you are about writing and how lousy I am, I reason that you can get everything done because you have so many people helping you with your life and I don't."

"Well, that's true," Grace concurred graciously.

"Yeah, but it's a cop-out," I admitted. "Please know that I would be the last person not to understand if you chose to limit your correspondence." With our hands still intertwined, I promised Grace that I would find a way to write more often.

Our second meeting on that trip was not nearly so serious, much more glamorous and a revelation for Don. We drove to Monaco for the Grand Prix ball late on a Saturday afternoon. Nadia Lacoste, who handled public relations for Monaco and its Princely Family, had booked a room for us at the Hôtel de Paris so we could drive in our street clothes and change there for the evening. The Palace invitation included a midnight supper, but we asked Nadia to join us for dinner at the hotel before we drove up the hill. I owned one truly beautiful Parisian couture dress, which I had saved for the occasion. My mother had it made for her the year before her death and, deciding it was too youthful for her, had given it to me. Made of eggshell silk surah, it had a high round neckline, huge puffed sleeves with smocked and ruffled cuffs, a belled skirt that fell just to the tops of my shoes, and a two-foot-deep circle of pleated smocking at the hem which was encrusted with gold, green and red jewels in a design reminiscent of the work Russian jeweler Carl Fabergé used to decorate his royal Easter eggs. Perfect, I decided, for a ball at the Palace. I packed it and my accessories in one hanging bag as Don assembled his dinner jacket and other belongings in his case.

Luckily, we had allowed more than enough time for the drive because the traffic to Monaco was horrid. Arriving at the hotel, we had just enough time to dress and meet Nadia in the bar for a pre-dinner drink. I could tell that Don was getting a bit nervous preparing for his first trip to the Palace. Just finishing my hair, I heard him yell out, "Oh, shit!" I spun around to see him holding up his shoes. He had black ones he wore with his dinner jacket exactly like those in his hands. But what he had packed was a brown pair! The only other shoes he had were the tennis shoes he'd worn for the drive over. All the stores were closed for the night. I assured him that with the low lighting and the crowd, nobody would even notice, but we left the room with Don convinced that his brown shoes with his black tuxedo would attract as much attention as flashing neon lights.

Nadia also tried to put Don at ease during our lovely catch-up dinner. He felt somewhat comforted as we waited in the long line of guests at the Palace gates for the guards to check invitations on the guest list. Perhaps there would be enough people so his shoes would not be noticed. As we neared the reception salon, though, seeing Grace and Rainier ahead of us receiving in a small line, I felt Don stiffen again. I suggested we let them in on the gaffe and Don agreed. After Grace kissed me on both cheeks and Rainier made a subtle little curtsy to remind me of our private joke from the first time we'd met, I introduced Don. "Don packed the wrong shoes when we left the Hôtel du Cap," I confided. Grace and Rainier looked down, then up again.

"This is embarrassing," Don admitted.

"Should we tell them?" Grace asked her husband.

"Absolutely," Rainier answered. "Why should Don be the only one who's uncomfortable?" His eyes were twinkling mischievously as were hers.

"Judy, dear," she cooed. "For once it is not you and I who are playing the Bobbsey Twins. But Christina de Camaran, who is already here, does have on exactly the same dress as you!" Grace pointed toward the crowded room behind me, and I turned to see the Countess, who was, indeed, dressed identically. "Later in the evening we can get the two of you to stand back-to-back and play bookends," she added. The four of us chuckled and the informality of the moment put Don immediately at his ease.

Before supper was served and the dancing began, Don and I visited with some of Grace's friends I had met on earlier trips. We also had the chance to have a chat with Ma Kelly, whom I'd not seen in years. I reminded her that the last time I had seen any of her children besides Grace was ten or more years earlier when I'd had lunch with Peggy while on my honeymoon with Tony in Philadelphia. Mrs. Kelly told us that Peggy was divorced from her second husband, Gene Conlan. She had already become a grandmother, I knew, when her younger daughter, Mary Lee, eloped and delivered twins while still in her early teens. Lizanne's two children, Gracie and Chris, were adorable, Ma Kelly said. Their father, Donald LeVine, had undergone serious stomach surgery some time ago, but was doing well and becoming more involved with the track and training horses, which he had always loved. When I inquired about Grace's brother Kell, Mrs. Kelly threw up her hands in despair. "I'm afraid that boy is never going to see the light," she moaned. I told her I had heard that Kell had divorced Mary, who had borne him six children.

Confessing that I'd always thought Kell suffered from many of the same problems that plagued the sons of other dynamic fathers, I added, "I suppose I presumed that when Jack died, Kell might find his own place in the sun, his own identity."

"I thought that might happen, too," she agreed. "But Jack has been gone for years now and Kell still can't seem to grow up. He's been active in local politics, and in business, but there's a lot of maturity still lacking." Pausing, Ma Kelly looked over at her daughter and son-in-law. "Gracie had her own rebellion." She turned to look at me. "Well, you know that, Judy." She looked back at Grace and Rainier again. "But look how nicely she settled down!" Mrs. Kelly sounded like any mother whose daughter had grown up to marry an account executive and was living in Westport, Connecticut. When I looked, what I saw was a beautiful princess in a salmon pink ball gown, erect under the weight of staggering jewels. She and her prince were mingling with famous and titled guests in a brocade-walled room while their footmen passed champagne on silver trays under the gleam of tall candles and pale bulbs that flickered from ormolu sconces and crystal-bobèched chandeliers. Every now and then, especially when she laughed, I could still see the old Gracie.

An elaborate midnight buffet was served as we danced both to traditional and more modern music. I had told Don about Ania Chervachidze, and was happy for the opportunity to introduce them. I had heard from Grace that Ania's fortunes had been reversed and that she'd been forced to sell her Villa Soulico, where she'd entertained so often for Grace. I knew that she was living in a smaller house near the Palace, but until she told me I did not know that the residence had belonged to Rainier and that Grace and he had put it at Ania's disposal in her time of need. Ania went on at great length about the loyalty and generosity of the Prince and Princess. She could repay that loyalty, she explained, only with her friendship and a promise to donate her Russian master art collection to the Principality upon her death.

On the drive home from the Palace, I told Don about Grace's other older friend, Milica Banek, who had died three years earlier. He interrupted me to note that he could easily understand why (as we'd heard from others who knew them) Prince Philip and, particularly, Lord Mountbatten were a little gaga over Gracie. Don admitted that just on one meeting, he had joined the long list of men who fell, inevitably, a little in love with her.

Not long afterwards, Grace and I found ourselves in a rather testy public exchange at a California dinner party Rupert Allan hosted for her at his home. Thirty or so friends had been invited for the evening. Grace was not with Rainier, but was accompanied by her divorced niece Mary Lee.

Several tables had been set up in Rupert's living room. Rupert had seated me across from Grace. During dinner Grace's old pal Bill Allyn asked me about *Jesus Christs,* the screen adaptation of A. J. Langguth's novel, which Don and I owned. As soon as she heard the title, Grace focused her attention on our conversation. I explained that the property was set in modern times, allegorically depicting Christ being forced to come back among us in the roles of various members of modern society—a TV show host, a truck driver, a Ralph Nader type testifying before Congress on the subject of genetic legislation. At the end of the first cycle, Christ was killed. Descending to a confrontation with Satan, he was then resurrected and had to return to begin a new series of roles in modern life. After three such life cycles, deaths, confrontations with Satan and resurrections, Christ's last rebirth allowed him to live as a simple man trying to build a home and family, a job presented as being—in itself—in the best image of God.

When I finished describing the property, Grace barked angrily, "Why would you make a picture like that today? Don't we have enough problems without sacrilegious films being made for mass audiences?" All conversation at our table came to a standstill. Everyone was listening. I looked down the table at Bill Allyn, wondering if he was as amazed as I to find Grace so quick to label and condemn, and so vehemently confrontational in public.

I chose my words carefully. "I agree, Grace, that the material is innovative. It's certainly not within the bounds of traditional Catholic or other Christian teachings. What it does offer is loving respect for the notion that modern humanity's greatest challenge is to build the family unit. I don't think that's sacrilegious."

It didn't work. "We need to confirm old values in these times. All this breaking down of traditional teachings has only succeeded in making the world more ugly, more hostile, even less loving than it was before. Our traditional teachings stabilized society. All we seem to do now is find ways to become less civilized," Grace announced regally.

I thought of a million things I would have said had no one else been present, or if this incident had transpired some years earlier. Throughout the evening, though, I had become aware that many of Grace's Hollywood acquaintances were beginning to treat her more like a princess than just a person whom they admired and respected. I was embarrassed for us all, but imparted the only remaining piece of information I believed was pertinent. "After we left you in Monaco last spring, Don and I went to Rome on business. We thought it a good idea to see whether the Vatican objected to our script."

"I should think they would!" Grace exclaimed.

"We submitted the screenplay," I continued. "A month or so after we got home, a letter came confirming that the script had been read. It said that while the material proposed ideas outside the traditional teachings of the Church, and while its humor might be regarded as irreverent, its subject matter reflected much of what was being questioned in new Catholic movements around the world. We were given Vatican approval to shoot in Italy."

The silence was so heavy and burdensome that I quickly changed the subject. It was a moment I hated. What possible satisfaction could I have had from the revelation that Grace had grown more conservatively Catholic than the Pope? What joy could come for any of us at the prospect that this intelligent and curious woman we had respected as an artist and a friend had shut off a part of herself that encompassed the world of ideas? I had always admired Grace's faith, the courage of her convictions. It disturbed me to sense that she had begun to convict before the trial— that, above all else, fear seemed to have become the shaper of her opinions. I wondered if, after all, the subject was one we could not have discussed any more successfully in private than we had in public.

Later that evening we were sitting on the sofa together dishing some mutual acquaintances. Gracie seemed at ease, relaxed, her old self again.

At one point she looked about the room to see how her niece was doing, but found her missing. Sotto voce, so only we could hear, Rupert mentioned that Mary Lee and Ryan O'Neal had strolled out into the garden a few minutes apart from each other some time ago and had not yet returned. Grace made one of her adorable comically sad grimaces. "Oh, to be young again," she sighed. "I wish it were me!"

In bed that night Don and I talked about the evening. "I feel as if I just had dinner with two people," I commented. "The only problem is they were both Grace."

During the early months of 1973, Grace called from Monaco to say that she, Rainier, their three children and her niece Gracie LeVine were going to spend their Easter holiday in Palm Springs at the Sinatras'. She wondered if we could arrange to be in the Springs, too, bringing as many of our children as were available. "They haven't been together in so long," she noted, "and Rainier and I are trying to avoid a lot of moving around, thus we have no plans to be in Los Angeles." Two weeks later I phoned her back to say we would come, had booked a bungalow at the Racquet Club, and would bring our housekeeper and two of our six children, Nina, who was nine and a year older than Stephanie, and Vicki, who was sixteen, Caroline's age.

My mother had left me her rather large pear-shaped diamond ring when she died. I had put it in a vault and left it there for a few years, entertaining the fantasy that I was too young to wear such a rock. Then reality dawned upon me that I was fast approaching my forty-second birthday, so I had taken to wearing the ring on special occasions. I decided to take it to Palm Springs for our holiday, knowing that Grace would have hers with her, that Barbara Sinatra and others of her friends there owned significant jewels, and that mine would not look out of place in that company. The day after our arrival, we and our children went to have lunch and spend the afternoon swimming at Frank and Barbara's.

In years past I had often visited the previous Sinatra home, a smaller, more traditional house. This was, however, Don's and my first visit to the new compound Barbara and Frank had developed. When we drove up, we found a huge, walled estate with several guards posted at the entranceway. Flags of both the United States and the state of California were flying, reminding me of the shift in Frank's political sentiments since the last time I'd been to one of his desert homes. Earlier, he had been a strong, visible supporter of the Kennedys and their liberal positions. In those days, when I'd first started working for the ACLU Foundation of Southern California, Frank and his close chums—many of whom were mine as well—had been among the Foundation's most generous supporters. Now, Ronald Reagan was Governor of California, the Watergate scandal was escalating daily, and Frank had become a staunch Nixon Republican, taking most of our old "rat pack" buddies along with him. I decided political discussion would best be avoided during the visit.

The children were all in the pool when we were ushered to it. Grace and Barbara had caftans on over their bathing suits; Rainier, Frank and the other men present were wearing trunks and open sport shirts or cotton trousers and polo shirts. Grace was her usual warm, affectionate self, making a great fuss over our two girls and spending the first half hour or so trying to get to know them a bit in their current phases of life. Over our informal buffet luncheon, served in the poolhouse and at neighboring outdoor tables, everyone howled at our reminiscence about the day at the Palace when Grace and I found Vicki and Caroline trying to stuff Stephanie, headfirst, down the toilet.

After lunch the three older girls wandered off to Caroline's room in one of the Sinatras' guesthouses while Albert occupied Stephanie and Nina in a game of water polo. Watching our younger daughters trying to keep up with Albie, Grace and I compared their mutual high energy and its sometimes exasperating manifestations. We discovered that both Stephanie and Nina were getting away with murder when we compared their upbringing to that of our older children. Grace and Rainier both were obviously much more tolerant and permissive with Stephanie than I'd remembered their being with Albert or Caroline. I knew the same was true of my attitude toward Nina. For all that Grace denounced these permissive times, I wondered why she indulged Stephanie as she did. The only common thread I could identify in her behavior and mine was that Steph and Nina were the youngest in both families, and certainly the last children each of us would have.

Barbara Sinatra came to join us, admiring my ring. I told her and Grace my family had named it "The Big Bopper" and that if I'd been prone to developing an attitude to accompany wearing it, nine-year-old Nina had taken care of that for me. Nina, I explained, had picked up an awful lot of rough language, primarily from being around her three older brothers. Though she was cautious about using it in company, on more than one occasion with only the family present, some of it slipped out. I told Grace and Barbara that the first time I had taken the ring out to wear it, I'd stopped in the dining room to say good night to the children, who were all having dinner together. I was wearing a pink taffeta dress with an off-the-shoulder ruffled collar. Nina was little, and I'd realized as I bent down to kiss her that my ruffle might dip into her tomato soup. In order to prevent that, I had held the ruffle close to my chest with my left hand, the ring on its third finger. As she kissed me good night, Nina looked admiringly at the ring. "Oh, Mommy," she'd said. "The ring is so beautiful, but if you'll pardon my saying so, it's bigger than your tits!" If Grace had seemed inordinately prudish some months earlier, she howled at this tale of my daughter's unvarnished honesty and the image of such a cherubic child uttering such language to her mother.

We had several other visits during the week. Grace brought the children to the Racquet Club one afternoon for lunch and swimming, and on one evening we dined with Nancy and Henry Ittleson. My parents had known the Ittlesons in New York. Henry was the head of CIT, the huge commercial credit and banking firm, Nancy, his young and lovely wife. Some years before, the Ittlesons had bought a villa near Monaco, where they spent their summers. Grace and Rainier were fond of them, and the two couples had become extremely friendly.

Nancy and Henry had a magnificent home in Palm Springs, where they always spent spring vacations. They hosted us there for drinks. Then we piled into cars heading to Don the Beachcomber, where we gorged ourselves on Polynesian food and fruity rum drinks. As the evening wore on, Stephanie and Nina got bored sitting around the table while the adults drank coffee. They disappeared to the ladies' room and remained gone for so long that Grace and I decided we'd best check on them. Nina had become very involved with figure skating, taking lessons throughout the week after school and beginning to join competitive junior training programs. Stephanie was a gymnastics devotee. In the hallways outside the rest rooms, we found the two girls teaching each other the tricks of their respective trades. Stephanie was busy tumbling, doing backbends and splits, Nina performing a landlocked slow-motion camel spin followed by a toe loop.

The trip was a congenial one—warm, easy and fun. Perhaps because so much of our focus was on the children, Grace and I had no opportunity to get into discussions that created either conflict or particular revelations. Then, too, perhaps because she, Rainier and the children were so far from home and only in the company of cozy old pals, they all seemed particularly relaxed. Friends from Monaco had mentioned to me on several occasions that Rainier was often short-tempered with Grace, too frequently in the presence of others. They said they felt bad for her when these outbursts came, that she never contradicted her husband nor called him on his tone. Grace was always deeply hurt, they had noted, but her brave silences seemed only to exacerbate and prolong the discomfort and embarrassment of such moments. I had seen no such incidents between Grace and Rainier in the Springs. But I did know that part of Grace's bargain as a European wife would never have permitted her to question or contradict her husband in public. If these stories were true, I also presumed, knowing Grace, she might even avoid confronting him in the privacy of their own bedroom.

That summer Robert, James and Sean became karate kids. They attended all the tournaments at the Chuck Norris School, where they took classes, and as many of the larger intraschool ones as we permitted. Don and I started seeing a bit of Chuck, for a while meeting together to see if we could jointly produce a documentary on the martial arts that he had been developing for several years. Late in the summer of 1974, we heard that a midwestern karate tournament promoter, Mike Anderson, was planning a huge event the next month in Los Angeles. We took our sons to a large national tournament held annually in August in Long Beach, and met Anderson there briefly. We also met a number of the leading point karate athletes, who sought our counsel on how they could develop karate into a professional spectator sport.

Don had secured back issues of a number of karate publications. There were nineteen of them on the newsstands in those days, one of them owned by Mike Anderson. We went out to talk with a friend, Jim Appell, who was then Director of the Inglewood Forum, asking for his thoughts on the potential of the sport going pro.

Mike Anderson had sold TV rights for a professional karate event to ABC through a contract he'd made months earlier with Universal Pictures. Universal was hosting a celebrity buffet at the studio before the event, busing over the stars to dress up the audience for the television coverage. Telly Savalas had been set as guest color commentator. We decided to get tickets and attend in order to explore the potential.

On Labor Day weekend of 1974, thirteen days before the First Professional World Karate Championships, a mutual friend called Don to say that Anderson, the promoter, wanted to meet with him. I was in bed with a 102 degree temperature and the flu when Don drove down the hill to meet Mike for lunch. When he came home five hours later, Don tossed a sheaf of papers on our bed and announced to me, "I'm co-producing the championships and all is chaos."

I suddenly realized the event was less than two weeks away. "What needs to be done?" I asked. "If it's a lot, I'd be willing to help on this one for the thirteen remaining days—but that's as far as my interest goes."

Unfortunately, everything needed to be done. We worked round-the-clock straight through the next thirteen days, stopping only to nibble on a snack before falling to sleep for an hour or so. I got over the flu and Don came down with it, but we kept going. Three nights before the championships, Don, Mike and I sat in our dining room. Actually it was nearing four in the morning on my husband's birthday. Tidying up the last details of that day, I heard Mike ask Don if he would like to promote more joint events when this one was finished. I had no such interest, but had not had time to ask Don what his feelings were. "I don't want to become a promoter of karate fights," he answered, "even if this one is a smash." I breathed a sigh of relief. "What would interest me, if this goes well," he went on, "is to create the superstructure for a whole new professional sport."

Don began to describe a vision that encompassed everything from the creation of comprehensive and standardized rules to trained officials to centralized record-keeping, from selling sports rights to television to licensed products, and to conforming the sport with government regulatory requirements. He envisioned eventual karate school franchises, along with professional full-contact training centers. As I listened to him talk, I had two reactions. The first was that fatigue had felled him and that he'd lost his mind. The second was that it all sounded challenging, difficult if not impossible—and terrific!

The launching of full-contact karate drew a huge number of enthralled spectators to the Los Angeles Sports Arena. Its tape-delayed TV debut on ABC over New Year's weekend out-rated NBC's Johnny Carson show. To celebrate the success of the live event, we rented Elvis Presley's old suite at the Beverly Wilshire Hotel and, at six in the morning as our party ended, stood rinsing the last plates and glasses the caterers had left in the sink. Don had on a suit. I was wearing my big ring and Missoni pajamas, which our youngest, Nina, had said were so beautiful "they should be in the Missonian Institute." A couple of late karate community revelers dressed in matching polyester "leisure suits" appeared in the kitchen doorway.

"Are you the caterers?" they inquired.

"No," we replied, "your hosts."

Unphased, the couple walked directly into the pantry, loaded up all the remaining liquor bottles on a dolly—those that had been opened and those still in cartons—and set off down the hotel corridor without so much as a "good night" or "thank you." Welcome to karate!

And that's where we were to spend the next twelve years of our lives. A far cry, perhaps, from the world of show business and its glamour. Further yet from Grace's life at the Palace and its super-fantasy aura. But it was a fascinating challenge and we would grow enormously dedicated to it, to the Professional Karate Association (PKA), which we founded as the sanctioning body Don envisioned, and to the related entities we formed which handled other aspects of the sport as it grew. Besides, as stand-up comic Ronnie Shakes approximately said, "I like life. It gives me something to do."

Grace so powerful during Lizzie's 1971 visit with the family in Roc Agel had begun to unravel by the middle of the decade.

Caroline had graduated from St. Mary's Convent school in England, which had given her the equivalent of an American high school diploma, when she was sixteen in 1973. But in order to enter advanced studies in Paris, where it was planned she would eventually go, Caroline still needed her *baccalauréat,* the equivalent of a French high school diploma. The Dames de St. Maur, whose convent school she'd attended for years in Monte Carlo, had another lycée in the Bois de Boulogne in Paris. Caroline chose to enroll there to pass her *bac,* and the family felt she had earned the right to have her preference accepted. Her grades had remained excellent all through the years, she had become proficient in Spanish and German as well as her native French and English, and had a more than passing knowledge of the literature written in the native tongues of several countries.

Caroline first suggested that she live with her grandmother, Princess Charlotte, during her lycée year in Paris, but this was unacceptable to her parents. It is not hard to understand why. Charlotte, or Mamou as her grandchildren called her, had never warmed to Grace. Mamou's affections were like a skipped-generation trust. Her own two children never received her devotion, which was distributed solely to her several grandchildren. To send Caroline to her at this point would probably have felt, to Grace and Rainier, a bit like giving the wicked witch their firstborn child. Most Europeans who knew about Charlotte's lifestyle gossiped about her passionate dedication to the rehabilitation of ex-convicts. She employed so many of them at the sovereign château in Marchais where she lived outside Paris that the townsfolk were said to be concerned for their own safety. Espousing her cause, Charlotte remarried before her death, this time to a former prison inmate who had also served for a while as her chauffeur.

It had been obvious since Caroline was small that she was impatient to graduate into adulthood. Though she clearly felt she came from a loving and happy home, she was not the kind of person who would recall being a child with any great sense of loss. In her desire to shape perfectly safe and happy kids, Grace felt compelled to enforce a proliferation of rules on even the smallest matters. Grace seemed to have forgotten how she herself had resented the thousand-and-one dos and don'ts imposed on her in her own youth, how much she had longed to be trusted herself, and how little trust she appeared to be vesting in her own firstborn child. (I think there was not one of us who didn't forget exactly the way that Grace did.)

When Caroline asked to stay at her family's Avenue Foch apartment in Paris with an approved female companion and whomever else Grace found acceptable while she attended the lycée, Grace said a firm no. Both Caroline and Rainier tried to change her mind, but Grace would not be swayed. I think the first thing she feared for was the most obvious— Caroline's physical safety.

Mindless violence, acts against person and property for no apparent reason, and political kidnappings or those for huge ransoms were rampant everywhere. Grace had reason to fear that her children—and Caroline in particular as the oldest and most visible of them—might be prime targets. There were other reasons Grace felt she should remain near to Caroline. The girl was obviously a beauty and at the age when she would begin to attract men. Grace wanted to help her daughter pick and choose the type of company she should keep.

As a solution, Grace proposed an arrangement that would divide her family during the weekdays, but still permit her to stay physically close to her two girls. She suggested that she and Stephanie would move into the family's Avenue Foch apartment in Paris, leaving Rainier and Albert in Monaco for the school week. She seemed so worried that this plan was accepted by everyone.

Upon reconsideration, however, Rainier and Caroline urged Grace to reject the cumbersome and difficult family subdivision she had recommended. Grace began to wonder whether she was doing the right thing. The tabloids had started to speculate on the frequency of her and Rainier's absences from each other. They might possess a photo of Grace looking startled, because their cameraman had leapt out at her from behind a bush. But they would run it with a caption attributing her expression to having just heard about an affair Rainier was "rumored" to be having. The following week they would use a shot of Rainier laughing with some friends at a party, crop out everyone but Rainier and whatever woman stood next to him, and caption that as the first photo of Grace's husband with "his new paramour." Was this a time, Grace questioned, when she should separate herself from her husband even more regularly?

Would that be wise, either for their relationship or for considerations of public opinion? Grace felt torn. Reconsidering, she decided to allow Caroline to stay with close family friends in Paris, Roger and Michelline Crovetto.

Almost from the moment Caroline landed in Paris, the paparazzi and the ever-increasing army of tabloid journalists began camping by the Crovettos' front door. When Caroline left the house for the simplest errand, to go to school or a lesson or a doctor's appointment, they followed her. They chased the car in which she was driving, overtook her, and shouted questions at her until she reached her destination. Every time the teenager alit from an automobile, she was surrounded by a swarm of reporters and blinded by flashbulbs. Caroline hated it. Perhaps there was a part of her that, as a budding young woman, was fascinated by all the sudden attention. But in one as independent as Caroline, that fascination soon faded, giving way to annoyance and distress.

Caroline-watching had started—the moment Grace and Rainier had dreaded, the moment when the first of their children would discover that the world intended to peek into and eavesdrop on every private moment of her life. Within weeks it became clear to Grace by the number of photos and stories circulated throughout the Continent, Great Britain and the States that this rabid attention being focused on her elder daughter was not going to abate.

Grace decided that she could not leave Caroline alone in Paris to face this new onslaught of the media. Reverting to her original plan, she packed her belongings and Stephanie's, and took Caroline with them to their own Paris home. The family planned to reunite each weekend, with either Grace and the girls going south to Monaco or Albert and Rainier flying north. Sometimes things did work out that way; often, though, they did not.

It was not long before Grace wrote me a letter describing life at Avenue Foch "like a retreat within a fortress." Grace's arrival did not diffuse the media's interest in her daughter, but added to it. Despite that, I am not sure that Grace's move to Paris was not in her own best interests at the time. She was beginning, I think, to feel trapped by her life as Princess of Monaco, beginning to realize that too many years had passed since she'd done anything but service the needs of others. Rainier's schedule had become ever more taxing, exacerbating his own quick temper. Grace had suffered silently over the years on the occasions when he barked at her without reason. She had counted on Rainier's anger subsiding as he aged. But that had not been the case. Instead, under the pressures of the enormous tasks he had undertaken, he grew moodier than ever.

During this period of the middle 1970s, they began to discover what most other parents in the Western world were also having to learn to live with—there was simply never enough time. Instead of families having some daily leisure hours in which to live out the comfortable home-life fantasies of the Fifties, everyone—including children—seemed to be constantly under the gun. None of us seemed to be able to stop the ball from rolling, nor even to share our feelings that it should be stopped. In this era of easy communication, we found it harder and harder to talk intimately with one another, harder and harder to even accommodate our own growth.

Grace was also beginning to tire more easily. Her move to Paris with the girls made her travel schedule heavier instead of lighter. Her colds became more frequent and lasted longer. She grew tired, but was unwilling to complain. But in photos printed of her during that era, you could begin to detect fatigue and disappointment. When the press saw it, they jumped on it.

For all the upheaval of the era that preceded it, the mid-Seventies were a time of tackiness and disillusion in which people dressed up like peacocks and shouted "me first" while they obeyed the disco singers' instructions to "get down" (whatever *that* meant). Instead, to "get up," too many young people turned to poppers or cocaine. Throngs of their elders, opposed to drugs, found a quick fix on the pages of the tabloids. There they could read about people in high places, disregarding the truth that what was written about them had virtually no basis in fact. Discovering that the marketplace had an insatiable craving for news of them, the tabloids simply began inventing stories about Grace and her family with the unbridled zest of dealers manufacturing synthetic drugs.

It was bad enough that these tactics and worse were being used on Grace and Rainier. But for parents determined to protect their children from the abnormalities that their position might impose on them, to see them used on Caroline was intolerable. Even little Stephanie's life was being affected. It frightened her to drive away from her own apartment to attend gymnastics class with so many reporters and photographers swerving in and out of the path of the car carrying her. For a period of more than three years, Grace watched her adolescent daughter being loaded into the trunk of the family car in order to get to gym class without being followed.

Restless, impulsive and tomboyish, Stephanie represented the only spirit in the family who had not yet been shackled by the concerns that burdened her elders. Perhaps, to her parents, she represented the child in each of them who had prematurely been crammed into their limiting, adult, public selves. That may be why Grace and Rainier exempted her from the intense molding and shaping that had befallen her sister and brother. For whatever reason, Stephanie was permitted to get away with almost any behavior.

Somehow, even with all the external turmoil and the bunker mentality that was developing within her household, Caroline passed her *bac* with a merit designation and enrolled in her father's alma mater, the Écoles des Sciences Politiques, called Sciences Po. She would have preferred attending the university in Provence, which was closer to home, but her mother was fearful that dorm life might expose Caroline to drugs and other dangers of modern collegians, and refused to allow that risk.

Watching Grace grow ever more anxious in the turmoil of the times, I sensed that she was imposing on herself and her family a burden that would further complicate their existence. In my view, during this period, she became, as the old French saying approximately goes, *plus royaliste que les royals.* It was not snobbery that drove her to this course of action, for Grace had not a snobbish bone in her body. It was fear. Fear that she would not be able to protect her children. Fear that their behavior would rekindle accusations that she was not a true princess, but simply an American movie star who couldn't manage her kids. Grace had created her own monument and had controlled its creation up to this point. But her own legend began to control her just when she should have begun chipping away at its constrictions.

My oldest daughter, Amy, was nearing the end of her college education at Sarah Lawrence. During her second year there she had taken a pre-med major. When I told little Nina of that major saying, "Amy thinks she might want to be a doctor when she graduates," Nina had corrected me, "No, you mean a nurse." I insisted that doctor was what I had meant, and we went back and forth with this until I realized the problem. Even in our so-called liberated household, as my youngest daughter had never known a woman doctor, the sole medical goal she could envision for her older sister was limited to nursing.

Amy reverted to her career interest in singing and songwriting. Vicki, meanwhile, was ensconced among the corn, the cattle and her books at Grinnell College in Iowa, where she majored in anthropology and minored in communications. Away at college, my two older girls made friends easily, fell in love, maintained excellent grades, and escaped some of the chaos that had begun to envelop us as our family life thickened at home. Our sons' mother was divorcing her second husband and was living with the man who would become her third. The two older boys, Robert and James, had started to get into some trouble during this difficult emotional upheaval. James had run away from his mother's home on several occasions, and even ran away from boarding school at the end of his stay there, winding up with a set of one-week foster parents in an upstate New York village. On his final runaway of the season, back in Los Angeles, we convinced him that coming to live with us was better than trying to be out on his own.

During the first part of his stay with us, James was driven to school each morning, but would soon depart the campus to sell marijuana on the local street corners. Don and I were beside ourselves, suspecting this activity but being unable to prove it. And James's permanent arrival in our home made the disciplining of Nina, two years his junior, a series of mixed messages. She was still expected to do things pretty much by the book. So far off his center, James needed rewards for the tiniest vestiges of progress. A double standard was developing that had nothing to do with age or behavior. As parents we were caught between the differing needs and developmental progress of two of our children.

One night when I was in Sacramento to attend a State Athletic Commission meeting and dinner, I received a message in my hotel box asking me to call the Governor's Office if I got in before midnight. Al Lowenstein answered my call and suggested I come right over to meet with him and Jerry Brown. On my way to the Governor's Office I figured out that, despite earlier printed denials, Jerry was going to run for President of the United States.

It was already spring, and as he was only just announcing, Jerry, Al and I agreed that there were a million things to be done. Unfortunately, I explained, I was swamped with work in my own business and had an eight-day trip east I wouldn't give up when the whole family was convening there for Amy's Sarah Lawrence graduation. I did, however, offer to make calls in New York while I was there in May if that would be helpful. It sounded casual enough when Al and Jerry said they might take me up on that offer when the time came.

By the time Amy had presented the senior class concert (which consisted solely of her performing her original songs with a band of fellow students) and tossed her tricorne into the air, I had become East Coast manager of the Brown for President campaign. Within twenty-four hours we opened a campaign office on Sixth Avenue in the Fifties, held a meeting in my hotel suite for all the earnest folks who had left messages saying they wished to serve, and began to create a New York schedule of delegate, media and fund-raising events. I had no idea how long this campaign would last or when I might extricate myself from it. Before too much time had passed, though, I began flying back and forth across the country for one-day meetings preparatory to the June primary on the Coast, the delegation meeting, and the convention planning required for the following month.

Somewhere between red-eye flights, I spoke with my family. I had been asked to serve as a Brown delegate and to be a floor leader for the California delegation at the convention. It would mean my staying in New York for five or six weeks, coming home only for one-day turnaround trips during the entire period. I told Don and the kids I would love to have this experience, but would not undertake it without their approval. Everyone urged me to "go for it." I did, little realizing that for the next two years, every time something went wrong in the family someone would date it back to "that time you were in politics."

Jerry Brown astonished the country, winning some primaries and placing respectably in others he entered at the last minute. Al Lowenstein and I were joined at the hip, working closely with Al's friend and political supporter, attorney Harvey Lippman, to raise the delegate count. Once a crew of Californians arrived to augment our New York office effort, tempers and frictions began to mount. There are always a group of people who use a campaign to position themselves high on the candidate's approval list, and in that process they think they gain strength by posturing arrogantly and belittling others. Though I had moved to the Dorset Hotel to be closer to the office, in the few wee morning hours when I returned to my room, I kept wondering what I was doing in all this frenzy. Campaigns, though, are like hurtling trains. Nobody thinks of how to get off, they only pray for deliverance at the end of the line.

During my stay in New York I heard that Grace, Rainier and their children were in New York for the Bicentennial celebration and the Tall Ships Sail. I immediately dialed the Regency Hotel. It was their last night in town, Grace said when she came on the phone. She urged me to attend a cocktail party a few hours later, when they would bid New York farewell.

The red and white Monégasque flag flew from the Loew's Regency flagpoles, alongside the red, white and blue. Security officers were positioned outside the hotel and throughout its lobby. One stood beside an attendant at the door to the reception room and cleared my name on the guest list before I was permitted entry to the party.

One of the first people I saw was Rita, who had brought her son Mike with her. I had not laid eyes on him since he was a baby and was astonished to find him so grown. Still a product of my era, I was even more surprised to see Mike without a tie and with brown, hippie-style sandals at such a formal occasion.

Rita told me she had finally found the strength to walk away from her married man, and was expanding her professional horizons by exploring ways in which she might become whole unto herself. She had developed the concept for a documentary on women to be filmed in Israel and, after finding funding for it there, was beginning to travel back and forth between New York, a California apartment she rented on her own and the Near East.

Within moments I turned to see Sally and John Richardson, whom I'd not seen since I'd moved to Los Angeles nineteen years before. They were very much as I'd remembered them—Sally her usual pleasant and composed self, John a little dour. When I could do so without interrupting them, I approached Grace and Rainier. It was obvious we'd have little chance to talk because of the crush of people. "Where are your children?" I asked Grace, who pointed toward a bar in the back corner.

Making my way through the throng, I thought about all the press coverage Caroline had received in the two years since I'd last seen her. If my own girls went nightclubbing in a low-cut dress, nobody made a fuss. Yet when Caroline wore one, she was accused of baring her breasts in public and being a tramp. Every boy she sat next to, drove with, or danced with had been rumored to be her latest lover. I wondered if she really did go to Parisian clubs more than other girls, or if it was just that each time she went, her photograph was wired to newspapers and magazines all over the world.

I saw before me an externally sophisticated young woman, no longer a child. I did not realize I was also looking at a girl whose few friends at college were foreigners, since her French peers looked upon her as epitomizing the very privileges, politics and prosperity that their revolution so condemned. Thinking this young woman might not remember me, I began to introduce myself when she bent over warmly to kiss me on both cheeks. Then she turned to a somewhat older man on her right and said, "Philippe, I'd like you to meet an old friend of mother's, Judy Quine. Judy, this is Philippe Junot." I'd not yet heard about their blossoming romance. But the moment was significant nonetheless. Junot was enough older than Caroline to conjure up for me a whole set of men who were likely surrounding her in those days. It struck me that he looked much like a certain type of man Grace had been attracted to in her single years—smooth, suave and just a touch too slick.

Within moments Stephanie turned from a group she'd been talking with to join our conversation. I got a fast impression of a restless tomboy, all dressed up in a pretty dress, with so much energy to burn that neither the dress nor perhaps even the body could contain it. While she rambled on amusingly, darting from one topic to another, she leaned over to lift her sister's cigarette from the ashtray, taking from it a long, deep drag. I half expected her to cough, and when she didn't, realized that she probably smoked whenever she could. I wondered whether her father (who did smoke) and her mother (who did not) knew about this, and if so, what they thought about it.

In fact, standing there with Grace's oldest and youngest children, I saw the schism in Grace, though I did not come to realize it until some time afterwards. For the restriction she placed on her one daughter was the measure of permissiveness she allowed the other.

Perhaps it was because they were our last babies, or because we shared the nagging guilt of every mother with an increasingly busy work schedule, but Grace and I were both raising our younger daughters differently than we had our older children. When they were together, Grace took Steph everywhere with her, just as I did with Nina. But when we were away, both Steph and Nina came home after school or outside classes to a house with help but no mother. Disregarding certain psychiatric warnings that children's sexual fantasies about their parents could be unduly aroused, both Grace and Rainier as well as Don and I allowed our youngest children to cozy up for the night in our beds far beyond the age when most kids were allowed to do that.

Perhaps we had grown tired of the cop role we had played out with our older children. Though we all intended our continuing permissiveness to impart understanding and unconditional love, I'm not at all sure any of us served these children well in the process. By creating the appearance of a reality that was not, in fact, available in the real world, we provided our most highly energized daughters with no boundaries for their complex energies. We made ourselves our youngest daughter's best friend in ways with which other, contemporary friends could not compete. And we unintentionally fostered the sibling schisms that arise when one set of kids sees others getting away with what they never could.

There were aspects of Grace's own conflict in that period that distanced her from certain of her old friends. She seemed caught between her enormous concern for appearances, on the one hand, and a suspicion, on the other, that a life led for appearance's sake was a betrayal of her own innermost convictions. At the root, I felt her experiencing a kind of self-doubt which I had seen none of for years.

One day, on a call from Monaco, Grace told me of a recent problem with an old chum. She had been in New York, attending yet another gala benefit at which she was being honored, and her friend was attending the same party. One or more of Grace's tablemates had pointed out that, during the evening, the woman seemed to appear at Grace's side whenever photographers were shooting or approaching, suggesting that Grace was being used. She had stewed about the incident, and returning home had written a strong letter, containing the accusation—the sort of letter that marks a clear interruption to a lifetime of easy camaraderie. But a few months had passed, and in that time Grace had had second thoughts. Perhaps, she reflected, those who had stoked the fire had acted out of jealousy, hoping to create the very wedge which had been formed. Even if their implications were accurate, Grace conjectured, was it such a big deal? She not only didn't mind sharing her limelight with others, usually she encouraged it.

Perhaps without completely understanding it all, Grace soon began sending her estranged friend warm postcards and notes from her world-wide travels. Both women were sufficiently generous to allow the schism to heal and to resume their former relationship, but the incident and the timing of it both seemed significant to me.

Not since Gant's banishment at the start of her marriage had I known Grace to actively create a rift in an old and valued friendship. Why now, at this stage of her life, was she prompted to do it once again? I recognized the possibility that Grace's lifelong inability to confront and her over-whelming desire to make and keep peace at all costs might no longer be serving her well. That part I thought beneficial. But I did hope she would come to pick her shots where they were more meaningful for her. When you've said yes and held your anger in for nearly fifty years, learning to say no and to deal straightforwardly with people who displease is not an easy thing to do.

Throughout the years since she'd married, Grace and Jay Kanter had remained close friends. Though the flood of scripts sent to Grace through Jay had diminished over the years, slowing to a trickle, it had never stopped entirely. If the project or its principals were interesting, Jay invariably forwarded the screenplay to Grace and phoned to discuss it with her. Over time, her refusals had become nearly automatic—until the mid-Seventies, that is, nearly fourteen years after Grace had relinquished her role in *Marnie* in what seemed to all to be a permanent abandonment of her acting career.

Jay and Alan Ladd, Jr., his former London producing partner, had both returned to the United States and were running the studio and production for Twentieth Century Fox, where they were preparing *Star Wars* and other mega-hits. Among the projects they were readying for production was a screenplay called *The Turning Point*, written by Arthur

Laurents, author of such fine works as *Time of the Cuckoo* and *West Side Story.* The plot centered on two mature women who had shared a close but competitive friendship when both were youthful ballerinas in a noted company, and conflicts between them which erupted when a series of events brought them together again in middle age. Herbert Ross, the choreographer-turned-director who was married to prima ballerina Nora Kaye, was set to direct the film. It dawned upon those casting *The Turning Point* that it might be material which could lure Grace back to the screen. Herb Ross asked Jay to send Grace the script and discuss the project with her.

It was the first time since 1962 that Grace did not say an automatic no. When she and Jay spoke, she told him she thought the screenplay was beautiful, forceful, moving and intelligent. "I won't say no today," she fudged. "Let me read it again." Then she added, "I'll talk to Rainier about it." Without asking her if she had, when she called again some time later, Jay knew that the rejection Grace gave him was uttered most reluctantly.

Perhaps it was that very reluctance which caused Jay to suggest, some months later when Fox was anxious to appoint its first woman director to its previously all-male board, that Grace be approached to serve. Dennis Stanfill, who was then Chairman of Fox, thought it a sensational idea, but Jay said he'd need to know it was approved by the entire board before he even so much as mentioned it to Grace. Her interest, if followed by a rejection, would have been both embarrassing and inappropriate. Of course, the board voted unanimously to issue the invitation. "Well," Jay started when he heard Grace's voice at the other end of his call, "we couldn't get you to make a picture for the studio, but how would you like to be on our board of directors?" It was clear she was provoked by the idea and was pleased to have been asked. She and Jay talked for quite a time, and again Grace signed off by saying she'd need to discuss it with Rainier.

While she did, word leaked out in Hollywood that Princess Grace might be joining the Fox board. Jules Stein, then still active in the MCA/Universal empire he'd founded and still friendly with Grace, called Rupert Allan. "I've just heard that Grace is going to go on Fox's board," Jules protested. "You can't let this happen! If she's going to become a director of an American film corporation, it's Universal's board she should serve on." Rupert promised to check with Grace to see what was happening. When he called Jules back, he relayed the information that Grace was pleased to know Jules and Universal wanted her, but that as Jay had called first and she had already told him yes, there was no way she'd go back on her word.

In 1976, Grace flew to Chicago to attend her first meeting. My hometown went crazy when Grace arrived. Dense cadres of police and other security forces lined the streets and accompanied her everywhere through the large crowds that had gathered around the city to catch a glimpse of her. Even for the sophisticated corporate magnates who comprised Fox's board, Grace's appearance was the social event of the era.

Serving as a director for Twentieth Century Fox brought Grace directly back in touch with the industry in which she had garnered all her original fame and respect. And it brought her back as a professional. For all her dedication to being a wife, a mother and a princess, Grace was also—to her very core—a true working woman. At Fox, she had a job—albeit not full-time—where she functioned as the equal of men, men of high accomplishment, corporate leaders who were the same kind of American men on the move she had known since childhood. The experience validated for her the maturity she had acquired over the years and the opportunities that existed because of it. I am unsure whether she recognized this at the start.

Writing to Bettina, Grace mentioned that she'd been traveling to the States more often now for board meetings. She matter-of-factly presumed this would offer them the opportunity to see each other after twenty years of separation. But Bettina, continuing to experience the failure of her marriage as a total failure of self, was still in hiding. The notion of joining Grace somewhere with a group of business tycoons and movie personages in attendance was, she felt, completely out of her league and could make her feel only more inadequate, more defensive and, thus, more abrasive.

Lizzie Gray seemed to have reached her own turning point in Nepal, where she'd hitchhiked from London in the company of an ex-marine who taught her how to trade on the black market, how to set up a tent and sleep with a knife, and how to learn to trust the very instincts for survival that polite society had drummed out of her. After two years of living with anthropologists and Shiite Muslims, mountain climbing expeditions and a near-fatal bout with amebic dysentery, Lizzie had come home to Massachusetts. Working as a secretary in the office at Harvard's Graduate School of Education, she settled down to study psychology and to housekeep with Thomas Hovey, a bond trader she'd met through her father, who was ten years her senior and the divorced father of two children.

The three Reybold girls, Jyl, Robin and Nyna, were trying to make the best of an increasingly more difficult family situation. The oldest, Jyl, had moved into New York City, where she was working as a modeling agent.

Sherman Fairchild had died, and Jyl missed her family's old and trusted neighbor. In a fatherly way, Sherman had taken time to invite her to sit in his office at the Lloyd Neck estate, where he had encouraged the developing Jyl to use her mind for independent achievement.

For a young girl, Jyl had assumed enormous responsibilities. She brought her sister Nyna from the unhappy and troubled house in the country to live with her in her Thirty-third Street studio apartment in Manhattan, and enrolled her in the Rhodes School. Money was in short supply then, so it was always touch-and-go as to whether Malcolm would or would not be able to meet the next tuition payment.

In the middle Seventies, on a business trip to New York, we accepted an invitation for drinks at the home of Diahn and Tom McGrath on Long Island. Driving up the driveway and parking at East Fair, which had formerly been Sherman Fairchild's home, I realized how close we were to the Reybolds' house. Once inside, I inquired whether our hosts knew them. They did, and had in fact called Malcolm to see if they would join us. Malcolm had told them, though, that it would not be possible. Carolyn had become increasingly more reclusive, venturing from her home principally to visit her mother and her spiritual advisers, both of whom were in Ohio.

Driving away from East Fair that night, I thought about Carolyn and about the years that were rolling by. I'd been part of many different groups in my lifetime, and no matter how often I tended to forget that one of them was called "the bridesmaids," someone or some publication would always be there to remind me. In the back of my mind as I grew older, I think I'd always presumed we would all be united with Grace once again, perhaps to review the twenty years of living we'd done since the wedding in Monaco, perhaps even when we were a bit older and could all sit around telling stories and comparing photos of our grandchildren. Like Grace, I tended not to lose people in my life, even if I was separated from them for long periods of time. Now I began to doubt whether I would ever see Carolyn again. I had already presumed that would be the case with Bettina. As not even Grace had laid eyes on either of them for nearly two decades and since it had been she who was their friend, not I, it seemed silly for me to be so sentimental about these women with whom I'd shared only one momentous occasion so long ago.

Though I'd seen Sally briefly at the Bicentennial cocktail reception at the Regency, I knew only from Grace what she was doing with her time. As Director of Volunteer Services of Beekman Downtown Hospital, Sally had risen admirably to her challenge. She brought volunteer assistants into the hospital's undermanned clerical department, assigned them to run specimens to and from the lab, and initiated a patient escort service. Work in the emergency room required some training, so Sally devised a program to bring in students to the hospital from both the New York University and Columbia University medical schools.

Since she'd married, Sally's adult life had seemed placid, self-contained and sedentary—very far afield from her early days as a world traveler and a pavement-pounding actress. But the yen for the theatre and the love of it had never completely left her. Throughout the years Sally had always been a faithful New York theatregoer, reading plays, analyzing them and—with the mark of a true actress—deciding how she would have played the parts differently. As her hospital work became more settled, Sally, then in her mid-forties, decided to join the New York Farce Company, a group that used several different Off-Off-Broadway theatres to house their productions. Delighted with her new hobby, Sally was pleased when Grace came to see her perform in *The Suicide,* an adaptation of a Russian farce that would later be presented by The Circle in the Square with a professional cast. After the performance, Sally and Grace chatted as they would have while at the Barbizon about the play, its production, direction and performances. But neither of them ever mentioned the possibility of going back to work again as a professional actress.

What Grace had begun to find by that time were more outlets for the artist in her soul. For years, while her children were growing up and she was building her monument as Princess of Monaco, she had kept her hand in the arts by providing the dynamism, drive, funding, coordination and direction for new or existing cultural endeavors with which she had indelibly stamped the Principality. But Grace was more than a patron of the arts—she was an artist. And artists don't make art possible, they make art. Not unlike Sally, Grace began to find this aspect of her personality rising to the fore. Without any particular notice, she began her own hobby. Collecting specimens of every kind of flower that she loved, she started to press and dry them so she could use them in collages she created. Rainier and the children used to tease her about the fact that in Paris, at Roc Agel and at the Palace every novel and telephone book they opened always spilled forth layer upon layer of her dried flowers. But they also thought her work was beautiful and let her know that as well. So did others, believing as her own family did that this was merely a charming and entirely appropriate hobby for a middle-aged princess.

CHAPTER 16

Growing Up Again

By the late Seventies, every one of us had either passed our fiftieth birthday or could, at least, see it edging up in the near future. On the one hand, we had accepted by then that life often consists of a series of crises. We prayed only that the ones we or our families had to experience would be less tragic than those we knew others had suffered. Some of our prayers were answered, some were not.

Whether or not we had taken on commitments and responsibilities outside our families' lives, there was a new clock that began to tick in each of us, a clock counting time in a way we had never before stopped to consider. Our time. Our own time. Time to do whatever it was we thought we should do with the rest of our remaining lives. Previously, it had been easy to entertain flights of fancy about things we might want to do later. When we were younger, "later" meant sometime in the future, five years from now, ten years from now, when the kids were grown, when our husbands grew more relaxed. Later. At fifty, or nearing it, five- and ten-year increments in the future did not stretch out before us as welcomingly as they had in the past.

The new recognition of time brought with it an inevitable need to look back at the patterns of our middle age, to reflect on how we could extricate ourselves from those patterns, distract ourselves from them, or see possibilities for unknown and as yet unexplored futures. Grace and I were the only two among the seven of us who had children in their mid-teens still at home. Yet underneath the busy schedules and the appearance that our individual courses were fixed and inviolable, even we could tell that something new was coming. There was no idle irony when we asked each other again at this age the same joking question we had asked when we were younger and thought we had it all down pat, "Who are we going to be when we grow up?" One arc of our lives was beginning to meet itself coming round at the other end. How we'd begin to draw a new circle was unclear, but what none of us could stop was the closing of one and the opening of the other.

For Rita, who had already started her new circle by developing documentaries, the new era reinforced comforting notions that had only just begun to dawn on her. It was all right to be without Mr. Right. There were things a woman might do with her own time that validated her more gratifyingly than a painful relationship could. If good acting roles were hard to come by, there were other ways in which to exercise her creativity, ways that empowered her more than waiting at the end of a telephone line for a call to work on someone else's project. Starting from scratch, using her own intelligence and talent, Rita discovered she could create jobs for herself, jobs that others responded to favorably.

At one point during the five years Bettina had spent in hiding from her failed marriage, she had read a Japanese haiku that expressed her feelings entirely. It approximately noted, "My boat is stuck in the reeds by the banks of the river, and I will wait patiently until the current starts me off again." When the currents came, they whisked Bettina off to all those parts of the world she had missed seeing during her itinerant childhood. She joined a number of tour groups advertising "third world countries" or "adventure travel." At home, when Bettina wasn't traveling, she was studying—reading Homer and the Greek playwrights, Nabokov, Mary McCarthy and mystic literature (like that which had always fascinated her daughter Lizzie) in continuing education courses. Once Bettina stopped looking inward at the quagmire that had bogged her down, she found the world around her waiting for her to come to it for pleasure, enlightenment and adventure. Though she was leery of dating, a kinship

commented in a critical tone when asked about her friend, "Well, Maree doesn't know what she wants!" as though criticizing her decision to separate from Bud. Though she never said anything directly to Grace, Maree wasn't sure at that point in her life that Grace was certain of what she wanted either.

At the start, Grace hoped that what was happening to Carolyn Reybold might free her to find a new path and direction. Carolyn wrote that she and Malcolm had been divorced. Grace wrote back sounding not a note of criticism for either party, knowing that however flawed Malcolm might seem to the rest of us, Carolyn had chosen to stay with him for all those years. Grace hoped, she said, that the divorce would prove best for all in the long run.

While her parents' divorce was in process, Jyl Reybold got a letter from her godmother in Monaco asking her to be present at a dinner party in New York. Jyl wrote back accepting immediately and began to assemble her best outfit for the occasion. She idolized Grace though she had not seen her since childhood. Arriving at Vera Maxwell's party, Jyl's first observation was that six of her tiny Thirty-third Street apartments could fit nicely into this one. Grace had never forgotten her own shyness as a young person in a roomful of accomplished and famous adult strangers. Noticing Jyl's anxiety, Grace immediately put her at ease by greeting her warmly and linking arms to keep her goddaughter close by her side.

Sally Parrish Richardson was at the dinner as well. Both she and Grace noticed not only Jyl's shyness but her unmistakable long-legged beauty. Jyl realized that Grace did not "work the room" as so many celebrated figures were wont to do. Instead, she remained in one spot, graciously receiving those who approached her. When someone appeared with a small camera and suggested memento snapshots, Grace put her arm around Jyl to include her in the photo, but just before it was taken she called a halt. "We've got to brush your hair!" Grace admonished in mock anger. The warmth of the moment melted Jyl's heart. She loved being cared about by Grace.

When Carolyn and Malcolm divorced, the only money to divide between them came from the sale of their 1950s suburban house. As Carolyn recalls what happened, she turned her money over to a broker at the same Manhattan investment firm that Malcolm used. After a few months the broker asked Carolyn to okay an investment plan that would place all her money in options. "Are they safe?" asked Carolyn. She knew nothing about the stock market. "This is all the money I have and I can't afford to do anything risky with it." With the broker's assurance that she couldn't lose anything, Carolyn consented to the transfer. Within months her account was wiped out. It is hard for me to know if this is what really happened to the money Carolyn had. Certain members of her family have told me that they thought she'd given most of it away to Kathryn Kuhlman and other Christian broadcasters.

Though Carolyn was pleased to be back in the city where she had enjoyed her youth, she began to worry about the germs she presumed were prevalent in Manhattan. When Jyl came to visit, and later moved in with her mother, she was cautioned to wash her hands before touching anything in the apartment after having been outside. Loving her mother as she did, Jyl chose not to argue. For a short time, their being together in the little walk-up seemed a respite for both women. Carolyn's youngest daughter, Nyna, had married her childhood sweetheart while both were still teenagers. They were living in nearby Queens. Robin, the middle Reybold girl, had stopped working for Vietnam veterans' causes and had moved to Philadelphia, where she was using her lovely folk-rock voice in an attempt to break into the music scene.

It was more peaceful and serene a time than the Reybold women had known for years, but Fate stepped in with the kind of horror that haunts every mother's dreams. Very early one morning in January 1979, Jyl and Carolyn woke suddenly to a hard, insistent knocking at their door. Stumbling out of bed to answer it, they found Malcolm, oddly dressed in a black business suit, a shirt and a somber tie. He had gotten a call, he said, a call from Philadelphia. The night before, after Robin finished rehearsing with a local band she'd joined, she'd gone out with a boy she'd been seeing a good deal of in recent weeks. The fellow had lost control of his car, which had hurtled off a railroad bridge, killing Robin instantly. Benumbed, the whole Reybold family drove to Philadelphia to arrange the funeral.

When she returned to New York, Carolyn found a letter from Grace waiting for her, a letter full of love, support and disbelief. In California, I got a call from Grace. "Doesn't each of us live in terror about the thought of such a thing happening to one of our children?" Grace asked. "How could this happen to Carolyn, the most fearful of us all?" she demanded, as though someone could give her an explanation. It was surely not I. And though Carolyn wrote to Grace to thank her for her sweet expressions and condolences, in her heart of hearts she knew it was not only Robin but Grace, too, whom she would never see again.

Knowing Grace, one could be sure that she would thank the Lord that she had been spared the kind of tragedy that had befallen her friend. By comparison, her own life seemed idyllic. Yet there was no denying that many of the inner questions about herself she had suppressed for so long began to color her vision of her present and her future.

It was just at this juncture that Grace became involved with Gwen Robyns, a British writer and biographer, and with Gwen's friend, John Carroll, who was organizing a poetry reading for the American Bicentennial celebration at the Edinburgh Arts Festival. Gwen had seen Grace read poetry on a Sunday religious broadcast, was impressed with her performance, and suggested to John that he invite the Princess to participate in the event planned for Scotland. John was as surprised as he was delighted when she agreed to join him. From that beginning, the possibilities of such appearances broadened. Grace accepted an invitation from the International Poetry Forum to do a 1978 reading in Pittsburgh. Her old friend and former secretary, Phyllis Blum Earl, was running an apartment referral service in London, but as she had a capable partner, was able to accept Grace's suggestion that the two women travel together for the trips that were starting to be penciled in on Grace's already crowded schedule.

They flew first to California for a Fox board meeting, then on to Pittsburgh. Without realizing yet that she was actually touring, Grace began to accept invitations to read poetry in Minneapolis, Washington, Princeton and Boston, often trying to time those dates with her Fox meeting schedule. All of these engagements were for charities; proceeds of the ticket sales went to support one worthy cause or another. The subject of Grace doing anything "commercial" was still a sore one in Europe, especially in Monaco.

Though she began to think about herself for the first time in years, Grace still felt compelled to say yes to anyone asking for a favor. Some of those favors were fun for her or dovetailed into her own interests for herself or her country. Bill Allyn, her old friend from the theatre, had become a producer. When Bill proposed a three-hour NBC-TV special on Monaco with Grace as tour guide, she jumped at the project. Of course she made sure that every aspect she needed to approve was within her purview, but she also knew that Bill was a tasteful and loyal friend, and that she could trust him to do the right thing. When she called me to ask if I would agree to be interviewed for "Once Upon a Time Is Now," I said yes. And when my friend Lee Grant was set as host and narrator for the show, it made the interview painless.

On the first day of filming at the Palace, though, Bill Allyn and his wife Sandy got to see both Grace Kelly and Princess Grace, each in their natural habitat. Grace had been slightly overwhelmed by being back in front of a 35mm camera. After the day's shooting in the main room of her Palace apartment, everyone, including the crew, had only a half hour to scatter, don black tie, and get to the Sporting Club. The show was to open with a shot of Grace and Rainier dancing together, and as Rainier dislikes dancing formally, he had been cajoled into having it filmed at that night's gala by camera operators who were to lie on the floor for their angles.

Before they scurried away to dress, Bill and Sandy stayed behind at the Palace to thank Grace for a wonderful first day. Her servants and aides were nearby as Grace, her hair in curlers, turned to the Allyns with tears already streaming down her cheeks. "I've let you down," she moaned apologetically. "I was terrible, just awful, my voice . . ." And again the tears fell. The three stood hugging one another while Bill assured Grace she'd been fine, that it was only an interview, and that if they didn't like what they saw in rushes it could be shot again. Racing to their hotel to change, Sandy and Bill were shaken that Grace had exposed such deep and painful insecurity to them. They were still trembling when Grace approached them in a receiving line at the Gala, wearing a greenish caftan-styled gown and carrying a silver purse given to her by Maria Callas. Though the Allyns were wrecks inside, Grace, when she got to them in the line, was as cool and collected as though she'd met them only once before on some formal occasion. There was not a trace of the woman who had been in their arms crying thirty minutes earlier. The moment said everything about the paradox of Grace.

But other favors she felt she could not refuse taxed Grace. On a poetry reading trip taking her from Washington to New England with a Fox board meeting in between, her brother Kell asked her to stop in Philadelphia to help him dedicate a scull. In terrible weather after no time to sleep,

Grace drove north to her hometown just in time to pose for pictures to help her brother, whom she had helped on many previous occasions like this one. Rainier tried hard to impress upon her that she did not always have to say yes, but Grace was a girl who could not say no. She had never been able to outgrow the childhood belief that it was easier not to disappoint anyone. For all her personal bravery as an adult, that area of cowardice would be present forever.

In the late 1970s, other friends began to see cracks in Grace's resolve. When John Foreman traveled to London to shoot his production of *The Great Train Robbery,* she called him there to urge him to be in the audience for a poetry reading she was giving at St. James's Palace. The huge cost of the tickets was all pledged to a worthy cause, but John's impression was that Grace was classier than the room. The Queen Mother had drab, flat curls pressed on the back of her head and an equally drab ball gown. After the reading, supper was served on round tables for all the guests. There was wine already in the glasses when the ticket buyers took their seats. No more was poured during dinner.

When John returned to his rooms at the Connaught that night, he found a message to call Grace immediately regardless of the hour. She was beside herself waiting for John's review! John sensed this was as important to her as her role in *The Country Girl,* and that she needed him to analyze the work as carefully as he had in the old days. Ah, Gracie, he thought, you've always known you belong "above the title," known you have to be good or better. For years, Grace had contented herself with princess reviews. Other sovereigns, sovereign advisers and sovereign watchers had given her those notices. Now, though she tried to downplay it, she was in fact acting again. And she wanted reviews from her peers in that field, the people who had always leveled with her in the past.

Late in 1978, John visited Grace in Paris. Usually on these occasions, they stopped at the Relais in the Hôtel Plaza-Athénée. John could remember several such days, recall exactly the entrance Grace always made into the room. Heads inevitably turned to stare, but Grace carried herself erectly, pretending not to notice the curiosity her presence evoked. John had always reflected that just like every other performance in her life, Grace performed lunch better than anyone else. On one rainy day, though, the kind of day that reminded John of how much he disliked Paris, Grace asked him to share a midday meal with her at her home. It was his first encounter with Stephanie since she'd been a baby, and he looked forward to meeting the fourteen-year-old.

Before he was in her presence for five minutes, John noted that this little girl, the same age as his daughter Mandy, was impossibly ill-tempered. She screamed when he came in, ignored him after the introduction, and quickly dragged Grace out of the room, slamming doors behind her. In amazement, John noted that Grace did nothing to restrain or reprimand her daughter, until finally, when Stephanie sort of spat on John and cuffed him on the back of his head, Grace quite literally sat on her! For a moment, John thought, "My God. This is like having lunch with Patty Duke in *The Miracle Worker*," but as the day wore on he realized that Steph was bright and capable of better. Like every other kid her age, he believed, she was testing her ability to manipulate her mother. Unlike most others, though, she had a mother who could be intimidated, who would not confront her. Perhaps, it dawned upon John as on other friends, Grace had been so exhausted by the controls placed on her own life and those she had felt obligated to place on Caroline's, that Stephanie represented the one remaining glimmer of adventurous free spirit Grace could locate in her immediate sphere.

Only a few months later, when John was shooting in Dublin, Grace and Rainier arrived there to stay at the Shelton Hotel. When the three adults dined together, Caroline's continuing romance with Philippe Junot was rumored to be leading toward marriage. Grace appeared in one of her ubiquitous turbans, and while they ate, John began to feel enormous sympathy for Rainier, who was spitting fire about his daughter's relationship. Throughout dinner Grace seemed to be maintaining a stoic lack of involvement. After coffee, the three decided to go for a walk, but as they were told the mist outside had turned to a soft rain, Grace said she needed to go to her suite for a raincoat. Rainier waited downstairs while John accompanied her. Waiting for Grace near her door while she fetched her coat, John determined he would not ask her anything about her own feelings during this tense period. But just as they were leaving the suite, Grace turned to face John, her eyes filled with tears. "I know," she said softly but with no small amount of desperation coloring her voice, "where I am going to be every single day for the rest of my life."

In spite of the interior struggle Grace waged during those years, her days were not always burdensome. There was a Fox meeting in Aspen,

Colorado, when Rainier and Rupert joined her, and the three of them had a grand old time. Fox had purchased an enormous amount of property in the resort town and wanted to show it off to its directors. The weather was temperate, and while Grace attended her board sessions, Rainier, who loves to shop wherever he finds himself, took off with Rupert to enrich the local boutiques. The threesome tooled around in a four-wheel-drive Jeep to take in the beauty of the countryside.

Though Grace made frequent trips to Los Angeles, my own business travel schedule meant I missed her more often than not. For one such trip, she was accompanied from Monaco by her niece, Tiny's youngest daughter, Christine. Aleco Noghes, who had fathered Tiny's three children and was *persona non grata* in Monaco, had settled in the San Fernando Valley, north of Los Angeles, where he made a career as a tennis pro. Christine, his daughter, was staying with him on the trip she made with Grace, while Grace herself was houseguesting with producer/director Mervyn LeRoy and his wife Kitty on the other side of the Santa Monica mountains.

Rupert gave one of his informal dinners for Grace, inviting eighteen or twenty chums, among them Rock Hudson. By 2:00 A.M., though most of the guests had departed, Grace, Rock and Christine were still chatting away. Frank McCarthy offered to drive Christine to her father's house in the Valley, and Rock volunteered to chauffeur Grace home. When the duo got to the bottom of Benedict Canyon, they both admitted to being ravenously hungry, so instead of heading west for the LeRoys' house, Rock drove east toward Hollywood. Ben Frank's, one of only two round-the-clock area dining spots in those days, is a rather garish modern coffee shop. It was there on the Sunset Strip that Rock and Gracie went to "pig out," ordering breakfast special combination plates that included ham, eggs, hamburger patties and pancakes. For nearly two hours, they ate and told each other old acting stories, roaring with laughter.

Just after four o'clock in the morning, Rock asked for the check. When the waiter brought it, Rock reached into his pocket to discover he'd left his wallet at home! He turned his pockets inside out, but no paper money nor change emerged. Grace was carrying no cash or credit cards, as she'd not presumed she needed them for the dinner at Rupert's. When the manager appeared, Grace told the man she did great dishes and Rock was proficient at other K.P. After asking if they could send someone with money the following day, they finally agreed to accept the manager's offer to consider the repast on the house. When I spoke with Grace from New York the next day, she told me the story, adding, "I've got this great new racket!"

My new racket, the PKA and karate, had begun to swamp me with travel and details. With only a small in-house organization, Don and I were trying to do everything, assisted by several volunteer promoters, officials and fighters around the country who were helping to build our sport. In the summer of 1977, Don told me he had to accompany our world middleweight champion, Bill "Superfoot" Wallace, to Europe. Bill was scheduled to do a week of clinics at an adult sports camp in the Italian Alps, and Don had arranged to meet with several European karate promoters there about activities on the Continent. I called Grace to tell her we would bring Nina and James, the only two children at home with us that summer.

We had a marvelous few days in Venice at the start of our trip. But I couldn't help noticing that Don was drinking more wine and hard liquor than ever before. During recent months in the States, I had felt his fuse growing shorter, his anger erupting more scathingly and rapidly over more insignificant matters. I had attributed that to the pressure of our work, which had us both snowed, and concerns for James and Robert, who were both having difficult adolescences. But as our holiday progressed, for the first time it crossed my mind that Don was drinking too often and too much.

Arriving in Monaco on a perfect morning, we found huge baskets of welcoming flowers from Grace in both our room and the children's. There was also a thick vellum card calligraphied with an invitation to attend a concert being held that evening in the Palace Court of Honor. I phoned Grace immediately to thank her for the flowers and accept the invitation, and when she asked if we could join her beforehand for a drink at her Palace apartments, I accepted that delightedly as well.

Before setting off to the Beach, where we had booked a tent, Nina and I went through my wardrobe, selecting a pair of my dinner pajamas that could be faked into a black-tie outfit for her that night. Don and James had dark suits and resolved to buy two black bow ties before the day ended. When it did and we returned to the Hôtel de Paris to dress, Nina decided her hair had been assaulted by too much sand, sea and sun. To refresh it, she poured a bottle of Johnson's Baby Oil into her tub and

elegantly set tables, Grace spent the entire day in a black one-piece bathing suit covered by an off-white, plain cotton caftan, her feet bared. In mid-afternoon, when she threw off the caftan to go for a dip in the pool, I noticed that she had put on weight, not a large amount, but just enough so she was not her familiar sylphlike self. In the sunlight, as her hair dried, I could see a small section of gray showing on both her temples. With no makeup save for a touch of waterproof mascara and a light lip gloss, her complexion was still flawless. At the Palace two nights earlier, fully made up and wearing a sedate dress of allover pleated ecru silk, she had looked older, more mature. In daylight, even with the extra pounds and her gray-rooted hair falling nearly to her shoulders, she looked almost like a teenager.

We begged Grace to get serious about her crystal ball, and to read to us from *The Art of Scrying*. As she did, it quickly became evident that scrying involved a great deal more advance preparation than either crying or screwing, because the first instruction read by the would-be seeress commanded her to wash her hair, her person and her linens twice a day for twelve days before trying to scry. As Grace read on silently to herself, she suddenly shrieked, "Hold it, everybody. No point in going any further. I've just seen the last instruction and have realized I'd never make it, so I'm abandoning this career before it starts." She read out loud mournfully, "It will be necessary to fast, without either food or drink, for six consecutive hours before images can be perceived from within the crystal." She tossed the booklet on the grass, exclaiming, "Forget it!" and flung herself like a defeated rag doll across the bottom of the chaise.

The following day she and I made arrangements to lunch together at the Beach. While Don and the children rafted in the clear Mediterranean waters, we seated ourselves by the railing at the poolside Terrace restaurant. The first thing I told her was that James had called her a fox. Gracie giggled like a teenager, and flipped her hair back from first one shoulder and then the other the way teenage girls do when they're feeling spiffy. She was wearing a rust and brown striped caftan, and after the waiter took our orders she noted, "I keep thinking I can take off some of this weight if I eat sensibly in the daytime. It's the dinners, though, that put it all right back on—and especially the caviar." When I insisted that she really had not gained so much weight, she responded, "I don't know, Judybird. Sometimes I see myself in the mirror and am startled, wondering who it is I'm looking at. I make great resolutions to fix it all immediately, but then other times I think, 'Why bother?' "

It was then that she told me about Caroline and Philippe Junot. "Just how serious is it?" I inquired.

"Very . . . unfortunately," Grace answered. "It's been going on for a while. She's convinced she's in love and definitely wants to marry him as soon as possible. If I seem anxious these days, it's because she convinced Rainier to allow her to take him on the Galápagos cruise, and I know she's going to be persuading him to okay a marriage after she finishes one more year at college. When it comes to something Caroline wants badly enough, you just know her father will permit it."

"Do you think she's too young to marry," I asked, "or are there other problems?"

"Well, of course, she's too young," Grace replied. "She's only twenty."

"Same age I was when I married Jay," I added, as we both made one of those "see what I mean" gestures.

"Caroline's always been so intellectually curious," Grace continued. "This man she's with really doesn't do anything. Oh, he's 'in investments' or something, but it doesn't sound very real to me. Mainly what he seems to do and Caroline does with him is go to nightclubs and parties. That's all very glamorous for a while, but it isn't the kind of life that could stimulate Caroline in the long run."

"She doesn't sound so different from most young girls her age, either back in our day or now. You protected her for an awfully long time, so it's only natural that being with slightly older people and hanging around glitzy nightclubs represents freedom and sophistication to her."

"I think," Grace corrected, "that she believes she can really make a home and family with him, that he'll change after they're married."

"Famous last words," I added caustically as Grace nodded assent.

"I've been trying to urge her to just go with him for a while longer before deciding about marriage, but she feels the time has come for that kind of decision."

"It's hard enough for young people to be patient even when nobody but themselves is interested in their relationship. But with the kind of spotlight and public conjecture Caroline is subjected to—everyone asking, 'What will she do next?'—it's even more difficult," I reflected.

"What would you do," Grace inquired, "if it were Amy or Vicki and you felt the way I do about the man?"

"We can't make a comparison, Grace," I replied honestly. "Even if I liked the fellow I'd urge a daughter of mine to live with him for a while before jumping into marriage. Live with him long enough to see what it's like when the daily routine of housekeeping blurs the romance of dating and all that."

"Of course Caroline can't do that," Grace sighed resignedly. "Can you just hear the talk that would start if it was known she and Philippe moved in together?"

"I can," I admitted, "and it wouldn't be pretty. But neither is the prospect of your daughter marrying someone you believe will prove to be a disaster. It's easy to say from where I stand, but I think I'd prefer some gossip to a broken marriage if it could be avoided. Otherwise, she's facing the same limited alternatives we did in our day."

"I can't do that," Grace said flatly.

"I know," I concurred, although I was not sure that I meant it.

What Grace dreaded did, indeed, happen on the cruise. Caroline was able to convince her father to allow her to marry Junot. The only concession she made was an agreement to finish out the following year studying philosophy and child psychology at the university. Likely both Grace and Rainier were hoping that before the next summer came, the bloom would be off the bush. The one thing that had never crossed either of their minds was to threaten to cut Caroline off or disown her. Both were firm in their resolve that parents should never close the door to their own children.

After leaving Monaco, Don and I took our children for a long weekend on Capri and then north to Rome. There I got a new job. Carlotta Mellon, who was then Appointments Secretary for Governor Jerry Brown's California State Administration, called me at my Roman hotel to tell me I'd been appointed a commissioner, or member, of the Contractors' State License Board and to tell me the date of my first meeting. Though I said I could not be back in California for that session, I accepted the appointment.

On the home front, it was not long after returning from our summer trip to Europe in 1977 that our son Robert left his mother's to join James at our house on a permanent basis. Like James, Robert had been getting into trouble and had reached an impasse at his other home.

Amy had decided to live in New York after her graduation from college, had worked for a while for a theatrical publicist there, and was busy trying to launch her music career. Vicki was off to finish her Grinnell education with a semester in London. With Nina almost a teenager and doing well at school, I had presumed things at our house would settle into relative calm. But with Rob and James both so troubled by the upheavals of their own early teens, I realized there was some truth to the words of Edna St. Vincent Millay, who had long ago said, "It is not true that life is one damn thing after another—it is the same damn thing over and over." Our kids, however, were the one blessed thing that mattered the most to me.

CHAPTER 17

Mothers-of-the-Brides

By the spring of 1978, I had given up keeping my makeup and hair supplies in two sets, one packed for travel and the other permanently arranged on my bathroom shelves for home use. The local set was utterly superfluous, considering I was always in transit for work on one side of the country or the other.

Our two oldest sons, Rob and James, had left home the previous winter, convinced that they were too old to be under the jurisdiction of parental discipline. They were in their middle teens, the age at which new laws did not permit parents to easily retrieve runaway or recalcitrant children, so Don decided to let them go out and learn what the big world really looked like. After James came home, he got himself into a bout of trouble with the law by stealing a stereo set from a house down the street. The scare of possible confinement in a juvenile facility and the realization that the only meaningful way to ever gain his mother's attention was to make a success of his life were enough to see him enroll in an alternative school program to complete his secondary education. Robert, too, decided his foray into independent living was much too premature, and he came home from a surfing sojourn in Hawaii to reenter high school.

Between trips to New York and Sacramento in late April, I found myself in Los Angeles at a small dinner for Grace, who was in town for a Fox board meeting. The only other guests I remember that evening besides Grace, Don and me were Maree and Princess Caroline, who had flown west with Grace, and Wayne Rogers. Caroline's promised school year had reached its conclusion and her wedding to Philippe Junot was being discussed.

But when I sat with Grace on a sofa a few minutes later while the other guests buzzed around making small talk, she admitted she was still hoping against hope that Caroline would change her mind about marrying Junot. It was an odd night, with Grace, Maree and me all being together. We three dashed off together to the ladies' room on several occasions just as we had done when we were Caroline's age, but now the young Princess's presence attested to the years that had passed since we ourselves were girls.

At the end of May, Don had to fly to Paris to supervise a world title fight we sanctioned there, and I flew to Iowa with Amy, Nina and the entire Kanter family so we could all see Vicki graduate from college. It has always been close to impossible to pick up a check when Jay is at the table, and he was especially unwilling to part with those in Iowa as I was alone, without Don. But it happened that at the same time that Don hosted one of our world champions and two officials for late-night pizza and beer on the outskirts of Paris for $94, I wangled one check at the country club outside Grinnell, paying the same amount for steak luncheons for fourteen!

In early June I flew to New York on business. Two days later, Don called from home to tell me that an invitation to Caroline's wedding had arrived. Together we assessed our schedules and realized there was little possibility of our attending. I called Grace to tell her we were forced to decline, but she was insistent. "Don't say no just yet. The wedding's quite small, and if you really can't be here, of course I understand. See what happens in the next few days. Maybe there's still a chance you can get free." I promised to call again with a final answer, but did tell Grace we'd surely be in Monaco in July, as a French promoter was producing a program of our sanctioned fights. Two days later a change in other PKA event plans enabled me to phone Grace again, this time to say we would be there to see Caroline married.

On June 23, a Friday, I flew up and back from Sacramento after a working day at the Contractors' Board. Two days later, on Sunday, Don flew home from a karate business trip to Florida, and sixteen hours later we were on a 747 heading for the second wedding in Monaco.

Waiting in line before the official gates at the Palace for our invitations to be cleared and our entry permitted to the pre-wedding ball, I kept seeing montages in my mind of the time that had passed since I first came to this enchanted land. A tearful reunion with Maree, and an introduction to her grown daughter, Louise, heightened my sentimental reverie. Once inside, we stood in orderly fashion being processed through the line where the bride and groom and their respective families were receiving. I could not help noticing that Stephanie was missing and asked Grace as soon as the line broke where she was hiding. "Hiding is the right word," Grace exclaimed. "I bought her a wonderful dress, but she said she would only come to the ball if I allowed her to wear pants or jeans." Grace threw her hands up in the air. "I had enough else to think about and do, so I just said if she got dressed correctly she could come and if she didn't, she could stay out."

"Didn't we all think," I asked, "that if we were easygoing and understanding, tolerant and sympathetic, our children would always be adorable and cooperative?"

Making a mock gesture of tearing her hair out and growling at the same time, Grace finally gathered her smile about her again. "This too shall pass," she muttered almost to herself, and moved along to resume playing the perfect hostess to a salon full of titled guests.

Footmen and butlers were setting a miraculous buffet on the groaning tables when the orchestra began to play a dreamy ballad for the first dance of Caroline and her fiancé. As she nestled her head along Philippe's shoulder, I noted that Caroline looked even more beautiful than when I'd last seen her in California a few months earlier. I glanced over to see Grace and Rainier bravely playing parents-of-the-bride, knowing they were less than thrilled with the man who was about to become their son-in-law. Rainier wore a polite smile, but the underlying slightly hardened set of his mouth reminded me how he'd learned to keep a stiff upper lip while being hazed at a British boarding school. Grace, the better actor of the two, wore a faultless beatific look. Her left arm was linked through

Rainier's right one, and I spotted the small woven gold *minaudière* she held in that hand. Her right hand, though, hung loosely at her side. Only her index finger frantically picking away at the cuticle area of her right thumb told me more about what she was feeling than she would have wished to reveal.

It was after four in the morning when we realized we had best leave, return to the hotel, and sleep a bit before an 8 A.M. breakfast meeting we had scheduled with the French karate promoter and his backer. Though the melon I carved on the Terrace restaurant of the Hôtel de Paris the following morning would set someone back $12, the contrast between the two parts of our lives became crystallized at that breakfast. The night before, our supper companions had included the tall and patrician Hubert de Givenchy, the revered Parisian couturier, and Countess Jacqueline de Ribes, of the impossibly long neck and impassably large sleeves. Our karate event producer was a retired officer of the French national police administration with a gold front tooth, his backer a self-made blue jeans merchant emperor from central France.

We had only the few stolen hours of wedding week festivities in which to settle a thousand details attendant to the fights in Monaco scheduled for less than a month away. By five-thirty that day we took off our martial arts hats and got back into the marital swing. First we met with Bill and Sandy Allyn for a reunion drink. A quick change of clothes saw us all off to the apartment of Grace's dear friend Jeanne Kelly Van Remoortel, who was hosting a cocktail party for the American wedding guests.

I had always thought of Jeanne as "the seventh bridesmaid." Most of the friends Grace had made since she moved to Monaco were either European, older or had worked for her. "Kelly," though, as Jeanne was still often called, was so distinctly American and contemporary that she could easily have been one of us. Her eyes were light and mine dark, but our red hair and pale freckles prompted others to ask repeatedly if she and I were related. It was Jeanne's full-of-beans appetite for life, though, and the way she rolled with the punches—which by then had mounted to near knockout proportions—that confirmed she could only be an American woman of our own generation.

Watching the lights twinkle on across the leviathan yachts gathered for the festivities in the Monte Carlo harbor below, I reflected on what it would really feel like to be an American girl living in Monaco and growing into a mature woman there. I realized that I had little sense of how anyone's life really felt but my own.

Leaving Jeanne's, we drove to the Bec Rouge to join Annie and Herb Siegel for dinner. Annie's parents had been close friends of the Kellys, and the slightly younger Annie had been thrilled when Grace asked her to be her attendant at her Stevens graduation many years earlier. By one that morning, Don and I had joined Ella and Robert de Balkany (Princess Maria Gabriella and the then son-in-law of ex-King Umberto of Italy) at Jimmyz in the Summer Sporting Club. The setting makes Jimmyz quite simply the most beautiful dancing club I have ever seen in my life.

The sun was already whitening the sky when we headed back to the hotel. So that the evening was not merely a hedonist's delight, I had worked with Régine to set the menu for a post-fight dinner we were giving the following month at Maona, her Polynesian restaurant in the Summer Sporting complex. Two hours after our heads hit the pillows, our wake-up call came, signaling a speedy café *complet,* a quick change and a traffic-snarled drive back up to the Rock for Caroline's 11 A.M. marriage.

Hoping to preserve the essence of a private family ritual, Grace and Rainier had limited the guest list to a couple of hundred. An abundance of uniformed and plainclothes security people guaranteed that neither aggressive press nor adoring fans would invade the enclave where the day's functions were to take place. The media would receive photographs taken by the Palace's own appointed photographer, and even the airspace above the Palace was being monitored to keep out trespassers.

The family's private chapel was situated at the northernmost end of the Court of Honor. That whole half of the courtyard had been made into a sort of outdoor room, blocked by high walls of flower- and vine-laden trellises. As guests entered through a smallish aperture, a uniformed Palace aide showed them to their preassigned seats. A lushly bedecked altar and ceremonial focus had been created just in front of the chapel doors ahead of us. As we waited for the rites to begin, breezes rustled through the ivies and flowers as soft music played. Those of us who knew one another nodded greetings up, down, and across the aisles. We had heard that Cary Grant had fallen in love with young Barbara Harris from England, with whom he'd been platonically friendly for a couple of years, but she had not been with him at the ball nor was she in attendance at the wedding. Rumor had it that as their relationship had not been made public, Barbara was remaining discreetly ensconced at the Pecks' villa in nearby Cap Ferrat. Greg and Véronique Peck came in, and I reflected back on the days when she and I had played with our baby children as newly settled wives in California. Hjordis and David Niven were shown to their seats, David making even his subtly nodded hello twinkle with his delight for mischief. Almost directly in front of us sat Barbara and Frank Sinatra.

Most of the women wore day-length, silk luncheon dresses and all wore hats. I had looked high and low for one in New York, but only found models appropriate for beach wear. When at last I did locate a proper and becoming hat at Bonwit Teller, the buyer said she'd be unable to order it in the right color for me in time for the occasion. I extracted the name of the local milliner who had created it and dashed to his salon only two blocks away. Flinging myself on the mercy of his rather protective receptionist, I explained I needed a hat custom-made before returning home to California briefly and setting forth for a wedding in Europe. An impeccably tailored gentleman suddenly appeared at my side. "Which wedding are you going to in Europe?" he queried, leaving me to think that only certain weddings passed muster for production orders.

Deciding I'd best use my strongest ammunition, I said, "I'm going to Monaco for Princess Caroline's wedding."

"Come in," the gentleman fairly swooped as he guided me into his small salon. "I'm Don Marshall," he added as I gave him my name. While I described the hat I wanted made, he kept looking at me with undue interest. Finally, he asked, "Forgive me, but how is it that you know Her Highness and have been invited to the wedding?" I thought he was being a bit pushy but explained that I was an old friend of her parents, having known Princess Grace before she herself married. A light bulb clicked on. "You were a bridesmaid for Princess Grace," Don Marshall exclaimed. I could not imagine the man's memory being so sharp that he remembered my youthful face from a yellowing newspaper, but he solved the mystery instantly. "I made your hat for the wedding in 1956!" Though I had not recalled his name, it had been Don Marshall whom Neiman-Marcus commissioned to create our original wedding hats twenty-two years earlier.

My reverie was brought to a close when the Princely Family and the bridal party began to walk down the center aisle. Caroline looked younger when she entered than she had even two nights earlier. I think we see the child in the brides we have known since infancy more on their wedding days than at any other time. Her rich, dark hair had been parted straight down the middle and pulled completely off her face to the back of her head where it was coiled. Semicircles of tiny flowers curved from behind her crown forward, across her temples and down over her ears. Her gauzy, collarless high-necked dress with its long sleeves and softly falling skirt gave her the look of a magical farm girl out of a fairy tale. Her deeply scalloped hemline, just below ankle length, revealed the tips of her graceful white silk pumps, and she was attended only by her cousin Gracie LeVine from Philadelphia, two small flower girls and two ring-bearing pages. Standing nearby, Stephanie looked utterly pained to have been roped into wearing a dress. Grace looked lovely in a filmy but sunny yellow dress that stopped just above her ankles and a matching wide-brimmed hat, and though she smiled with serene contentment I knew she would pray especially hard at her tufted prie-dieu for the happiness she feared—even now—might elude her firstborn child.

The softness and decorum of the ceremony lulled the guests into a kind of hypnotic trance of attention until a loud swoosh overhead caused us all nearly to jump to our feet. All heads quickly turned skyward to see what had caused the commotion. Something enormous had darkened the sky above us, something resembling a gigantic prehistoric bird that had come back down through the centuries to claim us one and all. Then we made out the figure of a daring photographer who had wafted himself into our midst on a homemade glider and the breezes from the sea. Though it was an entirely unwelcomed interruption, even the principals smiled a bit as Icarus and his Nikon passed over the eastern wall of the Palace and we once again focused on the marriage rites.

When the ceremony ended, several people began to make their way toward an entrance to the Palace garden and a newly concealed section of the public square. A few friends had told us they were invited to the luncheon but not to the ceremony, but as we had received no other invitation than to the wedding itself, it appeared we had not been included on the luncheon list. Leaving the Palace, Don and I conjectured about this. I noted it was customary to have a smaller ceremony and add additional people for the reception, so this turn of events seemed odd. We agreed, though, that with no invitation in hand, we would not consider getting into line to be turned away by the attendant checking credentials. That night, dining with Sandy and Bill Allyn, they said they were sure there must have been some mistake. So did Howell Conant, for years the Sovereign Family's favorite photographer, when I breakfasted with him the following morning on the Hôtel de Paris's terrace.

I had not called Grace, imagining her to be exhausted, but decided to write her a note thanking her and regretting that we'd had no opportunity to add our blessings in person to her, Rainier or the newlyweds. Lest we had been omitted intentionally, I made no reference to the lack of a luncheon invitation. Dropping the note off downstairs, I asked the concierge to have it hand-delivered to the Palace.

By the time we returned late that evening, there was a message from Grace asking that I call her first thing in the morning before leaving for home. "I almost dread the question because I think I already know the answer, but I have to ask it anyway," Grace remarked when I reached her by phone. "Why weren't you and Don at the wedding luncheon?" When I explained that we had not been invited, she almost cried, "Oh, God, no!" Going on, she said she asked a mutual friend if he had seen us and was told we'd been at the ceremony but seemed to have disappeared immediately afterwards. "I presumed you might have had a business emergency, as I know you had meetings all week for your promotion here next month, but when you didn't stop in to explain nor mention regrets in your note to me, I got suspicious." There was a long pause, during which she sighed resignedly. "I can't believe that after all these years of getting people here to be thorough about lists and details that we're still having some of the same problems that existed when Rainier and I got married."

In later years I heard that one woman had been invited to the luncheon, but as her fiancé's name did not appear on the door list, she'd been told that she alone would be permitted entry. A story also made the rounds that the Sinatras had left their invitation at the hotel and were also turned away by the staff, causing them to leave in a huff. I'm sure we all—the great and the near-great alike—managed to survive the pain of unintentional rebuffs by royalty.

*   *   *

Less than three weeks later we returned to the Principality for our karate fights. At noon on our second day there, Don and I slipped away from work and went over to the Palace for luncheon in the garden. There were only ten of us, including Wendell Niles, longtime producer of Monaco's annual celebrity tennis tournament, and our hosts' old friends, the Crovettos.

During lunch Grace asked me if I had yet read Joan Collins's recently published English version of her autobiography, *Past Imperfect.* As Rainier had been on the Galápagos cruise the summer before when we had all heard David Niven on this subject, she asked me to share that story with Rainier. David had asked me if I knew about the book, mentioning he'd heard that in it Joanie named everyone she had ever been to bed with. Knowing we were almost the same age, I had told David I was surprised that Joan had elected to do such a book at this point in her life.

"It sounds more like the kind of thing one might do in one's dotage," I said.

"Though I know what you mean," David pointed out, "the problem with waiting too long to write a book like that is that all the people who remember the names of the people you went to bed with have already died, and nobody young enough to buy or read your book knows who in blazes you're talking about!"

On the morning of Tuesday, July 18, it seemed that all the last-minute plans for the final day preceding that night's PKA karate event were going to run in smooth order. Grace, Rainier and Albert had accepted our invitation to watch the fights from ringside and to join us afterwards at a small dinner for the American champions. But by mid-afternoon, it became apparent that the troop of multilingual assistants whose services the promoter had promised to arrange was not going to materialize. This left only Don and me to do everything. As I attempted to conduct the mandatory rules' meeting with contingents from France, Italy, the Netherlands, Germany and Belgium, I realized that though my high school French had equipped me to find a hotel, a cab, a train, a steak and a bathroom, French I, II and III had never taught me to talk karate. There was no time to return to the hotel to change, but somehow a few of our necessary things made it over to the arena at the last moment.

Protocol demanded that we, as event hosts and family friends, be in attendance upon the Princely party's arrival to greet them formally and escort them to their seats. When the arena manager came to drag me by the arm, excitedly announcing the arrival of Their Highnesses, I was searching for a lost shoe and wearing a scarf on my uncombed hair with a face totally devoid of makeup. At least I was further along than Don, who was still in blue jeans. Tearing my scarf off my head and throwing it to an usher, and walking on the tiptoes of my one bare foot only minimally concealed under my pajama trousers, I rushed to the front door as though I'd been calmly awaiting the arrival for hours.

Several fights of varying lengths had been programmed for the evening, along with two *entr'acte* performances of a martial arts dance and weaponry exhibition. When I hustled back to my seat between Grace and Rainier as the first gong rang, Grace leaned over toward me. "I can't stand fights, you know, Judybird. Whenever Rainier and Albert go to the Stadium to see the boxing matches I always stay home. But I wouldn't have dreamed of missing this as it's your and Don's sport. Be prepared, though, to have me digging my nails into your arm, and if I start yelling, 'Stop hitting each other!' just clamp your hand over my mouth." The first bouts featured French fighters from a new stable in nearby Nice. A trained eye could see that these neophytes packed their three-rounders with wild flurries of action but no real power. Grace, however, could not tell the difference, and when any blow or kick was thrown she cowered, cringed and clenched my arm.

Between the second and third preliminaries Grace fanned herself with her program while Rainier, Albert and I discussed some of the strategies and talents required for the kicking and punching sport, comparing them with boxing. "Do the better fighters kick and punch harder than those we've seen?" Grace interjected. I nodded affirmatively. "Oh, my wud," Grace intoned, imitating a Southern belle, "I shall lahkley expiah! I actually did go once to see Albie compete in a judo tournament when he was studying. The very first time he fell to the mat I thought I was having cardiac arrest."

"Come on, Grace," Rainier cajoled, "you can get into this."

"I suppose I ought to start actually watching and learning something from Judy during the next fight. Maybe if I got more involved in the art of the sport and understood it better, I'd feel less apprehensive." From the minute the bell rang to signal round one of the third match, a cut above the first two, Grace began asking rapid-fire questions. "What does it mean," she queried, "when the cornerman yells, 'Double up!'?" . . . "What's a combination?" . . . "What are legal kicks or illegal ones?" . . . "Why do the men in the corners flipping the cards count the kicks?" . . . "How do they decide whether or not a kick should be counted?" . . . "Why do the fighters seem to stay at a greater distance from one another than boxers do?"

I answered every question as quickly as possible while her eyes never strayed from the action in the ring. By the fourth fight of the night, Grace was rising half out of her front-row seat, yelling out like any fight fan, "Double up! C'mon, double up!" and "Two more kicks. You need two more kicks!"

By the time Bill "Superfoot" Wallace began to throw his legendary sixty-mile-per-hour kicks in the final fight, using his foot like a jab with three kicks per second, Grace was cheering.

During the few days remaining while we attended to cleanup, settled accounts, and packed for a relaxed weekend on Giglio Island off the Tuscan coast, I also arranged to spend an entire afternoon with Grace at the Beach. Though we had been assigned a tent immediately next to hers for our whole stay, this was the only day of the trip when Don or I actually saw sand. When Grace arrived, we visited with Don for a half hour before he announced that he was going to keep himself busy for the rest of the day so we could have a long, private visit.

"That was so thoughtful of Don," Grace commented when she and I settled down into two chaises under her canopy. We were both still very guarded about saying anything disloyal to each other about our husbands, but without my planning it, something slipped out.

"He is thoughtful in so many ways," I agreed, "but then he changes and is extremely brusque and insensitive. Sometimes I can't put together the two sides of Don, that sweet thoughtful side and a side with a lot of rage."

Without turning her head, still looking straight ahead toward the sea, Grace added, "I don't understand why so many men are filled with so much anger. But they are, they most certainly are. How could a person feel right about the kind of dismissive criticism men so easily hand out?"

"Physically," I chimed in, "that kind of anger makes me so damned uncomfortable. I can't imagine how people with short fuses can tolerate the pain."

Still not moving her eyes, but shifting subjects nonetheless, Grace called my attention to the baby pool directly below us. "I kept a tent here so that I could watch the children splash about in that pool when they were little, though actually this section has far too many people socializing and watching one another for my taste. Now I can envision holding the little soft tummies of my children's children as they kick their legs in the same pool, and while it means I'll have to settle for this location, I can't wait." I asked Grace if she thought Caroline wanted to have children quickly. "I don't really know," she answered. "She thinks she wants to have them soon and settle down into a happy home life, but if that's what she wants I can't understand choosing someone like Philippe as a husband. I can't see him ever retiring from the nightclub circuit, at least not until several years have passed."

"Do you suppose," I asked Grace, "that your view of Philippe is not unlike the view your parents projected when they considered your marrying Oleg or a couple of other men to whom you were attracted before marrying Rainier?"

"I'm sure it's very similar," Grace responded candidly. "Only now that it's done, that they're married, I don't want to knock Philippe because I only pray she'll be happy and don't want any bad vibrations from me to influence her."

"What had you envisioned for Caroline at this point in her life?" I asked Grace.

"I suppose I hoped she'd have a career of some kind for herself," Grace replied. "She writes extremely well and has so very much potential in so many areas, I feel that such an early marriage will prevent her from finding her own talents and exploring how best to use them. Also, I wanted her to take charge of her responsibilities in the Principality."

"Being Princess Caroline of Monaco in itself doesn't offer her much opportunity to find a gratifying niche here." Grace looked at me quizzically, so I elaborated. "You are going to be around for a long time, Gracie, and you are an exceedingly powerful person with a potent image. By the time you are old, Albert will likely have married, and he and his wife will take over from you and Rainier. Where does that leave Caroline? Sort of in the role of Tiny," I observed. "With some small, local bailiwicks of her own to run, but that's not much for a girl like Caroline. You're right, if she had a career," and I couldn't avoid saying it, "one she would be permitted to pursue while maintaining her status as Princess, that would provide a more gratifying outlet.

"Vicki is getting married next month," I told Grace. "We're actually very fond of her fiancé, Ivano Colombetti, but nonetheless I think she's too young. I pressed her to abandon the thought of such a fast marriage and live with him for a while . . ."

"An option, as you reminded me last year, that Caroline did not have," Grace interjected.

"Vicki says they've been living together at our house for five months, but I keep saying that's not the same as being in a place of their own."

"You and I should have gotten as smart as Bettina about this wedding business," Grace laughed. "When Lizzie Gray got married last fall, Frank Gray arranged the entire wedding and gave it at his house. Why wasn't I that clever?"

"In our case, since Vicki and Ivano just decided to get married in August, we're going to have only immediate family on our lawn, with Ivano cooking his relished pasta."

"What is it with young people nowadays?" Grace asked after thinking a minute. "When we were girls all we wanted to be was instant matrons. Most of them now seem never to really want to grow up."

"I think neither approach is very useful," I said. "Both are too extreme."

For a while Grace told me what she knew about each of the other bridesmaids. "I don't know what it is that Maree thinks she's looking for," she volunteered.

"I surely would have no idea," I noted, "but I know it's my full work schedule that keeps me moving right along without questioning too much. If I didn't have that, I might dwell more on those other areas where I find a lack of fulfillment."

Commenting on the narration she had done for a documentary on the Kirov Ballet School in Leningrad, Grace described how dearly she had loved the feeling of being around the business again. "Of course," she added, "it wasn't really acting, only narrating, not even as close to acting as my poetry readings, but I loved it. I never publicly express my feeling about all the joys of really working in the business, as I've learned over the years that I'm always misunderstood when I mention it. It's wiser just to do what I can without making any statements. People don't seem to notice as much."

"I think all of us probably begin to take stock again just at about this point in our lives." I was thinking of Maree's separation, Rita's new career and my own work involvement. It was then that I mentioned to Grace an idea for a book which had come to me.

"I wasn't thinking about writing a book," I said honestly, "but on the plane coming over this last time I did get a thought which interests me. I'd like to do a book about the bridesmaids. Clearly it would have to be about you as well, but it couldn't be a Princess Grace biography because only you could tell us what your life has really been like."

"I have been thinking recently that one day I will write my autobiography," Grace admitted. "I don't know when the right time will be, but I'll hope to know it when it arrives. Tell me more about your idea for your book, though. It sounds fascinating." As I laid out the preliminary thoughts that had briefly spun around in my head, Grace became enthusiastic. "Do it, Judybird," she exclaimed. "You should just go ahead and do it!" I had some reservations, I explained. First of all, my hectic schedule, but mainly I was concerned that the book might be considered exploitive. "In what way?" Grace asked.

"Well, I probably could get such a book published, but we'd all have to recognize the interest would come from the fact that we were your bridesmaids, not the bridesmaids of Suzie Klutz in Piggott, Arkansas," I observed.

Grace paused to think. "I can only tell you what I tell my own children," she volunteered. "You were my bridesmaids, not Suzie Klutz's, and you can't change that nor would I. I tell my children they were born of their father and me, and there are things that go along with that, too. I don't think you should worry about people's interest in what was true. I don't think of it as exploitation, so you should write the book if you'd enjoy writing it." I was amazed.

"But, Grace," I cautioned, "when it comes to your side of the story, you've spent your entire life playing things close to the vest—being enormously discreet and private, even covering for any unhappiness among your friends and family on both sides of the ocean. Why would you suddenly think I could write this book without invading some of that privacy? We couldn't come off as Pollyanna and her six Glad Girls or the book would be dishonest."

Grace shook her head. "No, we couldn't," she concurred. "That *would* be dishonest. And you're right that I've covered for a lot of unhappiness around me. My brother Kell, for example, and all the brouhaha that happened when my mother aborted his mayoral race because he'd been photographed in the company of a female impersonator and she was afraid the scandal would be harmful to all our reputations. And my sister Peggy, who has been married twice and seems to harbor resentment toward me." When I raised my eyebrows quizzically as I had not seen Peggy in a long time, Grace added, "She hasn't come to any function in Philadelphia or New York where I've appeared for years. I know she doesn't go out much, but I do feel she stays away out of some unconscious hostility toward me. Only once did she comment that I had never really understood our father, but I wonder if the fact that he and I made some peace with one another before he died doesn't make her resent me." Grace was silent for a moment, before adding, "God, how I idolized Peggy as a child. Isn't it awful the way the feelings get all messed up as life moves along?"

"But, you see, if I interviewed Peggy, for example, and she said certain things to me about you or her, how would you feel about seeing that in print?" I asked pointedly.

For a long time Grace said nothing, and when she spoke she said two things. The first I never questioned, the second took me completely by surprise. "Oh, I'm sure Peggy will tell you everything if you decide to include her and interview her," was Grace's first observation. Her second, delivered with a sigh of such enormous release, was, "You know something, Judybird? It's all right now to say some of the things I've avoided saying."

One thing was clear: the utter exhaustion Grace was suffering from the burden she had so readily assumed and so impeccably carried all these years, exhaustion so debilitating that even she, the master of control of all in her life, was about to relinquish it in some way. Perhaps part of her letting go was caused by the recent wedding, where she watched her daughter marry a man she feared could never bring her happiness. But it was larger than that.

Don and I left Monaco to visit our friends Betty and Stanley Sheinbaum at their home in Italy. For the entire weekend on Giglio, I thought about what Grace had said. It haunted me as we strolled through the narrow, carless streets of Castello, Giglio's ancient hillside fortress town; as we ran hasty errands in Porto, its harbor village where the ferries docked, and as we danced in the local disco, which was originally a tiny church. What was Grace going to do with this resolve? I pondered that question as I lay quietly on the small beach or ate sandwiches in the little shack run by one local family who had controlled the tiny strand for generations.

During our last afternoon on Giglio, Don urged me to take the mask and snorkel he had purchased to explore undersea life in the swimming cove. Wading out into the temperate Tyrrhenian waters, I thought this sea was very like Grace. At first sight it appeared to be composed entirely of cool, serene, aquamarine liquid, its only visible bottom the pearlized, pliable sand that surrendered easily to the pressure of my step. As I waded out farther, though, the deepening water turned a darker teal blue and I donned the mask to see the encrusting of accumulated life on the seafloor. At first, the only detectable motion was the calm swaying to and fro of wavy eelgrasses. But on closer inspection the in-and-out breathing of jellylike combs revealed tiny crustaceans among the clumps of red, green and rust-tinted algae. Thousands of luminescent minnows tore off together in one direction before reversing course to pursue another with equal conviction. The more I looked, the more was revealed. This ocean, I thought, was like all of us—on the surface something you could easily recognize and describe, and beneath that, a million things you had to look carefully to find and even then could not classify. But more than anyone I knew, the calm sea and its complex underlife reminded me of Grace. She had for many long years stood firm between the tides, so firm that in the not-too-distant past she had almost seemed to be in stasis. But now her innermost self was beginning to break free once again and to course with its renewed life force. I could not guess, nor was I sure she could, where the tremulous re-creation of herself would lead, nor even how it could be affected. What I did know was that the fairy-tale mother-of-the-bride was about to change her life because it was no longer possible for her not to.

Other Voices, Other Rooms

*M*aree sat alone in her rented house, separated from her husband, Bud Rambo, knowing that he would not change his life for her. There were no more thriving holiday parties at the big house in Chestnut Hill, nor Christmas mornings-after when Maree felt utterly spent. Maree's only relief came from the invitations Grace extended to accompany her on her travels for a board meeting or a poetry reading.

Bettina had taken avidly to travel, finding new and more exotic spots around the globe to prepare for and investigate. It was as though Bettina, who had been locked inside herself for so long, had discovered the pleasures of making herself accessible, not only on an intellectual basis but on a personal one as well. Grace told me that though she never understood what had kept them apart for so many years, she was content with leaving that a mystery and simply enjoying "Tiners" now that they had found each other again.

Nothing had ever interrupted the affection nor the visits between Grace and Sally, who continued to work at Beekman Downtown Hospital. But though Carolyn had begun moving back and forth between New York and Philadelphia, her life and Grace's seemed even further apart. After Robin's death Grace had written a loving condolence letter, which had ultimately reached Carolyn, but now Grace was not even sure where Carolyn was living. For a while she and her oldest daughter, Jyl, had tried sharing a Philadelphia apartment, but for a number of reasons this was unsatisfactory. Carolyn, for example, was obsessed with germ warfare and required every object in the flat to be covered with airtight plastic. With her money gone either to reckless stockbrokers or relentless religious broadcasters, Carolyn was left with few residential options. After moving out of Jyl's place, she moved in for a while with the sisters at a Catholic shelter outside the City of Brotherly Love, where the Kellys had built their original fame and fortune. In town, close enough so that they could see each other, Jyl worked at a variety of different jobs.

As the decade neared its end and I reached my late forties, I found myself long on jobs and short on hours. I had served my second year on the Contractors' Board as its Vice Chairman, and during my third I was elected as the first woman Chairman in its fifty-year history. The CSLB absorbed most of my extracurricular schedule, as I had resigned from nearly every other board on which I'd served. The one exception was the ACLU Foundation of Southern California, which has always held a special place in my heart. The Foundation is the only nationwide organization singularly charged with the urgent mission of defending the Constitution by trying civil liberties cases in the courts.

In the autumn of 1979 our television agent sold a series of nine PKA fight programs to the newly launched sports cable network, ESPN. That number grew to forty-four two-hour shows in 1980 and remained at approximately that level for the next several years. There were now nearly three hundred PKA-sanctioned events a year. Don and I were working with a karate school owner, promoter and ex-fighter from Atlanta, Georgia, but even after we solidified our partnership there was still too much work for too few people. If Don and I had seen big egos (usually meaning damaged ones) in show business, we hadn't lived till we started the PKA! A sizable percentage of karate promoters and officials believe that their black belts make them not only good teachers or studio managers but also the world's greatest living authorities on every subject listed in the encyclopedia. The people I liked best in our sport were the fighters, for the most part a dedicated group of young men from diverse backgrounds who inspired me in ways for which I shall be eternally grateful.

At home, our children all seemed to have survived whatever difficulties had plagued them in their teenage years. Amy Kanter was in New York living with Bob Thiele, Jr., the son of my old friend, the immensely talented singer Jane Harvey. Amy and Bob wrote songs together, worked in each other's bands when either played the New York rock music clubs, and were recording an album of their songs on Atlantic Records with Amy singing and Bob playing and co-producing. Vicki and her husband Ivano lived not far from us in Beverly Hills. After graduating with honors, Vicki enrolled in postgrad courses at UCLA to study accounting, intending to sit for her board certification exams while her husband worked for a furniture company. Instead, Vicki became pregnant. Nina graduated from the Windward School and, after taking a year off to work, decided to study for a Bachelor of Fine Arts in Drama at USC. She had been acting since junior high school and studying in specialized summer programs. Robert was earning his living airbrushing clothes, linens, canvases and even rooms. James had abandoned all the alcohol and drug problems of his earlier teens and, after completing two years of credits in eighteen months at Santa Monica City College, enrolled as a junior at USC on academic grants he had won for excellence. Through high school, our youngest son, Sean, had lived with his mother and stepfather in Florida, but upon graduation he came to live with us and entered the University of Colorado at Boulder, where he was earning splendid grades.

With the children grown to the ages where they set off on their own vacations, Don and I simply stopped taking holidays and worked straight through every year. Though Don had initially carried the greatest load of company travel, our partner and I were now the ones who made the national rounds. Perhaps it was the fact that I began calling all the flight attendants on California trips and those on the L.A./N.Y./L.A. runs by their nicknames that prompted me to answer when anyone asked where I'd like to go on vacation, "My house!"

For a long while I had noticed changes in Don which I thought were due to the pressures of raising so many children and carrying such a burden with work. Though our company's activity increased by leaps and bounds, we were always juggling to balance expansion with available dollars, and though revenues improved with more consistent TV exposure, those dollars still remained small. Over the years, Don had always been the more explosive of the two of us. When the fur flew, I said what I needed to say, but often, as a natural peacemaker and problem solver, refrained from entering battle. But Don's increasingly taut, angry responses were, by now, becoming way too frequent and were provoked by small, insignificant things.

Gradually, I had begun to have a strange sense of Don being divided within himself. The loving, caring, reasonable and intelligent man I had grown to know and trust became a different person on too many occasions. I could tell, even by hearing him walking down the hall to our bedroom at night, which Don was going to enter the room. If his footstep was as I'd known it all these years, it was going to be the man I loved and trusted. But if his step fell harder and more purposefully on the ground, this other person was coming to bed.

About this time public service announcements and commercials began to appear on television for programs and facilities that treated people with addictive disease. Don didn't do any of the things those TV husbands did. He had never been physically abusive to me or the children. He neither wracked up cars nor wound up in drunk tanks. He remained functional during working hours which, in our cases, meant from early morning until late at night. He even stopped drinking and smoking for months at a time. It was hard for me to equate his problems with those of people called drunks or addicts, but gradually the children and I realized that all of our lives were suffering from Don's changes and that these were related to his consumption of alcohol and marijuana.

During two long business trips to New York, I realized that I had mixed feelings about being away from home. I missed my family, but enjoyed the relief of not having to run a house or deal with the thousands of daily details that arose in it or in our office. Yet on my two returns to Los Angeles, though I felt thrilled to see Don when we embraced at the airport, on the ride home I felt my shoulders tense up when it became clear that the wrong Don had come to collect me. Gradually, I began to confront him more often about his anger and the way he made me feel when he had smoked or drunk too much or too often. For a while he defended his actions as manly, but I made very certain he knew that I thought such defenses were, if not pure baloney, at least not the kind of manliness I was attracted to. Being able to acknowledge the problem together was somewhat helpful. But because neither of us knew what to do to solve it, and we were, like most people, engulfed in the thousand-and-one obligations of everyday life, we simply kept on keeping on.

Rita, too, was on the road nearly all the time during these years, writing articles and filming documentaries. On a night when we dined together at the California apartment she had taken, she told us she had been working on her autobiography. As the decade neared its close, Rita told us she'd also been gathering interviews while she traveled, for a book on world-acclaimed actresses. She and I talked about our schedules and Grace's—how we always seemed to be passing one another in the air flying in opposite directions. Both of us, though, sensed a loosening in Grace's tension of recent years, a resolve to consider more options for an even more self-determined approach to her life.

Many of Grace's friends were aware of her new path almost before she seemed to be conscious that she was pursuing it. There had been consistent flirtations with a return to show business, mostly unpublicized. One after another of us had been approached to see if we could make her original film treatment, *The Pattycake Man,* a viable project. When Grace's *Country Girl* director, George Seaton, was serving on the board of Los Angeles' Ahmanson Theatre, Grace had enthusiastically suggested to him a production of George Kelly's play *The Torch-Bearers,* identifying the role she wished to play. (Though her Uncle George had been dead for a number of years, Gracie could still quote his plays, almost line for line.) Seaton advised Grace against pursuing the production, insisting that the role she'd marked for herself was a character part and not at all what people expected to see her do in the theatre.

Having learned that it was often wisest to couch her artistic ventures as casual pastimes, Grace had already turned two such occupations into mini-careers. Nobody protested when her family and staff referred to her dried flower collages or her poetry readings as "lovely little hobbies." But any of us who saw Grace at work or heard her describe her preparations realized that she had really launched two professional occupations. At five-thirty in the morning, before the sun rose, Grace would often be up working on her next collage, pasting bits of Queen Anne's lace, forget-me-nots, periwinkles and primroses that had been pressed among the pages of the book stacks cluttering the floors of her glass-walled studio into elaborate designs.

In the late 1970s when her collages were shown as an official collection at a vernissage in a Paris art gallery, Bill and Sandy Allyn flew over from London to join Grace at the reception. It was an exciting evening. Huge posters advertising the showing were hung throughout Paris, bearing a sample of her work identified simply with her maiden initials, GPK. When the Princely party arrived on the Rue St. Honoré and tried to make their way down an alley toward a small courtyard and entranceway to the gallery, it seemed as though ten thousand paparazzi and fans were blocking their way. Inside, when the family posed for the cameras, Stephanie refused to be photographed, but Grace insisted. Grace explained to Bill and Sandy that Steph did not want to be like Caroline, whose picture was appearing daily in hundreds of worldwide publications.

All of Paris was in attendance. But it was not the status of the event, the glamour or prestige of the guests, nor even the verbal praise being heaped upon her that most elated Gracie. What she loved best were the small, round red stickers that gradually began to be pasted on the title cards next to her collages, telling her that people were actually paying real money for her work.

The value Grace placed on earned income was one facet of her I never thought Rainier understood. For a man, a European and a prince to boot, it would have been nearly impossible for him to have comprehended what that money meant to Grace. It was even a hard concept for affluent men in America to grasp—why their wives, for whom they provided well, sought jobs when they needed none, wanting to work when they could have played. But to many women, even those who had been raised with economic privilege, earned money was worth more than a hundred times its weight in gold. In Paris that night, what provided music to the soul of the woman behind the legend was the sound of somebody's cold, hard cash saying, "Good work, Gracie!"

On an immeasurable high, Grace and her party left the reception and decided, though they'd made no prior plans, to continue on to dinner. Once everyone was seated, the air of exultation emanating from Grace was still at its peak. Suddenly, Rainier plucked a handful of petals from a floral arrangement in the center of the table, grabbed a plate in his other hand, slapped the petals up against the plate and announced, "Sold. For three thousand francs!" Though the joke was funny and well-timed, and though Rainier had meant it to call attention to Grace's success, it drew only tense titters as everyone looked to Grace to see whether she felt complimented or belittled.

What happened the next day, though, got Grace really angry. Almost as soon as it had become known that her collages were for sale, the gossips began their work. Once the actual sales were announced by the gallery, the British and European press and public started to vilify Grace for stooping so low as to actually have entered commerce.

My correspondence to Grace had never improved and even hers to me had finally dwindled to a few letters a year, but we had taken to calling each other, sometimes at bizarre hours, from our various pit stops around the globe. When I congratulated her on her opening, she was fuming. "How infuriating," she exploded, "that all these people who live like kings are so hypocritical about money and commerce. What do they think they themselves live on, their good looks? Money is earned by work, and it's either their own or someone else's that provides them with their way of life. How dare they call money or commerce dirty or unsuitable!" I silently registered the fact that "these people who live like kings" now meant a class Grace had begun to see as different from herself.

"I suppose," I interjected, "you could diffuse or deflect all this talk by simply announcing you are giving the money to charity."

"No, not you, too, Judy!" Grace exploded. "Do you think I'm obligated to clean up my act by advertising my philanthropies?" Before I could answer she rolled forward. "I think that's the crassest sort of commercialism: 'Look at me, aren't I wonderful doing all these nice things for all these unfortunate people!' " I still couldn't get a word in as she continued, "Besides, I'm getting to the point where I don't care what you or anyone else, for that matter, thinks. Sometimes I'm tired of being the great diffuser or the great deflector, or whatever you want to call it!"

"Ahhhh," I sighed, stretching out the word in a long sigh of relief. "Bravo!"

What would Grace's new self-assertive moving-on mean? Was she going to leave her husband? Turn her back on her Principality? Begrudge worthy causes? Of course not! What she was going to do was to go back to work, as she understood it, as she loved it best, and as she believed was appropriate at that stage in her life, if not as a full-time actress, then as a project-by-project contributor, producing, directing, or even acting, if the right chance presented itself. She could not exactly take out an ad in *Variety* or *Dramalogue* worded, "Princess available for show biz–related work," but she got busy connecting herself to people and projects that would eventually lead to just those opportunities.

Life brings us new people and new chances when we're ready for them. In late 1976 a wealthy American had funded and produced a documentary at the Kirov Ballet School in Leningrad called *The Children of Theatre Street.* As his director, Earle Mack hired the poetic, leftist-leaning journalist-turned-documentary filmmaker, twenty-nine-year-old Robert Dornhelm, a divorced father of one child. Hearing about Grace's interest in the ballet, Mack mentioned to Robert that he was approaching the Princess to see if she would do the narration for their film. From New York, Mack wired Robert in Vienna, "GET YOUR REELS TOGETHER, FLY THEM TO PARIS, SHOW THEM TO THE PRINCESS AND SEE WHAT SHE HAS TO SAY AFTER SHE'S SEEN THE WORK."

After packing up his rough-cut 16mm print, Robert arrived in Paris on the appointed day to discover it was a national holiday. He was finally able to locate a screening facility and Grace met him at the CBS correspondents' editing site on the Rue Marbeuf. She was with Ania Chervachidze. Both were in a wonderful mood and seemed not at all distressed that the film would be viewed on the small screen atop the editing table. By this time, Robert had nearly a hundred films for Eastern European TV under his belt and was conversant in several languages. He was, however, fairly tongue-tied with Grace, until he heard the spontaneous, delighted laughs and cheers with which Ania and she greeted his latest project. Almost immediately after seeing the footage, Grace committed to doing the narration. By visit's end, Grace asked Robert to call her in Monaco in a week to begin making the necessary arrangements.

Once the crew arrived in the Principality, Grace invited Robert to the Palace so they could go over details before the first shooting the following morning. Realizing he'd need his most formal clothes, Robert donned his blue blazer, his gray slacks and the only white shirt he owned. Arriving on the Rock, he perceived that he was not dressed formally enough even to be a waiter, but when he asked the Princess what he should call her on the set the next day, she replied simply, "Grace. When I work, call me Grace."

The two-day shoot in the Monte Carlo Opera House, outside it and on the beach went smoothly. Robert noticed the enormous enthusiastic interest Grace lent every aspect of production. She was not only concerned with her lines, but also wanted to be sure the crew had the right hotel rooms and knew where to get a good, reasonable meal. Just as in her Hollywood days, Grace made relationships with all the crew members, not only the lighting and camera directors whose work could affect her appearance, but also the sound engineer and the grip who hauled the equipment.

Twenty-two years after Grace received her Oscar, *The Children of Theatre Street,* directed by her new friend Robert Dornhelm, took her back to the Academy Awards again, at least vicariously. On the night of the Academy's 50th Awards presentation, Grace stayed up, anxiously getting reports from Robert in America on whether or not it had, as a nominated feature documentary, won in its category. It did not, but Gracie was back in business in her old stomping grounds.

It was a time when Grace and I were both so crazed with activity that I could not remember when we last spoke together or even where we located each other when we did connect by phone. When we were both away from home, we'd speak in a kind of shorthand that we had mastered over the years, lest one or the other of our hotel operators had plugged themselves in to eavesdrop. I even lost track of the dates and times of our few hurried visits. They were never planned but occurred as though some fortunate accident had placed us near enough in New York or Los Angeles for a quick sandwich, a cup of tea or a drink.

In the spring of 1981, I had moved into the Wyndham Hotel on West Fifty-eighth Street for five weeks to produce an NBC karate event at Madison Square Garden's Felt Forum. Almost upon arrival, I saw in the paper that Grace was in New York and called her at her hotel. She immediately invited me to a function that evening—I believe yet another of the benefits *The Children of Theatre Street* had been having in countries around the world. I was already committed to an unbreakable business dinner, but was delighted to realize we'd be passing near to each other during the course of the day. Hastily, we agreed to meet between appointments at Manny Wolf's delicatessen on the corner of Sixth Avenue at Fifty-seventh Street.

I found Grace bubbling over with news, personally and professionally.

First she told me that Marie and Bud Rambo had reconciled, and then she went on to talk about her own family. Though I knew from prior contact how upset she felt when Caroline's marriage to Junot came apart, Grace seemed to have a perspective on the divorce that was better than I'd expected. Because of her Catholicism, Caroline had not seen divorce as a possible way out of an extremely painful situation. Her mother, though, that same mother who had been proposed as Catholic Mother of the Year, turned down her own accolade and convinced her daughter that she was not obligated to spend the remainder of her life in misery! Caroline was spending a good deal of time with her old friend Robertino Rossellini (son of Ingrid Bergman and Roberto Rossellini, the great Italian director), and Grace told me she was glad that this and other old, close friendships could help Caroline through this period when she was bound to suffer from a sense of failure and misguided youthful expectations.

When you're around fifty, have been a wife, mother, runner of things and doer of what needs to be done for a very long time, you grow accustomed to people who think you know everything, can come up with all the answers. Grace had grown used to the deference paid her by those of her own age and younger people as well. But having once again freed her curiosity, she longed to be challenged about what she did not know rather than to be revered for what she did. And so, to her huge retinue of old and contemporary friends whom she had inspired, she added new and younger ones whose candor and perspective inspired her.

Grace described two of her new friends to me, both younger men whom I'd not yet met, Robert Dornhelm and Jeffory FitzGerald. With Robert, she was planning a number of entertainment projects. She, Robert and Caroline were to do a film, with Sam Spiegel producing, commemorating the Year of the Child and focusing on child prodigies around the globe. Grace wanted Albert, too, to have a taste of film-making, and hoped to involve him on a project about Raoul Wallenberg, the World War II Swedish Red Cross hero who disappeared after aiding so many Jews in Budapest, and who was rumored to be still living in a Russian prison camp. She mentioned three or four more productions she had discussed with Bill and Sandy Allyn, and told me, too, about *Rearranged*, a small film project she and Robert had done together in Monaco. It was a frothy, mistaken-identity comedy set at the Monaco Flower Festival, which she had launched. Grace not only acted in it, but financed and produced it as well, in order to both promote and benefit her Garden Club and the Principality.

On February 25, 1980, wearing a warmly lined cloth coat over trousers and a sweater and carrying a mink coat over one arm, in addition to her jewelry and makeup cases, some magazines and a novel, Grace boarded a British Airways Concorde flight from London to New York. Her other arm was draped with an assemblage of brown paper shopping bags. As was her custom whenever she was rushed or simply unconcerned, her hair was concealed under a silk scarf that she had tied together under her chin in the favored babushka style of our youth.

Taking her 3A window seat, she unloaded her belongings on the adjoining seat and sat down for a breather before putting them away. As the flight attendants began to close the plane's doors, a young dark-haired man of twenty-nine streaked through the opening just in time to make the flight. The fellow glanced at his ticket and headed down the aisle for the third row. There he found a pleasant-looking woman near the window, glancing at a magazine, and an unpleasant load of her belongings occupying his assigned seat. "Excuse me, lady," he said, try-ing to be polite but suspecting that for all his good intentions his irrita-tion was visible. "Are these your things?" He pointed to the pile. Grace nodded yes and began both to apologize so profusely and move so quickly to clear her things that the man felt guilty for his stridency. "Just let me get my coat off and get rid of my briefcase," he offered, "so I can help you stow your stuff."

Once everything was neatly put away, Grace took out a crossword puzzle and began to work on it while the young man perused his London *Financial Times.* A voice came over the loudspeaker to announce a ten-minute delay. Grace looked at her neighbor, raised her hands in a gesture of futility, and made the same observation we all make under similiar circumstances, "Hurry up and wait!" The young man nodded and went back to reading his paper. Two or three more times, additional brief delays were announced. "I wish they'd just tell the truth in the first place," Grace commented after one such announcement.

Politely tapping her neighbor on the arm, Grace asked him if he could think of another word for one of the definitions in her puzzle. Offhand-edly, he offered a suggestion, but Grace said it didn't fit, thank you. For the next ten minutes, she repeatedly interrupted his reading to ask the young man's assistance. During this time the pilot announced spark plug trouble and an additional half hour's delay. Grace's seatmate put his *Times* away and extracted some work from his briefcase. "Madam," he said testily, meaning to dispel the possibility of further interruptions, "I don't think I can help you with your puzzle. I'm illiterate." Grace said nothing, but the corners of her mouth turned up in a nearly imperceptible, wry smile.

Finally, the plane took off. Both Grace and her seat partner put down their papers and began to eat. Noticing that she fairly dove into her caviar, the young man decided to make amends. "I don't really care for caviar," he said, "so if you'd enjoy my portion, too, I'd like you to have it." Grace and the impatient executive struck up a conversation. First they talked about the fact that people are never middle-of-the-road about caviar, they either love it or loathe it. Then they discussed the various types of caviar, and the young man revealed that he knew a good deal about it. Grace found herself giggling at the way he expressed himself. He found himself responding identically to her.

They began to chat more personally. "I'm a New Englander," he told her, thinking from her accent that perhaps she was from England.

"I like New England," Grace said. "Technically, I don't come from it, but I have a great many New England influences in my own background." For a while each of them volunteered their own observations about those influences, touching upon subjects including thrift, honor and strength of character. After a while Grace knew a fair amount about the young man. He worked for a leading executive search firm, and was flying home from a business trip to the Continent and Great Britain. Realizing that he knew precious little about her, he asked about her trip. "I'm going home, too," Grace responded, "to visit my family in Philadelphia, which is where I came from originally. I will stop in New York, where I also lived, and then I have to attend a board meeting on the Coast." No matter how long she'd been away, Grace still called California and the West "the Coast" just as she had always done and as everyone in show business does.

"Where do you live now?" the young man asked. Without knowing Gracie, he had no way of realizing how that innocent question delighted her.

"In Monaco," she answered simply.

"That's interesting," the man observed. "I do a lot of traveling in Europe, but I've never been to Monaco. How long have you lived there?"

"Twenty-four years," came Grace's reply.

"You must like it!" the man exclaimed. Grace nodded emphatically. "Tell me about it," her neighbor urged. So Grace tried to describe Monaco to the young man who, like herself nearly three decades earlier, had left his safe family nest to go off and make his fame and fortune in the Big Town. By now, it had become apparent to each of them that they shared a sense of humor which made both of them enjoy the conversation, whoever held it for the moment.

"Well," said the fellow, "it looks as though we'll be stuck together for the next few hours. My name is Jeffory FitzGerald. What's yours?"

"Grace," she answered succinctly, and then because he obviously was waiting for a second name, added, "Grace of Monaco." Jeff FitzGerald had not for one instant ever suspected who was in the seat next to him. When he realized it, he politely told the Princess it was a great pleasure to meet her and went right on with their former conversation as though nothing had been changed. Every subject they touched upon led to another of equal interest. Jeff was twenty-one years younger than Grace, not much older, she reminded him, than some of her children about whom she spoke at great length. But like men even younger and more foolish as well as those who were older and wiser, Jeff probably fell a little bit in love with Grace on that flight.

CHAPTER 19

Coming Round the Bend

When the Eighties began, I was in my late forties, still racing about with my own overloaded schedule without doing any serious self-questioning. But two things happened in 1980 which started to change that.

On March 13, I drove to a hotel in Anaheim where the Contractors' State License Board was holding one of its monthly two-day meetings and public hearings. Don had never been to a CSLB meeting before and decided he would drive down to join all of us for dinner after the first day's session and remain overnight to see me chair the Friday meeting. Toward the end of the second long day, Don signaled me that he was leaving the room to go upstairs, collect our belongings and check out. Once I concluded the official session, I waited for him to return, chatting animatedly with my co-workers and friends near the door. Looking up, I spotted Don heading across the lobby toward me. I knew instantly that something was terribly wrong.

When Don finally spoke, he said, "Al's been shot. He's in the hospital in New York in critical condition. Amy and Bob are there now. I said we'd start driving home and call when we get near the airport in case we should just get on a plane and go." Al Lowenstein had been shot in his Manhattan law office by Dennis Sweeney, who had worked for him and idolized him during the student movement of the Sixties. I knew that Dennis had become seriously unbalanced and had even seen him with Al a year or two earlier in New York, when I tried to convince Al there was nothing he could do to save Dennis.

When we tried calling the hospital from Anaheim, we couldn't get through, so we decided to drive home, pack and leave on the first flight the following morning. Driving my car up Rodeo Drive in Beverly Hills, I heard on the radio those persistent beep-beep-beeps that tell you an urgent bulletin is about to interrupt the broadcast. Then the solemn announcement came: "Former Congressman Allard K. Lowenstein has died in a New York hospital at the age of fifty-one after suffering multiple gunshot wounds earlier today."

Don and I flew east the next morning for the funeral. It was a weekend of almost intolerable shock and sorrow for a great many people, and some moments from it are still as clear to me as though they had occurred yesterday morning. I was an honorary pallbearer at Al's funeral, which was held at Central Synagogue. We arrived to see several thousand mourners unable to gain access to the rite because of overcrowding. As we passed them in the streets, nearly every stranger needed to stop us in the penetrating March wind to tell us that Al had been their own, personal best friend.

Inside, under the immense vaulted ceiling while Peter, Paul and Mary sang some of Al's favorite songs, I pondered how so many individuals from all walks of life could have personally felt so close to Al. Don grasped my hand while we joined the congregation to sing "Amazing Grace" through our tears.

Throughout that night and the next cold day, flying to Washington to bury Al on a slope under a tree at Arlington National Cemetery near the Kennedy memorial, where his old friends were interred, and flying home that night with a 103-degree temperature to my fluish sickbed, I knew I would have to start thinking of time in a new way. Four months later I was also forced to recognize more about my powerlessness than I had ever hoped to learn.

There was another two-day session of the Contractors' Board, this one in Long Beach, where I would preside as Chairman for the last time. My fellow board members had planned a tribute dinner for me on the night between the meetings, as well as a congratulatory ceremony for the second day's session. Don and our children were driving down to Long Beach to attend both events. My dinner was held at an Italian restaurant near the shore, at a long table prepared for us in a private room. My pregnant middle daughter, Vicki, was seated far at the opposite end of the room. Married for two years, Vicki had been working for a business management firm, and had been studying for her accountancy board exams. I had watched her slow transformation from a beautiful, fun-loving, energetic girl into a beleaguered matron, old before her time, disgruntled, overworked and unappreciated not only by others but by herself.

Glancing at her frequently down the length of the table, I realized that she also looked distant, frightened, ashen and thin. When dinner ended and everyone gathered round me to say good night, I looked down to see Vicki's arm next to mine. It was alarmingly narrow, gray, and bloodless, as though all life had been drained out of it. Not long afterwards, the truth became known. Vicki, who had dabbled with drugs since high school and had used them to stay up late for studying or partying at college, had become addicted to Quaaludes.

It is nearly impossible to confront one's child when she is adult, married, living away from home and self-supporting. When I tried to discuss her problem with her, Vicki inevitably dismissed me or insisted that she only took halves of pills. I was unable to convince Vicki that if other Quaalude users took whole pills and maintained stability and she took halves and walked into walls, the second piece of information was the only fact that should govern her concerns, but the more I talked, the further away from me she grew. From that time on, no matter what else was happening in my life, no matter what other successes accrued, I was consumed by a sense of failure for not having given Vicki enough self-esteem, and by a sense of impotence that I could in no way help her to recover.

In autumn 1981, I called Grace from an office apartment we had rented in New York. By then, Vicki had been through a full-term pregnancy and had delivered our first grandchild, Jason Colombetti, on September 21. She seemed better, so when Grace asked me how the children were, I said, "Wonderful!" We gurgled for a few minutes about Jason, before talking about the sadness of Bill Holden's death near to the time of Jason's birth.

"The Lord giveth and He taketh away," we remarked simultaneously.

Telling Grace that He seemed busier taking away than giving, I mentioned my old friend Cappy Yordan Badrutt Hand, whom Grace had known in Paris, St. Moritz and Monte Carlo. Grace said she had heard that Cappy was ill and asked what was happening. "Oh, Grace," I moaned, "Cappy's had one serious abdominal cancer surgery in Boston already. Yesterday I talked with her in Boston, where she's been hospitalized again. Her voice is only a pitiful wisp, and her husband confesses there is not much more time to go and nothing else to be done."

There was a long, weighted pause between us. "Time is precious," Grace noted solemnly.

"I've been thinking about that a lot, recently," I concurred. "Only I'm still rushing around trying to get too much done in too few hours. Now, though, losing Al Lowenstein and with Cappy so sick (I didn't mention Vicki's problem, which I prayed had ended), I realize that though I love my work and thrive on my schedule, I really miss being able to spend time with my friends."

"Well, Judybird," Grace cooed, "even you, the baby of the bunch, will be coming up to the big 5-0 soon. I've said this before, but getting to that age is what convinced me I had to add to my life whatever it was I'd feel sorry about missing if I died tomorrow."

It was my sadness, or perhaps that and the dirty gray rain that came streaking down my East Side Manhattan windows, which made me aware of how much Grace and I had shared since we'd met each other, and of how much our pride still demanded we keep from each other. Suddenly, that polite space, respectful as it was always meant to be, seemed like a waste of our time. "I love Don very much," I blurted out without any intention to do so, "and I've not even truly said this to him nor anyone, but I'm not sure I can go on living with him for the rest of my life if things keep going the way they are now." Grace said nothing, allowing me to continue. "I can't imagine wanting to be with anyone else, but I'm just not sure I can keep living with Don."

"Would you like to tell me about it?" Grace inquired, adding politely, "You don't have to."

"I'm not sure I understand it myself," I admitted. "But most of the wonderful things between us seem to have deteriorated on a slow but steady downhill slide."

"That happens a lot after the first glow of a new marriage fades," Grace offered.

"Thanks, Gracie," I responded a bit sarcastically, "but we've been together fourteen years! It's something else. A few months ago, after a terrible evening at our friends' beach house in Malibu where Don had too much to drink, we fought all the way home in the car and kept on with it in our bedroom. When we were all fought out, Don was sitting on the ottoman in our bedroom as I sat at the bottom of our bed facing him. 'It's got to have something to do with your drinking,' I told him. 'Your drinking or your marijuana, or both. For years you were a person whom I loved, respected and admired. But the booze and pot have changed you. I still love you, but I don't like or respect or admire you anymore, and that's a terrible way to feel about your husband.' "

"What happened?" Grace asked.

"Don thought for a while longer, then he lifted his head, looked me straight in the eye and asked outright, 'Do you think I'm an alcoholic?' The last thing in the world I wanted to do was label him that way," I told Grace, "and I'm not even sure that I know now what an alcoholic is since most of the ways we see alcoholics don't at all describe Don accurately, but he had asked me a straight question and I had to nod yes."

"Oh, God," Grace sighed deeply, her genuine sympathy evident in her voice, "how awful, how painful . . . for both of you. What are you going to do?"

"I don't know if there's anything I can do," I admitted. "I've shoved it all under the rug for so long, I suppose I could just keep busy and do that again, but it seems insane not to take time to address the most important thing standing between us, and between Don and the kids right now."

"Insane is a good word for it . . . isn't that the way, though, that most marriages go?" she asked rhetorically.

"But ours didn't for so long, that's just the thing. Now when we talk, I don't even seem to be talking to Don most of the time, but to a version of him manufactured by the pot or alcohol. I don't know what else I can do other than to stay or go, and I'm not sure I have enough time to really be able to stay, if you know what I mean."

"I do," Grace answered directly. "You know I do."

The late autumn of that year was weighted with an oppressive sadness in Beverly Hills. Though I was accustomed to feeling elated around November 24, when Nina's birthday came, I knew that it would inevitably be followed by the melancholy I always felt when my mother's birthday, November 29, arrived. In 1981 that date took on a new significance, for it was the day Natalie Wood drowned, and the town clung together in sorrow. Hollywood can be a fierce and bitter community, but nowhere do I recall it being more close-knit and comforting than at Bob Wagner's house in those days following Natalie's death. Stefanie Powers and I were old friends and neighbors. She had to bear the loss of Bill Holden two months earlier and now Natalie's death as well. Late one cold evening we talked for hours together about how slender the thread is that binds us all to life, and about the alcoholism that had plagued Bill throughout his own lifetime. Once again Don and I had not had time to talk before I left town for another Contractors' Board meeting in early December. Our last real discussion had been the one when he asked if I thought he was an alcoholic and I had finally admitted I did. My last thoughts on the subject had been shared with Grace—that Don was powerless and so was I, except for deciding whether to stay or go. But there was something else that could be done, and it was only Don who could do it.

When he picked me up at the airport two days later, Don noted casually, "Here's a new expression neither of us has heard before—high-bottom drunk." I looked at him quizzically. "That's what I am," he explained. "A high-bottom drunk is one who never really gets to the lowest kind of bottoms before deciding to stop using. I'm a recovering alcoholic," my husband announced, adding, "and a recovering addict." For a moment a rush of joy raced through me. Then I wondered if Don had simply heard all these expressions from a close friend who had just celebrated his first-year birthday in Alcoholics Anonymous. If it was only AA lingo Don was spouting, how would this prove to be any different from the times before when Don—even without urging from me or our children—had simply stopped drinking or smoking for several months? "I joined AA last week," Don went on, as though reading the suspicions in my mind. "I have to do my 90 in 90," he said, explaining his intention to attend three months' worth of meetings, one meeting each day, "and though I know I have to do this the way all other alcoholics or addicts do it—one day at a time—I seem to have lost all interest in drinking or smoking pot."

We had made a life together based on our mutual knowledge that there simply are no guarantees, that for ourselves individually and the two of us together, everything worked only if we worked at it one day at a time. But more than twenty-five hundred of those days have passed since that night, and my husband has never used a mood-altering substance again. Neither of us, though, has taken for granted the ease with which he relinquished his habits. Just as surely as any other AA member who has to struggle each day to refrain from his addictive disease substances, Don will be a recovering alcoholic and marijuana addict for the rest of his life. The "ism" of the disease is sometimes harder to beat than the substance itself. And though I joined Al-Anon for the families, friends and co-workers of those with addictive problems, it would be a long time before I was able to change the role I had so assiduously designed for myself in the dysfunction of our family.

I am always aware of two things about Don's courage. One is that he gave his own life back to himself and that allowed me to stay married to him and still have mine back, and that that same process began to evolve for our children as well. The other is how quickly he responded to the problem once we had been honest enough together to call it by its rightful name. Sitting in my first Al-Anon meetings, or at AA meetings I've attended in the years since, I am always struck by the same thoughts. What would have happened if I had been willing to say openly what I felt earlier? It took Don only two months to do the one thing that could solve the problem. If I'd had the courage to confront it before, might he not have joined AA sooner? Even when we did confront it, it was Don who raised the question head-on, not I. None of that troubles me any longer. In all of the twelve-step recovery program meetings, you hear a lot about spirituality, about a "higher power." Every member, even the agnostic and atheist among us, works hard to accept the existence of that higher power, to define it for his or her self, and to understand its place in his or her own life. That power is affirmed for me at each meeting, in each conversation I share outside meetings with friends or even acquaintances. For in those intimacies, I find constant proof that what we all dreamed of as children and later set aside as the fantasies of our youths is true. We can live on this planet together without hierarchical manipulation, supporting ourselves and one another with rigorous honesty and unconditional love. Do we deserve it? Of course we do. We deserve the pleasures we are able to create no less than the pain, not only for others but for ourselves. And it was precisely that subject which constituted the most intimate conversation that Grace and I shared in the nearly thirty years that we had known each other. It was to occupy our friendship until it was interrupted, and would—even then—last longer than life itself.

It was in that same year that Sally Richardson did an amazing thing. Beekman Downtown Hospital, where she had worked in Volunteer Services for several years, decided to merge with another hospital. Because of seniority regulations, Sally was unable to retain exactly the position she had designed for herself and executed so successfully. An uptown hospital, where the work would have been more palatable, was seeking her services, but Sally suddenly had a revelation. It had been nearly thirty years since she had acted professionally, and even so long ago her career had been modest and difficult to pursue. For five or six years recently, she had worked in her amateur theatre company in New York. What dawned upon Sally was that now that her kids were grown and her husband was accustomed to her having a real career, she ought to go and have the one she had always wanted. Well into her middle age, with no recent resumé other than as an active amateur, Sally Parrish Richardson became a professional actress again. Though she fully realized her hospital career guaranteed her a regular income and regular hours, and that her new career move was speculative in the utmost, she believed fully that she had talent to contribute to the theatre which she loved and ought to get out and start contributing it. And so she did. Before long she was being cast in rewarding projects!

Every now and then, Grace would fill me in by phone on the comings and goings of the other bridesmaids. All were accounted for save Carolyn, whose whereabouts were only rumored. We had been told she had remained in Philadelphia, consumed with anger that the young man who had been driving when Robin was killed had gotten off so easily. We had alternately heard that she had a room there, was living with friends, or was still in a Catholic shelter. Another story held the same set of possible details, but placed Carolyn outside New York. Malcolm, we knew, was living in a gatehouse on the estate of friends on Long Island.

The year 1981 was also the one in which Grace and Rainier celebrated their twenty-fifth wedding anniversary. By then Grace had hurled herself headlong into a schedule that would have felled a twenty-year-old. In September of the previous year, one week on Grace's calendar looked like this:

Sat., Sept. 6th	Founder's Society, Detroit, Michigan
Mon., Sept. 8th	Tennessee Performing Arts Center, Nashville
Wed., Sept. 10th	Duke University, Durham, North Carolina
Thurs., Sept. 11th	Johns Hopkins University, Baltimore, Maryland
Sat. and Sun., Sept. 13th & 14th	International Poetry Forum, Pittsburgh, PA
Mon. and Tues., Sept. 15th & 16th	Dallas Theatre Ctr., Dallas, Texas

Those dates were all for poetry readings. Between these engagements Grace popped into Los Angeles or wherever her Fox board schedule took her, joined the Honorary Board of the Salk Institute planning lectures and recitals, and stopped in New York, where she stayed with Vera Maxwell. Apart from the more formal occasions engendered in Manhattan for her visits, there were always dinners planned by Vera, whom Grace adored, and nights out on the town with old and new friends.

Her ever more frequent trips to America prompted Grace to make two decisions in 1981. One, that it made sense for her to establish a family apartment in New York. The other, that she wanted to create the Princess Grace Foundation-U.S.A. in order to assist emerging young artists in the fields of theatre, dance and film throughout the country of her birth.

Grace had begun to loosen up her life to make time for other things—for new attitudes. In some ways she grew more relaxed and supple, in others not. In a 1981 article in the Trust Houses *Forté* private publication for its own hotels, in an article entitled "Princess Grace, The Woman Behind the Fairy Tale," when asked about Caroline's divorce, she responded, "I wish I could have done something to prevent this heartbreak, but we can only do so much as parents . . . and then our young have to make their own experiences." Yet at the same time Grace made the statement, she could still not really let go of Caroline nor be unconcerned about her image.

Divorced, with a degree in psychology, Caroline grew intent upon pursuing her identity and potential through advancing her writing work rather than through another marriage. Caroline sought Grace's permission to study in London. She proposed to share an apartment there with a girlfriend, but Grace forbade the move. Though her oldest child was twenty-three and intelligent beyond her years, Grace believed it was still necessary to maintain the image that girls like Caroline did not simply go off and live with a friend in a foreign city, away from home. It was an odd decision for Grace, who four years earlier had spoken to me about wanting her daughter to develop her own identity, wishing she would not so quickly give herself over to a husband whom she felt could never make her happy. It was an odd decision, too, for a woman who, at that very moment, was finally untethering her own wings to take flight on her own career once again.

Her own artistic pursuits were compelling Grace forward, though, on a dozen fronts. In the autumn of 1981 she wrote to Bill and Sandy Allyn, inviting them to spend a week or more at the Palace in Monaco for the annual Circus Festival, which Rainier had created and so dearly loved. Upon their acceptance, Grace wrote again suggesting the Allyns stay an extra four or five days so they could be with her at the gala opening of one of her long-cherished dreams, The Monte Carlo Théâtre de Princesse Grace. Bill and Sandy had no doubt about Grace's devotion to the theatre and her plans to work in it in one capacity or another.

During the Circus Festival of 1981, the last pre-Christmas season of Grace's life, she and Rainier were surrounded by houseguests with whom they had enjoyed long friendships. Cary Grant and Barbara were at the Palace. From London came Fleur Cowles with her husband Tom Meir; and Rainier's chum Richard Bryant with his Lady Veronica Munster. Rainier's stepgrandmother Princess Ghislaine was present, as were Gant Gaither and the Allyns from America.

As usual, circus week was a busy time of parties and performances. When it concluded Grace took Bill and Sandy to tour the about-to-open theatre that had been named for her. Recalling all the cramped, empty spaces that she and Bill had used as actors in their early careers, Grace was particularly pleased to show off the spacious and well-equipped dressing rooms she had arranged. At three in the morning at the opening night party, she said to her table companion, Dirk Bogarde, "Bill and I acted together years ago in *Ring Around the Moon* by Christopher Frye." Bill Allyn was astonished then to hear Grace throw lines from the play across the table to him. Finding Bill's memory as good as her own, Grace was delighted to recite whole scenes back and forth, to the amazement of her other guests.

Within the next nine months following the opening of her theatre, Rita, Sally, Bettina, Maree and I all saw or spoke with Grace for the last time. Grace invited Rita to join her in the spring of 1982 when the Annenberg Institute of Communications honored her with a film tribute and retrospective in Philadelphia. As Rainier was unable to be with Grace for the occasion, Jeffory FitzGerald and other friends had motored down with her from New York. Many of Grace's former co-workers had been assembled for the benefit evening, among them Jimmy Stewart, whose remarks that night moved Grace to tears when she repeated them to me by phone.

For several years Grace had been battling and then succumbing to overweight. (The tabloids and later biographers would attribute her puffiness to alcoholism. But though Grace did like her glass or two of champagne, it was her caviarism that got to her, along with her love of other rich foods in abundant quantity.) In the early Seventies, I had told her Nina's expression for herself during the heavy periods of her childhood when she'd see too much girth in the mirror. "Blimposaurus Rex!" Grace exclaimed, recalling one of those Nina-isms. "Tyrannosaurus Blub!" she added, remembering the other, after I said I'd seen her photos from Philadelphia. Though I told her she looked gorgeous and glowing, I had to admit that her face looked more bloated than I'd ever seen it and I said so. "I've had this same ghastly cold for months," Grace moaned, and I could hear it even as she mentioned it. "Even when the worst of it subsides for a bit, it never really goes away. Have you ever felt permanently bloated . . ." I started to interrupt to answer in the affirmative, but Grace completed her own question, ". . . in the head?" Weight was on Grace's mind a lot in those days, not only her own weight but also the trimness of her friends. Jeffory FitzGerald had also put on heft during the two years they had known each other, so in letters or cards she mailed in from around the world Grace would peptalk him into taking and keeping it off. "Watch the lunch routine," she cautioned, ". . . iced tea instead of beer." Then she promised to be so thin by the time of her next U.S. arrival that she'd need to wear a red carnation so Jeffory would recognize her.

Over the years we had all grown accustomed to Grace's repeated observations about tyranny and repression wherever it was occurring in the world. But in the early Eighties she grew more candid about her broader sense of political manipulation. In one 1981 letter she'd spoken about the French election news and ". . . these phony politicians carrying on with their mud-slinging and their empty phrases . . . such a bore!" She wrote the letter while dining alone in Paris, ". . . surrounded by half-empty suitcases, piles of unanswered mail and trying to make sense on the telephone . . ." and had just finished eating ". . . fish and spinach and half an apple all by myself." Every horizon, every vista had seemed to open for her, all of the ones she had shut down or shrunk in the first half of the prior decade. The personal tribute in Philadelphia was an overwhelming experience for her, confirming that she had really acted in a body of film work, that she had been good and was always getting better. Throughout the evening, Grace took Rita firmly by the arm and fairly pulled or shoved her whenever a photographer approached, wanting to be sure that Rita was in the shot, generously insisting that this night was for all her friends and co-workers.

There was another such 1982 night in New York when Hildy Parks, whom Grace had known as an actress in their youth, and her husband, Alex Cohen, produced the Night of 100 Stars benefit. Calling me from the Helmsley Palace, where all the out-of-town celebrities were being housed, Grace giggled with surprise and delight. "You should see this suite, Judybird! You wouldn't believe the size of it. You could fly in and we could get bowling balls or bicycles and just play forever without running out of room!" After marveling again about Elizabeth Taylor's beauty, Grace told me how cozy she had been made to feel by so many new and old show business pals. Visiting with Sally on that New York trip, Grace told her it had been "like a great love-in." And it was on another trip to New York that year when, on the last day they were ever to spend together, Maree and Grace did something they had never done in all the years of their friendship. Having finished lunch at a small East Side German restaurant with Rainier, Albie and Howell Conant, the two old friends strolled together toward the corner. There, on Lexington Avenue, they kissed each other goodbye. Maree crossed the boulevard to head toward Fifth Avenue and some shopping. Grace waited for the light to change so she could continue south to a meeting. They had been friends for forty years, but for the first time—and for no known reason—both Maree and Grace turned at the same instant to catch one final glimpse of each other.

It was not, though, news of Grace's activities, nor my own, nor even news of others' comings and goings that tied Grace and me together during 1982. Instead, it was a single line from the last letter she ever wrote me, dated two days into the new year, which began the conversation that was to last nine months, until a day that following September when time ran out.

Grace had gone to Switzerland with her family following the Christmas holidays in Monaco. From her home in Gstaad she had written exactly the kind of letter I had come to expect from her throughout the years. It was filled with updates about her children, a compassionate note about the current crisis in Poland and an enthusiastic report on the new Princess Grace Theatre.

Along with her other friends, I had come to understand that Grace's letters were not the place where she could speak most confidentially. It seemed that she wrote with an ever-present awareness that what she put on paper might one day fall into unknown hands. Thus she always concentrated on chatty topics which, if ever they were to be seen by strangers and made public, could not be used to expose any matter that might embarrass her.

The most personal aspect of Grace's letters was always the style of them. They were written in sentence fragments, punctuated loosely, the way one would punctuate spoken thoughts, with equally casual attention paid to the use of capital letters, paragraphing and other grammatical conventions. They read the way Grace talked, so that, regardless of content, they always overflowed with her familiar warmth and coziness.

If the letter was of any length, however, somewhere within it Grace would usually drop a single line that told you more about what was really on her mind at that moment than a whole dissertation could have. Though the letters were offhand and couched in humor, I had learned to interpret these enigmatic lines like divining rods that would lead me nearer to Grace's soul. Her January 2, 1982 letter gushed about a recently received photo of our new grandson, Jason. It told me that her family had gone off skiing while Grace was lazing by the fire. Then, almost as an afterthought, Grace had added, "The menopause with its 'angry jaws' is catching up with me."

In the month or so that followed my receipt of that letter, I phoned her. "Grace," I said almost as soon as we had finished our hellos, "exactly what are the 'angry jaws' of menopause you said in your last letter were catching up with you?"

"It's not so much physical symptoms," Grace answered, "it's more an attitude, a feeling or an unexpected set of responses, you know what I mean?" Telling her that I didn't know and hadn't yet experienced anything like what she was describing, I asked her to continue. "I find I'm not as patient as I used to be, not with Rainier nor the children, not with others around me, even my friends, and I'd have to say even myself." I listened but said nothing, so Grace went on. "It's a kind of selfishness. I get rather testy and demanding for my own sake in a way I've never been before. I feel a bit mean and I don't like it."

"What makes you so sure it's menopause?" I asked.

"Well, don't you remember your mother or her friends getting weird that way when we were younger?"

"I do," I agreed, "but when I look back on what they were talking about when they were going through 'the change,' as it was so delicately called, and even when I think about what you've described as your own symptoms, I don't know that it has much to do with hormones and some mysterious 'angry jaws' afflicting women as it does with just the next natural cycle of life at this age."

"What do you mean?" Grace asked.

"I think it's natural that most of us committed our adult lives after we married to a lot of nurturing, caring and doing for others. We started with our husbands and our homes, and when the kids came we went for one helluva haul putting them first in every decision. I heard Mort Sahl say on a TV interview recently, 'When you have a child, you form a partnership with God' . . ."

"How wonderful!" Grace exclaimed. "And how true."

"Mort said another remarkable thing on that same interview," I added. "Speaking about why he felt marriage was perhaps the bravest act two people could jointly enter, he said, 'Women marry men hoping they'll change. Men marry women hoping they'll never change. Both are inevitably disappointed.' . . ."

"How about that for the story of all our lives?" Grace asked.

"That's just the point, Grace. Things change and we change unless we're stuck, and that's when we feel quite bonkers. We're supposed to change, not to try to stay in the process of life without affecting it and being affected by it. We just got out of the habit of ever thinking of ourselves first, so we have to learn again how to do it gracefully when it's appropriate. And we have to sort of edge our husbands and our kids into the old 'turnabout is fair play' game. I don't think it's selfish to begin to hope that it's now time for others to consider us. Not because we're old or doddering . . ."

"Speak for yourself," Grace interjected with dark humor.

"No, that's just it, Gracie. We've lived through the cycle of all these years gladly putting everyone else first. You, more than any of us, have made a career of it. There's nothing to feel guilty about just because, at this age, it's the natural time to feel that you—every now and then—get to come first."

"But, Judybird, all our lives we've heard of women getting this way during menopause. I'm sure you remember all the same talk I did behind cupped hands at the dinner table."

"I remember it all, Gracie," I concurred. "Only it strikes me that I don't hear as much about it today. Sure, part of that may be hormones. But another part, I think, is that more people accept the fact that the natural cycle of life changes naturally at this age. Mostly, as I remember it, those women they used to say were going 'gaga with the change' were only saying very sane, rational things. My mother wanted to do something meaningful for herself, in her own terms. She loved to sing, so when she hit menopause she began studying singing more seriously, even thinking about where she might sing other than in her own living room for herself and her voice teacher. My father thought she was a little looney, even though he never exactly said that, but you could see him wondering if she projected launching a career as a middle-aged chanteuse, perish the thought. I remember friends of hers wanting to go to work or back to work and their husbands thinking they were losing it. They sent women to sanitariums in those days, I think, just because they decided at that point in their lives to say what they wanted to say, or grew annoyed when nobody else listened."

"I never thought of it that way," Grace admitted. "I'm going to do that now, though, and maybe I'll find it's not all such a big deal."

We spoke again over the summer three or four times, and on a flight to New York, I wrote a twelve-page letter to Grace filled with personal observations based on the same theme. In every call, we talked about the "angry jaws" of menopause and specifically whether what Grace was feeling was the result of them snapping at her or of something else. "I love New York," Grace told me on one call. "I think I've missed it ever since I moved to Monaco, and I'm thrilled every time I get the chance to go back. Part of it is that in New York I'm able to be more anonymous, walk around and do the things I did when I was young without everyone gawking at me." Someone had recently confirmed to both of us that Carolyn Reybold had been living for a time in a women's shelter and Grace added, "Isn't it odd that there's something about Carolyn's life I actually think of enviously? Please don't take that wrong," Grace cautioned, "I know it might sound awful and insensitive, but the thought of just getting up every day and doing what that day brings you sounds wonderful to me in certain ways. I've also watched street people in New York and Paris and envied them, so I must be going 'gaga with the change.' "

"Oh, Gracie," I sighed, "that's not gaga. You just want a kind of privacy you haven't been allowed for nearly three decades. You just want to do for you because you feel like doing, and not think about the entire universe as your responsibility the way you have for so long. That's not gaga either."

There was a very long silence before Grace spoke again. "It scares me," was all she said. But when I answered nothing back, she asked, "Why, in God's name, should it scare me so?"

"I think that 'in God's name' is precisely why it does scare you," I offered.

"What?" Grace asked, as though she'd not heard me correctly.

"Let's face it, Gracie, on this one we've got two differing POVs," I noted, using the Hollywood abbreviation for points of view. "I can't stop thinking that comes from the fact that I'm not Catholic and you are. What was that expression we heard from Ricardo Montalban or

Gant Gaither that made us howl back when Gant produced *Seventh Heaven?*"

Grace recalled it immediately, now knowing where I was heading. "A piece of the true Cross!" she said, laughing both at the phrase and at the notion that I was insinuating it described her.

"The Church," I continued, "ain't exactly the place you go to get the message that a swell time on earth should be had by one and all." Grace giggled. "Our friend, the novelist Peter S. Beagle, wrote a book once in which he had a young man talking about the value our society placed on suffering. The character said something like '. . . it's almost as though we see billboards saying, Suffering Is Good for You. Get Some Today!' Well, I think there's a lot of that in your own Catholic background, the notion that you only prove your worth by sacrificing yourself to some cause or person larger, greater and more worthy than yourself."

Grace was at first abashed, as we rarely had talked about our religions in previous years. "Do you really think I think that?" she challenged.

"I do," I answered truthfully. There was another long silence, while I thought she might be gathering herself for a rebuttal.

"You're right," Grace said softly.

"There's another thing, too, that I suspect you're going through which we all experience in transitions. And that's the 'ohmygod-if-I'm-not-all-this-I'll-be-all-that' syndrome."

"I don't know what you mean," she answered.

"I don't know about you," I elaborated, "but when I decided I was going to put my foot down about certain things, I feared I'd be this hideous, grasping, demanding shrew . . . just the kind of person I've always loathed."

"Exactly," Grace concurred.

"But neither one of us, Gracie, could be that, not ever. We just don't got the equipment."

"You mean we go so far overboard in one direction fearing that if we try to balance that out with another side, we'll become what we've always despised?" Grace asked, but I could tell from the way she said it that it was more a confirmation than a question. "Take New York, for example," Grace shifted gears. "I adore it so, and have so many plans for touring and doing other projects in the States, I'm seriously thinking about taking a small apartment there."

"So?" I asked.

"So everyone is going to say I'm leaving Rainier, and abandoning my children and Monaco."

"So?" I offered again. "That's their problem. You can't live all the rest of your life making all our dreams of you come true and not taking care of your own."

"What about your dreams?" Grace asked pointedly. "Do you take care of them, feel entitled to them?"

"I feel entitled to them," I answered. "I think God meant me to take that responsibility. My kids are about the same ages as yours so we both have about the same notion of what we can or cannot do for them from here on in, no matter how much time we'd be willing to give or how much effort. I told you in my long letter that I still love working in our sport and care deeply about it, but I worry that it won't progress past a certain point and that a lot of the internal conflict in the community will ultimately kick it a fatal blow. I still want to work to avoid that, but I am starting to wonder if there are other things I'd like doing at least equally well. And now I have this blessing from Don, who, as I've told you, is in AA."

"It's incredible that he did that so quickly after you both admitted the problem to one another," Grace noted.

"Yes, that's true. And it's already made extraordinary changes in all our lives, in the kids, too. But if Don isn't hooked on alcohol and grass any longer, he still does seem hooked on his rage. He has a regular weekly stag meeting he goes to, and I know he's learning to be more intimate there with men friends than he's ever been able to be in his life. I'm hoping that will help him to be less hard on himself, because if he's not so hard on himself, I think he'll be easier on the rest of us."

"I know three years doesn't mean much at our ages," Grace offered, "but I can't help wondering how you'd feel if you were three years older and my age."

"I don't know where Don will be in three years, because he's six years younger than I, and, of course, I don't know how I'll feel either," I observed.

"Well, remember when the time comes to let me know," Grace insisted.

"I will," I agreed.

"Promise?" she countered.

"Promise," I confirmed, and because I could not help remembering all the letters I'd also promised but had never written, I added, "Not like the letters that never came. And I also promise both myself and you that no matter what happens this year, if I can find you somewhere between 'gigs' I'm going to take time off from whatever I think is so urgent and get to where you are so we can visit this way in person."

"Do you understand what I mean, Judybird, if I tell you that I am absolutely ready for that now?" Grace asked.

"Listen," I cajoled, "I've gotten used to reading your cryptic messages over the years, even when you think you're not sending them out."

"Cryptic!" Grace screamed with delight and surprise. "Oh, my word, have I really been cryptic all the time you've known me? Oh, how delicious, I've never thought about myself as cryptic before." Then like a child who was envisioning herself cast in the school play, Grace added, "Cryptic! What fun! A whole new me." I giggled with her but said nothing. Then, like a child who catches herself out on the wrong limb, Grace grew contrite. "Oh, no, cryptic is the old me, that's what you've been saying, isn't it? Cryptic is what I'm not going to be anymore, what neither of us is going to be when you find me 'between gigs.' "

I started to speak but could hear her laughing to herself about something, so I remained silent. "Between Gigs," she reflected, reciting it as if it were a title of a movie and still giggling in spite of herself, "The Life Story of Grace Kelly . . . oops . . . Princess Grace of Monaco." Other than "Bye bye, sweet Judybird," they were the last words I ever heard her utter.

Grace sent a postcard that summer saying that Rainier was the same, meaning that he had not yet recovered from losing two of his best friends, which, as she'd mentioned by phone, was making him feel old and disheartened, and that "S & P" were still the same, too, but that "S" was going to Paris that fall. The latter note meant that the devoted relationship between seventeen-year-old Stephanie and Paul Belmondo (son of the French actor Jean-Paul Belmondo) was still intense, and that Steph would be moving north, not only to be with him, but to attend the Paris School of Design to study fashion the following month.

When August came, Bettina flew from the States to join Vera Maxwell and Gant Gaither for a traditional Red Cross Gala week at the Palace. Then she, Grace, Rainier, Albert, Caroline and a few other friends departed for a cruise on the *Mermoz* through Norwegian waters. Returning from their cruise, Grace and Rainier sped to Roc Agel to enjoy the abbreviated weeks of their customary summer hiatus there.

The cold that had plagued Grace since the start of the year had grown worse, perhaps on the Scandinavian waters, and when Robert Dornhelm arrived to visit at Roc Agel on Friday, September 10, he found her complaining about it and about allergic problems. Like all of Grace's friends, Robert was accustomed to seeing her make an effort to pull herself out of her doldrums, so he was astonished to find Grace so depressed and unhappy that she seemed unable to conquer her gloom. Though, as friends, both were used to trying to cheer each other on a bad day, the depth of Grace's melancholy so unnerved Robert that he made no overt attempt to help alleviate it. The two were set to meet in Paris four days later, on Tuesday, September 14, to reedit and complete a longer version of *Rearranged* for ABC-TV, and Robert presumed that by the time they did, Grace's spirits would be elevated.

For years nearly everyone who knew Grace had teased her about her driving. It was the one practical thing in life that she had never done well. After one accident in Monaco some years earlier, Grace had nearly abandoned getting behind the wheel and had bought a taxi as a reminder to herself that driving was not her forte. But as her need for a sense of independence had been growing in recent times, Grace had started driving again.

On Monday morning, September 13, the weather greeting Grace when she arose at Roc Agel was as beautiful as though the high summer season of Monaco was still in full flower. Of all the family cars, Grace's particular favorite was the Rover 3500 that she'd had for years. Organizing herself for the eventful autumn that lay ahead of her, Grace had gathered together a whole slew of her dresses that required alteration for her upcoming travels. She had booked an appointment with her local seamstress and piled the clothes into the back of the Rover, stretching them across the seat so they wouldn't wrinkle. Stephanie, too, had things that needed to be transported down the hill, as she was only making a brief stopover at the Palace before setting off for her new adventure in Parisian fashion design. A family chauffeur offered to drive the Rover, but Grace, seeing how full the car had already grown, told him that would not be necessary. He reminded his employer of the serpentine, anfractuous route

that connected Roc Agel to the Palace and suggested her customary apprehension about it would be allayed if he were present for the short journey. "You can run behind us," Grace joked, letting him know that she really didn't want to be coddled, even though he meant well.

Shortly after nine-thirty in the morning, Grace and Stephanie waved to the guard stationed at the Roc Agel entrance and proceeded down the familiar Highway 53. The highway intersects the main route from Menton, where a French policeman acknowledged the two princesses when they passed, with Grace driving, only a few moments later. Grace drove exceedingly slowly, negotiating each hairpin turn with her customary restraint. French truck driver Yves Raimondo had been following the Rover for a while when the Palace came into view, less than five miles in the distance. Two hundred yards from the final perilous hairpin turn, the one where only a partial guardrail bordered the road, Raimondo saw the Rover begin to swerve both to the left and the right, zigzagging so dramatically that it sideswiped the mountain to the left of the road. Instantly presuming the driver had lost attention and could be startled back into vigilance, Raimondo blasted his horn. For a second or two, the Rover realigned itself and its course, but Raimondo suddenly realized its driver was making no preparation to make the dangerous turn that lay directly ahead. The Rover's brake lights did not come on, nor was there any other visible evidence that Grace was trying to control her speed or come to a stop. Raimondo watched in horror as Grace, within the flash of a second or two, drove the Rover with herself and her daughter inside it across the road, onto the bank, and over the side.

They soared out in the air for an instant before careening downward to a depth of a hundred and ten feet. When it landed, the Rover ploughed like a tank through dense underbrush, squashing small trees and shrubs as it somersaulted over and over again before it nearly righted itself and stopped at the edge of a small garden. Within seconds, four neighbors and laborers ran to the car. Steam gushed from its radiators and a figure, that of Stephanie, began to move and crawl through the left side of the car. A neighbor woman took her in her arms when she freed herself, as she sobbed hysterically, "Help my mother . . . my mother is in there . . . get her out!"

Stephanie identified herself just as the others recognized her. Calls were placed immediately to the Palace, an ambulance, the French author-

ities and the Monégasque hospital that bore Grace's name. Two ambulances arrived within moments. It was the difficult task of the attendants to extricate Grace from the car. In the crash, she had been hurled backward. Her feet were near the front window, her body stretched across the back seat toward the rear window. It was that glass which the attendants were forced to break in order to pull Grace out of the wreckage. She was not conscious. A small amount of blood emanated from a gash across the right side of her forehead, and her right leg was badly broken.

Both Grace and Stephanie were rushed to the hospital as Albert and Rainier sped from the Palace to join them there. Mother and daughter were both unable to be seen by either of them. Rainier phoned Caroline at a spa in northern France, asking her to come home immediately but telling her what he had been told—namely, that everyone would be all right. Stephanie's injuries were easier to assess. In addition to the obvious shock, she had suffered a concussion and a vertebra fracture that fortunately had just missed a spot so delicate that damage to it would have paralyzed her for life. Chief of Surgery Dr. C. L. Chatelin was easily able to determine that Grace had suffered a severe fracture of the femur in her right thigh, and that other fractures had damaged her ribs and her collarbone. Grace's breathing was excessively labored, so Dr. Chatelin had her hooked up immediately to a respirator and ordered injections of a fast-acting narcotic called Gamma O.H. Already concerned by what he saw, along with her pallor and apparent lack of reaction to external stimuli, the surgeon tested to see whether any reaction to light could be detected within Grace's eyes. None could, indicating the likelihood that brain injuries Grace had suffered internally were far worse than what could be seen on the outside of her body. Dr. Chatelin summoned Dr. Jean Duplay, an acclaimed neurosurgeon, from Nice, but it was nearly 1 P.M. by the time he arrived, three hours after the accident. Meanwhile Chatelin commenced surgery on Grace to repair what he could, his procedures including the opening of both her thorax and her stomach, the former to clear blood and bring air to her lungs, the latter to curtail internal abdominal bleeding.

Don and I had just finished running a four-day convention in Anderson, Indiana, for several hundred members of the karate community. On Monday morning, September 13, a van took us and our luggage to the Indianapolis airport so we could board a flight for New York, where we

had a hectic two weeks of work ahead of us. Halfway from Anderson, the driver began to turn the dial on the radio, looking for a station he liked. "If there's any news being broadcast, I'd love to hear it," I requested. "I've been too busy to read a paper or even have a clue to what's going on in the real world since we got here."

"Oh, that reminds me," said the young man, "you all know Princess Grace, don't you? Someone told me you're friends." Don and I both said we knew the Princess. "Well, I'll try to find this news for you now," he added, skimming past rock and wailing Western music stations, "but while I was waiting for you, I heard she'd been in some kind of accident." Don's heart must have skipped the same beat mine did, for we looked at each other in terror. "She's okay, though," the driver continued. "Some kinda car accident, but she's okay, just some minor injuries, I think they . . ." but he let the news broadcast he'd found tell us the rest of the story.

It didn't really make any difference where you were, or whether or not you knew Grace that day, for all of us heard the same thing: Sally and Rita in New York; Carolyn and Jyl in Philadelphia, where Jyl was riding high on the success of her roller skating shop, which was booming with the national craze; Maree in Philadelphia, too, at home and getting ready to run errands; Bettina and Lizzie Gray in Massachusetts. Grace had been driving her Rover down the tortuous La Turbie Road we knew so well. Stephanie was in the car with her as the two of them were returning from Roc Agel to the Palace preparatory to Steph's departure for Paris. There had been an accident. It was not described. Princess Grace was in the Monégasque hospital named after her, the one she had worked so hard and long to refurbish and modernize, and would remain there for a few days for observation. She had broken a bone in her thigh, a couple of ribs, and suffered a slight concussion or head wound from the impact of the accident. Princess Stephanie was also hospitalized and was being treated for a neck injury. Otherwise, all was well and we could rest easy.

Once Don and I started breathing normally again, he reached over and took my hand. "You've been promising yourself and Grace a long, close visit somewhere," he reminded me. "She'll probably have to cancel or postpone her trip to Texas for the poetry reading at Lynn Wyatt's. You really should find a way to make time to go and be with her in Monaco while she's recovering."

"You're right," I concurred. "Since she hadn't planned on being there next month anyway, and since it's the slow season in the Principality, it would be a great time to just go and spend a while together. I'll look at my book after we get through the first day or two in New York and call her to set a time."

"Honey," Don said, and I could tell a lecture was to follow, "don't put it off this time. I don't mean to pick on you, but you put off writing and visiting so much over the years. I don't care what's going on that's so important. There has to be time in your life to do this—for you and for Grace. Okay?"

"Okay," I said, and I made a mental note that I would find a way to get to Monaco within the next few weeks, come hell or high water.

In New York, I spent the next morning on calls with athletic commissioners from various states around the country and taking care of other business. At eleven-thirty our sport's publicity representative came by to collect us. At noon we met with Jim Forkan, an *Ad Age* journalist who was doing a PKA story, at the Assembly Steak House on West Fifty-first Street. By two, when Don headed back to the office, I was in Rockefeller Center being interviewed by Will Grimsley of the AP for another story on our sport and its upcoming events.

I had read the morning papers about Grace's accident, forswearing to myself and Don again that I would carve out whatever piece of time worked for her, to visit while she recuperated at home. Hailing a cab, I returned to the office, and while en route, borrowed the driver's early edition of the *Post,* the only Manhattan afternoon paper. Its description of the accident was a bit more lurid, but when you read past the sensational headlines, the news was identical to what we had already heard. Back at work, I returned two dozen phone calls, all the while thinking about Grace. We'd shared a few familiar punch lines over the years and little throwaway sayings related to admonishments doled out by the dancing teachers or musical directors of our youth. I suddenly recalled us standing on the deck of the *Constitution* twenty-six years earlier, when Grace screwed up her own courage and ours for the entrance to Monaco by instructing jovially, "This is it, girls, sing." Between business calls I dialed Western Union. To the operator, I dictated a gag line we had used over the years, plucked from a grab bag of giggling memories, and I knew it would tickle Grace to receive it while her leg was healing. The wire said,

"UP, UP, UP. DANCE, DANCE, DANCE. WILL CALL TOMORROW RE PROMISED VISIT WHILE YOU'RE A CAPTIVE AUDIENCE BETWEEN GIGS. LOVE, JUDYBIRD."

Near five-thirty that afternoon, my oldest daughter, Amy, called. When the receptionist answered, Amy asked her please to ring Don Quine's phone. Amy explicitly asked that only Don's phone should be rung, not mine, and said that if his line was busy she would hold until it cleared. Don was seated at a small round conference table, talking on his line. I was on the other side of the room, making notes about calls for that evening, while my phone sat unused by my side on a beige tweed couch. For some unknown reason, when it rang, it startled me. I picked up the phone. "Mom," Amy said, and I had not been her mother for all those years not to recognize not only her surprise at hearing my voice but the incredible sadness in hers. My heart stopped. "Mom," Amy said again, "are you alone?"

"No," I answered very softly, with the kind of calm you absolutely force upon yourself to prepare for survival when you doubt it most. "No, I'm not alone. Don is here, but on the other phone."

"Mom," my Amy said, her voice cracking with the tears she could not contain, "Grace is dead."

Although the next few minutes are missing from my recollection, others later told me what happened. My husband heard only my deep groan, loud enough to shock him into hanging up instantly. Then I started shaking my head, saying, "No, no, no, no, no, no, no, no, no," over and over again. I spun out of my office door into the hallway, where a multitude of secretarial stations were located, stopping at each desk I passed to beg for a radio, which nobody seemed to have. Picking up the phone and hearing Amy sob the news to him, Don fled down the hallway after me. By the fourth desk, someone asked what I wanted, what was the matter. "The news," I insisted, "I need to hear the news. It isn't true." One of the secretaries I knew well, two desks away, had already heard, though. As I looked up on my way to her, she nodded solemnly in the terrible affirmative. I remember that nod, but that is all, until some time later when I found myself standing in Don's arms in our office. When I could speak, what I remember saying is, "It's not fair. She didn't get to be a grandmother."

While I sat benumbed on that same beige sofa I'd been on a few minutes earlier thinking all was right with the world, Don called Amy back. "Rita," I said, but he was already asking Amy if she'd spoken with Kate Guinzburg. It was Kate who told Amy, as it turned out, and she had also called Rita, who nearly collapsed in the bulging packing boxes surrounding her on the floor of the New York apartment where she'd lived for the past fifteen years. As if by rote, Rita, Don, Kate and I all left immediately for Amy and Bob's apartment on Fifty-fifth and Sixth Avenue, just to cling together and get through the night.

We tried to call the Palace but could not get through. We tried Nadia Lacoste but could not find her. We thumbed through my book looking for numbers for Lizanne and Peggy, Grace's sisters. We spoke with both of them, but like everyone else in the world, they could not make sense of it all, nor even comprehend the reality. We called our other children and the Kanters and Foremans in California, and we talked about going to the funeral. Our first instinct was that we should not go. The grief overwhelming Rainier, Albert, Caroline and Stephanie seemed too private for us to invade.

Nobody—not a one among us—believed that Grace was no longer alive. We were trying to take care of the business at hand, but could not for an instant truly conceive of her death. I remembered the telegram I'd sent a mere few hours earlier. For an instant, I was flooded with remorse, so desperately wishing I could summon it back that I almost did not mention it. Then I told. Told that someone in Monaco was, either in this desolate hour or another, opening an envelope to Grace who lay dead, reading, "UP, UP, UP. DANCE, DANCE, DANCE." Rita did an amazing thing. She started to giggle. "I can't stop myself," she tittered, trying to control her laughter. "All I can think of is that Grace is checking us out right now to see what we're up to, and that hearing the wording of your wire and knowing the circumstances would absolutely make her collapse with laughter." Because I needed to feel less awful, and because I knew that what Rita said was true, I, too, began to giggle. Something about the bleakness of death juxtaposed with the silliness of the message, the paradox of the pain and pleasure combined so coincidentally would have brought forth those giggles that I could still hear ringing in my ears, those Gracie giggles every one of us would be able to hear in our hearts for the remainder of our days.

CHAPTER 20

Too Long a Sundown

At dusk the evening after Grace died, I returned to the exact spot where we had first met, a place I had not visited in the twenty-nine years that had since passed. Don and I had an appointment to meet with the banquet manager of the Plaza Hotel to settle arrangements for a karate reception to be held there the following week. We tried to locate an exit near his office on the Fifty-eighth Street side of the hotel, but taking a wrong turn led us into the reception area just outside the doors of the Grand Ballroom. I was walking a bit ahead of Don and stopped so short he nearly collided with me. "She was over there," I whispered, pointing to the exact place where Jay had introduced us in the receiving line. "It was 1953," I added, recalling the twinkling in Grace's eyes when we'd first caught sight of each other. "My first thought was that she noticed everything, maybe even more than she wanted to see. And inside there," I pointed to the ballroom doors, "she was dancing with Marlon when I first saw her laugh." Don tightened his arm around me.

"It doesn't seem real," we confessed simultaneously before turning to walk away.

It was the same for all of Grace's friends. Bettina had originally learned of Grace's death from her ex-husband Frank, yet only hearing about it over and over from local and national newscasters convinced her that the story was not a morbid hoax. She had spent the first terrible night alone, but on the second, she accepted Lizzie's invitation to drive to her place in Cambridge for dinner. The instant her mother arrived, Lizzie fed her two martinis, each strong enough to sink the *Sheffield*. The next morning Lizzie called Bettina to tell her she had reserved both plane tickets and a hotel room for their trip to Monaco. Bettina kept herself focused by simply folding each of her belongings over and over again before tucking them neatly into her travel bag. She was still worrying about having the right clothes, but when she found herself thinking about it, she muttered aloud, as much to Grace as to herself, "Can you believe it?"

Maree heard of the accident from Grace's sister Peggy, and it was Peggy, too, who phoned to tell her that their Gracie was dead. Maree's eldest, Linda, came over in two seconds flat, and among the many callers who rang in the subsequent hours, one was Virginia Gallico (Grace's Lady-in-Waiting since the death of her noted author/husband, Paul). Virginia invited Maree and her younger daughter, Louise, who intended to go with her to the funeral, to stay with Caroline at Clos St. Pierre, her home near the Palace.

It was John Richardson who had told Sally of Grace's death, only moments before she had to go onstage at the Old Vic Theatre in downtown Manhattan that Tuesday evening. Though her fellow actors could tell she had been crying, Sally continued for the ensuing days to do exactly what Grace would have wanted and expected her to do. She went on with the show.

On the night before Grace's accident, Carolyn had gone to sleep at the Chancelor, an apartment building in Philadelphia where she was staying temporarily. Some years before, Grace had sent her a photo of Stephanie in a pink ballet tutu. During her sleep Carolyn dreamed of a small creature in a fluffy pink outfit accompanied by a larger person. She could not stop the motion of her dream in which both kept tumbling and falling over and over again. The next day, she heard about the accident. And on the day following that, Carolyn knew she needed yet another miracle to add to the one that had pulled her through Robin's death.

On September 16, Rita, Jay and I met at Pan Am's JFK Clipper Club. Looking the same as he had nearly thirty years earlier, Jay was no more able to accept the necessity for this trip than we were. Walking to the plane, we took turns muttering, "It doesn't seem real," as though somehow the words would make the truth go away.

Halfway across the Atlantic, I picked up my neighbor's paper and saw the byline of Grace's friend and co-worker Gwen Robyns. I could not bring myself to read her article and only leafed through its pages as though they were pages of the past. Then my eye caught a small box in the lower corner of an interior double spread. And there it was—a poem written by a child, by the little princess of paradox, declaring a promise of what was to come, a promise on which she had, in fact, more than delivered.

> *Little flower, you're the lucky one*
> *you soak in all the lovely sun*
> *you stand and watch it all go by*
> *and never once do bat an eye*
> *while others have to fight and strain*
> *against the world and its every pain of living.*
>
> *But you too must have wars to fight*
> *the cold bleak darkness of every night*
> *of a bigger vine that seeks to grow*
> *and is able to stand the rain and snow*
> *and yet you never let it show*
> *on your pretty face.*

"Oh, Gracie," I sighed, "only you could have written your own epitaph when you were still a kid."

Jay had reserved a car and drove us from the Nice airport toward the Principality when we arrived on Friday, September 17. We had not discussed which road to take and without warning came to the signs halfway around the Nice harbor that point to the higher roads or to the shore road along the coastal towns. Jay stayed in the lane he was in and drove in silence across the mountains toward Monaco. The three of us realized simultaneously that we were descending the hills on the very road where Grace and Stephanie's accident had occurred earlier that week.

Before reaching the fatal turn, we could see it all ahead of us—the broken guardrail, the mangled trees, the police and the curious onlookers.

Even registering at the Hôtel de Paris hurt, standing at the same desk where we'd stood with such high expectations when we arrived for the first time for *le mariage du siècle.* And there was the same concierge who had winked at us on prior trips to signal that a message or invitation from the Palace was awaiting us in our rooms. Now, all he and we were capable of was a second's worth of eye contact before we were forced to lower our heads solemnly. Once inside my room, I walked to the ceiling-high glass doors, threw them open and stepped onto the balcony to stare at the familiar harbor below. Small lights were just beginning to appear along the lengths of the yachts, but even they could not relieve the gloom and stillness of the frozen, dim day's-end shadows.

We had read that Grace had been lying in state for two days so that every Monégasque citizen could have one last glimpse of their beloved Princess. Within minutes after we arrived, the phone rang. It was Milica Banek's granddaughter, Tessa Kennedy, to tell us that if we hurried, we were expected at the family chapel in the Palace courtyard for our own private moment.

I had seen people I love die before, or seen them only moments after death had taken them. The moment of death feels like riding away on a spirit that takes wing. You gasp from the force of the departure just as you do from the impact of arrival when you witness a birth. But I have always detested open coffins because a stranger has overlaid his or her reality on the person you knew, depriving you of the reality you want to hold in your memory. It was thus with Grace. Our small band formed a single-file line and inched very slowly around her. For an instant, I almost giggled with relief, because seeing Grace this way made her death seem completely unreal to me. She looked gussied up in a way she had never looked in life. "Edith Head and Virginia Darcy would never have allowed this, Gracie," I noted wordlessly. A rather old-fashioned wig had been selected and, of necessity, pulled down over Grace's natural hairline to hide the scar from the head wound suffered during her accident. I wished I could remove the wig and see the scar which would, at least, have been as real as Grace herself.

Grace's right hand lay across her abdomen. Over it and through the fingers on her left hand that covered it coiled a simple, crystal-beaded rosary. Her only jewelry was the plain gold wedding band that had brought her to Monaco twenty-six years earlier.

Back out in the Palace Court of Honor, while the others talked quietly, I stared up at the Galeries d'Hercule where we bridesmaids had stood with the bride on the morning of Grace's wedding. I saw the railing where she had paused to be photographed by *Paris Match* on the first day she and Rainier had met, and where she had hesitated briefly again for Howell Conant to capture her with his camera before setting off on her wedding procession. Whose fault is it, I wondered, that Grace felt so obliged to be so perfect? Ours or her own? A combination of both? Could any of us have expected or hoped for a better friend, a more devoted wife, a more loving mother, a more dedicated princess? What, in God's name, did we want from her? Or was all that had ever mattered only what Gracie had wanted from herself?

Later, as a group of us sat quietly at a table at La Rascasse overlooking the port, it was clear that Monaco was nearly drowning in a mist of tears. No matter where we looked, everything was dulled, as though an invisible veil of mourning had been stretched across the Principality from one end to the other. Only occasionally a sound came from the sea, something wrought by nature that could not be stilled along with the national heartbeat.

Grace's old friend Fleur Cowles Meir had arrived in Monaco from London earlier than any of us. She had tripped on the stairs at her hotel upon arrival, broken her leg, and was resting in a cast at the hospital where Stephanie, too, lay in her great and awful pain. After dinner we drove by so Tessa could visit Fleur and deliver a favorite local melon to her.

When we parked in front of the Princess Grace Hospital, the eerie night stillness was particularly pungent. Rita and I shared the backseat of the car and Jay sat alone in the front behind the wheel. We chatted for a while, but ahead of us, through our front window, the Rock rose upward toward Heaven and toward the Palace bathed in the lights we had come to know and love for their aura of mysterious grandeur and allure. The same thing happened that had been happening for the past three days. "It doesn't seem real," one of us would say. Talk, talk, talk. "It doesn't seem real." Tell this story, no that one, what about the time that. . . "It doesn't seem real." Did you pack your black gloves? "It doesn't seem real." Call me in the morning. "It doesn't seem real."

We had been staring silently at the Palace for three or four minutes when it was Rita's turn. "It doesn't seem real," she noted, as though that thought had just come to her for the very first time.

"I think that's because," Jay began to answer slowly in that precise, thoughtful way Grace had always admired, "for all these years since she left us we've always taken for granted that Grace was over there." Jay was right. Over there. When we were in the States we had learned to expect that she was in Monaco, at Roc Agel, in Paris, in Switzerland, in London or somewhere on the Continent. If she'd been in the East when we were in Los Angeles, then "over there" meant New York or Philadelphia. When we were in New York and she was in Los Angeles, "over there" simply switched coasts. Even when we'd been in Monaco throughout the years, Grace had been "over there" in her Palace. We had been learning to live without Grace since the day she sailed off on her honeymoon with Rainier on the *Deo Juvante,* perhaps knowing that nobody lasts forever and nobody that good ever lasts long enough. "Grace is over there," I thought to myself, repeating Jay's words and finding they gave me comfort, though I did not know any longer exactly where "over there" really was.

When we returned to the hotel that night, and left it again early the following morning, the same throngs of tourists and photographers stood tightly packed across from its front steps and around the Casino Square. Now, though, they waited in respectful silence, looking every bit as numbed as the rest of us. One aging Italian paparazzo whom I'd seen in Monaco for years pushed forward to the front of the crowd when he recognized us alighting from our car. "We are all so sorry," he called out, his voice cracking. "So sorry for everyone."

I had taken my children to see the Cathedral, but had never returned to it for any actual ceremony since the day Grace and Rainier were married there. At nine-thirty the following morning, a solid sea of black-clad mourners sat transfixed, fanning themselves with their programs against the oppressive heat that had already weighted the heavy day. Every familiar face reminded me of a moment spent with Grace. Cary and Barbara Grant, Hjordis Niven (David was already too ill to attend), Lynn Wyatt, Gant Gaither and countless others all sat solemnly, attesting to the years during which their friendships with Grace had been woven through time.

Gradually, a long, separated, slow parade of visiting dignitaries and local officials was led down the aisle, each guest shown to an assigned pew. If there had been a shortage of major presences twenty-six years earlier for her wedding, such was not the case for Grace's funeral. The King and Queen of Belgium had arrived the day after Grace died, the Queen of Spain the day after, as all had been extremely close to Grace, Rainier and their family. The procession included ex-Queen Anne Marie of Greece, Prince Bertil of Sweden, Princess Benedikte of Denmark, Prince Philip of Lichtenstein, Princess Paola of Liège, Grand Duchess Josephine-Charlotte of Luxembourg, ex-Empress Farah Diba of Iran, the Aga Khan and Begum Salima, and the Duc D'Aosta representing the Italian Royal Family. Madame Danielle Mitterrand, wife of the French President, was there, as was Madame Claude Pompidou, widow of the former President of France. Diana, Princess of Wales, walked down the aisle slowly, accompanied by her entourage, looking more beautiful than her pictures had ever made her out to be. Nancy Reagan wore an exceedingly stiff-brimmed black hat, but was without the sparkling eyes and vaguely beatific smile we had come to expect from her on all public occasions. I suspected what I saw on her face was more than merely the solemnity of the occasion, guessing that like almost all other women who had ever known Grace, Nancy (who knew her from their common MGM years) identified with her and felt her loss in an intensely personal way.

At 10:15 A.M. the utter silence that had muffled all the streets in the Principality for nearly four days was challenged briefly by a fanfare of trumpets announcing the procession of Grace's coffin and her family. The ebony box was swathed in a white pall bearing the arms of Monaco. Pink roses had always been Grace's favorite flowers, and four small bouquets of them had been placed atop her casket—one each, I suspected, from her husband and their three children. Dressed and gloved in black, wearing the medals and honors required by this state occasion but offered no solace by his rank, Rainier followed directly behind the casket, his grief so mighty it seemed to weigh him down like a burden he would be charged to wear for life. Completely covered in black, a long lace mantilla descending over her arms and shoulders, Caroline walked to her father's right, fighting back her tears by alternately biting at her lower lip or raising her tongue to her upper lip to prevent it from quivering. Albert walked on his father's left, his sober eyes filled with exactly the sort of committed resolution I had so often seen on the face of his beloved mother. Lizanne Kelly LeVine, Grace's younger sister, was directly behind Albert. Grace's brother Kell followed Rainier, and Peggy Kelly Davis Conlan—Jack Kelly's adored "Ba"—walked behind her niece Caroline. Though cadres of white-uniformed police guards were ready to hold back the crowds, in truth there would be no disrespect shown in the Principality by anyone this weekend. The Monégasques and the visitors mourned as one with Grace's stricken family.

Though I understood precious few of the words, the rites themselves were extremely painful. I tried hard not to stare, but my eyes kept wandering back to the faces Grace had loved best—Rainier's, Albert's and Caroline's. I could not help thinking, too, of Stephanie, lying in a nearby hospital room, her neck in a brace, knowing her mother had died in the accident she'd been unable to prevent. I had intended to do what I'd always done before at funerals—conduct my own private eulogy in my head and heart. Midway through the Mass, though, my high-necked silk blouse and black faille suit, wilted by the damp heat, began to cling to my body. For the first time in my life I felt claustrophobic, could understand why people who suffered from this ailment felt it necessary to stand, scream, run. "It doesn't seem real," I insisted internally. The Archbishop prayed. "It doesn't seem real." Rainier's head, heavy with grief, sunk farther down into his chest. "It doesn't seem real." Albert's pain grew too powerful, and he, too, was forced to lower his chin toward his breastbone. Caroline's face bore not only her own pain but also her father's. It distorted in such anguish that I was forced to avert my eyes.

Then we were all outside and it was over. Fanning ourselves with our programs, we formed a solemn parade back toward the Palace, where dignitaries and friends had been invited to a reception in the West Garden.

Rainier, Caroline and Albert had formed a receiving line just inside the entrance. Albert stood solemnly at the end of the short family grouping. He glanced upward, then to his right, and looked directly at me. If I live to be a thousand I shall never forget that moment when our eyes met, because I knew most assuredly that what I was seeing was a little piece of Gracie's soul. That same sweetness, the undeniable goodness was there in Albie's eyes. The lack of affectation was there, along with the values, the strengths, the humanity, the wonder of a God who could both give us such pure joy and then leave us so bereft. I saw the same confusion every one of us felt, but in Albert's eyes I also saw the man he was becoming, for somehow we knew that this loss was meant to make us all become more of ourselves than we had ever dreamed we could be.

We were not far from the entrance to the original "basement apartment" Grace and her family had occupied for so many years before claiming more of the Palace for their home. There had been many starfilled nights when we had gathered in this garden to enjoy buffet and conversation after the world's most beautiful music had been played in the Court of Honor under soft Mediterranean breezes. There was no breeze today, only the relentless heat of the sun and a binding notion that being together for a few hours would help us get through the day.

Princess Diana sat in the far left corner of the gardens, surrounded by her small entourage. Virginia Gallico took me over to present me, and I could not help staring at the best example of the fabled "English complexion" I had ever seen.

A few moments later someone else repeated a story the Princess had just told about her first meeting with Grace. In March 1981, only eighteen months earlier, Diana made her first public appearance since her engagement to Charles had been announced two weeks before. Prince Charles was patron of the Royal Opera House, Covent Garden, and Grace had flown to London to read from *Theme and Variations* for a gala benefit evening. Diana's entrance had caused quite a sensation with the press, as she was wearing a strapless black taffeta gown with a ruffle and matching ruffled shawl. The Princess said that on this night, the magnitude of how her life had just changed really descended upon her. For the first time she realized that she would never be a private person again. The thought frightened her beyond comprehension. At one moment when she felt quite panicked, Grace—whom she'd met only a few minutes earlier— appeared by her side to ask if she would like to go to the ladies' room. Once the two women were inside at the mirror, something about Grace prompted Diana to open her heart. She couldn't stand it, she told Grace, the way people yelled things at her, spied on her, invaded her every waking moment and even her nightmares. Grace, too, Diana realized, had been subjected to that kind of public scrutiny all her adult life. What could she do? the fledgling Princess near despair asked of her senior counterpart. When she had finished blurting it all out and was in tears, Grace put her arms around Diana, held her and patted her on the shoulder like a mother comforting a child. After a moment Grace backed away a bit, raised her hands and cupped them around Diana's tear-stained face. Grace had a way of cooing reassuring words that was among the most comforting sounds ever emanating from a human voice. "Don't worry, dear," she cooed to the soon-to-be Princess of Wales. Then in the same tone, she added quietly, "It'll get worse." The candor, the kindness and the wit had put Diana straight back on her required course.

"It doesn't seem real," we said over and over again as I strolled around the gardens stopping to talk with Lizanne, with Peggy, with Kell and his pretty new wife Sandy. "It doesn't seem real," Maree, Louise and I said as we hugged. "It doesn't seem real," Bettina muttered when she introduced me to her daughter Lizzie and we stood staring at one another in confusion. And for the most part, it still didn't. A sort of gauzy Felliniesque unreality descended on the gardens. Then an incident occurred which would have tickled Grace. I was crossing the garden to visit with Gant when I passed behind Cary and Barbara Grant, who were chatting with Nancy Reagan. Cary must have seen me coming, as he reached behind with one hand to grab my arm as I passed, gently pulling me around to join the group. I had known Nancy since our children were at John Thomas Dye together, but Cary didn't know that and started to make an introduction. Nancy, however, leaned forward to extend a condolence kiss as greeting. I leaned forward, too. The steely brim of her hard black hat hit me right between the eyebrows, straight across the bridge of my nose. I saw comic book stars and, almost blacking out, began to fall backward. Cary had heard the clang of steel-on-bone and quickly put his hand behind the small of my back to keep me from falling on the grass. Neither Nancy nor Barbara had noticed the accident and kept right on chatting. But as soon as Cary saw I'd recovered, he and I started to shake inside with silent and nearly uncontrollable giggles. Biting our lips to keep from laughing out loud, we turned slightly away from the others. I whispered, "See it now. First Lady decks bridesmaid with brim at Monégasque funeral." For an instant, the reason we were there became way too real. I whispered again, "Would she have loved that or what?"

Before the reception ended, Rita and I promised to meet Maree and Louise Rambo and Bettina and Lizzie Gray after dinner later that night. It was nearing midnight when we strolled across the Casino Square to join our compatriots. Though the mild September air invited al fresco dining, only two or three small tables were occupied outdoors at the Café de Paris. Monte Carlo was unbearably still. Every window of each designer and jewelry boutique had been hung with black draping, as had all the stores and restaurants throughout the Principality. We selected two round tables and wordlessly put them together, rearranging chairs to fit the new configuration. Rita and I were thinking about the four daughters we had between us and wishing we had brought them when we sat down to visit with Maree and her Louise, with Bettina and her Lizzie. "We're missing only Sally and Carolyn," Bettina noted as we ordered coffee and Evian.

Maree and Louise were the only people at the table with news of Carolyn. We four mothers shuddered, recalling her loss of Robin, every heart reaching out to Carolyn across the sea.

"When you first came to Monaco, you were all pretty privileged," Lizzie observed. We four older women nodded, then every one of us made a "so what" gesture at the same time.

"Not that we aren't grateful for it, but it doesn't buy you much, Lizzie—the privilege, I mean. Once you've got a roof over your head, can feed and clothe your family, and get a doctor when someone needs one, the rest is all icing and its importance melts away when the heat is on," I noted. For a while we all talked about that, agreeing it was never "things" we really wanted, only protection from worry, a guarantee that we'd be able to keep ourselves and our families safe. "Nobody's safe," we all said, speaking together again.

"Grace told me only recently," I mentioned, "that she was grateful for what she had but that sometimes—when she saw bag ladies on the streets—she envied their anonymity and their freedom." We sat silently, each with our private reflections.

"Oh, God," Maree sighed heavily. "I never thought we'd make this trip."

"How long ago was it when you all came here first, Mom?" Louise inquired.

"Twenty-six years," we four older women answered simultaneously because we had counted it often over the past few days.

Louise and Lizzie asked us to tell them about wedding week. Each one of us told our favorite stories. As we rambled on, I kept glancing at the two younger women. On the faces of both I saw a growing realization—

their own mothers had really been young once. Were any of us actually what we had formerly appeared to be? And if this was true of us was it also true of Grace? Lizzie finally asked. And though nobody answered her, the series of looks and sighs that circled the table announced that Liz had just asked the master question.

Gradually we began to speak. I noted that even before she met Rainier, I had always thought of Grace as the Princess of Paradox. "Trying to balance your own paradox," I added, "is probably what makes life such a great adventure, no matter how old you live to be." Suddenly all of us were stricken with the same thought, that Grace had only lived to be fifty-two, dying two months before her fifty-third birthday. Though her death had seemed totally unreal for the past ninety minutes, now it became achingly real.

As four o'clock in the morning approached, we talked about the next day. Once our travel plans had been detailed, everyone knew it was time to part. "I don't think I'll ever come back here again," Maree noted solemnly, and all our heads nodded in agreement. We paid the bill. The waiter brought change and for fully five minutes we sat in silence, all facing out to the Casino Square, the port beyond and the Palace beyond that. I could only think of what Jay had said, "She's over there." I kept reassuring myself. We sat quietly for another moment or two. "Say G'night, Gracie," I whispered, using the old familiar Burns and Allen sign-off that had been such a part of our history. We scraped our chairs back and rose slowly all at the same time.

"G'night, Gracie," answered Bettina, Rita and Maree.

Life Goes On

*J*ust as we wound differently, so do we heal in our own ways. Grace's family had their three months of official mourning. The only protection that time offered them was some distance from the public eye. Grace's friends went back to their normal lives. I was only able to grasp the reality of her absence in the method by which we let go and learn anything new of significance. I removed the layers of my disbelief, one by one, until I could gradually accept the fact that "over there" was a place with no telephones.

Mother's Day 1984
New York

Dear Grace,

Somewhere I read that Isak Dinesen told visiting students to "write because you owe an answer to God." Some days like today, though, I childishly feel it's God who owes me an answer. More of that later. . . . Can you believe that after not having written you for so many years I now start writing? Well, I promised when we last spoke in 1982 to let you know how I was feeling about things in three years' time. Though only two years have passed, I'd rather be early with this promised piece of correspondence than as late as I was in the old days. I have huge regrets about the time that passed over the years when my letters might have meant so much to you. Writing now may only mean a lot to me and, if so, I apologize for that selfishness.

So many things and people conspire to make me think of you so often. Eighteen months ago, when I returned to New York after your funeral, Don and I had dinner with Annie and Herb Siegel, and with Polly Bergen and Jeff Endervelt. Annie told us you had agreed to do the Pierre Salinger TV interview the previous summer. She knew you said yes just because you wanted to help her, even though you were already way too busy. By now, everyone has commented on the interview which ran back then, but when Annie told us about it, it was the first time we learned that Pierre had elected to ask you—two months before the accident—how you wanted to be remembered. Odd that he asked that question of one so young. Not odd that you answered ". . . as a decent human being and a caring one who tried to help others."

John and Rupert and other friends organized a memorial service for you on September 29, 1982, at Good Shepherd in Bev Hills, where you used to "hit the rail" when in town. The Grants, the Sinatras and the Stewarts were there, along with dozens and dozens of other pals. (Jimmy was so simple and eloquent when he spoke about you, saying what was in every heart.) This statuesque blond creature made an entrance all in snowy white. Remember Monique van Vooren? We always referred to her by the nickname one of her producers had given her, "Cuckoo the Bird Girl," remember? Brrp. Brrp.

You probably were aware that we celebrated your birthday with Jay, Amy and Bob and Elliott Kastner at "21" on November 12, 1982. It was so strange, Gracie, because as the limo drove me over the Triborough when I arrived in New York that evening, the radio first played "Your Eyes Are the Eyes of a Woman in Love" and followed that with "True Love." But at dinner when Jay raised his glass and said, "To Gracie," I added, almost under my breath,

"over there." You left us all quite mystified, you know. Old John-bones felt as if a steamroller had gone over him, and decided to ask John Huston, who's so much older, how he dealt with the deaths of so many of his friends. "I figure," Huston told John, "that if everybody I know is doing it, it can't be all that bad." Sounds like a great attitude, but I'm not sure most of the rest of us are ready for it. Were you?

Jeffory F., who is *so* young, really had the double whammy. A few months after you left, so did his beloved father. Finally, he did get some relief from reading over articles you had sent him about creative daydreaming, breathing to relax stress and the like. Remember the one you marked for him, noting about the author, "This guy knows what he's talking about!" Jeff thinks you did, too.

Maree told me about the time she spent after your funeral with Rainier and the children before leaving Monaco. Mostly, she felt that she was being a sounding board for Rainier. Over and over again he needed to repeat what the doctors had told him—that you had suffered a stroke and lost control of the car. He knew that if it had happened in your bedroom or your office or almost anywhere else, you'd have merely fallen to the floor. But it's impossibly hard for him to accept that it happened while you were driving, and because of that, it ended your life. Maree thought about it a lot when she and Louise visited with Steph in the hospital. Their hearts broke to see your seventeen-year-old (and most coddled) child lying braced and strapped to the bed. Thank God Paul Belmondo drove to Monaco in record-breaking time after hearing about the accident. He stayed at the hospital with Steph during the daytime hours and through all the longer ones at night when she was forced to deal with her own horror, knowing she had been unable to pull the hand brake in time to prevent the accident.

You can't believe how horrified we all are about the hateful headlines the tabloids still persist in running, all of their stories filled, as usual, with ghoulish lies. Though on-the-spot witnesses say she wasn't driving, and though we all know you would not have let her drive unlicensed, the rag sheets are constantly digging up "new witnesses" to say Steph was at the wheel. Not one of them considers that his lies make it all the harder for her to regain her emotional strength after the shock of losing you. Another story claimed that the Mafia killed you to avenge slights of Monégasque ordinances which prevented them from controlling the local gaming universe! And if that isn't crazed enough, another story accused your own family, at the least, of being involved with a cover-up and, at the most, of some foul play itself!

Haven't heard too much word about the other bridesmaids. Bettina, I believe, is still taking off on one adventuresome journey after the other. Sally, I hear, keeps getting terrific jobs in regional theatre. And Rita, after writing an article for *McCall's* on the early days you two shared in Hollywood, is traveling to assemble the rest of her interviews for her book on the world's great actresses. I haven't had any contact with anyone who knows where Carolyn is, but when I last heard, she was moving between Philadelphia and New York, trying to work out a permanent place to live.

I had hoped to see one or more of my fellow bridesmaids at the inaugural Gala the Reagans hosted in Washington a few months ago to kick off one of your special dreams—the Princess Grace Foundation-U.S.A. Many of your old friends have joined the board of trustees, and Lynn Wyatt chaired a perfect weekend to mark the kickoff! It began with a White House reception for the major donors, then a smallish dinner for them. The next day came a fashion show luncheon, followed by the Gala itself. A Sunday brunch at the State Department capped off the occasion. We brought Amy and Bob down from New York for it, and our son Sean (who is doing great at Georgetown) was there as well.

Oh, Gracie, Rainier is so sad. At the White House the first night, I asked him how he was doing. "I feel old," he said. "Old and tired all the time." When I asked him if a little relief came every now and then, he answered, "I wish it did, but it doesn't."

Rather stupidly I added, "We'll have to do something about that," but to tell you the truth, Gracie, I don't have any way to relieve the burden he so visibly carries.

Caroline has married Stefano Casiraghi and looks beautiful in her first pregnancy. Of course, that makes us think of you all the more often as we wait for the birth. Steph had way too much fear in her eyes in Washington, and I think it's going to take a long while for her to lose that, poor darling.

Speaking of fear, the amount I see in Vicki is perhaps why I feel I need an answer from God today. (Or maybe why I so desperately felt like talking to you.) Before her babies were born, when Vicki was on pills and finally attended an AA meeting, she was convinced she was not an alcoholic, since she took only "an occasional glass of wine." I had asked her if she didn't use the wine as a kicker to the pills, if it wasn't all part of the same craving that she had. She insisted not. Shortly afterwards she did stop taking the Quaaludes, but it was only a matter of months before she got hooked on cocaine and white wine. She and Ivano had a second beautiful son, Matthew, born in August of '83, but they have since separated. Though she goes to work, every decision she makes is based upon the rampant fear you can constantly detect in her. Of course she's "in denial," as they say in AA, but my heart breaks to see my beautiful, merry daughter looking like a walking nervous breakdown. I am angry, frightened and disconsolate.

Like Maree, I suspected in September of 1982 that I would not again return to Monaco, but Nina and I will be there this summer. She is going to spend five weeks in London doing a Shakespeare intensive at the Bear Gardens Museum site that you and Sam Wanamaker were working so hard to establish. Then she's got three plays to perform at the Edinburgh Festival. We're going to Monaco for the ten days in between. Your kids have made Rainier finish the boat he had started to have built two years ago, insisting it must be ready for your first grandchild, who will be born by the time we arrive. I don't know if any of your "little American friends" (as Jeanne Van Remoortel used to call us) matter to Rainier and your children any longer, but I want them to know they matter to us. Mostly, I think, I am longing to see Rainier smile.

I miss you,
Judy

Tues., July 17, 1984

Dear Grace,

Well, here I am back in Monaco for the first time since you left nearly two years ago. I can still feel the difference here in your absence, but unlike September of '82, the Principality has slowly begun to come alive once again. It would please you that people look like they're having fun here now, because no matter how seriously you took life, you knew enough to know that laughter saves us all.

Your grandchild Andrea is delicious! For all that Caroline seems so much less gooey than you about babies and all, hearing her coo to him in the garden today made the sound of your own sweet voice ring in my heart. Thank God for Rainier, for all your family, that he's here.

Vicki is so pitifully addicted to cocaine and wine now that I can't even describe it to you. Fear is an awful thing—her fears and ours. This disease, though, makes us all powerless, the users and their families alike.

On the brighter side, something so cute just happened: Albie picked up Nina and took her out for the evening. I can still see the two of them exactly as they were in the Palace pool all those years ago. They're still blond and adorable. Off to a dinner party and dancing and, you'd have loved this, practically keeling over with giggles as they left the hotel. Makes me think of what you said at Rupert's the night Mary Lee and Ryan O' disappeared in the garden—ah to be young again—I wish it were me!

Being older, though, ain't so bad. Don has finally given up his addiction to rage. He "saw the light" at a great retreat on spirituality we attended last spring with friends. The next morning, in our office, even our assistant noticed the change in his energy. "What happened to Don?" she asked midway through the morning. "It's sort of like reporting to work in the office of Mahatma Gandhi!"

Talked with Albert, Caroline and Rainier about the book I mentioned to you in '78, the summer Caroline and Vicki got married. Rainier and Albie are most supportive about my writing it, Caroline less so because she still resents some of the psychologizing in another book written about you published after the accident. Don't know how Stephanie will feel. It's time for a new collection and she's in Paris working for Marc Bohan at Dior, so I won't get to see her this trip. Bohan thinks she has a real flair for design and makes her hew the same lines of discipline as the other neophytes there, so the experience ought to be good for her. I worry, though, when I see her photos. Her eyes look terrified, and it's a sign I've come to dread. For one reason or another, too many of our children have lived in their own private hells way too young.

Albie seems in his usual fine form, although underneath I can still see him hurting. He's off to Paris in the morning en route to Los Angeles for the Summer Olympics. While he's there, I'm going to have a few of our old friends for dinner—Rupert, the Foremans with Mandy and Julie, my family (which takes up a lot of room when I get them all packed in) and the Kanters. Nina and I are staying on here through the weekend. Tomorrow night we'll be going to the opening concert in the Court of Honor. (Nina promises to "hold the baby oil" during her last rinse!) And sometime before we leave, Richard Bryant, Veronica and I, who are all here visiting, will plot a way to pry Rainier away from home base for a casual, local dinner at a favored spot.

Caroline told me that Sally's husband John died early this year. I'm in New York so often for work, I'm going to make sure to try to connect with her on my next trip.

I feel you very near to me everywhere, and more so as time goes on. Here, particularly, you are palpably close. Well, I need rest even if the kids don't. More later.

CHAPTER 22

...And On

Dear Gracie,

Sometimes I wonder if there were parts of it we got all wrong. I am aware that I've tried to do way too much for too long for my kids, particularly the girls. In trying to protect them, I've made them feel I don't believe in their own abilities to lead their own lives. I've gotten better about it with Amy and Vicki, but still find myself hooked on Nina in the same way you were on Steph. For so many years, we measured our worth by the quality of our mothering. Did letting go of our youngest scare us because we did not yet know what other measure to use? How often during a lifetime do we have to ask, "What am I going to be when I grow up?"

For years I've had this great rap about how growing up is becoming your own mother and father—how we all need to create the voices of each parent as we believe they *should* speak in order to become who we wish to be instead of who "they" made out of us. It's a swell theory, but it means Don and I have to stop talking for a while!

476

Some of my prayers, though, do get answered. Wonder of wonders, Vicki heard her own voices and picked herself up to join AA. She did her "90 in 90" and the transformation of her recovery, even this quickly, is miraculous to behold. She feels lucky to be able to take a year off before going back to work, allowing herself lots of time with her kids and lots of AA. With so many of us going to twelve-step meetings, for a while there it was almost impossible to find anyone in this huge family home at night. Happily, Amy and Bob are doing some work in L.A. and are staying with us. (Did I ever tell you that when they had their big wedding in 1983, they were married by a woman rabbi and Caroline sent flowers? Or that after Rita and Marlon shared a reunion there, Rita correctly noted, "Whoever said that fat men can't be sexy?")

I still see photos of Stephanie that concern me. Still a lot of fear in her eyes. God, but it was tough for her to lose you so suddenly at that particular juncture in her life. She had a brief but much-publicized modeling career which ended almost as quickly as it began. Recently, though, she's been garnering a great deal of favorable attention for the new company she started with her friend Alix de la Comble. They make marvelously inventive swimwear. Their firm is called Pool Position, and it's easy to see why Bohan thinks she has design talent.

Albert spent one season in New York working for Bill Rogers and another for Morgan Guaranty Trust. There are so many elements involved with ruling in Monaco, I know all of this will stand him in good stead when the time comes.

On the downside, we've been having dreadful problems with our business partner in the PKA. It's a bad time for internal rifts as the TV networks are starting to require that minor sports like ours bring in their own on-air sponsors. It's our weakest area and we should all be pulling together now. Instead, the schism on the inside which we always feared might rip the whole thing apart appears to be cutting across the community. It's been such a big part of our lives for a dozen years, but I don't know if it's salvageable.

Last spring I got a call from Barbara Grant asking if I would serve on a committee for the Princess Grace Foundation Annual Awards Gala being held here in November. Of course I said yes, but warned her that my work life limits my available time. Famous last words! Barbara and I have been joined at the hip or by phone wires ever since. She's wonderful! I can see why you were so thrilled that Cary has her in his life.

If this Gala weekend is anything like the one in Washington, I'll only get in a quick "hi-bye" to your family, but even so, I look forward to seeing them and to helping raise funds for the emerging artists for whom you cared so deeply.

Lots of love,
Judy

Tues., Nov. 12, 1985

Grace m'love,

Clearly I am thinking about you so much because it is your birthday, but the truth is, you couldn't have felt any closer these past few weeks than if you'd been breathing down my neck. Were you?

We were able to clear nearly $1 million at the Gala. Seeing the faces of the young artists on stage as your family handed out the awards made all the work seem more than worthwhile!

Albert and Stephanie preceded Caroline and Rainier into town, arriving on Halloween night. They dropped into our office at the Beverly Wilshire to say hello and couldn't have been sweeter. I'd been unable to hit Gene Kelly's and other familiar houses along the Beverly Hills trick-or-treat routing with my grandsons, so Vicki came by the office while Albie and Steph were there to show Jason and Matthew off in their ghost costumes.

As though there wasn't already enough scheduled for the weekend, once I realized that four of our original six-pack were to be here—some with their daughters—I planned another little "do," this one a small luncheon at the Bistro Garden, sandwiched in between a brunch and tennis matches. Rita was there with Kate, as was Maree with her eldest, Linda. Bettina came, too, as did Lizanne with your namesake, Gracie LeVine Packer, and with her daughter-in-law, Vicki McNeill LeVine. Amy, Vicki and Nina were all present from my side, and when Caroline accepted as well, it made the two hours we spent together even more special.

Here's an update on the younger generation. Jyl Reybold had a hard time for a while. It began when a tabloid she had never spoken with quoted her as saying your Philadelphia family thought your death was suspicious, and it went downhill from there. Fortunately, things seem to be better for her now. Nyna, her sister, has remarried and is living in upstate New York.

Sam Gray and his wife Gay are fine and hoping to start a family soon. Lizzie got her law degree and a divorce and, with some partners, is starting a wonderful new company to settle disputes among business and government entities.

Kate Guinzburg has a good career as a production associate in New York, but like Amy and Bob (with whom she became friendly at Sarah Lawrence), she's spending more and more time out here and may actually be moving soon. Mike G. has been traveling and continuing to write—both books and music. Like most young artists, this means a series of odd jobs. For Mike, they have included the following: Boston fish-packer, Alabama tree-planter, New Orleans private detective, Soho fruit-and-flower seller, and even "horse waste-matter" remover in Sagaponack, Long Island.

Linda and Peter Farnum are terrific, and Louise has apparently not heeded her mother's warning to avoid working "or you'll end up wearing corrective shoes," as she pursues one job or another. Nobody has news of Carolyn or of Sally.

On our end all is well. James and Sean both graduated Magna Cum Laude from USC and Georgetown, respectively. Robert still paints and recently had a couple of canvases in a museum exhibition of "rock art." The girls are fine. We hardly see Nina as she lives near college so she can make all her 8:00 A.M. classes and her nighttime play rehearsals.

It was so lovely for the two generations of women to be together, and as I'm sure you've already guessed, you were in every mind and heart at every moment.

We miss you. Love always,
Judy

Sun., July 27, 1986
Monaco

Grace darling,

Just as I feared, our sport did come unglued at the start of this year. Lawsuits erupted in all directions and so many fragments split off from the center that the karate community went back into the splinters it had been accustomed to twelve years earlier. Part of me was unwilling to let go. I still felt responsible for the sport we'd created and to those people who had been earning money working in it, but the degree of unpleasantness made it harder to remember the mission we had all set out together to accomplish in the first place.

Remember the book we talked about my writing way back in 1978 at the Beach? I've finally decided to write it. Part of that decision came from Don prodding me. Rainier, too, urged me to begin. "It would be nice," he noted, "to have a book written by somebody who knew Grace. Most of those which have been published were written by strangers."

Part of me is chomping at the bit to get at it; another part is pure chicken! I never did stick my neck out the way you did to be measured professionally for my own creative work, but spent most of my adult life encouraging or editing the work of others. Even when I was singing, I didn't really start letting go until I had retired from my brief career to become known as a talented amateur. It's a great routine—nothing to lose, perfect for those of us who never did like losing. It's comfortable, though, to find that none of that matters anymore. I measure success and failure very differently now than I did when we were younger. Step one is to start. I've had my toes over the edge for the past several years, as my surfing sons would say, hanging ten. Time to dive off the board.

Recently I thought of something I'd read, said by an eighty-two-year-old man who was nearing death and working to accept it, and of a conversation I had with Caroline recently. The old man said, "If I had my life to live over, I'd try to make more mistakes next time." I used to tell my children over and over to welcome their own errors, that it was only when I "bombed" that I ever really learned anything, that to be right all the time almost implied never learning anything new.

It's so miraculous to be able to discuss all this stuff with my own girls, with Vicki who's a mother herself, and (last week) with Caroline, now a mother, too. Nobody who knew you could have called you cautious when you bit off what you did after leaving Philadelphia, but from our kids' perspectives, perhaps you appeared that way. We talked about how incredibly successful you were at everything you did and how, considering your track record, you must have been all the more reluctant to break the patterns you formed along the way. C. would never be "sloppy" about life, but I think she, like my children, hopes to be a bit more free from care about small things than you and I seemed to have been.

Rainier, too, seems less conservative and meticulous about details, as do I—and all of us—since you left. "Fewer things seem to matter now," said Caroline, recalling an aphorism I read in the late Sixties in *Voices* by Antonio Porchia. "Some things," he wrote, "in order to show me their lack of importance, become mine."

You can even see Caroline's own self-assurance at Clos St. Pierre. It's decorated with a much bolder and more voluptuous stroke than anything you'd have done at the same age. We talked a lot about fun. Hers comes from a number of things—her paper, *The Egoist,* which she and a friend put out twice a year; her private time playing either flute or piano, both of which she still adores; her contemplative hours alone; her enormous appetite for studying and learning new things; and her time with Andrea, which she is fierce about protecting. She has taken on an increasingly heavier schedule of official duties, but even though she always wanted to have children young and seems very fulfilled now, I still wish she had gone off to London after her divorce from Philippe to explore the world of ideas. (Being a mother goes on so long!)

Caroline and I both recognize how much Ma Kelly there was in you, always having to be busy and active, but it's so clear to me that Caroline knows she was born a princess and does not feel obligated to validate herself in the role the way you did. Sometimes, I think she's even more of a stickler for manners than you.

Perhaps you defined that word differently and extended it to different limits, and that may be attributable to the difference in your generations combined with the fact of her European background and your American one.

Caroline did nod agreement, though, when I said there was a period in our lives where we forgot to have fun with our kids. Being a mother herself now, I think she can see how the world scared us, and we, in turn, imposed some of that fear on our children. For protectiveness, I think we forget to tell our kids a lot about our own youth—at least until they reach a certain age. But I'm not sure if anyone gets the benefit of such protection. Probably you, like me, would have given that up by now—if you were still here instead of over there.

Steph came home to Monaco the last week I was there, so I got a chance to visit with her, too. She has recently made a huge success as a recording star here on the Continent, but Rainier is scared about what the music business represents and wishes she'd focus only on her design work. She loved growing up the youngest, and still knows it had the effect of making her almost like an only child with you. She's still proud of the fact that you didn't make her into a sneak, but her outspokenness and willingness to be seen for what she is leaves her extremely vulnerable to criticism. Steph reminds me of you and your loyalty when she speaks with such devotion about Paul Belmondo. Though they split up a while ago, she will never forget that he got to her within hours after hearing about the accident and stayed with her at the hospital through every night and every day during the worst of worst times for her.

She's full of fight with a huge appetite for life. Her success in music is exhilarating to her, though she's aware that people expect more of her because of who she is. When she talks about how rock stars are getting off drugs and finding the natural high that comes from the camaraderie of creating together, she reminds me of you and your love for the same process in the company of actors. I heard that she was thinking of acting but had no appetite for the discipline necessary for such a career. That may have been the case previously, but when she talked with me she said that if she does decide to act, "I'll really have to work hard because I know I have to be really good. I can't be bad—for myself, for my family or for my mom's memory."

Albert and I had lunch alone together. It's amazing how much he reminds me of you! Do you remember a plane ride across the Atlantic while he was still at Amherst, when the two of you got to talk with complete intimacy? God, how he wishes there were more such times to share with you!

I visited with Ania Chervachidze one afternoon, her ever-present nurse/housekeeper Julie in attendance. She still visits with Rainier and the children for Christmas celebration, but her memory does seem dimmer. At one recent occasion Caroline bent down to have a small chat with her. When it was over, Ania's smile made it clear she had enjoyed herself, but she glanced upward at Albert, who was standing next to her chair and asked, "Who *is* that charming girl?"

We spent some time, too, with Princess Antoinette, who is still "Tiny," and met one of her baby grandchildren, one teenage one, and several of her dogs. Do you remember John Gilpin, who danced in the ballet during the Opera Gala when you and Rainier married in 1956? Tiny and he met again nearly thirty years later and confessed they had been in love since their first introduction. They married shortly after your accident, and were ecstatically happy for four months until—without any warning—John died. Rainier's one great loss and her two have brought them together. She marvels at his ability not to role-play in your absence, but to actually try to *be* father and mother, grandfather and grandmother as well. (I always spend good time with Nadia, too, when I'm here.)

On one late afternoon I strolled into the Cathedral and joined other tourists visiting your grave. As on the morning of your funeral service, there was not a drop of air. Your stone, flush with the floor, says simply, "Grace Patricia, wife of Prince Rainier III, died the year of our Lord, 1982."

"And therein hangs a tale," I reflected. I'd heard that Rainier had the body of another ancestor moved so you could be placed alongside the space reserved for him. Remembering how he loathed certain kinds of parties unless you were seated next to him,

I figured this was the old place card–switching routine taken to newer and greater heights.

Stopping home for twenty minutes, then on to the East to visit members of our old chorus line. Also have to be in Dallas for this year's Princess Grace Foundation-U.S.A. Gala there.

As they used to say on the radio, thanks for listening.

Hugs,
Judybird

Sun., Oct. 19, 1986
Dallas to L.A.

Am flying back home after a whirlwind L.A./Dallas/D.C./Dallas/L.A. trip. Did some pre-Gala work in Big D. for the Princess Grace Foundation, then took a one-day turnaround jaunt to Washington for the unveiling of your portrait bust by Kaes Verkade, which Rainier donated to the National Portrait Gallery of the Smithsonian Institution.

During cocktails Nancy Reagan received with Rainier, Caroline and Steph (Albie had to attend an International Olympics Committee meeting in Switzerland and was joining everyone in Dallas the next night). Maree was in Washington with her Linda and Peter, so we caught up fast before losing one another in the crowd. Your girls looked beautiful, Steph in one of her own designs, a long, black sleeveless clingy number made of stretch fabric marvelously draped across the hips. Caroline was also in black, but with a high, high collar—very sexy and elegant. Her hair was severely pulled back and parted in the middle, but because her face is now so soft, fabulously beautiful. Steph looks great, too. Hair still extremely short, bordering on punk, that wonderful androgynous beauty, sculpted head and face—it all works. You probably would not adore the current look, but then what are mothers for?

Nancy R. publicly accepted the gift, sweetly noting your meeting during the early days at MGM, before continuing, ". . . as the years went by we still remained close although our lives had taken us far apart in some ways . . . in some ways not." The girls' eyes moved from Rainier to the floor, but holding back tears and

seeming terribly vulnerable, they could not look at the depiction of you.

The Gala, chaired by Diana Strauss and Ann Lardner, was an immense success in every way. (Frank S. sang in top form and Jan Murray, though at first he seemed like an incongruous choice for such a formal night, kept the audience and particularly Rainier howling with his borscht belt stories.) Though your mom has been in a home for years, Lizanne bought her a raffle ticket and she won a trip to a spa for a vigorous seven-day workout. We all laughed at the irony, but figured she'd still probably perform the exercises better than any of us! Wept buckets when both Albert and Caroline addressed the Gala crowd. So like you—modest but with enormous presence. Bravo!

Hugs and love,
Judy

New Year's Eve 1986–87

Dear Gracie,

It's just a few minutes past midnight, making the technical date of this letter January 1, 1987. Doesn't that sound bizarre? When we first knew each other in the early 1950s, 1987 sounded like something out of a science-fiction movie. I'm still rehearsing the proper pronunciation and inflection for "Gort, Klaatu Barada Nicto." Remember when Pat Neal's movie *The Day the Earth Stood Still* taught us to say that so the Martians would know we were friendly when they landed? Being not only the child of my times, but of my particular parents as well, I for one intend to do exactly what they say in the movies.

Our darling Cary G. has joined you now over there. Likely you are sharing a giggle, dancing while the music swells in all the right places and the fireworks ignite just the way Hitch is telling them to, right on beat and better than ever. Keep the party going—we'll all be there eventually to join the fun! Albert called on Christmas Day. So dear of him, but then he thinks all your balmy friends are great. Your family spent the holiday together in Monaco before some of them headed off to St. Moritz. Steph's here, where she's now making her home, and Rainier's off to his favored Marchais.

Tonight a small group of us celebrated the close of '86 and the start of '87 at Linda and John's house. We raucous show-biz types had started at 7:30. By 11:30 we were all ready to turn in. Lots of warm, sweet good nights, then Don and I drove home. The New Year was actually born as we pulled the car into our garage. Don turned off the engine, and we sat together listening to a so-so band play the sweetest song I ever heard. We thought of you. "Should auld acquaintance be forgot and never brought to mind. Should auld acquaintance be forgot and days of auld lang syne. For old lang syne, my love, for old lang syne; we'll drink a cup of kindness yet . . ."

Happy New Year, love,

Judy

CHAPTER 23

P.S. We Love You

Wed., Nov. 11, 1987
New York

Sweetie,

It's the night before your birthday, thirty-one years after you married Rainier and moved away from here. Driving in from the airport tonight, I realized how much this city and you are bound together in my heart. It was so beautiful, Gracie—amber lights strung across the Triborough and a torrent of huge, unseasonably early snowflakes tumbling from the sky. It always looks so safe here when it snows—but wasn't the danger part of the fun? Speaking of fun, a friend of mine once said to my daughters on an airplane ride across the country, "Sorry to tell you this, girls, but people your age will just never have as much fun as your mother did!" And though I tried to silence him, the girls nodded, knowing it was true.

I've taken to referring to your original wedding attendants as "Les Girls" (remember how great Kay Kendall was in that film?). Anyway, "Les Girls" sounds just as dopey as "the bridesmaids" for women our age. Now that I've visited over the past eighteen

children, and I think she's right. But who in hell raised him anyway?

Spent three days with Jyl Reybold at the Don Cesar Hotel in St. Petersburg Beach, a renovated spot recalling all those glorious eastern seaboard resorts where our parents took us in the Thirties when the weather became too cold and gray. Jyl is finally off on her own, working and living near where we stayed. She's so beautiful, and talk about brave! Only last year she found she does have grand mal epilepsy ("Finally," she noted in mock triumph, "a real disease!"), but the medication she's on is allowing it to be controlled. She loves Carolyn so much and longs to make a success of her life so she can help her in any way possible. The feeling is mutual from her mother's POV. As she has no perspective of men in her father's era (almost two generations removed from her), Jyl harbors resentment about Malcolm. Lord knows, he was never one of my favorites and did suffer from terminal superficiality, but I explained how men thought they were supposed to be back then, hoping that seeing him in the context of his times would assist her to let go of him. She says it helped. I hope so.

Sally was opening in *The Foreigner* at the Spirit Square Theatre in Charlotte, North Carolina, when I flew there to visit and see her work. Do you realize that by the time we first met she had already given up acting to marry and start a family? Gracie, she's marvelous! Also still very private and insistent that the changing times never really affected her. Still, I see so much soul in her eyes and her work . . . I wonder.

Maree is another person who never seemed to have her Philadelphia universe shaken by the years. She is still every bit as trim and together as she ever was, and still as dry and witty. She and I gabbed our hearts out at the Regency in New York when she came up to shop, dine and dish with me.

I'm staying with Polly Bergen and Jeff Endervelt here. Never knew it until today, but Polly told me about meeting you again in Monaco after not seeing you since we were girls together in N.Y. It was just after she and Freddie had gotten divorced which, apparently, you knew about. Again you were on a yacht (Heavens, Grace, for a person who wasn't mad about shipboard, you sure spent a lot of time at sea). She has never forgotten your coming over to her as the party wore on to ask, "Are you okay? If you ever feel like it, I'm here and would love to be with you. Call me if you want to come over and just spend some quiet time."

Polly noted all the years that had passed between the Fifties and that meeting. Her eyes filled with tears as she added, "I hardly knew her." Did you ever have any idea how many people there were in the world who wanted to know you even better than they did?

The person I was happiest to get to know after so long a separation was Carolyn Reybold. I had sent a letter to her through Jyl, and though Malcolm said she wouldn't see me, we started a long correspondence by mail and phone which finally led to spending a week visiting together in New York. The minute I saw her I told her the bones are every bit as great as they were back then! We talked each other's ears off—one day in a small park which Carolyn assures me is blessed and a good place to seek miracles; another in Central Park, where we lounged against the same rocks I had played on during recess from Ethical Culture; and two others when it rained and we rented a room at—guess where?—the Barbizon! (No longer just for women, but we braved it anyway as long as our mothers and fathers weren't checking.)

Carolyn never complains about the shelter, though I get the feeling there's not a lot of communication between her and the others living there. She does refer to the inconvenience of having to stand in line for so long to secure three meals a day, but not complaining is something she learned in spades. Carolyn reminds me of our desire to be kind and sympathetic gone to extremes. There is no way that she will fault anyone for anything, at least not anyone she or I ever really knew. She's so up on news of the ballet and other cultural events in New York that at times I felt I was lunching with Brooke Astor and should have read up! I get the feeling, though, that being in a shelter embarrasses her. Labels again, ugh! The way I look at it, it could be any of us. She jokes about being at a good address in the heart of the city she, too, loves so well, and says she does still go around to Bloomies to check things out. We had a wonderful time.

There are still some of your Palace friends in Monaco who were afraid you were about to become something different than what they wanted you to be. If you were to read poetry, it was only suitable in their minds that you should do so under the auspices of Prince Philip of England or some equally exalted personage. That you planned to tour smaller U.S. cities with your readings threatened them in some way. It sounded as if you were a common trouper, hitting the road, and that wasn't "appropriate." This is not the case with Rainier and the children, though I do think, even now, he cannot quite comprehend your intense need to be a working artist.

I speak with Jeffory FitzGerald every few months, and Robert Dornhelm told me a while back that you had been reading *Pan* and *Victoria* by the Norwegian author Knut Hamsun during your *Mermoz* cruise in August of '82. I found copies of both and read them, Gracie. Exquisitely written but almost intolerably sad. Two tales of a man and woman who yearn deeply for the joys of loving each other, and in both, the lovers cannot unlock their pride, and thus eventually either destroy love or at least hold it at a safe—if relentlessly painful—distance.

Because Don and I have been able to reach such a miraculously close friendship, one in which we understand that the only proof of love is the active support of each other's growth, I believe again in all the possibilities.

I disagree with those who think that the kind of work you were beginning to do would have torn you and Rainier apart emotionally. I feel sure the space between you and the recognition that time together was precious and not to be taken for granted would have given you both the courage to be more open to each other than you had ever been. It is only letting go at the low points that leads us to the highest ones.

Love always,
Judy

Autumn 1988

Dearest Grace,

Thought you'd want to know that your Foundation's Gala this year will be held as the only tribute honoring dear Cary. As in '85,

Barbara Grant, Ruth Berle and I work so closely we feel like Patti, Maxene and LaVerne, the Andrews Sisters.

Spent a week in Monaco last June, where the summer sun illuminated just as much splendor as I've come to expect over the years. It's remarkable how Caroline has actually gotten the new and much-acclaimed Monte Carlo Ballet off the ground, a testimony to her devotion both to you and the cause. Stephanie has been living here for some time. She's studying acting with good old Nina Foch, and she told me she's in the studio daily preparing a new album for U.S. release. I've run into her occasionally at the Safeway, where she looks like any other gorgeous twenty-four-year-old shopping for dinner. Everyone seems finally to understand that she has to go on her own path to make the identity she can live with comfortably inside her own skin. I read a cute quote in a column a while ago where she allegedly said, "My mother gave up being an actress to become a Princess. I'm giving up being a Princess in order to become an actress." But she seems now to be able to do both. She has become President of the Théâtre Princesse Grace in Monte Carlo and Vice President of the Circus Festival there as well.

We were hoping to get to Canada last winter to see Albert compete in the two-man bobsled at the Winter Olympics, but couldn't get away for the trip. I marvel at his strength of character and his many talents. He placed exactly where he hoped to in the field for his event. By phone afterwards we both acknowledged that you, John B. and Kell must have been smiling down on him.

Thank goodness, I hear such enthusiasm again from Rainier in talking about the children and the grandchildren (now up to three with the arrival of Charlotte and little Pierre), as well as for his still-evolving plans for the future of the Principality. I think Americans have never truly comprehended what a brilliant businessman he is. Albert, too, has become such an important participant in Monaco's forward thrust that I think he'll be wonderful in the job and truly love it once it's all his.

Lord, but the world is so different now than it was when I visited Monaco the first time. Almost nobody believes anymore—as we did in 1956—that love conquers all, everyone's dreams come true, or that every life lived with a nobility of effort will reap its just rewards. But the miracle is that we go on loving and trying to learn how to do it better, that we still dream and that we live as nobly as we are able to anyway.

Bettina wrote a long reporting-in letter after her recent trip to China, and is only bummed out that people are shooting at each other in so many of the interesting new places she has yet to see. She spent the summer training for a bicycle trip through France, where she is now. There are rescue squads available along the way, but you know Tiner, she expects to be listed on the roster under "hardy." Sam Gray, his wife Gay and Katie their baby are all fine. Lizzie is still happily connected to Anthony Casendino, whom she's been with for the past few years. She visited recently and spent the night of Don's 50th surprise birthday party with us. Her business is extremely successful, but she admits to having cozy dreams of a husband, home and kids.

Speaking of visits and weddings, Sally was in L.A. for a month last winter with a company performing *I Never Sang for My Father.* She spent New Year's Day helping us celebrate Vicki's birthday, visiting with Rupert and Jay, and talking actor talk with Nina. And this past summer, her son Blair married a lawyer from North Carolina.

Maree invited us to Louise's wedding to Tony Adams last April. Bettina went, but we couldn't. Maree is happy with her new son-in-law and thrilled with the new grandchild Linda and Peter brought into her world. Such treats are useful because Bud has suffered a series of heart attacks, keeping Maree close to home most of the time.

Carolyn has become a grandmother again, thanks to her Nyna, and Jyl has moved to Long Island, where she works as a private investigator. They were all united last winter when Malcolm's heart and liver gave out, for his funeral. Carolyn and I spent a great day together in New York earlier this summer. She told me about a triptych in an East Side church in which the red-headed depiction of the Madonna reminded her of me. So we went by to see it, and stayed for a most wonderful sermon on fear and love.

Mike Guinzburg is living in New York, working as a cook-dishwasher and writing both his music and a book. Kate is ensconced in L.A. at Disney Studios. Rita's wonderful book on actors has been published, and she's currently writing another on ageless beauty. She did a production of *Hamlet* last year in New York, and Jean Dalrymple was quoted as saying that Rita was far and away the most brilliant and beautiful Gertrude she had ever seen! Rita also recently finished a movie here, and I went to the set with her before dinner one evening where she did a post-production TV interview. Just a dirty old Hollywood stage to most, filled with miles upon miles of electrical wiring wrapped in aging gray rubber, and with thousands of relic lamps on stands, waiting like prehistoric creatures for somebody's imagination to put them all back into use again. Why do such places still fill me with awe? Perhaps for the same reason they danced through your dreams—because magic gets made there.

At our end, all is well. James (who thought you were a fox) has found one closer to his own age, having become engaged to Elaine Pitzer, whom we adore. Sean is in London on a six-month stint for his company, living with a lovely girl named Nicki Giuliano (daughter of our friend Gail Carr) and her daughter from a prior marriage. Robert had some tough times this year but, thank God, seems to be maintaining the courage to make his own transition. Speaking of transitions, Nina (so talented) has just moved to New York. She wants to work in theatre there and we are both hoping I'll learn to keep my mommy hands off her at a distance of 3,000 miles! Vicki is still doing business management and busy being the adored mother of Jason (seven) and Matthew (five). She attended her 10th reunion at Grinnell this year (gulp!). People kept mentioning submitting Amy for roles in films, so she's been studying acting for a while, still sings gorgeously, writes wonderful songs and is also working for Marsha Mason.

Amy, Vicki and I, along with two contemporaries of theirs, meet together every other Tuesday night just to enjoy intimate talk of life and growth. Women learn younger these days about the pitfalls of losing themselves in the seductive eddy of falling in love. On the other hand, they know they eventually want to "take the plunge." Most young people I know, including Albert, openly say they want to marry their best friend.

Rainier seems happier now, at last. He has suffered deeply through these years with regret—regret that you were not together more, that there was always something to do or somebody between you. He said that his father once told him, "Marriage is not a great sexual experience—it's a long conversation." Almost every trip you took together, he recalls, was official or semiofficial, all boxed up and entirely too demanding. He felt so sad that he didn't learn to share more fully. He says he turns back the pages of the past over and over again asking, "Why didn't I do this that way, why didn't I do that better?" My heart breaks for him when he adds, "I think there's a lot of criticism for oneself, because one finds very few chapters where you can say you did well, or that you acted in the right way." I once asked him if there was anything he wished he could have had except more time. That was all, he answered, "Time meaning contact, exchange of ideas, opinions, feelings."

Could it be that men and women alike are coming to realize that the only gift we can give one another is that intimacy which so intimidated all of us? At one point we all seemed to realize it was what really mattered. But then we forgot, or never knew how to keep it going. That was when we stopped growing, either separately or together.

Last year Don and I saw an all-day version of a Peter Brook production, an adaptation of the Indian epic *The Mahabharata,* said to be the legend of all mankind. There were three lines in the text that made me yearn to talk with you. In the opening scene, a character playing the Hindu god Krishna addressed a young boy who is about to set out on the long journey with him. "If you listen carefully," Krishna promised, "at the end you'll be someone else." I thought it would make a swell sampler to tie on every crib in the world. Then, in a later scene, a young warrior asked Krishna a long list of questions on the eve preceding the start of the great war dividing all humanity. One of those questions was, "What is madness?"

"A truth forgotten," Krishna replied. There are all those infantile, egocentric truths we need to get rid of, but the ones that stemmed from the purity of our childhoods we should have clung to fervently. They were—and still remain—the engine driving our dreams, our own potential and our will to help others reach theirs.

The final question the young soldier put to Krishna was, "What is the one inevitable thing in life?" You could almost hear the wheels spinning out predictable answers in the heads of the audience. Pain. Suffering. Sacrifice. Death . . . and so on down the negativity trail.

A thousand strangers in a darkened theatre gasped as one when Krishna smiled, made a lovely small Hindu gesture with his right hand and answered simply, "Happiness."

Do you think it's because we are the only creatures able to contemplate our own aliveness that we get in our own way so much and so often fail to reach that state of grace? Maybe it's because I believe in what Krishna said and think you did, too, that when I think of you it is not of your legend (though it remains completely powerful to this day and will likely be inspiring people well into the next century) nor about the ways in which you became more than "just a person." What warms and reassures me is your irrepressible laughter. I see it in photos taken of you as a child and as a teenager. I have my own mental pictures of it over the years, taken since the Fifties when we first met, and there is no diminution of my ability to recall the sight and sound of it from our last meeting or our last conversation across a whole ocean.

If you had any flaw, Grace, it was your inability to allow yourself to be an equal-share beneficiary of your own unending compassion.

God, you were such a gift to our lives! Wouldn't it be wonderful if, in your memory, all of the men and women who loved you— whether or not they even knew you—could find a way to be intimate friends to one another? More later.

Love always,
Signed: Hopeful

Illustrations have been supplied and are reproduced by kind permission of the following:

p. i *(top)* Lizanne Kelly LeVine, *(middle)* The Museum of Modern Art/Film Stills Archives, *(bottom)* Jyl Reybold; p. ii *(top left and bottom right)* The Bettmann Archive, *(top right)* Springer/Bettmann Film Archive, *(bottom left)* Warner Bros. Inc., *(bottom middle)* Culver Pictures, Inc.; p. iii *(top left and right)* The Bettmann Archive, *(bottom left)* Springer/Bettmann Film Archive, *(bottom right)* Peggy Kelly Conlan; p. iv *(top)* Bradford Bachrach Studio/Judith Balaban Quine, *(bottom left)* Jyl Reybold, *(bottom right)* Rita Gam; p. v *(top)* Edward Quinn, *(bottom)* Lizanne Kelly LeVine; p. vi *(both)* AP/Wide World Photos; p. vii *(top)* Peggy Kelly Conlan, *(bottom)* Elliott Erwitt/Magnum Photos; p. viii *(top)* UPI/Bettmann Newsphotos, *(bottom)* Howell Conant; p. ix *(top and middle)* Howell Conant, *(bottom)* Peggy Kelly Conlan; p. x and xi *(all)* Howell Conant; p. xii *(top)* AP/Wide World Photos, *(bottom)* UPI/Bettmann Newsphotos; p. xiii *(all)* AP/Wide World Photos; p. xiv *(top)* *Paris Match*, *(bottom)* Howell Conant, *Life* magazine © 1956 Time Inc.; p. xv *(both)* Howell Conant; p. xvi–xvii *(top)* and p. xvi *(bottom)* Howell Conant; p. xvii *(bottom)* Howell Conant/Peggy Kelly Conlan; p. xviii *(top and bottom right)* UPI/Bettmann Newsphotos, *(bottom left)* AP/Wide World Photos; p. xix *(top)* Peggy Kelly Conlan, *(bottom left)* Howell Conant/Peggy Kelly Conlan, *(bottom right)* Howell Conant; p. xx *(top)* Photofest, *(bottom)* René Maestri/Sygma; p. xxi *(top)* Howell Conant/Sygma, *(bottom left and right)* Black Star; p. xxii *(top)* Lizanne Kelly LeVine, *(bottom)* René Maestri/Sygma; p. xxiii *(top left)* Lizanne Kelly LeVine, *(top right)* Photoworld/FPG International, *(bottom left)* Sygma, *(bottom right)* Howell Conant; p. xxiv *(top)* Gamma Liaison, *(bottom left)* Black Star, *(bottom right)* Lizanne Kelly LeVine; p. xxv *(top left)* Photoworld/FPG International, *(top right)* UPI/Bettmann Newsphotos, *(middle)* Black Star, *(bottom)* René Maestri/Sygma; p. xxvi *(top)* Don Quine, *(bottom left)* Jyl Reybold, *(bottom right)* Peter Basche/Rita Gam; p. xxvii *(top)* Adrienne and Elliott Horwitch, *(bottom left)* Maree Rambo, *(bottom right)* Bettina Gray; p. xxviii–xxix *(top left)* AP/Wide World Photos; p. xxviii *(bottom left)* Bertrand Laforet/ Gamma Liaison, *(bottom right)* James Andanson/Sygma; p. xxix *(top right)* Bettina Gray, *(bottom)* Dominique Isserman/Sygma; p. xxx *(top)* Gamma Liaison, *(bottom)* Coatsaliou/ Sygma; p. xxxi *(top)* Richard Melloul/Sygma, *(bottom left and right)* Alan Berliner Studios, Inc./Princess Grace Foundation-U.S.A.; p. xxxii: Jackie Korito for Alan Berliner Studios, Inc./Judith Balaban Quine.

Picture research by Toby Lee Greenberg and Carousel Research, Inc.